DEBATES IN GERMAN PUBLIC LAW

Germany's Constitution – the Basic Law of 23 May 1949 – created a democratic constitution which, despite amendments, has held up over the years, even providing the legal basis for German reunification in 1990. When it was written, the Basic Law was initially regarded as a temporary solution which would last until a pan-German constitution could be created, but over the years it has grown to become a mainstay of post-war stability and has even become one of Germany's most successful exports. Foreign scholars are particularly interested in the German conception of fundamental rights and the mechanisms in place for enforcing them in the courts, as well as in Germany's federal structure. Making and applying administrative law and working alongside the system of EU law are also subjects of great interest.

This book, developed by a group of scholars in honour of the 60th anniversary of the Basic Law, presents examples of fundamental aspects of current scholarly debate. The analyses found in this book present the latest scholarly discussions, specifically for a foreign audience, touching upon constitutional law, administrative law and the place of the Federal Republic within the system of European Union law, with constitutional law providing the constant framework.

Debates in German Public Law

Edited by

Hermann Pünder

and

Christian Waldhoff

•HART•
PUBLISHING

OXFORD AND PORTLAND, OREGON

2014

Published in the United Kingdom by Hart Publishing Ltd
16C Worcester Place, Oxford, OX1 2JW
Telephone: +44 (0)1865 517530
Fax: +44 (0)1865 510710
E-mail: mail@hartpub.co.uk
Website: http://www.hartpub.co.uk

Published in North America (US and Canada) by
Hart Publishing
c/o International Specialized Book Services
920 NE 58th Avenue, Suite 300
Portland, OR 97213-3786
USA Tel: +1 503 287 3093 or toll-free: (1) 800 944 6190
Fax: +1 503 280 8832
E-mail: orders@isbs.com
Website: http://www.isbs.com

Hart Publishing is an Imprint of Bloomsbury Publishing plc

British Library Cataloguing in Publication Data
Data Available

ISBN: 978-1-84946-472-7

Typeset by Hope Services, Abingdon
Printed and bound in Great Britain by
Lightning Source UK Ltd

Foreword

by Dr Hans-Peter Friedrich

Until a few decades ago, comparative studies of legal systems were undertaken primarily out of academic interest. Today, a country's legal system may be a key factor in determining whether a company chooses to base its operations there or not. Legal systems today thus find themselves in global competition. This competition is reinforced by an additional trend: social and political upheaval in many parts of the world lead to the creation of new legal systems. In the process, the legal systems of other countries are increasingly studied and their experience turned to advantage. This is another aspect of globalization.

Germany's Constitution – the Basic Law – from 23 May 1949 created a democratic constitution which, despite amendments to individual provisions, has held up over the years, even providing the legal basis for German reunification on 3 October 1990. When it was written, at a time of growing political division in post-war Europe, the Basic Law was initially regarded as a temporary solution until a pan-German constitution could be created. The German public at first viewed the Basic Law with scepticism, but its practical application and, not least, the rulings of the Federal Constitutional Court impressively demonstrated its structural advantages and the fact that it was flexible enough to deal with changing times. As a result, the respect of the German people for their Basic Law has steadily grown over the years.

This development has been carefully monitored abroad. Thanks to numerous contacts among scholars and an intense exchange of information at all levels, the structural principles of the Basic Law, the position and relationship of the constitutional bodies to each other, even the wording of individual provisions, have all served as models for the constitutions of other nations. As such, our Basic Law is one of Germany's most successful exports.

Numerous overseas delegations visit the Federal Ministry of the Interior, which is also one of two federal ministries responsible for constitutional matters, in order to gather first-hand information about Germany's Constitution and its system of public administration. Visitors from abroad are particularly interested in our conception of fundamental rights and the mechanisms in place for enforcing them in the courts, as well as in our federalist structure. Making and applying legislation in the field of administrative law and working within the system of European Union law are also subjects of great interest. The editors of this book, which I was pleased to assist with, report equally great interest among legal scholars.

The legal concepts developed in German public law are based on various dogmatic approaches and traditions of German jurisprudence. But this background is often difficult for foreign scholars and practitioners from the fields of policy-making and public administration to understand, not only owing to linguistic barriers, but also due to an occasional tendency towards extremely fine distinctions. So it is particularly important to present legal discourse in a more approachable way.

The project 'Debates in German Public Law', developed by a group of scholars in honour of the 60th anniversary of the Basic Law, does exactly that. Leading legal scholars of the younger generation present examples of fundamental aspects of current scholarly debate. The analyses touch on constitutional law, administrative law and the place of the Federal Republic of Germany within the system of European Union law, with constitutional law providing the framework. The aim is not to offer basic information about our system of government and law – numerous books already do that. Instead, these analyses focus above all on presenting the latest scholarly discussions specifically for a foreign audience.

Without the tireless efforts of the editors and authors, this innovative project would never have been realized in such exemplary form. I hope this book provides interested readers with a great deal of enjoyment as well as new insights and ideas.

Dr Hans-Peter Friedrich
Federal Minister of the Interior
Member of the German Bundestag
Berlin

Editors' Preface

'*Germanica non leguntur*'. It is often lamented that the international academic debate seldom notices literature in the German language. The book *Debates in German Public Law* aims to bridge this gap. In honour of the 60th anniversary of Germany's modern Constitution – the 'Basic Law' ('*Grundgesetz*'), enacted in 1949 – fourteen German law professors present to a foreign audience fundamental examples of contemporary scholarly discussions. The authors touch vital disputes in constitutional and administrative law and in respect to the place of the Federal Republic of Germany within the system of the European Union. References to leading cases and selected literature serve as a door opener for further research.

We hope that the book may add to a deeper understanding of Germany's public law system and of the German political culture as a whole. In a comparative perspective, the discussions in Germany might even provide food for thought to comparable legal and political debates in other countries. It may prove helpful that the authors have included comparative remarks in regard to other national jurisdictions and to the law of the European Union within their analyses of German constitutional and administrative debates.

The editors are grateful to the Federal Ministry of the Interior for funding the project and to Dr Hans-Peter Friedrich, the German Federal Minister of the Interior, for his insightful Foreword. Stylistic advice has been provided by Kevin Pike (Erlangen), and Helen Rhind (Singapore).

Hamburg/Berlin, October 2013

Hermann Pünder
Christian Waldhoff

Table of Contents

Part II – Administrative Law

Part III – European Integration

List of Authors

Professor Dr Christian Calliess, MAES (Bruges), LLM Eur, was born in 1964 and is Professor of public and European law at the Freie Universität Berlin. He holds the Ad Personam Jean Monnet Chair for European integration. He was in 2009 visiting professor at the Panthéon-Assas University (Paris 2) and in 2010 at the Lewis and Clark Law School in Portland (Oregon, USA). His main areas of research interest focus on European law, constitutional law and environmental law. Till 2013 he was Judge at the Supreme Administrative Court Berlin-Brandenburg. Since 2008 he is a member of the German Advisory Council on the Environment (SRU) which was established by the German federal government. He is as well editor of the Journal for European Environmental and Planning Law (JEEPL).

Professor Dr Wolfram Cremer was born in 1963 and holds a chair in public law and European law at the Ruhr University Bochum. In 2008 he was a visiting professor at the University of Tours in France. The main emphases of his publications are constitutional law, European law and environmental law.

Professor Dr Martin Eifert, LLM (Berkeley), was born in 1965 and holds a chair in public law at the Humboldt University in Berlin. He has led and participated in numerous international research projects for comparative law on questions of general administrative law, information law and administrative modernization. His main areas of research include administrative regulation law, information and media law as well as the relationship between the law and innovation. Until 2012 Martin Eifert held a chair at the Justus Liebig University in Gießen.

Professor Dr Bernd Grzeszick, LLM (Cambridge), was born in 1965. Since 2009 he holds the chair in public law, public international law, constitutional theory and philosophy of law at the faculty of law of the Ruprecht Karls University in Heidelberg. His main areas of interest concern constitutional law, international public law, comparative law, philosophy of law and media law. He is director of the Heidelberg Center for American Studies and an ordinary member of the social sciences class of the Heidelberg Academy of Sciences and Humanities. Before coming to Heidelberg, Bernd Grzeszick held chairs at the Universities of Münster, Erlangen and Mainz.

Professor Dr Matthias Jestaedt was born in 1961 and holds a chair in public law and legal theory at the Institute of *Staatswissenschaft* and Legal Philosophy at the Albert Ludwigs University in Freiburg. Until 2011 he held a chair at the Friedrich Alexander Universität Erlangen-Nürnberg. In 2005 he was a visiting professor at the Panthéon Sorbonne University (Paris 1) and in 2011 at the Panthéon-Assas University (Paris 2). The main focus of his research lies in the fields of constitutional law, legal theory and public law in other countries. Matthias Jestaedt is editor of the works of Hans Kelsen. Furthermore he is one of the editors of the journal *JuristenZeitung* (JZ).

Professor Dr Marcel Kaufmann, LLM (Nottingham), was born in 1966 and is a partner in the international law firm Freshfields Bruckhaus Deringer in Berlin. His field of work incorporates public commercial law in its European context. Marcel Kaufmann is adjunct professor at the Georg August University in Göttingen where he where he was awarded his Habilitation Doctorate in public law, European law and legal theory.

Professor Dr Thorsten Kingreen was born in 1965 and holds the chair in public law, social law and health law at the University of Regensburg. He is, inter alia, co-editor of the journal *Neue Zeitschrift für Sozialrecht* (NZS). The main emphases of his publications are in social and European law.

Professor Dr Hanno Kube, LLM (Cornell), was born in 1970 and holds the chair in public law, European law, finance and tax law at the Johannes Gutenberg University Mainz. His fields of academic work range from constitutional and European law to the law of taxation. As part of a research project, Hanno Kube spent time at the European University Institute (EUI) in Florence. In 2009 as well as 2012 he was a visiting professor at Cornell University New York.

Professor Dr Christoph Möllers, LLM (Chicago), was born in 1969 and holds the chair in public law and the philosophy of law at the Humboldt Universität in Berlin. He is a Judge at the Supreme Administrative Court Berlin-Brandenburg, a Permanent Fellow at the Institute for Advanced Study in Berlin, an ordinary member of the social sciences class of the Berlin-Brandenburg Academy of Sciences and Humanities and co-editor of the journal *Der Staat*. His main research interests focus on constitutional law, legal theory and comparative law.

Professor Dr Stefan Mückl was born in 1970 and lectures at the University of Freiburg as an adjunct professor. His publications are predominantly in the field of constitutional and administrative law as well as state-church law. Stefan Mückl has undertaken periods of research at the Universidad Complutense in Madrid, the University of Cardiff and the University of Strasbourg. He is currently working at the Pontificia Università della Santa Croce in Rome.

Professor Dr Hermann Pünder, LLM (Iowa), was born in 1966 and holds the chair of public law (including European law), science of public administration and comparative law at the Bucerius Law School in Hamburg. He has undertaken visiting professorships at the University of Oxford, the Pontificia Universidad Católica Argentina in Buenos Aires and Stanford University. In addition to this, he lectured at the Chinese Academy of Social Sciences (Beijing) and worked as an adviser in budgetary matters to China on behalf of the Deutsche Gesellschaft für

Technische Zusammenarbeit (GTZ). His principal areas of research are in public commercial law (especially public procurement law) and the modernization of the state and its administration.

Professor Dr Axel Tschentscher, LLM (Cornell), was born in 1964 and holds the chair of constitutional law, philosophy of law and constitutional history at the University of Bern (Switzerland). In his works he concentrates predominantly on the doctrines of fundamental rights, comparative constitutional law and the philosophy of law. Within the framework of postgraduate constitutional law programmes, he lectured at universities in Armenia und Georgia. He also recently undertook research at the European University Institute (EUI) in Florence.

Professor Dr Christian Waldhoff was born in 1965 and holds a chair in public law and the law of finance at Humboldt University Berlin, Faculty of Law. He was a director of the Institute for Ecclesiastical Law in the Faculty of Law and Economics of the University of Bonn where he held a chair in public law until 2012. In 2008 he was visiting professor at Osaka University in Japan. He is a member of the Advisory Board to the Federal Ministry of Finance, the Advisory Board of the legislative journal *Zeitschrift für Gesetzgebung* as well as being chairman of the Vereinigung für Verfassungsgeschichte (the Society of Constitutional History). Since April 2010 he has been deputy director of the International Centre for Advanced Studies 'Law as Culture' (Käte Hamburger Kolleg Centre for Advanced Study) in Bonn. His main areas of interest lie in constitutional law, public finance law, constitutional history and state-church law.

Professor Dr Bernhard Wegener, MAES (Bruges), was born in 1965 and is director of the Institute for Constitutional Law and Administrative Law and holds a chair in public law at the Friedrich Alexander University Erlangen-Nürnberg (FAU). His main areas of research deal with European law, the law regarding freedom of information, environmental law as well as the history of public law. Professor Wegener is editor of the environmental law journal *Zeitschrift für Umweltrecht*. In 2004 he was visiting professor at the Virginia Law School in the USA. His lecturing work has also taken him to Asia and the transition countries of Central and Eastern Europe.

Part I

Constitutional Law

1

Scope and Legitimacy of Judicial Review in German Constitutional Law – the Court versus the Political Process

CHRISTOPH MÖLLERS

I. INTRODUCTION

THE FOLLOWING CHAPTER will elaborate on a confusing observation: on the one hand the German Federal Constitutional Court (Bundesverfassungsgericht, 'BVerfG', 'FCC' or the 'Court') is arguably one of the most powerful national constitutional courts in the world, using its broad jurisdiction to apply wide interpretations to restrict the democratic legislature, in particular in respect of German basic rights. On the other hand, there is virtually no academic debate on the legitimacy of the FCC, as we know it from many legal discourses in other countries and in the context of the European Union. This chapter will address some of the historical origins of the Court's power of judicial review as well as the general lack of academic interest in its legitimacy. It will then introduce some of the characteristic elements of constitutional review by the FCC, in order to explain where specific problems tend to arise and why they are not couched in terms of legitimacy. This leads to an account of the functional equivalent doctrinal analysis of the Court's jurisprudence in German constitutional law and, finally, to a conclusion that paves the way for further debates.

II. ORIGINS OF A POWERFUL CONSTITUTIONAL COURT

A. The FCC and the German Tradition of *Rechtsstaat*

The establishment of a powerful constitutional court as a central element of a new constitution was largely uncontested during the deliberations of the constitutional assembly, the Parliamentary Council, in the winter of 1948/49.[1] The issue during the extensive but largely technical discussion was not what powers the FCC should have but how these powers should be designed. It was clear that the new FCC should have the power to review parliamentary statutes with regard to all constitutional provisions and particularly with regard to the basic rights. The Court was even vested with the power to review constitutional amendments in light of certain unalterable basic principles of the Constitution and the guarantee of human dignity. It was equally clear that access to the Court should be provided not only to particular parts of the federal organization, such as the federal government, certain parts of the federal Parliament and the federal states, but also to the lower courts (by way of preliminary ruling) and to every natural person who claimed his or her basic rights to be at stake.

The establishment of the FCC was the result of two historical factors. First, since the 1830s there had been a debate amongst German legal scholars about the merits

[1] (1951) 1 *Jahrbuch des öffentlichen Rechts* 664–738; M Kau, *United States Supreme Court und Bundesverfassungsgericht* (Berlin et al, Springer, 2007) 32–49.

of judicial review, in which many scholars argued in its favour as an important instrument to enhance the idea of the *Rechtsstaat* (legal state).[2] It was thus no coincidence that the civil courts slowly started to review statutes during the Weimar Republic, especially in cases concerning a revaluation of contracts affected by inflation.[3] It is notable that conservatives who distrusted the new democratic parliamentary system of the Weimar Republic favoured judicial review of the legislature. The more democratic the legislature became, the less loyalty was shown by the judiciary towards it.[4] During the Weimar Republic, this development was actively supported by the anti-parliamentary majority of German legal scholars who led important debates about judicial review.[5] Judicial review was also supported by Hans Kelsen's pure theory of law, which advocated a centralized constitutional court and which provided an important institutional role model for the German discussion through the establishment of the Austrian Constitutional Court in 1920.[6] However, whilst liberal Kelsen promoted this form of a specialized 'political' court, the conservative anti-parliamentarian constitutionalists preferred the model of decentralized judicial review by the normal courts.

Secondly, this long and intense debate on judicial review in the context of the German *Rechtsstaat* doctrine was finally resolved as a result of the experience of National Socialism. The Parliamentary Council interpreted the breakdown of the Weimar Republic and the subsequent Nazi rule as a failure of democratic self-government that had to be rectified by means of law, especially with regard to basic rights. Judicial review was a direct reaction to the decline of parliamentary government in the early 1930s. There is a certain irony in that the concept of judicial review that was mainly advocated in the 1920s by anti-parliamentary critics of the Weimar Constitution (with the exception of Kelsen) was now almost unanimously recommended in the late 1940s as an important safeguard for the protection of Germany's second attempt at a parliamentary political system.

[2] H Wendenburg, *Die Debatte um die Verfassungsgerichtsbarkeit und der Methodenstreit der Staatsrechtslehre in der Weimarer Republik* (Göttingen, Schwartz, 1984).

[3] PC Caldwell, *Popular Sovereignty and the Crisis of Weimar Constitutional Law* (Durham et al, Duke University Press, 1997) 153–55.

[4] F Kübler, 'Demokratische Justiz?' in RM Kiesow (ed), *Summa: Dieter Simon zum 70. Geburtstag* (Frankfurt/Main, Klostermann, 2005) 349, 355.

[5] H Triepel, 'Wesen und Entwicklung der Staatsgerichtsbarkeit' (1929) 5 *Veröffentlichungen der Vereinigung der Deutschen Staatsrechtslehrer* 2.

[6] H Dreier, *Rechtslehre, Staatssoziologie und Demokratietheorie bei Hans Kelsen*, 2nd edn (Baden-Baden, Nomos 1990) 131; R Walter, *Hans Kelsen als Verfassungsrichter* (Wien, Manz, 2005); C Neschwara, 'Kelsen als Verfassungsrichter' in SL Paulson and M Stolleis (eds), *Hans Kelsen* (Tübingen, Mohr Siebeck, 2005) 353.

B. The Beginning of the FCC – and the Influence of the Conservative Courts and the Political Process

Though the establishment of the Court was uncontested and fitted well with the legalist self-image of the early Federal Republic,[7] once the FCC came into being it faced two institutional challenges. Not only was there a general lack of experience of any system of constitutional review, but also the Court was largely filled with justices who had not belonged to the old German judicial and administrative establishment.[8] Many justices had been exiled or persecuted during the Nazi era, which was a clear contrast to the elites in the rest of the judicial system and in the federal Parliament and government. Lack of experience of such an institution and of the political background of the Court therefore led early on to open opposition to judicial review by the FCC by the federal courts of justice (the highest German courts in civil and criminal matters) and by the federal government. Members of the federal government, in particular the Minister of Justice, threatened not to 'accept' decisions of the FCC.[9] The conservative Federal Court of Justice openly disobeyed the FCC in one case that referred to the status of Nazi civil servants (including judges).[10]

It was in this conflict-ridden context that the FCC produced a remarkable document with amazing legal effects for its scope of review. Within the systematic structure of the German Basic Law (*Grundgesetz*) the FCC does not enjoy the status of a 'constitutional organ' (*Verfassungsorgan*) that is normally indicated by having its own subtitle within the Constitution, as is the case with the federal Parliament, the federal government and the federal President. Instead the FCC is explicitly mentioned as one part of the judicial power and, in this structure the highest court is just a court (rather than a constitutional organ).[11] However early in the Court's history, in 1957, the justices of the FCC published a *Status-Denkschrift* (a memorandum on status), which is a rather informal paper on the institutional status of the FCC within the Constitution.[12] In this paper the justices claimed the Court should have the status of a constitutional organ (*Verfassungsorgan*), with the same constitutional status as the other organs that are explicitly mentioned in the Basic Law. The paper's main author was the constitutionalist Gerhard Leibholz, who was a conservative and a victim of the Nazi regime. The paper's argument was somewhat unclear, oscillating between the role of the Court as a court and its political

[7] M Rainer Lepsius, 'Institutional Structures and Political Culture' in H Döring and G Smith (eds), *Party Government and Political Culture in Western Germany* (Basingstoke, Macmillan, 1982) 116, 124–26.

[8] U Wesel, *Die Hüter der Verfassung* (Frankfurt/Main, Eichborn, 1996).

[9] M Wild 'BVerfGE 2, 79 – Wiederbewaffnung III. Das BVerfG und "Hohe Politik"' in J Menzel and R Müller-Terpitz (eds), *Verfassungsrechtsprechung*, 2nd edn (Tübingen, Mohr Siebeck, 2011) 69, 71.

[10] N Frei, *Vergangenheitspolitik* (Munich, CH Beck, 1996) 93–98.

[11] G Roellecke, 'Aufgaben und Stellung des Bundesverfassungsgerichts im Verfassungsgefüge' in J Isensee and P Kirchhof (eds), *Handbuch des Staatsrechts der Bundesrepublik Deutschland*, vol III, 3rd edn (Heidelberg, CF Müller, 2005) § 67, para 15.

[12] 'Statusdenkschrift' (1957) 6 *Jahrbuch des öffentlichen Rechts* 144.

importance. Of most practical relevance were the passages about the necessary budgetary and organizational autonomy of the Court. All but one of the FCC's judges signed the paper and sent it to the federal government. Though there was academic as well as political criticism of the paper,[13] the Court finally prevailed and the parliamentary legislators explicitly accepted the status of the Court as a constitutional organ in the first paragraph of the FCC's procedural statute, even though the text of the Constitution has still not been amended to reflect this.

The status as a constitutional organ provided the Court (beyond budgetary and protocol privileges) with a certain institutional self-confidence with regard to the political process, which also had implications for its judicial review of legislative decisions, and more generally for its influence on the democratic process. Perhaps the most visible implication was another definition of the Court's role promulgated by the Court itself: the Court proclaimed itself to be the master of its own procedures (*Herr des Verfahrens*), enjoying procedural autonomy.[14] This claim is rather surprising because as a court the FCC is bound by all parliamentary statutes (unless the Court itself has deemed them unconstitutional) and there is much legislative regulation especially about the FCC's procedures in the *Bundesverfassungsgerichtsgesetz*.[15] In this context, the relevance of the claim to be a constitutional organ becomes clear. As the Court now has the same constitutional status as the legislators, it seems easier for the Court to interpret its own legal obligations more freely and flexibly. This is exactly what happened. The Court created procedural standards for itself that in many cases are not compatible with the statutory provisions.[16] We will come back to this issue.

III. JUDICIAL REVIEW BY THE FEDERAL CONSTITUTIONAL COURT

A. The Legal Basis

The Constitution and the statute regulating the Court authorize the FCC to review and strike down parliamentary statutes. For purposes of such reviews, the Court is to consider all parts of the federal Constitution. In one of its first decisions the Court made it clear that a plaintiff that claims that his or her constitutional rights are violated by the state can have this reviewed by the Court, not only with regard to the scope of his or her own rights but also with regard to all other constitutional provisions – even those that do not grant individual rights. A person who is affected by a federal statute can claim that the federal legislators made

[13] Especially: R Thoma, 'Rechtsgutachten betreffend die Stellung des Bundesverfassungsgerichts vom 15. März 1953' (1957) 6 *Jahrbuch des öffentlichen Rechts* 161; H Dreier, '"Unbeirrt von allen Ideologien und Legenden" – Notizen zu Leben und Werk von Richard Thoma' in H Dreier (ed), *Rechtsstaat – Demokratie – Grundrechte* (Tübingen, Mohr Siebeck, 2008) XIII, LVII–LIX.

[14] BVerfGE 1, 109, 110–11.

[15] BVerfGG.

[16] For a critique: A Voßkuhle in von Mangoldt/Klein/Starck (eds) *Kommentar zum Grundgesetz*, vol III, 6th edn (Munich, Franz Vahlen, 2010) Art 93, paras 27–29, Art 94, para 26.

the statute without having the constitutional competence to legislate in the matter.[17] The FCC wields complete control over all issues of constitutionality in a given case.[18] For example, when it had to determine the constitutionality of a statute that empowered the federal government to shoot down civil aeroplanes captured by terrorists, the Court held that the federal legislators had no competence to regulate the issue.[19] In addition, the Court found that the statute at issue was also unconstitutional because it breached several fundamental rights at stake, in particular the right of human dignity.

The FCC adheres to the Kelsen model.[20] That means that in almost all procedures of the FCC, constitutional law is the *only* standard of review and the Court is not entitled to interpret normal statutory provisions. Different from supreme courts in, for example, the US, Israel and India[21] and from the European Court of Justice,[22] the Constitution is the only standard for the Court. That means that every session of the Court and all of its rationes decidendi operate at least formally at the supreme level of constitutional law.[23] Everything the Court deals with becomes constitutional law. Therefore, when the FCC has to deal with the constitutionality of a judgment of a lower court, the following unsolved and probably unsolvable problem arises: on the one hand, is it the task of the Court to restrict its review to the question of constitutionality, but on the other hand, (according to Article 20(3) of the Basic Law) one of the foremost *constitutional* duties of all courts is to be bound by all parliamentary laws. Therefore, potentially every breach of a statute also constitutes a breach of the Constitution. The Court has made some efforts to define a standard of review of its own, claiming that it must restrict itself to specific constitutional questions.[24] However, this and other similar formulae have not solved the problem and the question remains unresolved, both within the Court and in legal doctrine. At the beginning of 2009 the FCC handed

[17] BVerfGE 1, 264. A rare critical analysis underlining the fact that this evidently constitutes a form of judicial review is E Franßen, 'Verfassungsbeschwerde – eine verkappte Normenkontrolle?' in E Franßen et al (eds), *Festschrift für Horst Sendler* (Munich, CH Beck, 1991) 81.

[18] E Benda, E Klein and O Klein, *Verfassungsprozessrecht*, 3rd edn (Heidelberg, CF Müller, 2012) 200–01; K Schlaich and S Korioth, *Das Bundesverfassungsgericht*, 9th edn (Munich, CH Beck, 2012) paras 280–333.

[19] BVerfGE 115, 118.

[20] For the typology: P Pasquino, 'Hans Kelsen: Verfassungsgerichtsbarkeit und Demokratietheorie im Licht der Kritik Carl Schmitts' in O Beaud and P Pasquino (eds), *La controverse sur 'le gardien de la Constitution' et la justice constitutionnelle – Kelsen contre Schmitt* (Paris, Pantheon-Assas, 2007) 19–31.

[21] For India: SP Sathe, 'Judicial Activism: The Indian Experience' (2001) 6 *Washington University Journal of Law & Policy* 29; for Israel: A Gundermann, *Die Rolle des Obersten Gerichtshofs bei der Entwicklung der israelischen Verfassung* (Baden-Baden, Nomos, 2002); R Hirschl, *Towards Juristocracy* (Cambridge, MA, Harvard University Press, 2004) ch 3 'Hegemonic Preservation in Action'.

[22] B Wegener in C Calliess and M Ruffert (eds), *EUV/AEUV. Das Verfassungsrecht der Europäischen Union mit Europäischer Grundrechtecharta*, 4th edn (Munich, CH Beck, 2011) Art 19 EUV, paras 3, 9–11.

[23] The scope of the binding effect is contested although this is not relevant in practice. For a critical account of a later judge: W Hoffmann-Riem, 'Beharrung oder Innovation – Zur Bindungswirkung verfassungsgerichtlicher Entscheidungen' (1973) 13 *Der Staat* 335, 340.

[24] BVerfGE 18, 85. For a critique: M Jestaedt, 'Verfassungsrecht und einfaches Recht' [2001] *Deutsches Verwaltungsblatt* 1309, 1315.

down a decision that judged the constitutionality of a decision of the Federal Court of Justice in criminal affairs that had reversed its standard jurisprudence on a procedural question after 130 years. In a five to three decision, the FCC remained divided about the issues and expressed a fundamental divergence of views with regard to the question of how to define constitutional limits of statutory interpretation and implicitly the jurisdiction of the FCC.[25]

B. Interpretation Conforming to the Constitution

Though the FCC has struck down many statutes in over 50 years of its work, there are even more cases in which it makes use of another mechanism of review. The Court tends to interpret statutory provisions which are questionable in light of the Constitution, by means of the so-called *verfassungskonforme Auslegung*, interpretation conforming to the Constitution.[26] In many cases this results in a statutory provision remaining in force which can only be correctly interpreted by knowing the rationale of the particular decision of the FCC. In the beginning of its jurisprudence, the FCC explicitly chose this approach out of respect for the legislature whose decisions the Court did not want to strike down if possible.[27] Meanwhile, it has become an open and much debated question as to whether the concept of interpretation conforming to the Constitution benefits the autonomy of the legislators.[28] A legislative norm that is spared by the Court, but the application of which is restricted by very specific constitutional limitations, is hard for the executive and the lower courts to interpret and even harder for Parliament to amend. In addition, a statute interpreted in this manner has lost much of its significance as it can only be understood in conjunction with the relevant Court decision. This is especially a problem with criminal statutes, where the constitutional standards of a written criminal rule are endangered by the practice of constitutional interpretation.

It is important to see that the German system of constitutional adjudication formally belongs to the Kelsen School in that the power to declare a democratic law unconstitutional is monopolized by the FCC. Other courts that consider a statute to be unconstitutional are obliged to submit a preliminary ruling to the FCC. This division of labour between the courts has been severely undermined by the practice of interpretation conforming to the Constitution.[29] The interpretation of a statute with regard to the Constitution is a different procedure from that

[25] BVerfG, 15.1.2009 – 2 BvR 2044/07; C Möllers, 'Nachvollzug ohne Maßstabbildung: Richterliche Rechtsfortbildung in der Rechtsprechung des Bundesverfassungsgerichts' [2009] *Juristenzeitung* 668.

[26] The best critique is by the now President of the Court: A Voßkuhle, 'Theorie und Praxis der verfassungskonformen Auslegung von Gesetzen durch Fachgerichte' (2000) 125 *Archiv des öffentlichen Rechts* 177, 182–84, 185–86.

[27] BVerfGE 2, 266, 282.

[28] See C Möllers, *The Three Branches* (Oxford, OUP, 2013) 137.

[29] Voßkuhle, 'Theorie und Praxis der verfassungskonformen Auslegung von Gesetzen durch Fachgerichte' (n 26) 185–87.

relating to the nullification of a statute. The delineation between constitutional law and statutory law as well as between judicial review and simple legal interpretation is blurred.[30] This is partly the case because the FCC has become very restrictive in accepting preliminary rulings, which results in the lower courts being forced to interpret the Constitution themselves.[31]

C. Three Case Examples

As it is not possible to give a comprehensive overview of the vast jurisprudence of the FCC, we will look at three groups of cases that raise serious and much debated questions with regard to the limits of judicial review.

i. Abortion Case

Shortly after reunification in 1989, the German Parliament made an effort to reform the law on abortion and to partially liberalize some of its criminal sanctions. This attempt was generally felt necessary because the German Democratic Republic had much more liberal regulation of abortion than West Germany. West Germany's stricter rule, which it was felt should not be simply applied to what had previously been East Germany, was itself the result of an older decision of the FCC in which the Court had struck down a social democratic reform of the abortion law in 1975.[32] After the reform statute had been passed by an all-party coalition dominated by female members of Parliament, a parliamentary minority asked the FCC to conduct a constitutional review of the statute. The Court struck down the statute because it violated the constitutional rights to life and the protection of human dignity.[33] Moreover the Court issued an interim regulation that applied between the time of the decision of the Court and the implementation of new legislation imposing a criminal ban on abortion.[34]

This decision gives two remarkable insights into the standards of judicial review and their implementation by the FCC. First, in its jurisprudence on abortion, the Court developed a doctrine of constitutional duties to protect, according to which certain fundamental rights like the right to life are accorded an *objective* dimension which obliges the legislators to pass certain measures to specifically protect them, like criminal sanctions for abortion. Without going into the details of the doctrine,[35] it is obvious that this objective understanding of rights (which is

[30] For critique of this effect see A Stone Sweet, *Governing with Judges* (Oxford, OUP, 2000) 114–16.

[31] Schlaich and Korioth, *Das Bundesverfassungsgericht* (n 18) paras 134–64 on Art 100(1) of the Basic Law.

[32] BVerfGE 39, 1.

[33] BVerfGE 88, 203. cf Stone Sweet, *Governing with Judges* (n 30) 109–12.

[34] BVerfGE 88, 203, 335. P Lerche, 'Das Bundesverfassungsgericht als Notgesetzgeber' in M Heinze (ed), *Festschrift für Wolfgang Gitter* (Wiesbaden, Chmielorz, 1995) 509.

[35] The most elaborated critique is R Poscher, *Grundrechte als Abwehrrechte* (Tübingen, Mohr Siebeck, 2003).

generally accepted) makes it possible for the Court to strike down a statute as violating a basic right without any plaintiff claiming that his or her rights are violated. Note that in the abortion cases nobody actually made a claim in respect of his or her own rights. The plaintiffs were a parliamentary minority, whose own individual or institutional rights were not at stake. In addition, the doctrine of a duty to protect gives a new institutional dimension to judicial review. With the creation of a constitutional duty to specifically protect basic rights, the Court gives itself an agenda-setting role in which the Court not only reacts to legislative decisions in its review, but also initiates them.[36]

The second remarkable element of the decision is also procedural. The Court issued a regulation of its own and thus established itself as an intermediate legislator. This has been widely criticized, although this is not the only case in which the Court has acted this way.[37] As in other cases in which plaintiffs sought injunctive relief, the Court demonstrated significant freedom, which was consistent with its own doctrine of procedural autonomy. The Court has even issued injunctions in cases in which the plaintiff has not requested one[38] and the Court has issued verdicts despite the plaintiff having withdrawn its claim.[39] These and other cases give an impression of a court that claims a remarkable double function, not only as the protector of the plaintiff's rights but also as the guardian of the objective constitutionality of any public action. The abortion case with its sensitive political context that was totally ignored by the Court is a good example of the role the Court has developed for itself.

ii. Parliamentary Vote of Confidence

A second group of cases that arose in different historical contexts may help to better understand the FCC's strategy of review. In 1982 after the German Liberal Party had changed its coalition partner, the German Bundestag elected Helmut Kohl as the new federal Chancellor. Although his election was completely constitutional, Kohl sought fresh political legitimacy by a popular vote. As the German Parliament has no authority to dissolve itself, Kohl made use of the following procedure. He sought a vote of confidence in Parliament and made the members of his own party and of the Liberal Party abstain from voting, in order to achieve a no confidence result.[40] This enabled the Chancellor to ask the federal President to dissolve Parliament, and for new parliamentary elections to follow. Despite certain constitutional doubts on the part of the then federal President (a former professor of constitutional law), this happened. The whole procedure was brought

[36] C Möllers, *Gewaltengliederung* (Tübingen, Mohr Siebeck, 2005) 148–50; Möllers, *The Three Branches* (n 28) 138.

[37] BVerfGE 93, 181. See C Möllers, 'Legalität, Legitimität und Legitimation des Bundesverfassungsgerichts' in M Jestaedt and others, *Das entgrenzte Gericht* (Berlin, Suhrkamp, 2011) 281, 380–81.

[38] BVerfGE 1, 74, 75; 1, 281, 283; 35, 12, 14.

[39] BVerfGE 98, 218, 242–43.

[40] H Kistler, *Die Bundesrepublik Deutschland* (Bonn, Bundeszentrale für politische Bildung, 1985) 411–12.

to the FCC by some members of Parliament, who claimed to be unconstitutionally deprived of their four-year term in Parliament. The plaintiffs argued that although the procedure was formally correct, the constitutional norms that governed a vote of confidence implicitly require a 'genuine' substantial lack of confidence on the part of the parliamentary majority in the Chancellor. Otherwise the parliamentary majority would have the power to dissolve Parliament whenever it wanted.

In a remarkable move, the Court accepted this point on its merits, but explained in a long and not very concise decision that it was in particular members of the Liberal Party who lacked confidence.[41] It held that as long as the majority had 'substantial confidence' in the Chancellor, Parliament could not be constitutionally dissolved. The Court added a new substantial and unwritten criterion to the highly political constitutional procedure in which three constitutional organs must consent to the dissolution of parliament. This was a very difficult legal argument. To determine whether there is a genuine lack of substantial confidence, the Court needs to discover the 'true' political relationships between Parliament and the Chancellor. The Court thus has to second-guess the political attitudes of the majority of the German Bundestag. It is therefore not surprising that the reasoning in the decision was so long, unstructured and of dubious methodology. In a second similar case the majority of the Court kept to this standard, at least in principle.[42] However, the Court never actually dared to stop federal elections that were underway during the Court procedure. It appears that the Court is torn between a strict refusal to restrain the democratic legitimacy of the politicians and a refusal to recognize that there are certain limits to constitutional review – a dilemma resulting in the irony that the Court imposed a strict standard of review which it effectively could not live up to.

iii. Judicial Review of European Integration

Although the relationship between domestic and international law is far from settled in most democratic legal systems, the approach of the German FCC towards the European process can be regarded as quite activist and relatively unusual. Since its decision on the Treaty of Maastricht,[43] the Court claims not only to be the guardian of human rights in Germany, it has also developed a control standard for the political process of integration that claims to define absolute limits for the process of integration that cannot even be overcome by means of a constitutional amendment. The FCC continued on this path with its recent decision on the Treaty of Lisbon.[44] This is not the place to review the decisions, but it is worth noting that the orientation of both decisions towards the future is remarkable.

[41] BVerfGE 62, 1, 52.

[42] BVerfGE 114, 121, but the discourse has become more critical.

[43] BVerfGE 89, 155.

[44] BVerfGE 123, 267; for a critique: D Halberstam and C Möllers, 'The German Constitutional Court says "Ja zu Deutschland"' [2009] 10 *German Law Journal* 1241.

The Court even defines certain core areas of state activity that should not be integrated too much.[45] In its data retention case, the Court quoted the *Lisbon* decision, holding that further huge data collections by the EU could violate the identity of the German Basic Law. In other words, the Court does not merely decide cases that have already happened, but it additionally places restrictions on the agenda, claiming to restrict even constitutional majorities in order to limit the process of European integration. This claim has even gained more relevance in the most recent cases concerning the European rescue mechanisms, in which one of the central assumptions of the Court, that every relevant decision has to pass the German Parliament, will effectively block the installation of European bonds as an instrument against the Euro crisis.[46]

iv. Interim Conclusion

These three groups of cases, therefore, illustrate at least three important and problematic elements of the standards of review of the FCC. The creation of new and intrusive procedural means that conflict with the written legislative procedural standards; giving subjective rights an objective dimension that makes it possible for the Court to become an agenda-setter which acts not only at the end but also at the beginning of the political process; and, finally, substantiating the political procedure to allow the Court to intervene in decisions that have a degree of political legitimacy of their own.

D. Patterns of Self-restraint

In addition to these (two) spectacular and by no means atypical decisions, there are certain patterns of judicial self-restraint in the Court's jurisprudence that should be mentioned to provide a complete picture. First of all, the words 'judicial self-restraint' were used once by the Court in another highly political decision of the 1970s, in which the Court upheld the political decision of the federal government to start cooperating with the German Democratic Republic.[47] The Court's use of the expression 'judicial self-restraint' in this decision provoked academic discussion about whether it should be used again.[48] All in all, the decision, though consistent with the government's policy, was by no means an expression of self-restraint. By defining German reunification as a constitutionally mandated goal, the FCC developed strong standards for the political relationship between East and West Germany that remained relevant for many political decisions until

[45] BVerfGE 123, 267, 358–63.
[46] BVerfGE 129, 124.
[47] BVerfGE 36, 1, 14.
[48] See eg D Blumenwitz, 'Judicial self-restraint und die verfassungsgerichtliche Überprüfung von Akten der Auswärtigen Gewalt. Zur Rezeption eines amerikanischen Rechtsbegriffs durch das BVerfG' [1976] *Deutsches Verwaltungsblatt* 464.

reunification in 1989. Although this and other decisions of the 1970s in which the FCC struck down many social democratic reform projects (like the liberalization of abortion), provoked some public anger (including a famous response in a law review article by the then federal Minister of Justice[49]), there was never fundamental criticism of or political resistance to the Court, either in academic debate or amongst the public.

Of even more importance than the semantic episode mentioned above is a restraint that has been systematically applied by the Court since the 1970s.[50] Within the four-step proportionality test,[51] the most important element of its basic right standard of review is the question of appropriateness (*Geeignetheit*), which is raised in the second step. Is the legislative instrument appropriate to achieve the objective that it wants to achieve? This is obviously a factual question, and (as supported by more recent research on the institutional abilities of courts[52]) the Court has accepted that the assessment of socio-economic factors and determining which developments require legislation is a task for the legislators. Therefore, in most cases the question of appropriateness has only been reviewed according to a very weak standard. The Court has explicitly accepted that it is the government's and the legislators' prerogative to assess such facts.[53]

However, problems remain, at least when one accepts that it is logical to review the proportionality of legislative decisions. In many cases determining the legislative goal and the question of the appropriateness of the legislation are intricately connected with the other elements of the proportionality test. This is especially true for much anti-terrorism legislation, in which goals such as the protection of lives have such a high constitutional status that, given their appropriateness there is no real angle for any further constitutional review. For this reason, there are individual cases in which the Court has waived its general restraint against intervening in the appropriateness test and struck down a statute because it was not convinced that the measures would be effective.[54] More importantly, the FCC has established procedural standards which require Parliament to regularly assess the factual basis of a given piece of legislation. It has become common for the Court to require the government to provide it with statistics and to constantly re-assess and re-evaluate the facts.[55] This makes it possible for plaintiffs to get a further

[49] H-J Vogel, 'Videant judices!' [1978] *Die Öffentliche Verwaltung* 665.

[50] BVerfGE 30, 292, 316; 33, 171, 187.

[51] The FCC's standard of review for alleged fundamental rights violations is the proportionality principle, the conformity with which the Court assess in four parts: 1) the adopted measure has a lawful purpose, 2) the measure is suitable to achieve that purpose, 3) there is no less restrictive measure available that achieves the intended purpose to the same extent, and 4) the benefits sought with the adopted measure are not disproportional to the restrictions that the measure causes.

[52] A Vermeule, *Mechanisms of Democracy: Institutional Design Writ Small* (Oxford, OUP, 2007).

[53] BVerfGE 50, 290, 332–36. cf R Schmidt, 'Das Mitbestimmungsgesetz auf dem verfassungsrechtlichen Prüfstand' (1980) 19 *Der Staat* 235, 242. Also BVerfGE 57, 139, 159–60; 62, 1, 50; 68, 193, 220; 99, 367, 389; 102, 197, 218; 107, 62, 151; 108, 282, 311.

[54] BVerfGE 115, 118, 154–57.

[55] For a critique: S Huster, 'Die Beobachtungspflicht des Gesetzgebers' (2003) 24 *Zeitschrift für Rechtssoziologie* 3, 17–25.

review of the appropriateness of a legislative decision after some years. Generally, there has been little research on the use of facts or factual assumptions by the FCC (which is a classic question of legal realism).[56] The particular care with which the Court treats the government's use of facts remains the main example of judicial restraint in the Court's jurisprudence.

IV. THE ACADEMIC DISCOURSE

A. The Question that has Never Been Properly Debated: Democratic Legitimacy

Academics have often neglected the question of the political legitimacy of the FCC. At least since the 1950s there has been criticism of the Court (albeit marginal) that may be understood as a specific (and problematic) German version of the discourse on the counter-majoritarian difficulty. The Weimar constitutional debate is still remembered for quite a fundamental argument about the value of constitutional review and the question of who should be the 'guardian of the constitution' – a constitutional court to be established (Kelsen)[57] or the President of the Reich (Carl Schmitt). Schmitt's existentialist and anti-pluralist account of national politics rejected the possibility of any judicial review of a political constitutional question.[58] For him, a constitutional court as an institution was not reconcilable with any legal methods.[59] Schmitt's school still wielded some intellectual influence in the post-war Federal Republic.[60] Its criticism of a court which is forced into the political arena with no better standards of review than moralizing and ill-defined constitutional values was common and can still be heard. Though there may be seeds for analysis in these complaints,[61] the members of the Schmitt School failed to develop a normative concept of a democratic political process that went beyond Schmitt's own Weimar political existentialism. It is interesting that though the fundamentally critical attitude towards judicial review characterized the Schmitt School, its more constructive contributions to the debate focused on particular characteristics of judicial review, especially criticizing the Court's extensive human rights adjudication, rather than criticizing the legitimacy of the Court itself.[62]

The question of the democratic legitimacy of the Court was again raised much later by an influential outsider to the previous legal discourse. In 1992, Jürgen

[56] Lepsius, 'Sozialwissenschaften im Verfassungsrecht – Amerika als Vorbild?' [2005] *Juristenzeitung* 1, 2–4.

[57] H Kelsen, *Wer soll Hüter der Verfassung sein?* (Berlin, Rotschild, 1931) 12–40.

[58] C Schmitt, *Der Hüter der Verfassung* (Tübingen, Mohr, 1931) 36–48.

[59] C Schmitt, 'Die Tyrannei der Werte' in *Säkularisation und Utopie* (Stuttgart, Kohlhammer, 1967) 37; E Forsthoff, 'Die Umbildung des Verfassungsgesetzes' in H Barion, E Forsthoff and W Weber (eds) *Festschrift für Carl Schmitt zum 70. Geburtstag* (Berlin, Duncker & Humblot, 1959) 35.

[60] D van Laak, *Gespräche in der Sicherheit des Schweigens: Carl Schmitt in der politischen Geistesgeschichte der frühen Bundesrepublik* (Berlin, Akademie Verlag, 1993).

[61] Developed in B Schlink, *Abwägung im Verfassungsrecht* (Berlin, Duncker & Humblot, 1976).

[62] E-W Böckenförde, 'Grundrechte als Grundsatznormen' (1990) 29 *Der Staat* 1, 26–31.

Habermas dedicated a whole chapter of his book *Between Facts and Norms* to the legitimacy of judicial review.[63] Because Habermas' Rousseau-type concept of basic rights has no pre-political core but is oriented towards guaranteeing participation in the political process, his account of constitutional review was rather critical. For Habermas any judicial review of the legislative process must be justified by reference to the process itself. In other words, constitutional courts do not have to protect a given core of individual freedoms, but they have to protect the integrity of the democratic process that has defined the scope of individual subjective rights.[64] Habermas' concept obviously draws from American concepts of judicial review, like the idea of representation reinforcement by John H Ely.[65] Habermas' book provoked some discussion in constitutional literature, which mainly revolved around the American origins of the debate but did not deal with the actual jurisprudence of the FCC.[66] No use was made of the opportunity to follow up on this approach to discuss the legitimacy of the institutions, which was theoretically quite demanding. We will now consider why there was a lack of interest in pursuing these theories.

B. Reasons for the Lack of Theoretical Analysis in Germany

Constitutional adjudication has been perceived as a problematic instrument in many countries with a long democratic tradition, most notably in the United States, Great Britain, the Netherlands, the Scandinavian states and France.[67] The long history of the discussion about the 'counter-majoritarian difficulty' in the United States shows the same democratic sensitivity,[68] as does the very recent

[63] J Habermas, *Faktiziät und Geltung* (Frankfurt am Main, Suhrkamp, 1992) 292–348.

[64] T Lieber, *Diskursive Vernunft und formelle Gleichheit* (Tübingen, Mohr Siebeck, 2007) 195–96.

[65] JH Ely, *Democracy and Distrust: A Theory of Judicial Review* (Cambridge, MA, Harvard University Press, 1980).

[66] J Riecken, *Verfassungsgerichtsbarkeit in der Demokratie* (Berlin, Duncker & Humblot, 2003); U Haltern, *Verfassungsgerichtsbarkeit, Demokratie und Mißtrauen* (Berlin, Duncker & Humblot, 1998).

[67] See for the United States eg: A Bickel, *The Least Dangerous Branch* (Indianapolis et al, Bobbs-Merrill, 1962); LD Kramer, *The People Themselves* (Oxford, OUP, 2004); for Great Britain eg: J Goldsworthy, *The Sovereignty of Parliament: History and Philosophy* (Oxford, OUP, 1999); for The Netherlands eg: L Besselink, 'Grundlagen und Grundzüge staatlichen Verfassungsrechts: Niederlande' in A von Bogdandy (ed), *Handbuch Ius Publicum Europaeum I* (Heidelberg, CF Müller, 2007) § 6; J ten Kate and PJ van Koppen, 'Judicialization of Politics in The Netherlands: Towards a Form of Judicial Review' (1994) 15 *International Political Science Review* 143; for France eg: A Stone Sweet, *The Birth of Judicial Politics in France* (Oxford, OUP, 1992); for Scandinavia eg: E Smith, 'Pays scandinaves' in L Favoreu and J-A Jolowicz (eds), *Le contrôle juridictionnel des lois* (Paris, Economica, 1986) 225; O Krarup, 'Zur neueren Verfassungsentwicklung in Dänemark' (1988) 37 *Jahrbuch des öffentlichen Rechts* 113 (Denmark); G-C von Unruh, 'Die Eigenart der Verfassung des Königreichs Norwegen' (1989) 38 *Jahrbuch des öffentlichen Rechts* 277 (Norway); H-H Vogel, 'Grundlagen und Grundzüge staatlichen Verfassungsrechts: Schweden' in A von Bogdandy (ed), *Handbuch Ius Publicum Europaeum I* (Heidelberg, CF Müller, 2007) § 9 (Sweden).

[68] B Friedman, 'History of the Countermajoritarian Difficulty, Part Four: Law's Politics' (2000) 148 *University of Pennsylvania Law Review* 971.

introduction of judicial review of statutes in France.[69] There is historically much less fundamental criticism of constitutional courts in post-totalitarian or post-authoritarian political systems, like Spain, Italy, Hungary or South Africa,[70] and the same is true for Germany.

The central answer to the question of the legitimacy and scope of judicial review in German constitutional law depends upon the doctrine and systematic interpretation of the constitutional text. Despite the fact that many constitutional questions remain highly debated between academia and the Court, and even within the Court, there is one feature of the American debate on the counter-majoritarian difficulty that is not shared by many constitutional lawyers in Germany, namely a fundamental distrust in the methods of constitutional interpretation.[71] As a result, the question of legitimacy is less oriented towards procedure and democratic accountability, and instead relates to the substance and authority of the Constitution itself. The legitimacy of the Court lies in its claim to the possibility of an objective interpretation of the Constitution and follows from the Constitution-makers' decision to establish constitutional rules and to explicitly establish a court to enforce these rules against the legislative process.[72] This point is not so much part of an argument regarding the status or institutional role of the Court, but rather it is implicitly made within a discourse which criticizes the Court's misunderstanding of certain constitutional questions in specific cases (which is by no means uncritical of the Court's decisions). In other words, the criticism of the Court remains restricted to the merits of particular cases, rather than the institution of the Court itself.[73]

One has to add that though this take on the Court might be considered methodologically naïve, it has a stable basis in the very legal origins of constitutional review under the German Basic Law. A comparison with the US debate may make this clear. Although one reason for the extensive discussion of judicial review in the US may be a distrust of classic legal methodology, another reason for the debate is the dubious origins of the practice of judicial review itself in the American system. The interpretation of *Marbury v Madison* and its political context lie at the heart of even many contemporary contributions to this problem.[74] However, the FCC does not have to refer to anything similar to Justice Marshall's very particular art of constitutional construction to justify judicial review as such. Despite initial protests about the way the power was used, it was generally uncontested

[69] Stone Sweet, *The Birth of Judicial Politics in France* (n 67); M Troper, *La separation des pouvoirs et l'histoire constitutionnelle française* (Paris, Librairie Générale de Droit et de Jurisprudence, 1973); Louis Favoreu, *La politique saisie par le droit* (Paris, Economica, 1988).

[70] For this idea I thank Pasquale Pasquino.

[71] M Kelman, *A Guide to Critical Legal Studies* (Cambridge, MA, Harvard University Press, 1987) 46–48; S Breyer, *Active liberty: Interpreting our democratic constitution* (Oxford, OUP, 2006).

[72] The radical counter-argument is J Waldron, 'The Core of the Case against Judicial Review' (2006) 115 *Yale Law Journal* 1346. One feature is just the political concept of rights. In other words, Waldron's argument wins some of its force from the assumption that there is no point in a constitutional definition of rights.

[73] Stone Sweet (n 30) 147.

[74] B Ackerman, 'The New Separation of Powers' (2000) 113 *Harvard Law Review* 633; Bickel, *The Least Dangerous Branch* (n 67); Ely, *Democracy and Distrust* (n 65); Kramer, *The People Themselves* (n 67).

that the FCC should have the power to strike down statutes.[75] Therefore, the rather nonchalant approach of the German constitutional debate towards questions of legitimacy stems from the design of the German Basic Law and the general expectations of all participants of the German legal discourse in respect to the Court's performance. Any reference to constitutional 'origins' as such is very questionable. However, it is clear that the formalistic nature of the German legal discourse and the shorter history of the German Constitution make any reference to constitutional 'origins' more plausible for Germany than for America.

C. Internal Solutions

The lack of theoretical solutions to the problems within the German legal discourse does not mean there is a complete lack of interest in the question of the limits of constitutional review. To the contrary, there is much literature which at least attempts to develop constraints for judicial review by the Court. However, these are purely doctrinal solutions that do not touch on the question of the Court's institutional legitimacy.

i. Limitations of the Basic Rights' Doctrine

As a consequence of the established constitutional foundation of judicial review, as we have seen above, the discussions take place in the field of substantive law, in particular in connection with the doctrine of basic rights. Questions relating to two main areas are regularly discussed with regard to both the substantive law and also the power of the Court. First, in relation to the doctrine of proportionality (especially the balancing test at the fourth and last step of this standard), in which advantages and disadvantages of constitutional rights are balanced against each other. Secondly, in relation to the objective dimension of basic rights that makes them a determining element of the whole legal system and that even leads in some cases (like abortion) to constitutional duties of protection.

Since the early criticism by the Schmitt School[76] the balancing test has remained one of the most disputed elements of the jurisprudence of the FCC, and is seen by many critics as the foremost expression of the Court's methodologically unlimited powers. However, systematic alternatives are hard to find, and it is perhaps not surprising that the German system of proportionality is quite successful outside the realm of German constitutionalism.[77] The most discussed alternative to balancing is a concept of basic rights that develops a narrower scope of protection. Rights should become strictly defined and strictly protected, unlike in contempor-

[75] (1951) 1 *Jahrbuch des öffentlichen Rechts* 665–66, 669–82.
[76] Böckenförde, 'Grundrechte als Grundsatznormen' (n 62).
[77] J Mathews and A Stone Sweet, 'Proportionality Balancing and Global Constitutionalism' (2008) 47 *Columbia Journal of Transnational Law* 73.

ary jurisprudence where they are wide in scope but weak in individual protection when balanced against other rights or other constitutional norms.[78] One of the dilemmas of the dominating jurisprudence for the scope of judicial review stems from the fact that in the overwhelming majority of decided cases, although the plaintiff claiming a basic right finally loses his case, the balancing reasoning of the Court contains constitutional restrictions for the legislature and the administration. This problem becomes even more acute because many issues are decided in sub-divisions of the Court (namely chambers consisting of three justices). However, the alternative of a narrower interpretation of the scope of basic rights does not fit with the long-standing doctrine that explicitly acknowledges that any form of action is protected by the basic rights. It is, therefore, unlikely that any such substantial reversal of the approach will offer a solution to the problem.

The same holds true with regard to the objective dimension of basic rights. The interpretation of rights as values has resulted in constitutional law influencing all parts of German law. Every part of the German legal system has been under strict constitutional review and has been strongly influenced by the Court's jurisprudence. Attempts to establish a new liberal and negative concept of basic rights are regularly made in academic literature,[79] but it is again quite unlikely that there is a way back. To the contrary, both features of the German doctrine seem to be used more and more frequently at the European level, as elements of the jurisprudence of both the European Court of Justice and the European Court of Human Rights.[80]

Any reform or reversal of the basic rights doctrine could significantly affect many of the problems we observe regarding the scope and depth of judicial review. However, this kind of fundamental change is unlikely to happen. Balancing tests and the objective dimension of human rights are too deeply engrained in the jurisprudence of the FCC and the lower courts and they are too closely linked to many other current elements of German constitutional interpretation. If possible, solutions have to be found at a procedural level.

ii. Functional-Legal Limits of Constitutional Adjudication

A different attempt to narrow the scope of judicial review refers to a contemporary version of separation of powers, called the 'functional-legal limits' of constitutional

[78] E-W Böckenförde, 'Schutzbereich, Eingriff, verfassungsimmanente Schranken: Zur Kritik gegenwärtiger Grundrechtsdogmatik' (2003) 42 *Der Staat* 165; W Hoffmann-Riem, 'Enge oder weite Gewährleistungsgehalte der Grundrechte?' in M Bäuerle (ed), *Haben wir wirklich Recht?* (Baden-Baden, Nomos, 2004) 53; W Hoffmann-Riem, 'Grundrechtsanwendung unter Rationalitätsanspruch' (2004) 43 *Der Staat* 203.

[79] B Schlink, 'Freiheit durch Eingriffsabwehr: Rekonstruktion der klassischen Grundrechtsfunktion' [1984] 11 *Europäische Grundrechte-Zeitschrift* 457; Poscher, *Grundrechte als Abwehrrechte* (n 35).

[80] C Walter in D Ehlers (ed), *Europäische Grundrechte und Grundfreiheiten*, 3rd edn (Berlin, de Gruyter, 2009) § 1, para 43; W Hoffmann-Riem, 'Kontrolldichte und Kontrollfolgen beim nationalen und europäischen Schutz von Freiheitsrechten in mehrpoligen Rechtsverhältnissen' [2006] 33 *Europäische Grundrechte-Zeitschrift* 409.

adjudication.[81] The systematic point of departure for this approach is to remember the fact that the Federal Constitutional Court is a court which interprets the Constitution. Both its institutional role as a court and the constraint that it is limited to constitutional review may result in a more general limitation on the Court's activity. This approach clearly leads one to question the fact that the Court has given itself the status of a constitutional organ.

As a court that interprets only the Constitution, the FCC has to make sure that its standards of review influence the interpretation of statutory law as little as possible. There are solutions to this problem, but they are rather technical.[82] They are especially important with regard to the relationship between the FCC and the lower courts. The FCC has to make sure that the object of its review is not a legislative statute as such, but the way the statute is handled by the lower courts, in particular with regard to the basic rights. This kind of constitutional review by the FCC is generally restricted to a review of the lower court's reasoning in a particular case, without further regard to the actual decision. One important element of this restriction is a new relationship between the direct appeals procedure (*Verfassungsbeschwerde*) to the FCC and the procedure of preliminary rulings from lower courts. As we have already seen, the FCC is very open towards the former and more restrictive towards the latter. But respect for the parliamentary statute and its related procedures ought also to mean that the Court should give greater consideration to the constitutional doubts of the lower courts than to those of private parties. In addition, we have seen that a restrictive handling of preliminary rulings invites the lower courts to a constitutional-oriented interpretation of their own, which again leads to more (albeit unintended) restrictions on the legislators. Finally, the German Constitution refers to the FCC as part of the judicial branch,[83] which has consequences for how the FCC decides cases. This means, first, a rather literal interpretation of legislative rules concerning the Court's procedure. The Court is not the master of its own procedure.[84] The Court cannot make decisions without a party bringing any motion before it. Above all, as an institution that has to act as a court, the FCC has to restrict the scope of its judgments to the decisions of the particular cases. For the American constitutional system the argument has been made that because of their very specific institutional legitimacy, the American constitutional courts should avoid adopting a

[81] H Ehmke, 'Prinzipien der Verfassungsinterpretation' (1963) 20 *Veröffentlichungen der Vereinigung der Deutschen Staatsrechtslehrer* 53, 73; GF Schuppert, *Die verfassungsgerichtliche Kontrolle der auswärtigen Gewalt* (Baden-Baden, Nomos, 1973) 162–65; K Hesse, 'Funkionelle Grenzen der Verfassungsgerichtsbarkeit' in *Festschrift für Hans Huber* (Bern, Stämpfli, 1981) 261.

[82] N Luhmann, *Legitimation durch Verfahren* (Neuwied et al, Luchterhand, 1969); CR Sunstein, *One Case at a Time* (Cambridge, MA, Harvard University Press, 1999); O Lepsius 'Die maßstabsetzende Gewalt' in Jestaedt and others, *Das entgrenzte Gericht* (n 37) 159.

[83] Art 92 of the Basic Law.

[84] Voßkuhle (n 16) Art 93 para 29, Art 94 para 26.

broad scope in their reasoning[85] and instead decide 'one case at a time'[86] without burdening the legislative process by creating broad rules or rationales. With regard to the US Supreme Court, this well taken point referred to the reasoning of the decision. In the German system this argument works for both the reasoning and the holding of the decision. In some cases the FCC is inclined to deliver judgments that take the form of a positive legislative decision and of a general and abstract rule. To decide a case in this context means that the Court has to find a less general ruling for the judgment itself.

iii. Legitimacy of the Court and the Role of Legal Academia

Even if a convincing argument for tighter constitutional review can be made, it is highly improbable that it would become the practice of the Court. There are two apparent reasons for this. First, the German public attributes a high level of informal political legitimacy to the Court. Respect for the Court seems often to be expressed as a general scepticism against political processes and as the desire for wise and apolitical institutions that should guide the country without the efforts of self-government.[87] The Court is very sensitive to the public's reception of its decisions and may even gain some legitimacy as a result of decisions that are directed against the political systems.[88] A formal reconstruction of its role as a court, therefore, misses its rather political self-image and misses the mechanism on which its popularity is founded, especially the fact that everybody has direct access to the Court.[89]

Secondly, there is the rather affirmative role that legal academia plays with regard to the FCC. As already mentioned, there is only little institutional criticism of the Court. It may not come as a surprise that a court composed of many professors of law does not serve as a prime target of academic criticism. More surprising, however, is that German legal academia has widely forgotten the fact that we are dealing with the decision of a concrete case in a certain political and historical context.[90] Instead, decisions of the FCC are regularly treated like general laws. Certain legal elements are derived from a decision and integrated into the systematic doctrine. The facts of the case do not play any role in the academic analysis of the case

[85] See the structural parallels in Luhmann, (n 82) 121–28; Sunstein, (n 82) 24–45. For Germany: A Brodocz, *Analoges Begründen: Über den Beitrag von Verfassungsrechtsprechung zur symbolischen Integration demokratischer Gesellschaften* (talk given in Darmstadt, May 2002); Lepsius (n 82).

[86] Sunstein, *One Case at a Time* (n 82).

[87] This is further elaborated in: C Möllers, 'We are (Afraid of) the People' in M Loughlin and N Walker (eds), *The Paradox of Constitutionalism: Constituent Power and Constitutional Form* (Oxford, OUP, 2007) 87–105.

[88] This is most obvious in its jurisprudence on the meaning of equal protection for tax breaks: BVerfGE 122, 210 and the critique in O Lepsius [2009] *Juristenzeitung* 260–63.

[89] For an analysis see Möllers, 'Legalität, Legitimität und Legitimation des Bundesverfassungsgerichts' (n 37) 297–99.

[90] Critically observing a methodological lack of experience with case law is O Lepsius, 'Zur Bindungswirkung von Bundesverfassungsgerichtsentscheidungen' in R Scholz and others (eds), *Realitätsprägung durch Verfassungsrecht* (Berlin, Duncker & Humblot, 2008) 103–17. For an American perspective on European legal academia, see again Stone Sweet (n 30) 146–49.

law. The most remarkable indicator that decisions are not confined to their particular context is the fact that the Court's decisions are normally quoted without reference to the year of the decision. Treating cases in this way automatically results in a broadening of their scope. The Court is reconstructed as a legislator.

D. American Alternatives: Ely and Sunstein in German Constitutional Law?

This chapter has been quite sceptical so far about the application of more abstract arguments stemming from the theory of the counter-majoritarian difficulty. Although the FCC seems to be far from being the 'least dangerous branch' of German constitutional law, this chapter has tried to argue that more general points about its legitimacy neglect the institutional basis of the FCC that is much more closely connected to the text and origin of the Constitution than in the American case.

Given this, one might still wonder how much scope remains in the German system for more general arguments concerning the legitimacy of judicial review by the FCC. We will look (at least briefly) at two important theories of judicial legitimacy from the American legal discourse that both (albeit in very different ways) try to outline the possibility of limiting judicial review by reference to democratic theory. The important role that Robert Alexy's interpretation of Dworkin's theory of rights[91] plays in German constitutional law shows that a meaningful application could be possible. The following comments will not address the theories in detail, but will merely touch on some of the possibilities and limits of a more general solution to the problem.

John H Ely's theory of representation reinforcement argues that judicial review of democratic decisions is legitimate when the democratic process itself fails to produce adequate democratic representation.[92] In such cases it is the duty of the judiciary to apply stricter standards of review. Ely's theory is especially tailored to protect minorities' rights in the political process. However, at least two characteristics of the German system of judicial review make it unlikely that this concept could ever be usefully applied in Germany. First, there are virtually no cases that are based on the difference between a minority and majority. Apart from the distinction between citizens and foreigners (which distinction is irrelevant for most of the basic rights), a theory that is based on the difference between a minority and majority does not fit into the German system of rights and entitlements. That obviously does not mean that there is no discrimination of minorities in Germany, but that legal solutions for these problems are generally sought by applying general standards, not by developing specific rules for minorities. This feature is closely connected with the second problem with Ely's theory, namely that German constitutional law does not have different tests within its standards of review. The

[91] R Alexy, *A Theory of Constitutional Rights* (Oxford, OUP, 2002).
[92] Ely (n 65) 103.

application of a constitutional rule to a case is not governed by different grades of intensity, as is, for example, the case with the American doctrine of equal protection. It seems, therefore, that it would not be feasible to implement Ely's concept into the concrete mechanisms of judicial review in Germany.[93]

As already mentioned, Cass Sunstein's concept of judicial minimalism[94] may provide a more promising solution for our problem. Sunstein's idea that courts should make use of 'incompletely theorized' arguments and leave more general problems to the legislators is obviously designed for a common law system.[95] Only common law systems leave the reasoning and factual distinction to the courts.[96] However the point that courts can only fulfil their tasks in a legitimate way when they strictly 'individualize' their reasoning has been made for civil law systems as well.[97] Moreover, we mentioned that the FCC clearly sees itself as far less bound by procedural constraints of its own rationes decidendi. In fact, we have seen that the way in which decisions of the FCC are used by the FCC itself, by other courts and by the doctrine may justify a quest for judicial minimalism, although the way in which this could be integrated into the judicial decision-making process would have to be specific to the German system of judicial review. Whilst for the US Sunstein tries to argue against legal arguments that are too fundamental in their theoretical approach, this is not the problem for the FCC, with its text-based and structural jurisprudence. More problematic is that the factual and historical circumstances of single decisions of the FCC have little relevance. Judgments of the FCC are read rather like statutes than like the decisions of single cases.[98] The structure of the Court's reasoning allows a clear distinction between a general decision and its application to the particular facts.[99] It is the general decision that is applied in a statute-like way by the lower courts. The common law art of distinguishing cases by reference to the facts is, as we have seen, unknown in the German legal tradition. In this context, the concept of judicial minimalism has to be understood in a different manner. However, it would be difficult to implement necessary changes to the way decisions of the FCC are interpreted and applied. A culture of focusing on the particular context probably has to start in academic discussions.

[93] For a contextualization of Ely's concept, see also Möllers (n 28) 130.

[94] Sunstein (n 82) 4.

[95] Sunstein argues that constitutions are 'incompletely theorized agreements' that have not been enacted on the basis of a coherent political and legal philosophy and that courts should adjudicate cases accordingly and refrain from engaging in broad philosophical-type of reasoning; C Sunstein, 'Incompletely Theorized Agreements' (1995) 108 *Harvard Law Review* 1733.

[96] O Lepsius, *Verwaltungsrecht unter dem Common Law* (Tübingen, Mohr Siebeck, 1997) 39.

[97] Luhmann, *Legitimation durch Verfahren* (n 85) 121.

[98] According to § 31(2)(1) BVerfGG (Federal Constitutional Court Act), certain FCC decisions are accorded the legal force of a statute.

[99] O Lepsius, 'Die maßstabsetzende Gewalt' (n 82) 168–71 and throughout.

V. CONCLUSION

Theories of democratic legitimacy of judicial review are important instruments, not only to assess the normative achievements and disadvantages of counter-majoritarian institutions, but they also constitute forms of dialogue between disciplines (like law and political theory) and between different legal systems. The higher level of conceptual abstraction that can be found in general theories of judicial review may serve as a common language that translates between the specifics and technicalities of particular legal systems. Obviously, there is also a danger of reaching too abstract a level and starting to talk in a theoretical Esperanto that is ultimately useless for all concrete questions relating to specific legal systems.

For those constitutional systems that, like the German, are the result of a totalitarian political experience, the American theory of the legitimacy of judicial review is of relatively little use only.[100] The variety of American theories on the counter-majoritarian difficulty (which is perhaps the most developed theoretical argument on the status of courts in a democracy) depends too strongly on the founding history of the US Constitution and, above all, on the self-aggrandizing story of Chief Justice Marshall in *Marbury v Madison*. States like Germany (as well as Spain, Italy, Poland, Hungary, South Africa and Chile) have made a deliberate choice to establish a powerful constitutional court whose standard of review is defined separately from the rest of the court system. These differences make it more difficult, though not impossible, to integrate democratic theory and legal doctrine in a way that may function as a useful check on the constitutional court's activity.

CASES

BVerfGE 1, 264 – *Bezirksschornsteinfeger* (1952)
BVerfGE 2, 266 – *Notaufnahmegesetz* (1953)
BVerfGE 18, 85 – *Spezifisches Verfassungsrecht* (1964)
BVerfGE 30, 292 – *Erdölbevorratung* (1971)
BVerfGE 36, 1 – *Grundlagenvertrag* (1973)
BVerfGE 39, 1 – *Schwangerschaftsabbruch I* (1975)
BVerfGE 62, 1 – *Vertrauensfrage I* (1983)
BVerfGE 88, 203 – *Schwangerschaftsabbruch II* (1993)
BVerfGE 89, 155 – *Vertrag von Maastricht* (1993)
BVerfGE 98, 218 – *Rechtschreibreform* (1998)
BVerfGE 108, 282 – *Kopftuch für Lehrerin* (2003)
BVerfGE 115, 118 – *Luftsicherheitsgesetz* (2006)
BVerfGE 123, 267 – *Vertrag von Lissabon* (2009)
BVerfGE 129, 124 – *Griechenlandhilfe/Eurorettungsschirm* (2011)

[100] Comparably critical: A Barak, *The Judge in a Democracy* (Princeton, NJ, Princeton University Press, 2006).

SELECTED LITERATURE

Benda E, Klein E and Klein O, *Verfassungsprozessrecht*, 3rd edn (Heidelberg, CF Müller, 2012)

Böckenförde EW, 'Verfassungsgerichtsbarkeit: Strukturfragen, Organisation, Legitimation' [1999] *Neue Juristische Wochenschrift* 9

Ebsen I, *Das Bundesverfassungsgericht als Element gesellschaftlicher Selbstregulierung* (Berlin, Duncker & Humblot, 1985)

Forsthoff E, 'Die Umbildung des Verfassungsgesetzes' in H Barion, E Forsthoff and W Weber (eds), *Festschrift für Carl Schmitt zum 70. Geburtstag* (Berlin, Duncker & Humblot, 1959) 35

Habermas J, *Faktizität und Geltung: Beiträge zur Diskurstheorie des Rechts und des demokratischen Rechtsstaats* (Frankfurt am Main, Suhrkamp, 1993)

Haltern U, *Verfassungsgerichtsbarkeit, Demokratie und Mißtrauen* (Berlin, Duncker & Humblot, 1998)

Jestaedt M and others (eds), *Das entgrenzte Gericht* (Berlin, Suhrkamp, 2011)

Kelsen H, 'Wesen und Entwicklung der Staatsgerichtsbarkeit' (1929) 5 *Veröffentlichungen der Vereinigung der Deutschen Staatsrechtslehrer* 30

—— *Wer soll Hüter der Verfassung sein?* (Berlin, Rothschild, 1931)

Möllers C, *The Three Branches* (Oxford, Oxford University Press, 2013)

Roellecke G, 'Aufgaben und Stellung des Bundesverfassungsgerichts im Verfassungsgefüge' in J Isensee and P Kirchhof (eds), *Handbuch des Staatsrechts der Bundesrepublik Deutschland*, vol III, 3rd edn (Heidelberg, CF Müller, 2005) § 67

Schlaich K, 'Die Verfassungsgerichtsbarkeit im Gefüge der Staatsfunktionen' (1981) 39 *Veröffentlichungen der Vereinigung der Deutschen Staatsrechtslehrer* 99

—— and Korioth S, *Das Bundesverfassungsgericht*, 9th edn (Munich, CH Beck, 2012)

Schmitt C, *Der Hüter der Verfassung* (Tübingen, Mohr, 1931)

—— 'Die Tyrannei der Werte' in *Säkularisation und Utopie* (Stuttgart, Kohlhammer, 1967)

Triepel H, 'Wesen und Entwicklung der Staatsgerichtsbarkeit' (1929) 5 *Veröffentlichungen der Vereinigung der Deutschen Staatsrechtslehrer* 2

Voßkuhle A, 'Theorie und Praxis der verfassungskonformen Auslegung von Gesetzen durch Fachgerichte' (2000) 125 *Archiv des öffentlichen Rechts* 177

2

Dimensions of Fundamental Rights – Duty to Respect versus Duty to Protect

CHRISTIAN CALLIESS

I. INTRODUCTION

GENERALLY SPEAKING, GERMAN theory distinguishes between three objective and three subjective dimensions or functions of fundamental rights.[1] Objectively, they contain decisions on values,[2] for instance for human dignity or freedom,[3] which are fundamental constitutional decisions, applying to all areas of law, eg to statutory interpretations of private law.[4] Furthermore, one distinguishes between *Institutions* of public law, such as the professional civil service in Article 33(5) of the German Constitution (the 'Basic

[1] An introduction: B Pieroth and B Schlink, *Staatsrecht II*, 26th edn (Heidelberg, CF Müller, 2010) paras 75ff; K Stern, 'Idee und Elemente eines Systems der Grundrechte' in J Isensee and P Kirchhof (eds), *Handbuch des Staatsrechts der Bundesrepublik Deutschland*, vol V (Heidelberg, CF Müller, 1992) § 109, para 27; W Cremer, *Freiheitsgrundrechte* (Tübingen, Mohr Siebeck, 2003) 8ff, who speak of functions.

[2] K Hesse, *Verfassungsrecht*, 20th edn (Heidelberg, CF Müller, 1995) paras 290ff.

[3] *Lüth* BVerfGE 7, 198, 205.

[4] ibid; C-W Canaris, 'Grundrechte und Privatrecht' (1984) 184 *Archiv für die civilistische Praxis* 201, 210ff.

Law'[5]) and *Institutes* of private law, such as private property or the law of succession in accordance with Article 14(1), sentence 1 of the Basic Law.[6]

The subjective dimensions of fundamental rights that are of special interest with regard to the subject of this chapter are referred to as *status negativus, status positivus* and *status activus*, notions introduced by Georg Jellinek.[7] *Status negativus* describes the fundamental rights in their 'classical' function as an individual's rights of defence (*grundrechtliches Abwehrrecht*) against interferences from state authorities, which in turn have a corresponding duty to respect these fundamental rights. On this basis, citizens can demand an omission by the state.[8] Contrary to this, the *status positivus* considers the fundamental rights as the individual's right to demand an action from state authorities. This action can consist in a single benefit (eg of the mother, Article 6(4) of the Basic Law), the granting of participation in a benefit (deriving for example from Article 12(1) of the Basic Law, eg the entrance into a public university)[9] or in the protection against private third parties (duty to protect, for instance from Article 2(2), sentence 1 of the Basic Law for the *nasciturus*,[10] ie an unborn child, against abortion).[11] Finally, the *status activus* signifies participatory rights, eg the right to vote set down in Article 38(1), sentence 1 of the Basic Law and the right of access to public offices pursuant to Article 33(1–3) and (5) of the Basic Law.[12]

On the basis of these dimensions, which correspond to the doctrine of *Georg Jellinek* and are generally accepted nowadays (yet still controversial), multipolar conditions of constitutional law emerge.[13] The latter can usually be found in the area of subjective dimensions of fundamental rights, especially in the constitutionally guaranteed *status negativus* and *status positivus*.

The *status negativus*, guaranteed by the fundamental right of defence, considers the individual's freedom as a limit to the actions of state authorities. They have a *duty to respect* the freedom guaranteed by this fundamental right. The *duty to respect* aims at protecting fundamental rights from unjustified interferences committed by the state. State authorities unilaterally act as a 'counterpart to the fundamental rights'. Their actions become relevant when they depreciate the freedom's potential contained within the scope of protection of a fundamental right.[14]

[5] Pieroth and Schlink, *Staatsrecht II* (n 1) para 76.

[6] On property: *Hamburgisches Deichordnungsgesetz* BVerfGE 24, 367, 389; on groundwater *Naßauskiesung* BVerfGE 58, 300, 339; on the right to inherit: BVerfGE 19, 202, 206.

[7] G Jellinek, *System der subjektiven öffentlichen Rechte*, 2nd edn (Tübingen, Mohr, 1905) 86ff; more detailed and critical: R Alexy, *Theorie der Grundrechte* (Frankfurt am Main, Suhrkamp, 1986) 229ff; differentiating Cremer, *Freiheitsgrundrechte* (n 1) 8ff.

[8] cf *Lüth* BVerfGE 7, 198, 204–05.

[9] BVerfGE 66, 155, 182ff.

[10] *Schwangerschaftsabbruch I* BVerfGE 39, 1, 41.

[11] On the terminology: Stern, 'Idee und Elemente eines Systems der Grundrechte' (n 1) paras 41ff.

[12] ibid para 48.

[13] C Calliess, *Rechtsstaat und Umweltstaat: Zugleich ein Beitrag zur Grundrechtsdogmatik im Rahmen mehrpoliger Verfassungsrechtsverhältnisse* (Tübingen, Mohr Siebeck, 2001) 256ff.

[14] J Isensee, 'Das Grundrecht als Abwehrrecht und staatliche Schutzpflicht' in Isensee and Kirchhof, *Handbuch des Staatsrechts der Bundesrepublik Deutschland* (n 1) § 111, para 2; more detailed: B Schlink, 'Freiheit durch Eingriffsabwehr: Rekonstruktion der klassischen Grundrechtsfunktion' [1984] *Europäische Grundrechte-Zeitschrift* 457; Alexy, *Theorie der Grundrechte* (n 7) 272ff.

In contrast, owing to the *status positivus*, state authorities have the duty to guarantee the integrity of goods that are protected by the fundamental rights from interferences from other individuals. Instead of being repressed, like in the case of the duty to respect, the authority is called into action by a duty to protect.[15] It becomes clear that the duty to respect and the duty to protect as the basic dimensions of every fundamental right can safeguard the same good, but represent directly opposed functions of a freedom right.[16] The interferences have different origins; in the case of the duty to respect they derive from state authorities, whereas the duty to protect applies in the case of actions deriving from private persons, ie other individuals. Nevertheless, the duty to respect and the duty to protect share the same addressee: the state and its authorities.

Owing to this conflict of interests the respective state authority is pushed into a contradictory position. It must fulfil its duty to protect and meet the interests of defence at the same time.

The *status negativus*, the *status positivus* as well as the multipolar constitutional condition that they create find their principal foundation in the 'Basis Fundamental Right' of Article 1 of the Basic Law, which reads:

> Article 1
>
> (1) Human dignity shall be inviolable. To *respect and protect* it shall be the duty of all state authority.
>
> (2) ...
>
> (3) The following basic rights shall bind the legislature, the executive and the judiciary as directly applicable law

According to its wording, Article 1(1), sentence 2 of the Basic Law contains a dimension of defence ('*achten*', ie to respect) and a dimension of protection ('*schützen*', ie to protect). These dimensions draw a scope of protection around each fundamental right which protects it from any interference, regardless of whether it derives its origin from an act undertaken by state authorities or from an act of other private persons. Since all fundamental rights have a core, which is related to human dignity, the double dimension of defence and protection forms a fully-fledged 'ring of freedom' around every good or interest protected by fundamental rights. Hence, the duties to respect and to protect derive from the core of every fundamental right.

Via human dignity, which forms the core of every basic right (cf Article 79(3) of the Basic Law), the state authorities' duty to respect and to protect is transferred to all basic rights. Thus, the scope of every right's dimension of defence and of protection has its starting point in a common objective rule[17] which is expressed by every fundamental right. This objective rule – one might also call it the guarantee of the

[15] Isensee, 'Das Grundrecht als Abwehrrecht und staatliche Schutzpflicht' (n 14) para 3; more detailed: Alexy (n 7) 410ff.

[16] Calliess, *Rechtsstaat und Umweltstaat* (n 13) 307ff; Cremer (n 1) 504ff.

[17] cf BVerfGE 6, 32, 40; 35, 79, 114.

fundamental right[18] – is defined by the interest or object that is to be protected by the right.[19]

On the basis of Article 1, paragraph 3 of the Basic Law, the fundamental rights have a protective effect not only towards legislation, but also towards the application of rules and their interpretation.[20]

II. THE DIMENSION OF DEFENCE OF FUNDAMENTAL RIGHTS (*DIE GRUNDRECHTLICHE ABWEHRDIMENSION*)

In a state governed by the rule of law, the fundamental rights serve as a benchmark for the assessment of all public action that interferes with individual freedom.[21] They create a duty to justify every interference from state authorities. As a consequence, the burden of proof lies with the state authorities with respect to the legitimacy of their action in the light of individual freedom.

Within this context, a particular dogmatic scheme (the so-called *Eingriffsschema*) was developed in a process involving jurisdiction and legal scholars.[22] This scheme distinguishes between three constituent elements:

First, there is a distinction between the scope of protection and the possibility to restrain the fundamental right.[23] In most rights guaranteed by the Basic Law, this latter element is laid down by the consecutiveness of the guarantee and the possibilities of limitation expressed. This distinction is already expressed in the wording of most basic rights:

> Article 5
>
> (1) Everyone has the right to freely express and disseminate his opinion . . .
> (2) These rights shall find their limits in the provisions of general laws, in provisions for the protection of young persons and in the right to personal honour.

Another example:

> Article 14
>
> (1) Property and the right of inheritance shall be guaranteed. Their content and limits shall be defined by the laws.

[18] cf Alexy (n 7) 224ff.

[19] cf Isensee (n 14) paras 40–41; Hesse, *Verfassungsrecht* (n 2), para 310 who talks about 'Normbereich'.

[20] G Lübbe-Wolff, *Grundrechte als Eingriffsabwehrrechte* (Baden-Baden, Nomos, 1988) 28–29; Alexy (n 7) 100ff and 300ff; P Lerche, 'Grundrechtsschranken' in Isensee and Kirchhof (n 1) § 122, paras 3ff.

[21] BVerfGE 7, 198, 204; M Sachs, 'Abwehrrechte' in D Merten and H-J Papier (eds), *Handbuch der Grundrechte in Deutschland und Europa*, vol II (Heidelberg, CF Müller, 2006) § 39, paras 6ff; Cremer (n 1) 74ff; the approach of R Poscher is too far-reaching: R Poscher, *Grundrechte als Abwehrrechte* (Tübingen, Mohr Siebeck, 2003) 167ff.

[22] More detailed: Lübbe-Wolff, *Grundrechte als Eingriffsabwehrrechte* (n 20) 25ff; Alexy (n 7) 249ff; Isensee (n 14) paras 37ff; P Lerche, 'Grundrechtlicher Schutzbereich, Grundrechtsprägung und Grundrechtseingriff' in Isensee and Kirchhof (n 1) § 121, paras 11ff and Lerche (n 20) paras 1ff.

[23] cf Alexy (n 7) 272ff; Cremer (n 1) 74 and 136ff.

This also demonstrates that an interference in a right does not automatically constitute a violation of the right, insofar as a distinction is made between the scope of protection of the fundamental rights and their effective scope of guarantee.[24]

It is this scope of guarantee to which the second element of the scheme refers, the distinction between the fundamental rights' formal and substantial function of protection. From a formal point of view, this function requires that any interfering measure must either be a law/statute or – in the case of an individual act – be based on a law/statute.

The substantive function of protection results from the interplay between the fundamental right and the limiting statute, which finds its concrete shape in the test of proportionality.[25] In the light of this principle (following from the idea of fundamental rights and their limits as well as from the rule of law) every state action has to pass a three-level test:[26] first, state action needs to be suitable for reaching the intended aim. Secondly, state action has to prove to be necessary, in order to reach the intended aim. This means that no other available measure can reach the intended aim in a similarly effective but less freedom-limiting way. Thirdly, state action has to be appropriate. To that end, a fair balance between the intended aim and the protected interest enshrined in the fundamental right in question has to be proven by state authorities.

The third element in the dogmatic scheme is the notion of interference.[27] It is the connection between the aforementioned formal and substantive functions to protect.[28] With regard to a changing environment and the new challenges to the protection of individual rights, the notion of interference has been extended over the years. Today it does not matter anymore if the interference of state authorities is made intentionally (*finaler Eingriff*) or merely de facto (*faktischer Eingriff*).

These elements of the 'interference scheme' constitute the conditions for the legitimation, the lawfulness or unlawfulness of interferences in fundamental rights and thereby of any action taken by state authorities. Hence, any action taken by state authorities is considered as an intervention in individual freedom and, as such, faces the pressure of legitimation.

In this relation of rule and exception, which works in combination with the guarantee of each fundamental right, the citizen's freedom and the state authorities' corresponding responsibility are expressed. As a consequence, any measure taken by state authorities constitutes an interference in a fundamental right which must then be legitimated from a formal perspective by statutory law and from a substantive perspective with regard to the citizen's constitutional rights.[29]

[24] Lübbe-Wolff (n 20), 25–26; Alexy (n 7) 251ff.

[25] BVerfGE 7, 198, 205 and 208–09; BVerfGE 19, 342, 348f49.

[26] BVerfGE 7, 198, 205 and 208–09; Lübbe-Wolff (n 20) 29; Alexy (n 7), 267ff.

[27] cf U Di Fabio, *Risikoentscheidungen im Rechtsstaat* (Tübingen, Mohr, 1994) 425ff; Lübbe-Wolff (n 20) 42ff; Cremer (n 1) 162ff with more references.

[28] Lübbe-Wolff (n 20) 30ff.

[29] Isensee (n 14) para 47; Lübbe-Wolff (n 20) 125ff; Schlink, 'Freiheit durch Eingriffsabwehr' (n 14) 457, 467–68.

To that end, the fundamental rights dimension of defence and the state authorities' corresponding duty to respect work in favour of the maintenance of the status quo. However, the status quo is not conserved forever by the fundamental rights, but is preconditioned as legitimate. As a consequence, state authorities in general – and especially the legislator – must balance every attempted reform with the citizen's protected rights and prove its 'better right'.[30] Thus, the burden of legitimation is not on the state authorities because they want to change the status quo, but because they want to defy the citizen's fundamental rights. This is where the fundamental rights' dimension of protection comes into play: when state authorities want to interfere in the scope of protection of a fundamental right, they are obliged to legitimize their action, whereas the beneficiary of that right does not need to justify his acts or omissions, as long as he acts within the limits of his right.[31]

III. THE DIMENSION OF PROTECTION BY FUNDAMENTAL RIGHTS (*DIE GRUNDRECHTLICHE SCHUTZDIMENSION*)

A. The Jurisdiction of the Federal Constitutional Court ('BVerfG')

Threats to and interferences in fundamental rights are not merely caused by state acts but also by acts of private persons.[32] Based on the objective dimension of fundamental rights, the doctrine of values contained in fundamental rights (the so-called *objektive Wertordnungslehre*),[33] the Federal Constitutional Court developed in 1958 the objective duty of the judiciary to interpret private law in the light of the values enshrined in the Constitution. With the first judgment of the Federal Constitutional Court on the punishability of abortion in 1973,[34] a duty of the legislator to protect fundamental rights (in this case it was the life of the unborn child) was introduced into German constitutional law. According to the case law[35] of the Federal Constitutional Court, the duties to protect derive on the one hand from the objective values contained in the affected fundamental right, the aforementioned *objektive Wertordnungslehre*.[36] On the other hand, the state authorities' duty to protect stems from human dignity as enshrined in Article 1(1) and 1(3) of

[30] Isensee (n 14) para 47.

[31] With reference to Isensee (n 14) para 47.

[32] More detailed: D Murswiek, 'Freiheit und Freiwilligkeit im Umweltrecht' [1998] *JuristenZeitung* 985, 987ff; Isensee (n 14) paras 83ff; Calliess (n 13) 307ff.

[33] See *Lüth* BVerfGE 7, 198, 205; U Di Fabio, 'Zur Theorie eines grundrechtlichen Wertesystems' in Merten and Papier, *Handbuch der Grundrechte in Deutschland und Europa* (n 21) § 46, paras 4ff; critical Cremer (n 1) 191ff.

[34] *Schwangerschaftsabbruch I* BVerfGE 39, 1, 41.

[35] *Schleyer* BVerfGE 46, 160, 164; *Kalkar I* BVerfGE 49, 89, 140–41; *Mülheim-Kärlich* BVerfGE 53, 30, 57; *Fluglärm* BVerfGE 56, 54, 73; *Schwangerschaftsabbruch II* 88, 203, 251; BVerfG [1998] *Neue Juristische Wochenschrift* 3264 and BGHZ 102, 350, 365 – on damages to forests.

[36] *Schwangerschaftsabbruch I* BVerfGE 39, 1, 42; *Schleyer* 46, 160, 164; *Kalkar I* 49, 89, 141; *Mülheim-Kärlich* 53, 30, 57; *Fluglärm* 56, 54, 73.

the Basic Law. This has been explicitly confirmed by the Federal Constitutional Court in its second judgment concerning the punishability of abortion:

> The reason for the duty to protect lies in Article 1, paragraph 1 of the Basic Law, which explicitly obliges the State to respect and to protect human dignity; its object – and, through this, its extent – are specified by Article 2, paragraph 2 of the Basic Law.[37]

These two lines of dogmatic reasoning are obviously linked by the idea that Article 1(1), sentence 2 ('and protect') and Article 1(3) of the Basic Law oblige state authorities to ensure the implementation of the value-decision contained in the objective contents of the fundamental right in question. On this basis, the Federal Constitutional Court acknowledged a duty to protect not only with regard to unborn life from abortion,[38] but also with regard to the threats of peaceful use of nuclear energy,[39] chemical weapons,[40] road traffic noise and aircraft noise[41] and other aspects of environmental pollution. The central point of these decisions is the basic right to life and physical integrity enshrined in Article 2(2) of the Basic Law. Even so, it is also accepted that – like in the cases of damage to the environment (forests) by air pollution – duties to protect can derive from the right to property in Article 14(1) of the Basic Law.[42]

Naturally, not every duty to protect acknowledged by the Court has led to concrete consequences. When examining whether a duty to protect has been fulfilled, the Federal Constitutional Court[43] stresses the legislator's margin of appreciation to weigh up and to balance the different protected interests that may conflict with each other. However, the jurisprudence is inconsistent with regard to the criteria of examination. The Court distinguishes between a control of obvious interference (test of evidence), of tenability and of content.[44] Usually, it only carries out a 'control of evidence', which means that it examines whether there is an 'obvious' violation of the basic right in question.[45] In recent times, the Court has on occasions referred to the benchmark of the prohibition of insufficient means (*Untermaßverbot*).[46] According to this principle, a sufficient and appropriate protection is necessary when taking conflicting interests into account; the crucial point is that the protection is effective. The provisions made by the legislator must be sufficient for an appropriate and effective protection and must be based on a

[37] BVerfGE 88, 203, 251–52.
[38] *Schwangerschaftsabbruch I* BVerfGE 39, 1, 41–42; *Schwangerschaftsabbruch II* 88, 203, 251.
[39] *Kalkar I* BVerfGE 49, 89, 140ff; *Mülheim-Kärlich* BVerfGE 53, 30, 57ff.
[40] BVerfGE 77, 170, 214–15; more precisely: *Straßenverkehrslärm* 79, 174, 201–02.
[41] *Straßenverkehrslärm* BVerfGE 79, 174, 201–02; *Fluglärm* 56, 54, 73–4.
[42] BVerfG [1998] *Neue Juristische Wochenschrift* 3264, 3265–66.
[43] *Fluglärm* BVerfGE 56, 54, 81.
[44] BVerfGE 50, 290, 332–33.
[45] BVerfG [1996] *Neue Juristische Wochenschrift* 651 and [1996] *Europäische Grundrechte-Zeitschrift* 120.
[46] *Schwangerschaftsabbruch II* BVerfGE 80, 203, 254; on the *Untermaßverbot* debate in detail, see C Calliess, 'Die Leistungsfähigkeit des Untermaßverbots als Kontrollmaßstab grundrechtlicher Schutzpflichten' in R Grote and others (eds), *Festschrift für Christian Starck* (Tübingen, Mohr Siebeck, 2007) 201ff.

careful investigation of the facts as well as on an acceptable appraisal.[47] Unlike the control of evidence, the control based on the prohibition on insufficient means enables a more precise extent of control. Whether the minimum standard of protection is guaranteed is examined by the Federal Constitutional Court in a check on justifiability, which requires a careful investigation of the facts.[48]

Since the Federal Constitutional Court's decision on chemical weapons[49] it has generally been accepted that the violation of the duty to protect constitutes a violation of the fundamental right. Only from then on has it been explicitly clear that the state authorities' duty to protect corresponds to a subjective right to remedy through protection,[50] which can be claimed by a constitutional complaint if state authorities should omit to protect.[51]

B. The Debate in German Doctrine

A large part of the German doctrine has agreed to the Court's jurisprudence on the duty to protect;[52] only some authors reject any constitutional duty to protect based on fundamental rights. One major argument is the principle of separation of powers and the fear of too much influence of the constitutional judiciary to the detriment of the Parliament.[53] However, predominantly the Court's dogmatic reasoning – not the duty to protect in itself – has been criticized.[54] First, the Federal Constitutional Court's theory of an objective order of constitutional values as well as the objective content of fundamental rights that is based on this dogmatic argument is criticized.[55] Moreover, the Federal Constitutional Court is criticized for the fact that it has not sufficiently clarified how a subjective duty to protect can derive from the fundamental rights' objective content.[56]

[47] *Schwangerschaftsabbruch II* BVerfGE 88, 203, 254.

[48] See the dissenting opinions of Mahrenholz and Sommer JJ BVerfGE 88, 203, 355.

[49] BVerfGE 77, 170, 214–15; more precisely: *Straßenverkehrslärm* 79, 174, 201–02.

[50] ibid.

[51] Cremer (n 1) 326ff and 355.

[52] J Dietlein, *Die Lehre von den grundrechtlichen Schutzpflichten* (Berlin, Duncker & Humblot, 1992) 51ff, especially 64ff; Hesse (n 2) para 350; Alexy (n 7) 410ff; Stern (n 1) para 59; Isensee (n 14) para 82; E Klein 'Grundrechtliche Schutzpflicht des Staates' [1989] *Neue Juristische Wochenschrift* 1633; HH Klein, 'Die grundrechtliche Schutzpflicht' [1994] *Deutsches Verwaltungsblatt* 489; G Hermes, *Das Grundrecht auf Schutz von Leben und Gesundheit* (Heidelberg, CF Müller, 1987) 58ff; M Ruffert, *Vorrang der Verfassung und Eigenständigkeit des Privatrechts* (Tübingen, Mohr Siebeck, 2001) 141, 152ff; Calliess (n 13) 437ff; Cremer (n 1) 228ff; E-W Böckenförde, *Staat, Verfassung, Demokratie* (Frankfurt am Main, Suhrkamp, 1991) 159ff.

[53] Schlink (n 14); Poscher (n 21) 167ff.

[54] Cremer (n 1) 229ff; M Jestaedt, *Grundrechtsentfaltung im Gesetz* (Tübingen, Mohr Siebeck, 1999) 42ff; Böckenförde, *Staat, Verfassung, Demokratie* (n 52) 159ff, 190 with more references.

[55] K Stern, *Das Staatsrecht der Bundesrepublik Deutschland*, vol III 1 (Munich, CH Beck 1988) 945ff; Isensee (n 14) para 81; Cremer (n 1) 191ff, 217.

[56] See the dissenting opinion to BVerfGE 39, 1, 68, 73ff; Stern (n 55) 945; Klein, 'Grundrechtliche Schutzpflicht des Staates' (n 52) 1635; C Starck, 'Grundrechtliche Schutzpflichten' in C Stark (ed), *Praxis der Verfassungsauslegung* (Baden Baden, Nomos, 1994) 46, 72.

Against this background, a part of German doctrine explains the duty to protect by the responsibility of state authorities to ensure security. Referring to Thomas Hobbes' philosophy of a contract between state (King) and citizens, which forms the basis of the state's monopoly on the use of force and its corresponding duty to ensure the peace of its citizens, state authorities are obliged to guarantee protection among the citizens themselves. Citizens have a fundamental right to be protected (*Grundrecht auf Sicherheit*).[57] Other authors[58] suggest on the basis of these arguments an approach that puts the duty to protect on a level with the dimension of defence of fundamental rights, the state authorities' duty to respect, by extending the notion of interference. If state authorities allow, by statute, certain acts or behaviour to the citizens, they interfere at the same time with fundamental rights of other citizens. The aforementioned obligation to the peaceful settlement of conflicts forces citizens to tolerate these lawful interferences. As a consequence, the non-prohibition of these (originally private) interferences can be treated as an action by state authorities. Thus, what state authorities do authorize is in their responsibility and therefore – in a wider sense – a public interference. By extending the understanding of public interference, an attribution of private behaviour to state authorities should be attained in order to activate the fundamental rights in their dimension of defence.

The attempts to extend the notion of interference primarily result from the convincing analysis that the efficiency of the fundamental right's dimension of protection (duty to protect) remains weak compared to the fundamental right's dimension of defence (duty to respect).[59] In that sense, the extended notion of interference constitutes a possible reaction to the new threats to positions protected by the fundamental rights. But this can only be convincing to a certain extent.[60] Faced with the fact that a wide scope of protection in conjunction with a wide notion of interferences leads to a precondition that every interference committed by the state must be based on a law (so-called *Totalvorbehalt*), an unlimited widening of the understanding of public interference would undermine the administration's efficiency and flexibility and considerably decrease the legislator's freedom of scope. Ultimately, such an unlimited extension of the dimension of defence would lead to a shift of power to the judiciary, which would not only

[57] cf J Isensee, *Grundrecht auf Sicherheit* (Berlin, de Gruyter, 1983) 34ff; Isensee (n 14) paras 83ff; Stern, *Das Staatsrecht der Bundesrepublik Deutschland* (n 55) 932ff; E Klein (n 52) 1635–36; Klein, 'Die grundrechtliche Schutzpflicht' (n 52) 492–93; fundamental critic: C Möllers, *Staat als Argument* (Munich, CH Beck, 2000) 207ff.

[58] cf J Schwabe, *Probleme der Grundrechtsdogmatik* (PhD thesis, University of Darmstadt, 1977) 19, 40, 213ff; D Murswiek, *Die staatliche Verantwortung für die Risiken der Technik* (Berlin, Duncker & Humblot, 1985) 61ff, 88ff, 102ff; T Koch, *Der Grundrechtsschutz des Drittbetroffenen* (Tübingen, Mohr Siebeck, 2000) 72ff; Poscher (n 21) 156, 167ff.

[59] In that sense: A Roth, *Verwaltungshandeln mit Drittbetroffenheit und Gesetzesvorbehalt* (Berlin, Duncker & Humblot, 1991) 132–33; B Weber-Dürler 'Der Grundrechtseingriff' (1998) 57 *Veröffentlichungen der Vereinigung der Deutschen Staatsrechtslehrer* 78.

[60] See W Roth, *Faktische Eingriffe in Freiheit und Eigentum* (Berlin, Duncker & Humblot, 1994) 261ff; Weber-Dürler, 'Der Grundrechtseingriff' (n 59) 75–76; A Roth, *Verwaltungshandeln mit Drittbetroffenheit und Gesetzesvorbehalt* (n 59) 141–42, 210ff; Calliess (n 13) 410ff; Cremer (n 1) 99, 162ff.

threaten the separation of powers, but also the legal security.[61] However, in order to avoid an excessive extension of the dimension of defence, the potential of the dimension of protection needs to be further examined dogmatically.

C. Conclusions

For the abovementioned reasons it is necessary to understand the state authorities' duty to protect as a dogmatic dimension of protection of human rights of its own. Of course the state's monopoly on the use of force and the corresponding private duty to peace cannot be the dogmatic basis for a fundamental right to be protected; this argument can only explain their origin in a historical sense.[62] Constitutionally the derivation and reasoning of the duty to protect from human dignity, as enshrined in Article 1 of the Basic Law, is of importance. In accordance with Article 1(1), sentence 2 of the Basic Law, every fundamental right contains a dimension of defence *achten*, ie to respect) and a dimension of protection (*schützen*, ie to protect).[63]

According to the constitutional conception that fundamental rights are rules conferring subjective rights,[64] the state's duty to protect must correlate with a claim of the right holder to demand omission or protection. As a consequence, the state is obliged to ward off any private interference in a third party's goods or interests protected by fundamental rights or to prevent the threat or risk of any such interference.

The concrete determination of the legal consequences of the duty to protect depends on the quality of the good or interest protected by the Constitution. Concerning the goods protected by Article 2(2), sentence 1 of the Basic Law, the situation is unproblematic. Life is the precondition for the exercise of all fundamental rights, the physical integrity for some of them. Therefore, both of them have a superior rank within the Basic Law.[65] Compared to this, the right of property in Article 14(1) of the Basic Law ranks lower.[66] Furthermore, the quality of the existing rules needs to be taken into account.

In the event that there is no statutory law, or that the statutory law does not provide efficient protection for the affected goods and interests, a duty of state authorities, especially the legislature, emerges to protect these from private inter-

[61] Roth (n 59) 163ff; A Scherzberg, '"Objektiver" Grundrechtsschutz und subjektives Grundrecht' [1989] *Deutsches Verwaltungsblatt* 1128, 1130; Weber-Dürler (n 59) 76–77; H-U Gallwas, *Faktische Beeinträchtigungen im Bereich der Grundrechte* (Berlin, Duncker & Humblot, 1970) 75, 94–95; Stern (n 55) 1207; differentiating Lübbe-Wolff (n 20) 72ff, 228ff, 308ff; Cremer (n 1) 86 , 99, 162ff with more references.

[62] Möllers, *Staat als Argument* (n 57) 207ff; Calliess (n 13) 88ff; in detail Cremer (n 1) 258ff.

[63] Calliess (n 13) 437ff; in detail Cremer (n 1) 234ff.

[64] See Alexy (n 7) 159ff; U Ramsauer, 'Die Rolle der Grundrechte im System der subjektiven öffentlichen Rechte' (1986) 111 *Archiv des öffentlichen Rechts* 502, 513ff.

[65] cf Isensee (n 14) para 98.

[66] H-H Trute, *Vorsorgestrukturen und Luftreinhalteplanung im Bundesimmissionsschutzgesetz* (Heidelberg, v Decker, 1989) 239; Isensee (n 14) para 141.

ferences.[67] When private persons interfere in goods or interests protected by fundamental rights, the affected person can claim a sufficient protection against risks by state authorities.[68] However, the content of this claim cannot be easily determined in an abstract way, since duties to protect – unlike the duties to respect which aim at a particular action by state authorities – cannot be fulfilled by only one action. As a consequence, the duty to protect leaves to the state authorities, especially the primarily responsible legislator, a margin of appreciation concerning the way of fulfilling the duty. However, the aim of the state authorities' discretionary power is always the efficient accomplishment of the duty to protect, so that a minimum standard of protection must be guaranteed. The benchmark for this minimum standard is the prohibition of insufficient means (the so-called *Untermaßverbot*). Thus, the effective extent of the duty to protect must be determined by the prohibition of insufficient means, which corresponds to the principle of proportionality, but is not identical with the latter.[69] Both have different concepts corresponding to their respective dogmatic origin and their different dogmatic functions (on the one hand, an omission or the limitation of a state action is desired, on the other hand, an action from the state is demanded), but there are similarities in their structure.

Just as it is the case with the principle of proportionality, the prohibition of insufficient means can be examined with the help of a three-step test:[70]

preliminary question: is there a concept of protection by the state with regard to the good or interest protected by the respective fundamental right that is affected by private action?

if yes, is this concept of protection able to protect the good or interest effectively? (first step)

if yes, is there a concept of protection that ensures a more effective protection than the concept that is in use without interfering in a stronger way in the rights of third parties or having an impact on public interests? In other words: is there a more efficient concept that is (just) as mild (second step)? In this way, parts of the concept of protection can also be examined on their effectiveness and possibly be considered as violating the prohibition of insufficient means due to their lack of effectiveness.

if yes, is the protection appropriate with regard to the conflicting goods or interests (third step)? It has to be examined whether it is just and reasonable to have the affected person consent to the remaining threats and risks for the protected good or interest with regard to the conflicting private and public interests with

[67] cf BVerfGE 53, 30, 57–58, 65ff.

[68] cf ibid.

[69] J Dietlein, 'Das Untermaßverbot' [1995] *Zeitschrift für Gesetzgebung* 131, 134ff; Calliess, 'Die Leistungsfähigkeit des Untermaßverbots als Kontrollmaßstab grundrechtlicher Schutzpflichten' (n 46) 201ff; different opinion K-E Hain, 'Der Gesetzgeber in der Klemme zwischen Übermaß- und. Untermaßverbot' [1993] *Deutsches Verwaltungsblatt* 982, 983.

[70] See Calliess (n 13) 577ff with further references.

which it needs to be brought in balance. Here, at the third step, the relevant aspects of the principle of proportionality and the relevant aspects of the prohibition of insufficient means come together.[71]

However, state authorities do not comply with their duty to protect just by an act of legislation. With regard to the rule of law, a statute is a necessary step, but pursuant to Article 1(3) of the Basic Law they also have to ensure the law's effective implementation and acceptance. To this end, the duty to protect is a benchmark for the executive and judiciary for the application and interpretation of statutes to the effect that in cases of doubt, they must be interpreted in such a way that they provide effective protection. Indeed, according to the dynamic character of the duty to protect, the legal provisions must be adapted to the technical and social changes.

IV. FUNDAMENTAL RIGHTS AND PROCEDURE (DUE PROCESS)

The procedural guarantee of fundamental rights complements the rights' dimensions of defence and of protection.[72] Since German understanding of public law generally follows in general a rather substantive approach, procedural elements are understood rather as a supplement. Against this background, procedural aspects of law primarily possess a compensatory function. Therefore, the procedural supplement is more mandatory, the weaker the substantial power of control of the fundamental right is in the individual case. From that point of view, the procedural protection of fundamental rights has a particular significance in the field of duties to protect, which – as mentioned above – necessarily leave a relatively wide margin of appreciation to the legislator.[73]

The procedural protection of fundamental rights can be achieved via information, participation and legal protection.[74]

This procedural *triad* is not only reflected in German environmental and technical law, but is also defined by European and public international law. As the European Court of Human Rights in Strasbourg declared in *Guerra*,[75] the effective accomplishment of the duty to protect deriving from Article 8 of the European Convention on Human Rights confers a right to information to the concerned person. Such a right to information can also derive from the fundamental rights:

[71] Critical with regard to this third step Cremer (n 1) 314ff.

[72] See K Hesse, 'Bestand und Bedeutung der Grundrechte in der Bundesrepublik Deutschland' [1978] *Europäische Grundrechte-Zeitschrift* 427, 434; P Lerche, 'Vorbereitung grundrechtlichen Ausgleichs durch gesetzgeberisches Verfahren' in P Lerche and others (eds), *Verfahren als staats- und verwaltungsrechtliche Kategorie* (Heidelberg, CF Müller, 1984) 97, 101ff; E Schmidt-Aßmann, 'Grundrechte als Organisations- und Verfahrensgarantien' in Merten and Papier (n 21) § 45, paras 5ff; Cremer (n 1) 394ff; see as well BVerfGE 24, 367, 401; 53, 60, 65; 88, 203, 281ff.

[73] Schmidt-Aßmann, 'Grundrechte als Organisations- und Verfahrensgarantien' (n 72) paras 12, 20–21.

[74] See Calliess (n 13) 467 ff.

[75] *Guerra and others v. Italy*, App no 14967/89 (ECtHR, 19 February 1998) paras 58ff.

without information, the persons concerned cannot assess the consequences or risks that are caused by a state authority's action. However, this is an indispensable condition for an action taken by the person concerned, so that any protection of the affected interests remains ineffective without the necessary information. The right to information is therefore a necessary precondition for the protection of fundamental rights.

In the same way, participation of concerned persons (eg in the authorization procedure of an industrial or infrastructure project) belongs to the minimum of procedural protection of fundamental rights.[76] Participation is recompense for the lack of influence on the decisions within the administration and for the limited protection of individual rights owing to the usually low degree of control,[77] which is almost typical for the fundamental rights' duties to protect. This applies particularly in fields where the legislator leaves a wide margin of appreciation to the executive and administration by the use of undefined notions. In this case, the decisive definition of the fundamental rights of the person concerned is not made by the legislator, but during the administrative procedure. The effective participation is a necessary compensation for the indefiniteness of legal rules and the low control by courts that is caused by it.[78]

The access to justice is an important element of the procedural protection of fundamental rights. Corresponding to a tendency in European law, a widening of individual legal protection which lowers the exigencies on the claimant to be affected in its own rights becomes important. Different from German law which entitles claimants access to court only when they can prove to have been potentially violated in an individual right, European law entitles claimants to take action when individual interests are infringed, interests that belong to those protected by the applicable law.[79]

V. DUTY TO RESPECT VERSUS DUTY TO PROTECT – ONLY A GERMAN DEBATE?

Apart from merely bipolar relations, the fundamental rights' dimensions of defence and of protection and the corresponding state authorities' duty to respect and to protect are inseparably connected. With the duty to protect, state authorities become a guarantor of fundamental rights with regard to private interferences. But when they execute their duty, state authorities have to intervene in the fundamental rights of third parties. Against this background, the extent of individual freedom is reflected in the double dimension of fundamental rights,

[76] BVerfGE 53, 30, 66.

[77] cf BVerfGE 61, 82, 115; BVerwG [1985] *Neue Zeitschrift für Verwaltungsrecht* 745.

[78] The Federal Constitutional Court is not that explicit. But in that sense, see the dissenting opinion of Heußner and Simon JJ BVerfGE 53, 69, 75, 77ff; as well as D Grimm, 'Verfahrensfehler als Grundrechtsverstöße' [1985] *Neue Zeitschrift für Verwaltungsrecht* 865, 871.

[79] On the specifications of European Law: BW Wegener, *Rechte des Einzelnen* (Baden-Baden, Nomos, 1998) 295–96.

between the duty to respect and the duty to protect. From this point of view, the scope of protection of a fundamental right can be determined only in a multipolar context by passing a multipolar test of proportionality including a balance of interest.[80] The principle of proportionality on the one hand (duty to respect, dimension of defence) and the prohibition of insufficient means of the duty to protect (dimension of protection) on the other, form a kind of corridor[81] within which the legislator has a margin of appreciation, how to weigh up the conflicting interests and to bring them into balance. This margin of appreciation ensures the separation of powers, especially between legislature and judiciary. Concerning the Court's extent of control, it must be congruent with regard to the state authorities' measures in question, in order to ensure the necessary symmetry between the conflicting dimensions of fundamental rights in multipolar constitutional relations – in concrete terms, the duty to respect and the duty to protect.

Is that concept of a multipolar perspective on fundamental rights including a state authority's duty to protect only a 'German affair'? To a certain extent it is, because the debate has its origin and strongest supporters in German jurisdiction and doctrine. On the other hand, a state authority's duty to protect that derives from fundamental rights can not only be found in Germany but also in Austria[82] and – at least partially – in France[83] and Ireland.[84] Moreover, the European Court of Human Rights in Strasbourg has acknowledged a state authority's duty to protect under the term of 'positive obligations'.[85] In the case of *López Ostra,* the Court developed a duty to protect with regard to the right to respect for private and family life guaranteed by Article 8 of the Convention.[86] However, the Strasbourg Court repeated its remarks made in the case of *Powell and Rayner*[87] which – from

[80] Calliess (n 13) 566ff.

[81] Critical: Hain, 'Der Gesetzgeber in der Klemme zwischen Übermaß- und. Untermaßverbot' (n 69) 984; such a model is indicated by the opinions of C-W Canaris, 'Grundrechtswirkungen und Verhältnismäßigkeitsprinzip in der richterlichen Anwendung und Fortbildung des Rechts' [1989] *Juristische Schulung* 161, 163–64; HD Jarass, 'Grundrechte als Wertentscheidungen' (1985) 110 *Archiv des öffentlichen Rechts* 363, 382ff; A Scherzberg, *Grundrechtsschutz und Eingriffsintensität* (Berlin, Duncker & Humblot 1989) 221–22; Isensee (n 14) paras 165–66; explicitly on such a corridor: W Hoffmann-Riem, 'Reform des Allgemeinen Verwaltungsrechts: Vorüberlegungen' [1994] *Deutsches Verwaltungsblatt* 1381, 1384–85; Cremer (n 1) 310.

[82] cf R Feik, 'Staatliche Gewährleistungspflichten und Nachbarrechte im gewerblichen Betriebsanlagenrecht' in C Grabenwarter and R Thienel (eds), *Kontinuität und Wandel der EMRK: Studien zur Europäischen Menschenrechtskonvention* (Kehl, Engel, 1998) 205ff with more references.

[83] CD Classen, 'Die Ableitung von Schutzpflichten des Gesetzgebers aus Freiheitsrechten – ein Vergleich von deutschem und französischem Verfassungsrecht sowie der Europäischen Menschenrechtskonvention' (1987) 36 *Jahrbuch des öffentlichen Rechts* 29, 30ff; M Ruffert, *Subjektive Rechte im Umweltrecht der Europäischen Gemeinschaft – unter besonderer Berücksichtigung ihrer prozessualen Durchsetzung* (Heidelberg, v Decker, 1996) 52ff; Peter Szczekalla, *Die sogenannten grundrechtlichen Schutzpflichten im deutschen und europäischen Recht* (Berlin, Duncker & Humblot 2002) 919ff.

[84] Szczekalla, *Die sogenannten grundrechtlichen Schutzpflichten im deutschen und europäischen Recht* (n 83) 917ff.

[85] cf R Schmidt-Radefeldt, *Ökologische Menschenrechte: Ökologische Menschenrechtsinterpretation der EMRK und ihre Bedeutung für die umweltschützenden Grundrechte des Grundgesetzes* (Baden-Baden, Nomos, 2000) 66ff; Szczekalla (n 83) 712ff.

[86] *López Ostra v Spain*, App no 16798/90 (ECtHR, 9 December 1994) para 51.

[87] *Powell and Rayner v UK*, App no 9310/81 (ECtHR, 21 February 1990) para 41.

a dogmatic point of view – blur the distinction between dimension of defence and of protection:

> Whether the question is analysed in terms of a positive duty on the State – to take reasonable and appropriate measures to secure the applicant's rights under paragraph 1 of Article 8 (art. 8-1) – as the applicant wishes in his or her case, or in terms of an 'interference by a public authority' to be justified in accordance with paragraph 2 (art. 8-2), the applicable principles are broadly similar. In both contexts attention must be paid to the fair balance that has to be obtained between the competing interests of the individual and of the community as a whole – however in any case the State enjoys a certain margin of appreciation.[88]

In *Guerra*,[89] on the other hand, the Strasbourg Court explicitly stressed that an effective protection of the right to private and family life also covers positive obligations (in that case an obligation to information). According to this, duties to protect deriving from the European Convention of Human Rights are acknowledged, even without a clear dogmatic foundation.[90]

Finally, with regard to EU law, the European Court of Justice acknowledged that intra-Community trade is as likely to be obstructed by a positive act as by

> the fact that a Member State abstains from taking action or, as the case may be, fails to adopt adequate measures to prevent obstacles to the free movement of goods that are created, in particular, by actions by private individuals on its territory aimed at products originating in other Member States.[91]

Thus, Article 34 TFEU in combination with Article 4(3) TEU obliges Member States to take all necessary and adequate measures in order to ensure the respect of this fundamental freedom. On this ground, Member States have a duty to protect with regard to the fundamental freedom of trade. The judicial control was restricted by the European Court of Justice on a control of obvious infringement.[92] Now that the EU has obtained a comprehensive catalogue of fundamental rights by the Charter of Fundamental Rights, it is likely that the duty to protect deriving from fundamental rights will become an element of European protection of fundamental rights as well. Article 1 of the Charter, which is influenced by the wording of Article 1(1) of the Basic Law, contains a sound dogmatic foundation in the formulation 'Human dignity is inviolable. It must be respected *and protected*'.

Against this background, the dogmatic approach of the German judiciary and the doctrine to attribute a fundamental right a dimension of defence and a dimension of protection with a corresponding duty to respect and duty to protect by state authorities[93] does not just seem to be another sophisticated German debate. Instead it might offer an important perspective for a fundamental protection of

[88] *López Ostra v Spain*, App no 16798/90 (ECtHR, 9 December 1994) para 51.

[89] *Guerra and others v Italy*, App no 14967/89 (ECtHR, 19 February 1998) paras 58ff.

[90] R Desgagné, 'Integrating Environmental Values into the European Convention on Human Rights' (1995) 85 *American Journal of International Law* 263, 265ff, 293–94.

[91] Case C-265/95 *Commission v France* [1997] ECR I-6959, para 31.

[92] See also Szczekalla (n 83) 223.

[93] Cremer (n 1) 501ff proved correctly, that these both are the only functions (dimensions) of fundamental rights.

rights that increases the possibilities of establishing a fair balance between different interests of freedom in complex decision-making processes. This might become of some importance in a time where society is longing for additional legitimation beside the democratic process in parliaments.

CASES

BVerfGE 7, 198 – *Lüth* (1958)
BVerfGE 39, 1 – *Schwangerschaftsabbruch* I (1975)
BVerfGE 46, 160 – *Schleyer* (1977)
BVerfGE 49, 89 – *Kalkar I* (1978)
BVerfGE 53, 30 – *Mülheim-Kärlich* (1979)
BVerfGE 56, 54 – *Fluglärm* (1981)
BVerfGE 79, 174 – *Verkehrslärm* (1988)
BVerfGE 81, 242 – *Handelsvertreter* (1990)
BVerfGE 88, 203 – *Schwangerschaftsabbruch II* (1993)
BVerfGE 89, 214 – *Bürgschaftsverträge* (1993)

SELECTED LITERATURE

Alexy R, *Theorie der Grundrechte* (Frankfurt am Main, Suhrkamp, 1986)
Calliess, C, *Rechtsstaat und Umweltstaat – Zugleich ein Beitrag zur Grundrechtsdogmatik im Rahmen mehrpoliger Verfassungsrechtsverhältnisse* (Tübingen, Mohr Siebeck, 2001)
Canaris CW, 'Grundrechte und Privatrecht' (1984) 184 *Archiv für die civilistische Praxis* 201
Cremer W, *Freiheitsgrundrechte* (Tübingen, Mohr Siebeck, 2003)
Dietlein J, *Die Lehre von den grundrechtlichen Schutzpflichten* (Berlin, Duncker & Humblot, 1992)
Isensee J, 'Das Grundrecht als Abwehrrecht und staatliche Schutzpflicht' in J Isensee and P Kirchhof (eds), *Handbuch des Staatsrechts der Bundesrepublik Deutschland*, vol V (Heidelberg, CF Müller, 1992) § 111
Jellinek G, *System der subjektiven öffentlichen Rechte*, 2nd edn (Tübingen, Mohr, 1905)
Jestaedt M, *Grundrechtsentfaltung im Gesetz* (Tübingen, Mohr Siebeck, 1999)
Koch T, *Der Grundrechtsschutz des Drittbetroffenen* (Tübingen, Mohr Siebeck, 2000)
Lerche P, 'Grundrechtlicher Schutzbereich, Grundrechtsprägung und Grundrechtseingriff' in J Isensee and P Kirchhof (eds), *Handbuch des Staatsrechts der Bundesrepublik Deutschland*, vol V (Heidelberg, CF Müller, 1992) § 121
Lübbe-Wolff G, *Grundrechte als Eingriffsabwehrrechte* (Baden-Baden, Nomos, 1988)
Poscher R, *Grundrechte als Abwehrrechte* (Tübingen, Mohr Siebeck, 2003)
Schlink B, 'Freiheit durch Eingriffsabwehr: Rekonstruktion der klassischen Grundrechtsfunktion' [1984] *Europäische Grundrechte-Zeitschrift* 457
Schmidt-Aßmann E, 'Grundrechte als Organisations- und Verfahrensgarantien' in D Merten and H-J Papier (eds), *Handbuch der Grundrechte in Deutschland und Europa*, vol II (Heidelberg, CF Müller, 2006) § 45
Stern K, 'Idee und Elemente eines Systems der Grundrechte' in J Isensee J and P Kirchhof (eds), *Handbuch des Staatsrechts der Bundesrepublik Deutschland*, vol V (Heidelberg, CF Müller, 1992) § 109

3

Interpreting Fundamental Rights – Freedom versus Optimization

AXEL TSCHENTSCHER

I. THE IMPORTANCE OF THE BALANCING DISPUTE

'MORE FREEDOM, LESS balancing!' That is the battle cry in contemporary human rights law. It sounds throughout public international law and has a knock-on effect in national constitutional law. The German version of this debate emanates from the case law of the Federal Constitutional Court (Bundesverfassungsgericht, 'BVerfG', 'FCC' or 'Court'). The Court has adopted a broad variety of balancing measures in its interpretation of fundamental rights, thereby encouraging the theory that basic rights generally have the structure of principles rather than rules.

Ronald Dworkin introduced the theory of principles in the United States. In Germany, the theory of principles is most strongly advocated by Robert Alexy. The German version has a specific flavour. While the Anglo-American discussion of principles focuses on judicial activism and mostly glances over the structural analysis of principles, Alexy introduces additional characteristics to the concept, namely the duty to optimize the principles' normative impact. Structure, optimization and balancing are seen as an interrelated functional framework, forcing courts (and that is, *all* human rights courts, nationally and internationally) to adopt a balancing approach with fine-tuned control as their major tool of adjudication. As a matter of fact, most courts now follow this jurisprudential guideline.

II. BALANCING IN GERMAN CASE LAW AND IN JURISPRUDENCE

A. A Matter of Principle: Balancing Endangers Freedom

Moving from legal rules to legal principles endangers freedom. This view is rarely questioned, even by proponents of the theory of principles, and it holds true in a double sense.

In the libertarian sense of freedom meaning 'absence of restrictions', freedom is endangered because principles are more pervasive in their scope of application than rules tend to be. As Dworkin pointed out when characterizing the somewhat distorted image of 'positivism' he was criticizing:

> To say that someone has a 'legal obligation' is to say that his case falls under a valid legal rule that requires him to do or to forbear from doing something. . . . In the absence of such a valid legal rule there is no legal obligation [1]

For Dworkin, this is all the more reason to resort to principles because he considers the absence of obligations to be a danger for individual rights. The judge's discretion is 'not bound by standards set by the authority in question', and therefore his decision 'is not controlled by a standard'.[2] However, the libertarian reading of the situation is quite the opposite. Where a judge has no legal rule to apply, the court's power to impose state law ends and individual freedom reigns. By moving from a system of legal rules limited in scope to a system of legal principles with much wider potential application, freedom is therefore reduced.

In the liberal sense of freedom meaning 'freedom by protection', the move from rules to principles endangers freedom in a different way. Legal rules work as safeguards of the law and against state intervention. If a basic right is protected by a rule, the protection tends to be stronger than the protection afforded by a matter of principle. A legal rule can only be compromised by explicit exceptions specified in the law. In contrast, a legal principle is always subject to balancing against other principles, so its protection cannot ever afford the same degree of legal

[1] R Dworkin, *Taking Rights Seriously* (Cambridge, MA, Harvard University Press, 1977) 17.
[2] Dworkin, *Taking Rights Seriously* (n 1) 32.

certainty. Accordingly, the rule 'Human dignity is inviolable' (Article 1(1), sentence 1 of the German Constitution, Basic Law, *Grundgesetz*, 'GG') results in stronger protection than any (hypothetical) equivalent principle to the effect that 'The principle of human dignity is to be protected'. As another example of this effect, within international human rights law, the rule of non-refoulement would be compromised if questions of extradition were submitted to balancing against the principle of national security.[3]

B. German Federal Constitutional Court Case Law

Notwithstanding the risk of endangering freedom, the German Federal Constitutional Court has generally adopted balancing in its interpretation of fundamental rights. The interpretation of the German Constitution took a decisive turn with the *Lüth* decision in 1958. When the Court upheld the plaintiff's right to call for a boycott on grounds of free speech, it opened the floodgates for broad control over private law. This was achieved by interpreting constitutional rights as 'an objective order of values', intended to strengthen the effect of these rights.[4] The term 'order of values' was subsequently no longer used and was replaced by the notion that basic rights have an 'objective dimension' in addition to their subjective dimension as individual claims. The Court now no longer refers to values and instead refers to 'the principles [. . .] expressed by constitutional rights'.[5]

Collisions of principles are resolved by balancing. For this task, the Court resorts to an even more general principle in constitutional interpretation: the meta-principle of proportionality. The three tenets of this meta-principle are well known in international and national human rights law: suitability, necessity and proportionality in the narrower sense. The suitability requirement prohibits any means being adopted which are unhelpful for or obstruct promoting the legislative goals. It puts a stop to self-contradictory laws. The necessity requirement demands that if an alternative, less interfering and equally suitable means is available, this must be adopted. This requirement calls for efficiency in the sense of Pareto optimality for the law. Finally, the requirement for proportionality in the narrower sense is synonymous with balancing. The Court weighs the advantages to the public of implementing the means (eg national security) against the disadvantages to the individual of having his or her freedom reduced (eg by phone tapping). In cases where competing basic rights apply, the Court weighs the basic rights of the one group (eg the right to publicly call for a boycott) against the basic rights of the opposing group(s) (ie economic freedom of merchants). Whenever the advantage achieved is out of proportion to the disadvantage inflicted, the means is considered to be an

[3] M Scheinin, Statement of the Special Rapporteur on the Promotion and Protection of Human Rights and Fundamental Freedoms while Countering Terrorism (Security Council Counter-Terrorism-Committee, New York, 24 October 2005) www.un.org/sc/ctc/pdf/ ScheininCTC2005.pdf.

[4] *Lüth* BVerfGE 7, 198, 205.

[5] *Handelsvertreter* BVerfGE 81, 242, 254.

unconstitutional infringement on basic rights. Almost every decision of the German Federal Constitutional Court that strikes down a statute on the basis of substantive control has its roots in this balancing procedure.

'Optimization' has been mentioned by the German Federal Constitutional Court as the overall purpose of the balancing procedure. When considering whether a book should be classified as pornography, the Court balanced artistic freedom on the one hand with the state's interest in protecting minors from pornography on the other hand, 'with the goal of optimization' for both principles.[6] The same formula had already been applied in the conflict between artistic freedom and state symbolism in a flag case[7] and had been taken up by other courts, most notably the German Federal Administrative Court.[8] Optimization in this series of rulings was however explicitly distinguished from 'maximization'. A variety of television programmes is in the interests of optimizing the freedom of journalists, but this must be distinguished from 'maximizing' this right.[9]

C. Dworkin's Principle as a Generic Term for Non-Rules

What constitutes a principle and may thus be subject to balancing? According to Dworkin, principles are legal considerations that lack the 'all or nothing' applicability of legal rules.[10] Such considerations can be part of the law, ie binding on officials, without stating the conditions for their application or their relative strength compared with other considerations. A principle such as 'No man may profit from his own wrong' only implies one reason (amongst others) for the principle; it may prevail today and yet be superseded by a competing consideration tomorrow. A rule such as 'A will is invalid unless signed by three witnesses' applies provided the specific set of conditions is satisfied; it is definitive in application as long as it is not overruled by superior law.

Dworkin never draws a clear line between 'principles, policies and other sorts of standards', but uses the term 'principle' generically to refer to everything but rules.[11] The examples he gives of circumstances where general legal principles overrule rules are cases of strong principles. For example, he refers to a will being invalidated as a result of the principle 'no man may profit from his own wrong', and a contract clause about limited liability being declared void as a result of the principle 'no man may unjustly take advantage of the economic necessities of others'. Not all principles in Dworkin's broad sense are so strong and have this power. In not attributing a specific force to legal principles, he leaves unanswered the question as to what a legal principle requires judges to do.

[6] *Josephine Mutzenbacher* BVerfGE 83, 130, 143.
[7] *Bundesflagge* BVerfGE 81, 278, 292.
[8] *Glykolwein* BVerwGE 87, 37, 45–46.
[9] *Rundfunkentscheidung* BVerfGE 83, 238, 321–26.
[10] Dworkin (n 1) 24.
[11] Dworkin (n 1) 22.

D. Alexy's Principles as a Duty to Optimize

Alexy's theory of principles specifies the requirement missing in Dworkin's theory. Principles require balancing, ie the application of the meta-principle of proportionality, and this necessarily involves optimization.[12] Wherever legal principles exist, the duty to optimize their normative impact follows. In particular, the meta-principles of suitability and necessity address optimization relative to what is *factually* possible. The necessity requirement, for example, dictates that if an alternative means exists that is equally suitable in promoting the state interest and yet interferes less with individual rights, this means must be chosen. Since this does not diminish any of the interests being realized and one interest is further promoted by the alternative means, the sub-principle expresses Pareto optimality.

The specific balancing procedure that implements the third sub-principle is the rule called the 'law of balancing': 'The greater the degree of non-satisfaction of, or detriment to, one principle, the greater must be the importance of satisfying the other'.[13] Press freedom can, for example, legitimately be curtailed in the interest of national security as long as the weight of the security principle at least equals the weight of the infringement and thereby compensates for the loss. In always choosing the principle of greater weight, the law of balancing makes sure that optimization takes place to the extent that public policies, if implemented, always increase the total level of interest satisfaction, and never decrease it. Alexy calls this an optimization relative to what is *legally* possible.[14]

But how does one weigh principles, even relatively? According to Alexy, three factors relating to interest satisfaction have to be considered within a weighing formula:[15] the *importance* of the objective and of the right, the *probability* of realizing the objective and of the interference with the right, and the *intensity* of the loss for either the objective (if the measure is not applied) or for the right (if the measure is applied). Applied to the example of national security versus press freedom, on the one side, how important is the part of national security protected by the measure, how certain is its protection, and how far does the protective effect carry? On the other side, how important is the part of press freedom affected by the measure, how likely is the measure to result in a loss of freedom, and how intensely does this affect the general operations of the press? Even though there is no binding determination of the relative weights of the various interests, the law of balancing identifies what is significant for balancing.[16] By way of illustration, both sides of the balancing could be considered as a product of the factors' importance, probability and intensity in favour of or against the proposed

[12] R Alexy, 'Constitutional Rights, Balancing, and Rationality' (2003) 16 *Ratio Juris*, 131, 135.

[13] R Alexy, *A Theory of Constitutional Rights*, J Rivers tr (Oxford, OUP, 1985) 102.

[14] Alexy, 'Constitutional Rights, Balancing, and Rationality' (n 12) 136; R Alexy, 'Die Gewichtsformel' in J Jickeli and others (eds), *Gedächtnisschrift Jürgen Sonnenschein* (Berlin, de Gruyter, 2003) 772.

[15] ibid 790.

[16] Alexy, *The Argument From Injustice: A Reply to Legal Positivism*, L & B Paulson tr (Oxford, OUP, 2002) 105.

measure. The total weight in favour of the state's side must be equal to or greater than the opposing total weight in favour of the individual's side.

E. Carrying the Argument Even Further

Alexy is not satisfied with identifying the optimization within balancing. He links all parts of his legal philosophy to this interpretive approach, even deducing the necessity of non-positivism.[17] If principles are *optimizing commands* whereas rules are *definitive commands* (and free from balancing), then any incidence of legal balancing implies the existence of principles. 'A criterion for whether or not a judge appeals to principles for support is whether or not he undertakes to strike a balance'.[18] Accordingly, every legal system that is at least minimally developed necessarily includes principles (the incorporation thesis). This leads Alexy to refute legal positivism. If every legal norm, every legal decision, and every legal system as a whole necessarily claims to be legally correct (the correctness argument) and if principles, as optimizing commands, require a realization to the greatest possible extent (the principles argument), then at least some of the contents of the arguments with which the judge justifies the balance he strikes must have the character of moral arguments.[19] A non-justifiable norm is either defective (the qualifying connection) or, in the case of extreme injustice, even lacks legal character (the classifying connection).

III. CRITICISM OF THE BALANCING APPROACH

A. Early Criticism in General

Since the first decisions of the Federal Constitutional Court, there has been emphatic criticism of the balancing approach, including the following allegations: 'The freedom of the legal subject is replaced by the objectivity of a value'.[20] Court practice leads to a 'purposeful interpretive reversal of basic rights'.[21] Critics feared all along that an objective order of values or principles (which was later combined with a duty on all state powers to optimize) would subject the entire legal system to the jurisdiction of the Federal Constitutional Court.[22]

[17] ibid 68.
[18] ibid 72.
[19] ibid 77.
[20] E Forsthoff, 'Zur heutigen Situation einer Verfassungslehre' in H Barion and others (eds), *Epirrhosis: Festgabe für Carl Schmitt* (Berlin, Duncker & Humblot, 1968) 190.
[21] C Schmitt, 'Die Tyrannei der Werte' in *Säkularisation und Utopie* (Stuttgart, Kohlhammer, 1967) 37.
[22] E Forsthoff, *Der Staat in der Industriegesellschaft: Dargestellt am Beispiel der Bundesrepublik Deutschland*, 2nd edn (Munich, CH Beck, 1968) 149; EW Böckenförde, 'Grundrechte als Grundsatznormen: Zur gegenwärtigen Lage der Grundrechtsdogmatik' in EW Böckenförde, *Staat, Verfassung, Demokratie: Studien zur Verfassungstheorie und zum Verfassungsrecht*, 2nd edn (Frankfurt am Main, Suhrkamp, 1992) 187.

B. Criticism of Fundamental Rights as Principles

Nearly three decades later, Jürgen Habermas raised similar concerns, claiming a downgrading of constitutional rights to the level of policies. 'For if in cases of collision *all* reasons can assume the character of policy arguments, then the fire wall erected in legal discourse by a deontological understanding of legal norms and principles collapses'.[23] By understanding most, if not all, constitutional provisions as principles, everything becomes a matter of balancing and hardly any decision of the Federal Constitutional Court can be effectively criticized. 'By being open to everything and excluding only the obvious, nearly everything is possible'.[24] The theory has little structure and is very dogmatic, and as it draws so many conflicts into the realm of constitutional court adjudication, it works like a 'constitutionalization trap'.[25] Similarly, the notion of basic rights as principles is criticized as undermining the effective *material* protection of individual rights in sub-constitutional law. It also undermines the *institutional* protection of individual rights achieved by the separation of legislative and adjudicative functions. The Constitution determines everything; the Constitutional Court rules supreme. Overall, the application of the balancing approach, even if it were well suited to explain contemporary court practice, results in 'dogmatic and methodological collateral damages'.[26]

Notwithstanding this criticism, the meta-principle of proportionality and the balancing procedure it incorporates are broadly accepted in German academic literature and court practice. There remains strong controversy, however, as to whether these elements should be based on a theory of principles and, moreover, whether principles should be understood as duties to optimize. When the German state governments recently argued against the Federal Constitutional Court's control over the specific rates for funding public broadcasting, they challenged the Court's 'optimization of value judgements' as a fundamental contradiction to their legislative powers.[27] Some commentators emphasize that the principle of proportionality does not require optimization at all.[28]

C. Criticism of Organizational Principles

Germany 'is a democratic . . . state' (Article 20(1) GG). This provision can be read as a rule with strong formal properties, eg that any authoritative decision must

[23] J Habermas, *Between Facts and Norms: Contributions to a Discourse Theory of Law and Democracy*, W Rehg tr (Cambridge, Polity Press, 1996) 258–59.

[24] R Poscher, *Grundrechte als Abwehrrechte* (Tübingen, Mohr Siebeck, 2003) 75–76.

[25] ibid 81–82.

[26] M Jestaedt, 'Die Abwägungslehre – ihre Stärken und ihre Schwächen' in Otto Depenheuer and others (eds), *Festschrift für Josef Isensee* (Heidelberg, CF Müller, 2007) 260.

[27] *Rundfunkfinanzierungsstaatsvertrag* BVerfGE 119, 181, 203.

[28] C Starck in *von Mangoldt/Klein/Starck: Kommentar zum Grundgesetz*, vol I, 5th edn (Munich, Franz Vahlen, 2005) Art 1(3), 162.

ultimately be based on an act of the people themselves or on the activity of officers democratically elected by the people. It can also be read as a principle requiring as much citizen participation as possible in the circumstances, ie the highest possible 'level of democracy' rather than a mere 'label of democracy'. This 'principalization' approach has been criticized as endangering the 'normativity of the constitution'.[29]

IV. SOME ANALYSIS

The following analysis will first test the merits of the two groups of criticism and then look for alternatives to the Alexy-type theory of principles prevailing in German constitutional law.

A. How Arbitrary is Balancing?

Even among the few critical voices, the criticism falls into two opposing directions regarding the impact of fundamental rights when interpreted as principles. Some critics fear an inappropriately *strong* impact of fundamental rights if they were to rule every part of the legal system. Other critics focus on the *weak* protection of the rights themselves. Taking account of both schools of thought, the conclusion is that the theory both endangers the structure of the legal system whilst also failing to protect the individual holder of rights.

A two-pronged counter-argument has been raised against the criticism that balancing renders everything possible. In its radical form, the scepticism is simply not persuasive because it would imply that balancing could *never* yield rational results. There are clear cases where balancing gives rational outcomes – for example, the unconstitutionality of a law imposing the death penalty for littering.[30] On the other hand, no proponent of balancing ever claimed that *every* case could be decided by this procedure or that there was only ever one definitive rational way. The procedure is helpful, but not foolproof.

B. What Remains Exempt from Balancing?

Notwithstanding the ubiquitous presence of principles in German constitutional law, some areas remain exempt from balancing. Most notably, the protection of human dignity is absolute (Article 1(1), sentence 1 GG) and it follows a different pattern of adjudication and is not subject to any balancing. Furthermore, the core meaning of basic rights is to be protected irrespective of how strong the state's

[29] S Unger, *Das Verfassungsprinzip der Demokratie: Normstruktur und Norminhalt des grundgesetzlichen Demokratieprinzips* (Tübingen, Mohr Siebeck, 2008) 164.

[30] cf M Borowski, *Die Glaubens- und Gewissensfreiheit des Grundgesetzes* (Tübingen, Mohr Siebeck, 2006) 209.

interest in regulation may be (Article 19(2) GG). The Basic Rights section of the German Constitution provides that some forms of restrictions may only apply in specific conditions, whilst others are prohibited altogether. Censorship and the death penalty are absolutely prohibited (Article 5(1), sentence 3 GG, Article 102 GG). Forced labour may only be imposed on persons who are deprived of their liberty by court sentence (Article 12(3) GG). In expropriation cases, the extent of the compensation is subject to balancing, but the requirement for compensation as such is a rule, not a principle, and therefore it is mandatory that the state give compensation (Article 14(3) GG). Similarly, the protection of German citizens against extradition to a country outside the European Union (Article 16(2), sentence 1 GG) and the guarantee of citizenship (Article 16(1) GG) are not subject to balancing. These are examples of rules which are protected as fundamental rights. They establish islands of absolute protection within a sea of balancing.

In addition to explicit rules within the law, unwritten rules result from jurisprudence or court practice. The duty to optimize, for example, is itself a rule and does not share the basic right's character as being a principle.[31] Most importantly, the results of balancing tend to take the form of rules. While the German legal system does not contain a doctrine of formally binding precedent like the common law systems, a material notion of stare decisis nevertheless underlies court practice. Therefore in practice the rules achieved by balancing are materially binding for future decisions. A balancing decision that acknowledges the superior weight of free political speech as expressed in the public distribution of pamphlets, notwithstanding that such activity disturbs the free flow of commerce in a marketplace, is a rule. This rule will be applied whenever the same conflict arises in future cases. Citizens, therefore, are not submitted to the uncertainties of balancing over and over again, but can rely on a progressively more extensive system of rules about the effective extent of their freedoms.

Another argument about the limited extent of balancing has been presented by Alexy for some time. Agreeing with his critics, he insists that the Constitution should not always be understood as a determinate *foundation* of law, but also at times as an indeterminate *framework* for law. Within his 'theory of leeway' he acknowledges institutional and substantive discretion, which he considers to build a counterforce to the duty to optimize. Where, for example, the Constitution does not determine legal rules by prohibitions or requirements, the legislator has a structural leeway and is (at least in this context) exempt from the control of the Federal Constitutional Court.[32] Structural leeway gives the legislators freedom, within bounds, to choose the goals, determine the means and – most importantly – even set the stage for balancing because, in Alexy's view of constitutional law, there can be more than one correct outcome of the balancing procedure. Parliament may, for example, deem the prohibition on tobacco advertisements to be an adequate means of fighting smoking-related illnesses. The weight of this

[31] M Borowski, *Grundrechte als Prinzipien* (Baden-Baden, Nomos, 1998) 76–77.

[32] R Alexy, 'Verfassungsrecht und einfaches Recht – Verfassungsgerichtsbarkeit und Fachgerichtsbarkeit' (2002) 61 *Veröffentlichungen der Vereinigung der Deutschen Staatsrechtslehrer* 16.

measure and of its interference with economic freedom will be adjudicated according to a rough assessment (ie low, middle or high) of the relative weight of the factors' importance, probability and intensity. Accordingly, this might very well result in a draw between both sides, ie a shortfall in the structural leeway of balancing. In such a case, the balance determined by the legislators takes precedence over any criticism. The structural leeway theory is reinforced by the view that the Constitution does not provide for fine-tuned control.

In addition to structural leeway, epistemic leeway results from the inability to determine the applicable conditions for prohibitions and requirements. Empirical uncertainty about causes and effects does *not* automatically lead to an optimization of basic rights.[33] On the contrary, taking into account the principles of the separation of powers and democracy, the legislators should be given discretion in adopting empirical premises for law-making.

C. Is Law by Rules and without Principles Possible?

Modern law relies strongly on the flexibility of its application. Not only are judges conscious of the leeway they have in interpretation, but the legislature and government (being the other powers within the institutional balance) also require this flexibility, in order to focus on the general objectives of political decisions rather than the detail. Drafting legal precepts in the form of principles fits nicely with this collective interest in flexibility. The theoretical question of government by rules leads to the pragmatic question of whether or not rules alone are suitably flexible for modern legal systems.

Owing to their difference in structure, rules tend to be less flexible than principles. By definition, they either apply or do not apply automatically if the relevant criteria are satisfied. There may be certain exceptions to a rule's application, but no balancing requirement disturbs the definitive application of a rule. If on the facts the criteria stipulated for the rule (ie its conditions) are satisfied, then the legal answer it supplies (ie its consequences) follows automatically, based on the rule's validity within the legal system.

With principles, however, even where the conditions for the legal precept are satisfied, the principle's application remains subject to balancing. The principle will have no impact on the outcome if a countervailing factor outweighs it during balancing. Accordingly, the principle 'press freedom . . . is guaranteed' (Article 5(1), sentence 2 GG) establishes a legal 'guarantee' that will, however, in many cases be outweighed by the superior weight attributed to the right to privacy. The legislature is free to establish any number of conflicting principles without considering their relative impact a priori. Since conflicts of principles are not considered to exclude their application, many principles can be applicable at the same time. The Court will resolve the issues of material conflict when applying them.

[33] Alexy, 'Verfassungsrecht und einfaches Recht' (n 32) 27–28.

Given the broad scope of their applicability, legislators make use of the fact that principles are more flexible by design.

Many principles are also vague with respect to the conditions in which they apply. The principle 'press freedom . . . is guaranteed' does not specify what falls within the term 'press freedom'. It might or might not include internet blogs and the like. The legal meaning of the term 'press freedom' might very well deviate from ordinary language. In summary, principles are always flexible in the manner in which they are applied (the output side) and often also with respect to the conditions for their application (the input side).

It is only possible to give similar flexibility to rules on the input side. The conditions as to when a rule applies can be vague, whilst the manner in which a rule is applied is always definitive – and if the criteria for the rule's application are satisfied, the rule will apply in all circumstances. The rule 'A contract violating morality is void' (§ 138(1) German Civil Code, 'BGB') is strict in its application, but very flexible with respect to the vague conditions in which it will apply. There are quite a few similar general rules. The rule 'ownership follows possession in good faith' (cf § 932(1), sentence 1 BGB) and the rule 'parties are liable for failing in their duty to observe due diligence' (cf § 276 BGB) are further examples. Dworkin claims that rules and principles can play much the same role, and that the difference between them is 'almost a matter of form alone'.[34] The example he gives from the Sherman Act is quite similar to the morality rule mentioned above, namely 'every contract in restraint of trade shall be void'. The US Supreme Court treated this provision as a rule, but added flexibility by introducing the notion of 'unreasonable restraint' into its conditions. This allowed the provision to function as a rule, but in practice also substantially as a principle because a court has to take other principles into account in order to determine the 'unreasonableness' of the restraint. In summary, adding flexibility to the conditions of a rule can achieve quite similar results to relying on the balancing procedure used with principles.

D. Can we have Legal Principles without the Notion of Optimization?

The duty to optimize principles is what distinguishes Alexy's view on principles from Dworkin's concept. Optimization is the most contested aspect of the theory of principles in German jurisprudence. For many scholars and judges, it would be most appealing to abolish the notion of optimization whilst adhering to the balancing approach where unavoidable with respect to fundamental rights.

To illustrate the issue, let us consider three cases relating to the regulation of protest marches. In the first case it is claimed that the march should be prohibited because the protesters trespass on private property. Here the combined principle of free speech and assembly is weighed against the principle of the state's duty to protect private property. The 'goal of optimization' of both principles results in

[34] Dworkin (n 1) 27.

the principle of free speech not being fulfilled at all in this case because the court will grant precedence to property protection and prohibit the march. In the second case it is claimed that the march should be prohibited because it reduces the amount of business at local stores. Here the combined principle of free speech and assembly is weighed against the state's duty to protect economic freedom. The court will allow the march to take place, thereby giving precedence to free speech over business interests. However, the principle of economic freedom still protects the local store owners' interests to a certain extent. The 'goal of optimization' of both principles forces the state to regulate the time, place and manner of the protest march to accommodate the interests of business and the marchers as far as possible. In the third case it is claimed that the march should be prohibited because the protesters are critical of local government. Here the combined principle of free speech and assembly is effectively not weighed against anything, because the government's political interest in reducing criticism is not a legitimate state interest, and therefore is incapable of legitimately interfering with free speech. The protesters will win.

How would these cases be affected if we retained principles, but abolished the notion of optimization? The outcome of all three cases would be the same. The protesters would lose the first case, but win the second and third cases. Furthermore, the combined principle of free speech and assembly in these cases would not be realized to any lesser extent if we abolished the notion of optimization. Protest marches would take place with no modification whatsoever. The only difference would occur in the second case and would affect only the business interests, ie given the countervailing principle. While the notion of optimization on both sides of the scales would force the state to try to accommodate the protesters' interests as well as economic freedom as far as possible, in a legal world without optimization the court may resort to an 'all or nothing' decision. Accordingly, only the combined principle of free speech and assembly would be decisive in the second case. As it would outweigh the countervailing principle of economic freedom in balancing, all other considerations would be irrelevant. This would relieve the government from any duty to regulate the time, place and manner of the march. It would also relieve the court from any need to suggest specific measures to accommodate both the business interests and the marches. In effect, the court's balancing procedure is linked to the positive law established by the government.

Many other case constellations are possible, but there is no need to consider these here because the general direction of what the answer will be is clear from the few examples given above. We can in fact have legal principles without the notion of optimization. The outcome of the balancing procedure will not change without optimization. However, the control of the Federal Constitutional Court over government regulation would be less fine-tuned. Its decisions would be restricted to an 'all or nothing' statement regarding the relative weight of the principles involved with regard to the specific facts of the case.

Is the notion of principles without optimization the right way to think about fundamental rights in German constitutional law? The Federal Constitutional

Court would disagree. Its jurisdiction is full of examples of fine-tuned control, even where the term 'optimization' is never mentioned. It has been used or misused, depending on one's perspective, to call for very specific limitations on legislation. For example, the constitutional principle about the protection of private property (Article 14(1), sentence 1 GG) has been interpreted as a duty on the government to leave at least half of income free from taxes or burdens.[35] The Court's jurisdiction now extends to all areas of public and private law, leaving hardly any details untouched. Therefore, abolishing the notion of optimization might appear to be an attractive way to scale back the Court's influence and re-empower the legislature.

V. CONCLUSION

This chapter challenges the balancing approach as a danger to individual liberty. It finds that there are good reasons to interpret much of the contents of the fundamental rights as rule-based rather than principle-based; flexibility in a legal system does not require a structure of principles but can also be achieved with properly drafted rules; principles can be understood without the notion of optimization in order to reduce the courts' preponderance over legislative power.

CASES

BVerfGE 7, 198 – *Lüth* (1958)
BVerfGE 81, 242 – *Handelsvertreter* (1990)
BVerfGE 81, 278 – *Bundesflagge* (1990)
BVerfGE 83, 130 – *Josephine Mutzenbacher* (1990)
BVerfGE 83, 238 – 6 *Rundfunkentscheidung* (1991)
BVerwGE 87, 37 – *Glykolwein* (1990)
BVerfGE 115, 97 – *Halbteilungsgrundsatz* (2006)
BVerfGE 119, 181 – *Rundfunkfinanzierungsstaatsvertrag* (2007)

SELECTED LITERATURE

Alexy R, *A Theory of Constitutional Rights*, J Rivers tr (Oxford, OUP, 1985)
—— *The Argument From Injustice: A Reply to Legal Positivism*, L & B Paulson tr (Oxford, OUP, 2002)
——'Verfassungsrecht und einfaches Recht – Verfassungsgerichtsbarkeit und Fachgerichtsbarkeit' (2002) 61 *Veröffentlichungen der Vereinigung der Deutschen Staatsrechtslehrer* 16, 8–33
——'Constitutional Rights, Balancing, and Rationality' (2003) 16 *Ratio Juris* 131–40

[35] *Halbteilungsgrundsatz* BVerfGE 115, 97.

——'Die Gewichtsformel' in J Jickeli and others (eds), *Gedächtnisschrift Jürgen Sonnenschein* (Berlin, de Gruyter, 2003) 771–92

Böckenförde EW, 'Grundrechte als Grundsatznormen: Zur gegenwärtigen Lage der Grundrechtsdogmatik' in EW Böckenförde, *Staat, Verfassung, Demokratie: Studien zur Verfassungstheorie und zum Verfassungsrecht*, 2nd edn (Frankfurt am Main, Suhrkamp, 1992) 159–99

——'Grundrechtstheorie und Grundrechtsinterpretation' [1974] *Neue Juristische Wochenschrift* 1529–38

Borowski M, *Grundrechte als Prinzipien* (Baden-Baden, Nomos, 1998)

——*Die Glaubens- und Gewissensfreiheit des Grundgesetzes* (Tübingen, Mohr Siebeck, 2006)

Dworkin R, *Taking Rights Seriously* (Cambridge, MA, Harvard University Press, 1977)

Forsthoff E, 'Zur heutigen Situation einer Verfassungslehre' in H Barion and others (eds), *Festgabe Carl Schmitt* (Berlin, Duncker & Humblot, 1968) 185–211

——*Der Staat in der Industriegesellschaft: Dargestellt am Beispiel der Bundesrepublik Deutschland*, 2nd edn (Munich, CH Beck, 1971)

Habermas J, *Between Facts and Norms: Contributions to a Discourse Theory of Law and Democracy*, W Rehg tr (Cambridge, Polity Press, 1996)

Jestaedt M, 'Die Abwägungslehre – ihre Stärken und ihre Schwächen' in O Depenheuer and others (eds), *Festschrift für Josef Isensee* (Heidelberg, CF Müller, 2007) 253–75

Poscher R, *Grundrechte als Abwehrrechte: Reflexive Regelung rechtlich geordneter Freiheit* (Tübingen, Mohr Siebeck, 2003)

Scheinin M, Statement of the Special Rapporteur on the Promotion and Protection of Human Rights and Fundamental Freedoms while Countering Terrorism (Security Council Counter-Terrorism-Committee, New York, 24 October 2005) www.un.org/ sc/ ctc/ pdf/ ScheininCTC2005.pdf

Schmitt C, 'Die Tyrannei der Werte' in *Säkularisation und Utopie* (Stuttgart, Kohlhammer, 1967) 37–62

Unger S, *Das Verfassungsprinzip der Demokratie: Normstruktur und Norminhalt des grundgesetzlichen Demokratieprinzips* (Tübingen, Mohr Siebeck, 2008)

4

The Basic Right to 'Free Development of the Personality' – Mere Protection of Personality Development versus General Right of Freedom of Action

WOLFRAM CREMER

> 'Every person shall have the right to free development of his personality insofar as he does not violate the rights of others or offend against the constitutional order or the moral law (Article 2(1) Basic Law).'*

* Art 2 Abs 1 GG: Jeder hat das Recht auf die freie Entfaltung seiner Persönlichkeit, soweit er nicht die Rechte anderer verletzt und nicht gegen die verfassungsmäßige Ordnung oder das Sittengesetz verstößt.

I. INTRODUCTION

THE PURPOSE OF basic rights is generally to provide protection for certain freedoms, namely those that are included in the respective constitution's bill of rights. Freedoms which are not included in the respective bill of rights do not have this constitutional privilege of being protected by the basic rights. This also applies to the Basic Law of the Federal Republic of Germany (*Grundgesetz*, referred to as the 'Basic Law'). Only the freedoms included in the basic rights norms of the Basic Law have (in accordance with Article 1(3) of the Basic Law)[1] the privilege of being protected against actions by the state. This does not touch on the content and scope of the particular protection, but only whether basic rights' protection applies at all.

To define the freedom afforded by a particular basic rights norm, the norm must be investigated. This investigation is required for every basic rights norm, including Article 2(1) of the Basic Law. The distinction is that Article 2(1) of the Basic Law is, without a doubt, the default basic right in the Basic Law's bill of rights. From this it follows that only through interpreting Article 2(1) of the Basic Law can it be ultimately determined whether a particular human behaviour[2] enjoys protection through the basic rights at all. In other words, the scope of protection[3] of a basic right indicates the subject matter which is protected through a basic right.[4] In any particular case, it is necessary to define the scope of protection of the particular basic right. If a particular human behaviour falls within the scope of protection of a so-called specific 'liberty' basic right (*spezielles Freiheitsgrundrecht*), it is not necessary to examine Article 2(1) of the Basic Law any further as a result of the principle of subsidiarity.[5] If on the other hand the particular human behaviour does not fall within a specific liberty basic right, then Article 2(1) of the Basic Law should be used

[1] Art 1(3) of the Basic Law reads as follows: 'The following basic rights shall bind the legislature, the executive and the judiciary as directly applicable law'.

[2] Art 2(1) of the Basic Law includes the protection of behaviour (natural doing) as well as the protection of integrity of a natural being. See further section II.

[3] In light of the facts of the particular case it must be decided if the defined area of life is comprehensively protected through the basic rights norm. At times it is necessary to distinguish between the scope of protection and the scope of regulation of the basic right. A famous example is Art 8(1) of the Basic Law, where the scope of regulation and the scope of protection differ. The subject of regulation of Art 8(1) of the Basic Law is the right to assemble, but its scope of protection is limited to only peaceful and unarmed assemblies; cf also the discussions relating to other constraints on the scopes of protection in K Stern, 'Grundrechte und ihre Schranken' in P Badura and H Dreier (eds), *Festschrift 50 Jahre Bundesverfassungsgericht*, vol I (Tübingen, Mohr Siebeck, 2001) 11ff.

[4] The scope of protection is divided into an objective, thematic scope of protection and a personal scope of protection. This chapter will not discuss the personal scope of protection but it should be noted that the personal scope of protection must take into consideration the wording of the respective basic right as well as Art 19(3) of the Basic Law. Art 19(3) of the Basic Law reads as follows: 'The basic rights shall also apply to domestic artificial persons to the extent that the nature of such rights permits'.

[5] As the default basic right, Art 2(1) of the Basic Law also covers the objective protection of the specific liberty basic rights. Art 2(1) of the Basic Law does not apply in instances where certain specific constraints of freedom are covered by specific basic rights, as a result of the principle of subsidiarity. See H Dreier in *Dreier: Grundgesetzkommentar*, vol I, 2nd edn (Tübingen, Mohr Siebeck, 2004) Art 2, para 1, para 30.

to determine whether it is necessary to legitimize the particular state action in accordance with a basic right at all.

Given this background, for cases where it is assumed there is no applicable specific liberty basic right, it is necessary to consider the scope of protection afforded by Article 2(1) of the Basic Law. In particular, does Article 2(1) of the Basic Law guarantee a general right of freedom of action or simply a limited scope for development of the personality? Whilst this article refers to specific criteria of the German Basic Law, this does not mean that the German discourse and the thoughts presented here could not be applied in other jurisdictions, especially in jurisdictions with comparable or similar laws. Note in particular the laws and jurisdictions cited in the appendix: Article 5(1) of the Constitution of Greece, Article 10(1) of the Constitution of Spain, Article 26(1) of the Constitution of Portugal, Article 31(1) of the Constitution of Poland, Articles 4 and 5 of the French Declaration of the Rights of Man and of Citizen, § 19(1) of the Constitution of Estonia and Article 23 of the Constitution of the Ukraine.[6] Despite comparable or similar provisions in the texts of the constitutions in these other jurisdictions, in comparing such laws one has to keep in mind that the evolutionary history of Article 2(1) of the Basic Law is important for its interpretation (as explored further below).

II. ARTICLE 2(1) OF THE BASIC LAW AS A GENERAL RIGHT OF FREEDOM OF ACTION: CONTENT AND PROCEDURAL RELEVANCE

According to the principles developed in the *Elfes* judgment of the German Federal Constitutional Court on 16 January 1957,[7] the prevailing view interprets Article 2(1) of the Basic Law as a general right of freedom of action in a broad sense.[8] As a general right of freedom of action Article 2(1) of the Basic Law not only protects a limited area of development of the personality, but also every form of human act and omission, regardless of the importance attached to such behaviour in the

[6] The relevant articles of these constitutions (in their original language as well as in English and German) are reproduced in the appendix. See also A Kukk, *Verfassungsgeschichtliche Aspekte zum Grundrecht der allgemeinen Handlungsfreiheit: Art. 2 Abs. 1 GG* (Stuttgart, Kohlhammer, 2000) 34ff; D Richter in T Marauhn and R Grote (eds), *EMRK/GG-Konkordanzkommentar* (Tübingen, Mohr Siebeck, 2006) ch 9, paras 4ff; Dreier, *Grundgesetzkommentar* (n 5) paras 5, 7 and 19; A Haratsch, 'Allgemeine Handlungsfreiheit' in S Heselhaus and C Nowak (eds), *Handbuch der Europäischen Grundrechte* (Munich, CH Beck, 2006) § 18, paras 1ff.

[7] BVerfGE 6, 32, 36–37; subsequently BVerfGE 54, 143, 144, 146; 74, 129, 151–52; 80, 137, 152ff; BVerfGE 2, 237, 265–66 favours a narrower understanding of the scope of protection; BVerfGE 4, 7, 15–16 left the definition of the scope of protection open.

[8] R Alexy, *Theorie der Grundrechte*, 2nd edn (Berlin, Suhrkamp, 1994) 311; M Cornils,'Allgemeine Handlungsfreiheit' in J Isensee and P Kirchhof (eds), *Handbuch des Staatsrechts der Bundesrepublik Deutschland*, vol VII, 3rd edn (Heidelberg, CF Müller, 2009) § 168, para 37; W Höfling in *Berliner Kommentar zum Grundgesetz*, Art 2, para 53; U Di Fabio in *Maunz/Dürig: Grundgesetz Kommentar*, 63rd edn (Munich, CH Beck, 2011) Art 2 para 1, para 9; D Murswiek in *Sachs: Grundgesetzkommentar*, 5th edn (Munich, CH Beck, 2009) Art 2, para 43.

context of development of the personality[9] – the freedom 'to do or not to do what one wants'.[10] In light of the dissenting judgment of Judge Grimm in the *Riding in the forest* judgment in 1989, the other judges in the case again confirmed the overall position of the German Federal Constitutional Court in their judgment as follows:

> Any attempt to limit the area of protection would lead to loss of freedom for the citizen. This cannot be permitted simply because other basic rights have a protective area which is narrower and of greater importance and for which no other compelling grounds are evident. For instance, limiting it to a guarantee of some narrower personal sphere of life (even purely spiritual or moral development) or according to similar criteria, would bring with it difficult demarcation problems which would be hard to resolve satisfactorily in practice.[11]

In terms of a comprehensive guarantee of natural freedom,[12] Article 2(1) of the Basic Law covers the behavioural component (doing or not doing) as well as the integrity of the natural being.[13] The basic rights of the Basic Law guarantee an active, dynamic element and a static element. The active, dynamic element refers to the freedom to determine one's own behaviour in terms of a so-called natural doing.[14] The static element refers to the integrity of the natural being in different circumstances[15], or rather human characteristics and situations.[16] For instance, Article 5(1) of the Basic Law (freedom of expression) and Article 8 of the Basic Law (freedom of assembly) only protect the natural ability of a person to act (natural doing), which in addition to the ability to be alone, includes a person's wish to mix with others (eg the right to assemble). Article 10 of the Basic Law (privacy of correspondence) and Article 13 of the Basic Law (inviolability of the home), on

[9] cf *Reiten im Walde* BVerfGE 80, 137, 152.

[10] Alexy, *Theorie der Grundrechte* (n 8) 311; Murswiek, *Sachs* (n 8) para 43.

[11] In the original text: 'Jeder Versuch einer wertenden Einschränkung des Schutzbereichs würde danach zu einem Verlust des Freiheitsraums für den Bürger führen, der nicht schon deshalb geboten sein kann, weil andere Grundrechte einen engeren und qualitativ abgehobenen Schutzbereich haben und für den auch sonst keine zwingenden Gründe ersichtlich sind. Eine Einschränkung etwa auf die Gewährleistung einer engeren, persönlichen, wenn auch nicht auf rein geistige und sittliche Entfaltung beschränkten Lebenssphäre oder nach ähnlichen Kriterien würde überdies schwierige, in der Praxis kaum befriedigend lösbare Abgrenzungsprobleme mit sich bringen'. *Reiten im Walde* BVerfGE 80, 137, 154.

[12] It is not necessary to discuss here the extent to which the basic rights assure protection of rights derived from laws other than the Basic Law. See G Lübbe-Wolff, *Grundrechte als Eingriffsabwehrrechte* (Baden-Baden, Nomos, 1988); W Cremer, *Freiheitsgrundrechte* (Tübingen, Mohr Siebeck, 2003) 86ff.

[13] C Degenhart, 'Die allgemeine Handlungsfreiheit des Art. 2 Abs. 1 GG' [1990] *Juristische Schulung* 161; W Schmitt Glaeser, 'Schutz der Privatsphäre' in J Isensee and P Kirchhof (eds), *Handbuch des Staatsrechts der Bundesrepublik Deutschland*, vol VI (Heidelberg, CF Müller, 1989) § 129, para 18, who talks about a 'double-layered' protection for the object of protection.

[14] The active element also includes the freedom not to act, ie an omission.

[15] cf for the application of the term 'situations', Alexy (n 8) 311; Schmitt Glaeser, 'Schutz der Privatsphäre' (n 13).

[16] Alexy (n 8) 174ff; Degenhart, 'Die allgemeine Handlungsfreiheit des Art. 2 Abs. 1 G' (n 13). For similar terminology, see W Roth, *Faktische Eingriffe in Freiheit und Eigentum* (Berlin, Duncker & Humblot, 1994) 161–62; T Koch, *Der Grundrechtsschutz des Drittbetroffenen* (Tübingen, Mohr Siebeck, 2000) 72ff; W Brugger, 'Der moderne Verfassungsstaat aus Sicht der amerikanischen Verfassung und des Grundgesetzes' (2001) 126 *Archiv des öffentlichen Rechts* 337, 369.

the other hand, protect the inviolability of situations and therefore only the integrity of the natural being.[17]

Article 2(1) of the Basic Law combines (at least in the sense of the general right of freedom of action) both scopes of protection (natural doing and natural being) in one norm.[18] The protection of the natural being is exclusively covered by Article 2(1) of the Basic Law in conjunction with Article 1(1) of the Basic Law. The case law of the Federal Constitutional Court developed this general right of personality development (*allgemeines Persönlichkeitsrecht*). It also developed the right to information self-determination (*Recht auf informationelle Selbstbestimmung*), which can also be seen as a specific element of the general right of personality development, rather than a separate right.[19] In the following the term 'general right of freedom of action' will be referred to as expressing a comprehensive protection of natural doing and natural being (regardless of the static element).

The consequences of interpreting Article 2(1) of the Basic Law as the general right of freedom of action will be discussed from a substantive and a procedural perspective. From a substantive law perspective, almost every act of state intervention[20] needs to be justified.[21] The determination that an act of state intervention has occurred results in only prima facie protection and should not be confused with a determination that there has been a violation of a basic right. Nevertheless, the prima facie protection requires the state to provide justification in the form of a legitimate reason each time it intervenes in the freedom of a person. Furthermore the state intervention must be proportionate (suitable, necessary and adequate) in light of the weight of the legitimate reason. The Federal Constitutional Court generally respects the legislature's assessment of what is proportionate to a large extent. In addition to there being a legitimate reason and the state intervention being proportionate, as a consequence of the *Elfes* decision the Federal Constitutional Court additionally requires that any act of state intervention (including parliamentary laws) must be formally and lawfully implemented (the so called *Elfes* doctrine). In other words, a person's basic right as set out in Article 2(1) of the Basic Law is violated by, for instance, a federal law, even if the legislature has a legitimate reason and the intervention is proportionate, if the law has a jurisdictional or procedural error.[22] In this way, an intervention into the right of general freedom of action enables anyone to seek general legitimacy

[17] Within the integrity of natural being a distinction can be made between the protection of the character (eg health, agility) and protection of situations (eg inviolability of correspondence and of the home).

[18] cf for the additional function of the general right of personality/development BVerfGE 54, 148, 153.

[19] Degenhart (n 13) 161; Schmitt Glaeser (n 13); Alexy (n 8) fn 11.

[20] The classification of state information activities (including state warnings) is disputed. On the one hand *Glykol* BVerfGE 105, 252 and *Osho* BVerfGE 105, 279 and on the other hand W Kahl, 'Vom weiten Schutzbereich zum engen Gewährleistungsgehalt' (2004) 43 *Der Staat* 167, 173ff.

[21] 'Political shareholder' rights do not follow out of Art 2(1) of the Basic Law.

[22] The highly disputed question of the ability to contest a violation of the basic rights of a third party will not be discussed; BVerfGE 96, 375, 398 and BVerfGE 85, 191, 205–06 have not finally decided this question either.

control in the form of a constitutional complaint. The constitutional complaint, Article 93(1)(4a) of the Basic Law, was incorporated into the Basic Law in 1969. In addition to this protection offered by the Federal Constitutional Court, an individual can bring a claim relating to Article 2(1) of the Basic Law to an administrative court if an administrative action is incriminating him.

III. OTHER CONCEPTS AND CRITICISM OF THE INTERPRETATION OF ARTICLE 2(1) OF THE BASIC LAW AS A GENERAL RIGHT OF FREEDOM OF ACTION – THEORIES REGARDING A NARROWER SCOPE OF PROTECTION

The interpretation of the scope of protection of Article 2(1) of the Basic Law as a general right of freedom of action is well accepted, but still has some harsh critics.[23] There are essentially two groups of critics: on the one hand various approaches which emphasize the relevance of the personality (referred to as 'relevance of personality theories') and on the other hand the approach that attempts to exclude behaviour that harms others from the scope of protection provided by Article 2(1) of the 1 Basic Law (referred to as the '*neminem laedere* theory'). These two groups of theories will now be discussed in relation to the interpretation of Article 2(1) of the 1 Basic Law as the general right of freedom of action, as developed by the case law of the Federal Constitutional Court.

A. Relevance of Personality Theories

The 'relevance of personality theories' only acknowledge the protection of human behaviour through Article 2(1) of the Basic Law if there is a certain 'personality relevance'[24] or a relevance with respect to the 'narrow personality sphere'[25] or the 'core personality area'.[26]

[23] cf more recent discussion, Cornils (n 8) paras 37ff; M Hochhut, 'Lückenloser Freiheitsschutz und die Widersprüche des Art. 2 Abs. 1 GG' [2002] *JuristenZeitung* 743, 744. In the first few years after the Basic Law came into force, even the basic rights quality of Art(1) of the Basic Law was in dispute; D Haas, 'Freie Entfaltung der Persönlichkeit' [1954] *Die Öffentliche Verwaltung* 70ff; W Wertenbruch, 'Der Grundrechtsbegriff und Art. 2 Abs. 1 GG' [1958] *Deutsches Verwaltungsblatt* 481ff.

[24] cf with respect to this expression the dissenting judgment of Grimm J in *Reiten im Walde* BVerfGE 80, 137, 169. The subjects which are to be legally protected by Art 2(1) of the Basic Law must be similarly relevant for personal freedom to the subjects to be legally protected by the specific liberty basic rights; see also W Schmidt, 'Die Freiheit vor dem Gesetz: Zur Auslegung des Art. 2 Abs. 1 GG' (1966) 91 *Archiv des öffentlichen Rechts* 42, 77–78.

[25] K Hesse, *Grundzüge des Verfassungsrechts der Bundesrepublik Deutschland*, 20th edn (Heidelberg, CF Müller, 1999) para 428. His opinion regarding the content is not different from Grimm's J, as is evident from Grimm J refering to Hesse in his dissenting judgment to BVerfGE 80, 137, 166 and Hesse refers to Grimm J at para 428, fn 74.

[26] H Peters, *Das Recht auf freie Entfaltung der Persönlichkeit in der höchstrichterlichen Rechtsprechung* (Opladen, Westdeutscher Verlag, 1963) 47ff, in particular 49; H Peters, 'Die freie Entfaltung der Persönlichkeit als Verfassungsziel' in D Constantopoulos and H Wehberg (eds), *Festschrift für Rudolph Laun zum 70. Geburtstag* (Essen, Girardet, 1953) 669ff. This so-called 'personality core relevance theory' approach attempts to protect only a very small amount of freedom of action, but is no longer used.

i. Article 2(1) of the Basic Law has no Substance as a Basic Right of Freedom from Interference; and the Constitutional Complaint as a Procedure for Objective Law Control

The proponents of the 'relevance of personality theories' argue that the comprehensive scope of protection concept makes Article 2(1) of the Basic Law meaningless[27] and without any substance.[28] From this point of view Article 2(1) of the Basic Law guarantees not freedom of action, but freedom from interference.[29] Accordingly Article 2(1) of the Basic Law creates a basic right of constitutionality to which all state actions are subject and therefore renders the 'fundamental principle of the constitutional state' a basic right[30] – a 'right not to be unlawfully stopped by the state from expressing one's own will'.[31] Furthermore this interpretation of the scope of protection should be procedurally questionable.[32] It would contradict Article 93(1)(4a) of the Basic Law and § 90(1) of the Federal Constitutional Court Act (*Bundesverfassungsgerichtsgesetz*, 'BVerfGG'), because this would mean that any state law would violate Article 2(1) of the Basic Law and could therefore be attacked by way of a constitutional complaint alleging that it violates the Constitution.[33] This would mean that any incriminating action of the state would potentially be subject to a review of its compatibility with the Basic Law by way of a constitutional complaint.[34]

The criticism is correct in that the concept that broadly interprets Article 2(1) of the Basic Law as a general right of freedom of action (with respect to the scope of protection) does not give any criteria to finally assess restrictions on freedom as valid or invalid. However, it should be borne in mind that there is also a lack of definitive criteria to assess state action with respect to the scope of protection for other liberty basic rights.[35] It would therefore only be correct to criticize the lack of assessment criteria and lack of substance with respect to the weighing of the balance of interests in the context of the proportionality test.[36] However, there is at least no convincing alternative to a proportionality test on the consideration

H-U Evers, 'Zur Auslegung von Art. 2 Abs. 1 des Grundgesetzes, insbesondere zur Persönlichkeitstheorie' (1965) 90 *Archiv des öffentlichen Rechts* 88, 94–95, argues correctly against Peters when saying that Peters' interpretation of Art 2(1) of the Basic Law only protects 'effects of the human race in the sense of an occidental understanding of culture'. Evers says that this approach is not shared by the Basic Law because it refers to a pluralistic approach. Grimm J also argues emphatically against the 'personality core relevance theory' in his dissenting judgment to BVerfGE 80, 137, 166.

[27] Schmidt, 'Die Freiheit vor dem Gesetz (n 24) 48.

[28] Schmidt (n 24) 47, 49.

[29] Dissenting judgment of Grimm J in BVerfGE 80, 137, 168; Schmidt (n 24) 49.

[30] H Ehmke, 'Prinzipien der Verfassungsinterpretation' (1963) 20 *Veröffentlichungen der Vereinigung der Deutschen Staatsrechtslehrer* 53, 84.

[31] Dissenting judgment of Grimm J in BVerfGE 80, 137, 167.

[32] ibid 168; Dreier (n 5) paras 44–45.

[33] Ehmke, 'Prinzipien der Verfassungsinterpretation' (n 30) 84–85.

[34] Dissenting judgment of Grimm J in BVerfGE 80, 137, 168; Dreier (n 5).

[35] Alexy (n 8) 314–15.

[36] The suitability and necessity assessment are not an issue with regard to Art 2(1) of the Basic Law; Alexy (n 8) 319.

level.[37] The intensity of the intervention into basic rights is connected with the importance of the reasons justifying the intervention, as the reasons justifying the intervention have to be more important when the intervention into basic rights is more intense. In any case, the criticism that Article 2(1) of the Basic Law as a general right of freedom of action lacks criteria is not specific to Article 2(1) of the Basic Law because the weighing of the balance of interests is the same as for other liberty basic rights. The proportionality test in a narrow sense always requires consideration of all arguments on a case-by-case basis to justify a restriction of a basic right. In this respect Article 2(1) of the Basic Law and the specific liberty basic rights structurally follow the same concept.[38] The 'relevance of personality theories' however, require an even more comprehensive assessment and weighing of the balance of interests than the theory which interprets Article 2(1) of the Basic Law as a general right of freedom of action. The reason for this is that attempts to define the scope of protection of Article 2(1) of the Basic Law with the help of increased personality relevance are already confronted with difficult assessment questions when determining the scope of protection. Only when behaviour does not have sufficient personality relevance is it no longer necessary to weigh up the opposing interests. The personality relevance theories therefore often lead to complex assessment at both levels; at the scope of protection level and again when weighing up the balance of interests.

From a terminology perspective it would be correct to call the interpretation of Article 2(1) of the Basic Law as a general right of freedom of action, 'a right of freedom from intervention'.[39] This criticism does not object to the contents or methodology of the comprehensive scope of protection theory, but simply suggests that the labelling of this concept as a freedom from intervention discredits it. Arguably this criticism itself and the procedural argument also lack substance.[40]

ii. The Human Dignity Argument (Article 1 of the Basic Law)

Attempts to use a link to Article 1 of the Basic Law to justify a narrower interpretation of Article 2(1) of the Basic Law[41] are not persuasive either. Just because these basic rights are located next to each other in the Basic Law's bill of rights does not justify why the narrow interpretation given to the scope of human

[37] Alexy (n 8) 315ff.

[38] E Grabitz, *Freiheit und Verfassungsrecht* (Tübingen, Mohr Siebeck, 1976) 120.

[39] Grabitz, *Freiheit und Verfassungsrecht* (n 38) 126; B Pieroth, 'Der Wert der Auffangfunktion des Art. 2 Abs. 1 GG' (1990) 115 *Archiv des öffentlichen Rechts* 33ff.

[40] R Uerpmann, 'Annahme der Verfassungsbeschwerde zur Entscheidung' in Badura and Dreier, *Festschrift 50 Jahre Bundesverfassungsgericht* (n 3) 673, 676, criticizes the consequences of narrowing Art 2(1) of the Basic Law's scope of protection in light of the protection afforded by the various courts.

[41] Hesse, *Grundzüge des Verfassungsrechts der Bundesrepublik Deutschland* (n 25) para 426; Grimm J, dissenting vote in BVerfGE 80, 164, 166–67; D Suhr, *Entfaltung der Menschen durch die Menschen* (Berlin, Duncker & Humblot, 1976) 74–75: 'General human dignity acts as a regulator to ensure that with the precise and perhaps overly perfectionist basic rights protection, the very reason for this legal protection is not forgotten'.

dignity should extend to the following right and reduce its scope of protection.[42] Without a doubt, the protection of human dignity is of foremost importance within the Constitution (not only from a chronological perspective) and (as the order implies) requires prime consideration. The Federal Constitutional Court requires that when defining the content and scope of Article 2(1) of the Basic Law, Article 1(1) of the Basic Law must be considered.[43] However, according to case law of the Federal Constitutional Court, the requirement to give serious consideration to Article 1(1)of the Basic Law does not result in a narrowing of the scope of protection of Article 2(1) of the Basic Law. Reduced protection of freedom cannot be deduced from Article 1 of the Basic Law.[44]

iii. The Significance of the Historical Origins

So far several interpretations arguing against an understanding of Article 2(1) of the Basic Law as a general right of freedom of action have been rejected; however, we have yet to see a positive justification for this broad scope of protection interpretation. The genesis of the Basic Law is often referred to in demonstrating that the legislators intended Article 2(1) of the Basic Law to be interpreted as a right 'to do or not to do what one wants'; in other words, as a general right of freedom of action. The Federal Constitutional Court also placed significant importance on the historical origins when interpreting Article 2(1) of the Basic Law as a general right of freedom of action in the key *Elfes* decision.[45] However, this interpretation of the historical origins is not undisputed, so this chapter will now consider the genesis of Article 2(1) of the Basic Law further.

a. Historical Origins: a Précis

The historical origins of Article 2(1) of the Basic Law were influenced by various differing drafts.[46] Article 2(2) of Herrenchiemsee's draft[47] states: 'Everyone has the freedom to do anything within the bounds of the legal system and moral law, unless it hurts others'.[48] Following this, the 'Basic Principle Committee' (Grundsatzausschuss) and the 'General Editing Committee' (Redaktionsausschuss)

[42] Alexy (n 8) 321, says that Art 1 of the Basic Law can be used as an argument in favour of a comprehensive interpretation of the scope of protection because 'without negative legal freedom there would be no human dignity in a legally relevant sense'; Alexy's principle of negative freedom, 318–19

[43] BVerfGE 32, 373, 379; 34, 238, 245.

[44] The 'core of personality relevance theory' is abused to make the constraints of Art 2(1) of the Basic Law obsolete.

[45] cf to this evaluation of the *Elfes* decision, T Dehler, 'Zur Entstehungsgeschichte des Art. 2 Abs. 1 des Grundgesetzes' [1960] *JuristenZeitung* 722, 727.

[46] (1951) 1 *Jahrbuch des öffentlichen Rechts* 54ff; Dehler (n 45) 722ff; H-C Nipperdey and G Wiese, 'Freie Entfaltung der Persönlichkeit' in KA Bettermann and H-C Nipperdey (eds), *Die Grundrechte: Handbuch der Theorie und Praxis der Grundrechte*, vol IV 2 (Berlin, Duncker & Humblot, 1962) 741, 774–75; Suhr, *Entfaltung der Menschen* (n 41) 51; Kukk, *Verfassungsgeschichtliche Aspekte* (n 6) 207.

[47] The so-called 'Herrenchiemsee Convent' (Konvent von Herrenchiemsee) prepares a draft for the Basic Law for the Federal Republic of Germany in August 1948 as basis for the work on the German Constitution of the 'Parliamentary Council' (Parlamentarischer Rat).

[48] *Der Parlamentarische Rat* II, 580 (text), 513–14 (descriptive part).

of the 'Parliamentary Council' (Parlamentarischer Rat)[49] stated that anyone can 'do or not do', anything that does not violate the rights of others,[50] but they added the 'constitutional order' as another constraint. The expression 'right of freedom of personality development' first arose in the 'Basic Principle Committee's' proposal on 19 November 1948 (its 23rd session) when referring to the respective UN drafts.[51] Although the 'General Editing Committee' used the original formulation again on 13 December 1948, the 'Basic Principle Committee' confirmed its amended version ('right of freedom of personality development') in its 32nd session on 11 January 1949. Hermann von Mangoldt, a member of the 'Parliamentary Council' and the 'Basic Principle Committee', stated that the reasons for the amendment were that the original text was not well worded and did not have an appropriate tone.[52] At this time von Mangoldt is not thought to have been opposed, but his subsequent criticism of the original text in the second reading of the 42nd session of the head committee on 18 January 1949 is famous. He stated: 'It seems to us that the expression "Everyone has the freedom to do or not to do what he wants" sounds too vulgar and we think that this version would destroy the dignity of the draft of our basic rights'.[53] Even a further alternative proposal of the 'General Editing Committee' on 25 January 1949 did not change the expression 'the right of freedom of personality development'.[54]

b. Interpretation of the Historical Origins

Scholarly literature generally concludes that the legislature wanted the comprehensive scope of protection concept and therefore an interpretation of Article 2(1) of the Basic Law as a general right of freedom of action. The historical origins, and in particular the words of Mangoldt, state that the reason for changing the original version was purely linguistic.[55]

[49] The Parliamentary Council (Parlamentarischer Rat) first met on 1 September 1948.

[50] Questions relating to the draft of the fourth session of the 'Basic Principle Committee' on 23 September 1948; (1951) 1 *Jahrbuch des öffentlichen Rechts* 55; *Der Parlamentarische Rat* V, 62: 'He can do or not do what does not violate the rights of others or the constitutional order of the community'. The 'General Editing Committee' on 16 November 1948, (1951) 1 *Jahrbuch des öffentlichen Rechts* 56: 'Everyone has the freedom to do anything within the bounds of the constitutional order and moral law, unless it hurts others'. The quote in BVerfGE 6, 32, 36–37 is not accurate.

[51] (1951) 1 *Jahrbuch des öffentlichen Rechts* 57; in detail *Der Parlamentarische Rat* V, 604, 608. Von Mangoldt was explicitly referring to Art 23 and 27 of the UN drafts on the declaration of human rights on 7 October 1948. On the impact of these documents, see H Dreier, 'Kontexte des Grundgesetzes' [1999] *Deutsches Verwaltungsblatt* 667, 672; H Wilms, *Ausländische Einwirkungen auf die Entstehung des Grundgesetzes* (Stuttgart, Kohlhammer, 1999) 138–39.

[52] *Der Parlamentarische Rat* VII 2, 918 ('wenig schön') and 924 (sounds 'sehr schlecht'); (1951) 1 *Jahrbuch des öffentlichen Rechts* 60.

[53] In the original text: 'Uns will es scheinen, daß die Fassung: "Jedermann hat die Freiheit zu tun und zu lassen" zu vulgär klingt, und wir meinen, daß das Würdevolle im Klang, das wir in die Fassung unserer Grundrechte hineinlegen sollten, durch die Fassung durchbrochen würde', (1951) 1 *Jahrbuch des öffentlichen Rechts* 61.

[54] Referring to the various drafts and stages, (1951) 1 *Jahrbuch des öffentlichen Rechts* 57ff; *Der Parlamentarische Rat* VII 2, 36, 92, 135, 205, 340; Dehler (n 45) 727ff.

[55] H-D Horn in *Grundrechte-Kommentar* (Cologne, Carl Heymanns, 2010) Art 2(1), (2); Murswiek (n 8) para 2; C Starck in *Bonner Kommentar zum Grundgesetz*, 5th edn (Heidelberg, CF Müller, 2009) Art 2(1), (8).

However, some argue that the historical origins of Article 2(1) of the Basic Law are not really possible to interpret.[56] Horst Dreier refers to the report of Thomas Dehler, a member of the 'Parliamentary Council' and the 'General Editing Committee', and argues that the 'General Editing Committee' removed the previous reference to the ability to be restrictive based on the general legal system, only because it wanted a narrower understanding of Article 2(1) of the Basic Law.[57] This interpretation of Dehler's report is difficult to justify. Dehler's report states that the 'General Editing Committee' was against including a general reservation of statutory powers, but this does not mean at all that the 'General Editing Committee' wanted a narrow understanding of the scope of protection of Article 2(1) of the Basic Law. Dehler was not attempting to establish a narrower scope of protection either. Dehler highlights in his report more than once that the character of the basic right is a 'general right of freedom of action' and the 'core basic right'.[58]

Dieter Suhr has argued, without distinguishing between the different committees, that the legislature dismissed the first version not only because of linguistic reasons, but also because of its content. He stated that it was not the linguistic form of the first version that caused aesthetic concerns, but that there was concern about the legal ethics of the content.[59] This interpretation of the historical origins is not plausible either. The actual content of Suhr's criticism does not conflict with the interpretation of the historical origins of the prevailing view. It is more that Suhr disagrees with Mangoldt's view that the first version sounded too vulgar (as mentioned above). 'The individual liberal freedom of arbitrariness could not have been put in better terms'.[60] In support of his view, he deduced that the 'creators of the Basic Law' could not have considered the tone to be too vulgar, but rather that the content of the expression was too vulgar. Suhr clearly expresses this assumption when saying: 'This discontent with the contents of the Article was subjectively perceived as a vulgar tone'.[61] This is only an assumption of what the creators of the Basic Law thought and therefore does not suffice to dismiss the generally held interpretation of the origins of Article 2(1) of the Basic Law.[62] The creators of the Constitution did not want to change the factual content of Article 2(1) of the Basic Law, but rather Suhr wishes that they had wanted to do so. Suhr's criticism that the Federal Constitutional Court's understanding of

[56] Dreier (n 5) para 9; dissenting judgment of Grimm J in *Reiten im Walde* BVerfGE 80, 137, 165.

[57] Dreier (n 5) para 9 and fn 35, 45.

[58] Dehler (n 45) 728–29.

[59] D Suhr, 'Die Freiheit vom staatlichen Eingriff als Freiheit zum privaten Eingriff?' [1980] *JuristenZeitung* 166, 173.

[60] Suhr, 'Die Freiheit vom staatlichen Eingriff' (n 59) 173.

[61] ibid.

[62] For a different view, but without explanation, Pieroth (n 39) 33, 35, who thinks that the genetic and systematic arguments which Grimm J expresses in his dissenting judgement in *Reiten im Walde* BVerfGE 80, 137 are relevant.

Article 2(1) of the Basic Law is determined by preconceptions alone, rather than through interpretation,[63] can be applied to him instead.[64]

An interpretation of the origins of Article 2(1) of the Basic Law concludes that Article 2(1) of the Basic Law should be interpreted as a general right of freedom of action, because the creators of the Constitution did not want to change the factual content of the original draft.

iv. Analysis of the Wording of Article 2(1) of the Basic Law

Beyond the systematic, systematic-teleological and historical origin objections described above, sometimes the wording of Article 2(1) of the Basic Law is used as a basis to refute an understanding of the norm as a general right of freedom of action.[65] Dieter Suhr analysed the wording of Article 2(1) of the Basic Law in detail. He did not conclude that his analysis led to a narrow scope of protection, but others have.[66]

Suhr started his analysis with a comparison between the wording of the original draft and the present wording of Article 2(1) of the Basic Law. He concluded that the 'to do or not to do phrase' only refers to a single action of doing or not doing, without considering that these actions are 'somehow combined' and that every human being is developing through these actions. 'Development of the personality' not only considers the freedom in respect of each individual action or omission separately, but also considers the relationship between the many actions and omissions. In contrast to the present wording of Article 2(1) of the Basic Law, the 'to do or not to do' phrase ignores any connection between individual actions and therefore any consistency in behaviour.[67] Suhr comments: 'The freedom of the individual to do or not to do is related to the development of the personality just as the ability to make tones is related to playing a melody'.[68] Suhr analyses the meaning of the wording in the individual characteristics of Article 2(1) of the Basic Law thoroughly and meticulously. Development conveys the image of processes that are transformed from a 'budding to a blossoming state, from a seed to maturity'. In German there are two different words that mean 'development' and, according to Suhr, the one used in Article 2(1) of the Basic Law infers a deeper meaning, with positive foundations. Development is not necessarily pre-determined, but neither is it arbitrary; rather it is a 'procedural process'.[69]

[63] Suhr (n 46) 71.

[64] J Esser, *Vorverständnis und Methodenwahl in der Rechtsfindung* (Königstein im Taunus, Athenäum, 1970), writes about the meaning of and problems relating to the pre-conceptions in light of the interpretation and use of law.

[65] Hesse (n 25) para 426.

[66] cf eg dissenting judgment of Grimm J to *Reiten im Walde* BVerfGE 80, 137, 165; Hesse (n 25) para 426.

[67] Suhr (n 46) 65ff.

[68] ibid 66.

[69] ibid 78–79.

With his interpretation, Suhr requires that social contexts should be integrated, which leads to a 'communicative' understanding of Article 2(1) of the Basic Law.[70] He continues his analysis from a comprehensive sociological perspective,[71] which leads him to an interactive understanding of basic rights.[72] He uses this interactive understanding of basic rights to interpret the basic rights norm text,[73] which he ultimately relates to an institutional understanding of liberty and basic rights in general.[74] His considerations (which are rich in content) need not be expanded upon here because they are not aimed at narrowing the factual scope of protection of Article 2(1) of the Basic Law; but rather (from a dogmatic perspective) at establishing a guarantee of basic rights beyond their defence function. Suhr is primarily interested in the triangular relationship between 'the citizen, the citizen and the state' and in particular in the state's perspective. He says:

> A state does not consist of one random individual developing, but rather consists of a situation where several citizens develop together in an interactive manner. The state is therefore bound by the principles of common good and indivisible freedom. In this respect basic rights have the function of an organisational principle and a measure of whether the state can exist in accordance with the concept of basic rights.[75]

It appears that Suhr makes no conclusions concerning the definition of the scope of protection of Article 2(1) of the Basic Law, despite his criticism of Article 2(1) of the Basic Law being understood as a right of freedom of individual choice.[76]

Indeed, Suhr's analysis has no consequences for the interpretation of the scope of protection of Article 2(1) of the Basic Law.[77] Suhr did not state that personality can only develop through 'beneficial' behaviour. Rather he stated that in reality 'development' of the personality means more for many people than mere protection against state intervention. The formation of a 'consistent' concept of life for individuals requires not only the 'establishment of a community' by the state, but also the individuals' right to have effective protection against state intervention. Article 2(1) of the Basic Law can therefore not be interpreted as being restricted to 'beneficial' behaviour, because this would mean the state excluding certain forms

[70] ibid 81–82.
[71] ibid 83ff.
[72] ibid 95.
[73] ibid 105ff.
[74] ibid 119ff.
[75] Ibid 125. In a later report it states that his understanding of liberty basic rights and basic rights in general is not only important with respect to constitutional justification of state intervention, but also with respect to establishing human relationships. In this context he considers a situation where a private individual constrains another private individual against his will and his legally protected basic rights, for example a smoker may constrain a non-smoker, Suhr (n 59) 174. For further development of his ideas, see D Suhr, *Gleiche Freiheit* (Augsburg, Mette, 1988).
[76] D Suhr, 'Freiheit durch Geselligkeit' [1984] *Europäische Grundrechte-Zeitschrift* 529, 536, concisely shows that the intention is to clarify the understanding of freedom. He contrasts this intention with the common understanding of freedom as a sphere of individual arbitrariness without a state or law. He states that freedom is a process of human actions which have to obey legal rules.
[77] His analysis is useful with respect to state obligations, providing appropriate measures to ensure private autonomy in legal transactions. Cremer (n 12) 188ff.

of personality development completely from the scope of protection of Article 2(1) of the Basic Law. The result would be, first, that the legislature could prohibit actions such as 'feeding doves'[78], 'riding in the forest'[79] and other activities that are less recognized and accepted by society as a whole without any objective reason, and secondly that the administration could also prohibit these actions even without any legal authorization. Prohibiting behaviour which is allegedly less beneficial and important can also cause long-term harm to an individual's life from the individual's subjective perspective. The following theoretical question illustrates this: do 'feeding doves', 'riding in the forest' or playing sport have less personality relevance than, for example, watching television programmes on topics such as horse racing, dressage, soccer matches or car racing, which are mass phenomena?

B. Exclusion of Behaviour which Violates Others: '*Neminem Laedere* Theory'

The *neminem laedere* theory is another criticism of the prevailing view of the concept of the scope of protection of Article 2(1) of the Basic Law. This theory states that behaviour which violates the legally protected rights of others is not protected by basic rights, including Article 2(1) of the Basic Law.[80] Basic rights protection of freedom exists only if it is used in a peaceful and non-physically violent way. The general prohibition against violence violates the freedom of an individual, but does not violate the freedom protected by the basic rights.[81] There is no such thing as basic rights protection of murdering or stealing. The prohibition against stealing and murdering does constrain an individual's freedom, but does not constrain the freedom protected by basic rights.[82] This is not because of an isolated observation of the relevance and worthiness of the behaviour (as is the case with the personality relevance theories), but rather because of the impact of the behaviour on society.[83]

[78] cf BVerfGE 54, 143.

[79] cf BVerfGE 80, 137.

[80] This approach has a special meaning with respect to the so-called inviolable basic rights – ie basic rights which have no explicit constraint in the text of the Basic Law, such as Art 5(3) of the Basic Law – because according to the prevailing view stricter standards apply to justify any intervention. These stricter standards would be partially side-stepped if there were a narrower scope of protection. cf J Isensee, 'Das Grundrecht als Abwehrrecht und als staatliche Schutzpflicht' in J Isensee and P Kirchhof (eds), *Handbuch des Staatsrechts der Bundesrepublik Deutschland*, vol V, 2nd edn (Heidelberg, CF Müller, 2000) § 111, para 177.

[81] Starck, *Bonner Kommentar zum Grundgesetz* (n 55) para 13; Isensee, 'Das Grundrecht als Abwehrrecht' (n 80) paras 176ff; H-U Gallwas, *Der Mißbrauch von Grundrechten* (Berlin, Duncker & Humblot, 1967) 17; KA Schwarz, 'Der Gleichheitssatz, die gesetzgeberische Gestaltungsfreiheit und das Geld der öffentlichen Hand' [2000] *JuristenZeitung* 126, 128.

[82] Isensee (n 80) para 181, states that sanctioning these breaches would be an intervention in the scope of protection of the respective basic right.

[83] However, any behaviour which violates others would also lack sufficient personality relevance for the purposes of the aforementioned theories. The personality relevance theories therefore narrow the scope of protection further than the approach which attempts to exclude behaviour which violates others.

This theory may be intuitively convincing, because from the very outset it denies basic rights protection (including the formal protection) where there are significant violations of the legally protected rights of others.[84] As with the personality relevance theories, the *neminem laedere* theory also already raises difficult evaluation questions at the scope of protection level. Decisions have to be made as to which behaviours are likely to be harmless and which behaviours may violate others (for example, running a factory with emissions) and where behaviour does violate others, how strong the violation has to be in order for the behaviour to be excluded from the scope of protection of Article 2(1) of the Basic Law. These difficult evaluation questions at the scope of protection level would be acceptable if this theory was generally convincing. However, it is not because the theory lacks a methodical constitutional justification capable of overcoming the historical argument.[85]

IV. CONCLUSION

It has been shown that the prevailing assumption that Article 2(1) of the Basic Law offers comprehensive prima facie protection against any state intervention that burdens the individual is persuasive. The scope of protection of Article 2(1) of the Basic Law covers the so-called general right of freedom of action in the sense of comprehensive protection in respect of natural doing and natural being. One could therefore talk about a basic right of freedom from intervention, but one has to bear in mind that infringement of the scope of protection does not necessarily mean that there is a violation of the basic right. The state may still be able to justify state intervention where there are legitimate reasons, and is highly likely to succeed in justifying state intervention where this seeks to prohibit individual actions which have less personality relevance or where the individual's actions violate the rights of others.

CASES

BVerfGE 2, 237 – *Hypothekensicherungsgesetz* (1953)
BVerfGE 6, 32 – *Elfes* (1957)
BVerfGE 54, 143 – *Taubenfütterung* (1980)
BVerfGE 80, 137 – *Reiten im Walde* (1989)

[84] Gallwas, *Der Mißbrauch von Grundrechten* (n 81) 105, however believes that the objective legal principle must be considered with respect to any constraints of law; Isensee (n 80) para 179.

[85] cf other contra arguments Koch, *Der Grundrechtsschutz des Drittbetroffenen* (n 16) 105; Alexy (n 8) 313; Lübbe-Wolff (n 12) 87; Murswiek (n 8) para 53.

SELECTED LITERATURE

Alexy R, *Theorie der Grundrechte*, 2nd edn (Berlin, Suhrkamp, 1994)

Degenhart C, 'Die allgemeine Handlungsfreiheit des Art. 2 Abs. 1 GG' [1990] *Juristische Schulung* 161

Dehler T, 'Zur Entstehungsgeschichte des Art. 2 Abs. 1 des Grundgesetzes' [1960] *JuristenZeitung* 722

Evers HU, 'Zur Auslegung von Art. 2 Abs. 1 des Grundgesetzes, insbesondere zur Persönlichkeitstheorie' (1965) 90 *Archiv des öffentlichen Rechts* 88

Grabitz E, *Freiheit und Verfassungsrecht* (Tübingen, Mohr Siebeck, 1976)

Haas, D, 'Freie Entfaltung der Persönlichkeit' [1954] *Die Öffentliche Verwaltung* 70

Kahl W, 'Vom weiten Schutzbereich zum engen Gewährleitsungsgehalt' (2004) 43 *Der Staat* 166

Kukk A, *Verfassungsrechtliche Aspekte zum Grundrecht der allgemeinen Handlungsfreiheit (Art. 2 Abs. 1 GG)* (Stuttgart, Kohlhammer, 2000)

Peters H, *Das Recht auf freie Entfaltung der Persönlichkeit in der höchstrichterlichen Rechtsprechung* (Opladen, Westdeutscher Verlag, 1963)

——'Die freie Entfaltung der Persönlichkeit als Verfassungsziel' in D Constantopoulos and H Wehberg (eds), *Festschrift für Rudolph Laun zum 70. Geburtstag* (Essen, Girardet, 1953)

Pieroth B, 'Der Wert der Auffangfunktion des Art. 2 Abs. 1 GG' (1990) 115 *Archiv des öffentlichen Rechts* 33

Schmidt W, 'Die Freiheit vor dem Gesetz – Zur Auslegung des Art. 2 Abs. 1 GG' (1966) 91 *Archiv des öffentlichen Rechts* 42

Schwarz K, 'Der Gleichheitssatz, die gesetzgeberische Gestaltungsfreiheit und das Geld der öffentlichen Hand' (2000) *JuristenZeitung* 126

Suhr D, *Die Entfaltung der Menschen durch die Menschen: Zur Grundrechtsdogmatik der Persönlichkeitsentfaltung, der Ausübungsgemeinschaften und des Eigentums* (Berlin, Duncker & Humblot, 1976)

——'Die Freiheit vom staatlichen Eingriff als Freiheit zum privaten Eingriff?' (1980) *JuristenZeitung* 166

Uerpmann R, 'Annahme der Verfassungsbeschwerde zur Entscheidung' in P Badura and H Dreier (eds), *Festschrift 50 Jahre Bundesverfassungsgericht,* vol I (Tübingen, Mohr Siebeck, 2001)

Wertenbruch W, 'Der Grundrechtsbegriff und Art. 2 Abs. 1 GG' [1958] *Deutsches Verwaltungsblatt* 481

APPENDIX: REGULATIONS IN OTHER JURISDICTIONS SIMILAR TO ARTICLE 2(1) OF THE BASIC LAW[86]

Article 5(1) of the Constitution of Greece: Καθένας έχει δικαίωμα να αναπτύσσει ελεύθερα την προσωπικότητά του και να συμμετέχει στην κοινωνική, οικονομική και πολιτική ζωή της Χώρας, εφόσον δεν προσβάλλει τα δικαιώματα των άλλων και δεν παραβιάζει το Σύνταγμα ή τα χρηστά ήθη

[86] Translations on www.verfassungen.eu/eu/index.htm.

English translation: 'Each person is entitled to develop his personality freely and participate in the social, economic and political life of the country, provided that he does not encroach upon the rights of others, the Constitution or *bona mores*'.

Article 10(1) of the Constitution of Spain: 'La dignidad de la persona, los derechos inviolables que le son inherentes, el libre desarrollo de la personalidad, el respeto a la ley y a los derechos de los demás son fundamento del orden político y de la paz social'.

English translation: 'The dignity of the person, the inviolable rights which are inherent, the free development of the personality, the respect for the law and for the rights of others are the foundation of political order and social peace'.

Article 26(1) of the Constitution of Portugal: 'A todos são reconhecidos os direitos à identidade pessoal, ao desenvolvimento da personalidade, à capacidade civil, à cidadania, ao bom nome e reputação, à imagem, à palavra, à reserva da intimidade da vida privada e familiar e à protecção legal contra quaisquer formas de discriminação'.

English translation: 'Everyone's right to his or her personal identity, civil capacity, citizenship, good name and reputation, image, the right to speak out, and the right to the protection of the intimacy of his or her private and family life is recognized'.

Article 31(1) of the Constitution of Poland: 'Wolność człowieka podlega ochronie prawnej. Każdy jest obowią zany szanować wolności i prawa innych. Nikogo nie wolno zmusza´c do czynienia tego, czego prawo mu nie nakazuje'.

English translation: 'Freedom of the person shall receive legal protection. Everyone shall respect the freedoms and rights of others. No one shall be compelled to do that which is not required by law'.

Article 4 of the Declaration of the Rights of Man and of Citizen: 'La liberté consiste à pouvoir faire tout ce qui ne nuit pas à autrui: ainsi, l' exercice des droits naturels de chaque homme n` a de bornes que celles qui assurent aux autres membres de la société la jouissance de ces mêmes droits. Ces bornes ne peuvent être déterminées que par loi'. Article 5: 'La loi n'a e droit de défendre que les actions nuisibles à la société. Tout ce que n'est pas défendu par la loi ne peut être empêché, et nul ne peut être contraint à faire ce qu'elle n'ordonne pas'.

English translation: Article 4: 'Liberty consists in the freedom to do everything which injures no one else; hence the exercise of the natural rights of each man has no limits except those which assure to the other members of the society the enjoyment of the same rights. These limits can only be determined by law'. Article 5: 'Law can only prohibit such actions as are hurtful to society. Nothing may be prevented which is not forbidden by law, and no one may be forced to do anything not provided for by law'.

§ 19 of the Constitution of Estonia: 'Igaühel on õigus vabale eneseteostusele. Igaüks peab oma õiguste ja vabaduste kasutamisel ning kohustuste täitmisel austama ja arvestama teiste inimeste õigusi ja vabadusi ning järgima seadust'.

English translation: 'Everyone has the right to free self-realization. Everyone shall honour and consider the rights and freedoms of others, and shall observe the law, in exercising his or her rights and freedoms and in fulfilling his or her duties'.

Article 23 of the Constitution of Ukraine: 'Верховним органом власти Української Народньої Республіки являються Всенародні Збори, які безпосередньо здійснюють вищу законодавчу власть в Українській Народній Республіці і формують вищі органи виконавчої й судової власти Української Народньої Республіки'.

English translation: 'Every person has the right to free development of his or her personality if the rights and freedoms of other persons are not violated thereby, and has duties before the society in which the free and comprehensive development of his or her personality is ensured'.

5

The 'Serving' Freedom to Broadcast – Subjective versus Objective Dimensions of a Fundamental Right

BERND GRZESZICK

I. The Special Status of Public Broadcasting under Constitutional Law
II. Data Concerning Broadcasting in Germany
III. The Stages in the Development of the Broadcasting Corporations in the Federal Republic of Germany
  A. (Re-)construction
  B. The Constitutional Underpinning of Public Monopoly Broadcasting
  C. The Continuing Development into a Dual Broadcasting System
  D. Digitalization, Convergence and Internationalization
IV. The Position under German Law: an International Comparison
V. Special Path and its Perspectives

I. THE SPECIAL STATUS OF PUBLIC BROADCASTING UNDER CONSTITUTIONAL LAW

IN COMPARISON TO most other countries, public broadcasting corporations – that is, broadcasting corporations which are subject to public law – stand out in Germany not only de facto but also legally. The fundamental right of the freedom of broadcasting is interpreted by the German Federal Constitutional Court (Bundesverfassungsgericht, 'BVerfG') as being a 'serving freedom' (*dienende Freiheit*) which, as a consequence, extensively and constitutionally guarantees public broadcasting. German constitutional law finds itself on a *Sonderweg* (a separate path) in this respect, the grounds for and borders of which are the subject of this chapter. This chapter does not concentrate in too much detail on the discussion of individual dogmatic problems with reference to the character of this 'serving freedom', a notion which was developed by the BVerfG, but rather it deals, first, with the actual grounds for the development of this separate path which Germany has taken. This will be demonstrated by throwing light on the political and historical environment of the decisions of the BVerfG which were authoritative in developing the German legal position within this sector. Against this backdrop, the question will also be posed as to what advantages and disadvantages this separate path taken by the 'serving freedom of broadcasting' involves and whether this has now reached its end in the light of the actual changes in the use of media itself and in media technology, as well as in view of changes to the EU state aid legislation. On the basis of a roughly outlined comparative law overview, it will then be discussed whether, or to what extent, this doctrine can, on an international scale, be deemed a separate path of its own and whether the objectives which are linked to it can also be achieved as a 'serving' freedom, even without an understanding of the fundamental rights guarantee.

II. DATA CONCERNING BROADCASTING IN GERMANY

In Germany, the levels of distribution, use and the degree of effectiveness of the classic media, ie radio and television, still largely remain at a considerably high level despite the advance of the internet. Of the 35.6 million recorded German households in 2007 (average size: 2.1 people), 33.9 million of them – that is, 95.3 per cent – had an appliance for the purpose of receiving television programmes.[1] In fact, evaluations based on the data of the consumer behaviour of German citizens concerning the media even showed an increase in television consumption over the previous figures. As such, the total consumption of television programmes in 2007 for the viewer group of 3-years-old and above amounted to 208 minutes per day (compared with 144 minutes in 1988), and among adults above 14-years-old, also in 2007, the figure was 299 minutes per day (compared with 216 minutes in 1988).[2]

The public broadcasting corporations assume an extraordinary position within the landscape of German radio and television. They are made up of the nine broadcasting institutions of the *Länder* (the German federal states) which are combined in the Working Group of the Public Broadcasting Institutions of the Federal Republic of Germany ('Arbeitsgemeinschaft der öffentlich-rechtlichen Rundfunkanstalten der Bundesrepublik Deutschland' – ARD), the Second German Television ('Zweites Deutsches Fernsehen' – ZDF) as well as the German radio. In 2008 these were responsible for running a total of 65 radio stations and

[1] VIP International Marketing Committee (CMI), *Television 2007 – International Key Facts* (Luxemburg, IP and RTL Group, 2007) 176.

[2] This and the following information are taken from: Arbeitsgemeinschaft der Landesmedienanstalten in der Bundesrepublik Deutschland (ALM), *Bericht über die wirtschaftliche Lage des Rundfunks in Deutschland 2006* (Berlin, Vistas, 2007) 23; Arbeitsgemeinschaft Fernsehforschung (AGF), *Fernsehzuschauerforschung in Deutschland* (Frankfurt, AGF, 2008) 54ff; Arbeitsgemeinschaft der Landesmedienanstalten in der Bundesrepublik Deutschland (ALM), *Jahrbuch 2009-2010* (Berlin, Vistas, 2010) 8, 53ff., 86; Arbeitsgemeinschaft der öffentlich-rechtlichen Rundfunkanstalten der Bundesrepublik Deutschland (ARD), *ARD-Jahrbuch 2009* (Hamburg, Hans-Bredow-Institut, 2009) 176ff.

22 television channels for the national audience. In addition to that, there are the foreign channels of the federal broadcasting institution 'Deutsche Welle'. The market share of the public broadcasting corporations – that is, the relative share of the complete duration of consumption of all the channels at a given time – is considerable. In the television sector, the public broadcasting companies were able to achieve the following market shares as a daily average in 2009 in the group of viewers aged three and above: ARD 12.7 per cent, ARD third channels 13.5 per cent and ZDF 12.5 per cent. If all the public broadcasting channels are included (inter alia 3sat, Phoenix, KiKa and arte), the public television corporations achieve a considerable market share of 43.6 per cent (based on 2007).

Public broadcasting is financed through licence fees, advertising and other sources of income. In 2008, there were revenues of €8.6 billion for the entire public broadcasting corporations in contrast to an expenditure of €8.7 billion during the same period of time, thus resulting in a deficit of €157 million. The entire revenue of the combined ARD *Länder* broadcasting institutions alone amounted to €6.181 billion in 2008. The decisive share of the financing of public broadcasting is thereby provided by the licence fee,[3] which comprises a standing charge and a television fee and which was increased in 2009 to €17.98 per month (€215.76 per annum). The revenue which is obtained from this accounts for €7.1 billion, which corresponds to 83 per cent of the total revenue of the public broadcasting corporations. In 2008 ARD and ZDF generated a total of €506.4 million gross advertising revenue in television (6 per cent of the total television advertising market), whereby marginally increasing net revenues in TV advertising were confronted with corresponding losses in radio advertising.

The largest share of the finances for broadcasting as a whole in Germany is allotted to television. The total receipts for all the German television channels (private and public) reached a figure of €9.2 billion in 2009. Of that, €4.5 billion was apportioned to the public broadcasting corporations' licence fees, €3.6 billion to net TV advertising revenue and €1 billion to Pay-TV revenue. The private television companies, who are primarily dependent upon advertising revenue, were able to achieve total revenues of approximately €7.4 billion in 2008. The leading media groups in the private television sector, RTL Group and Pro Sieben Sat 1 Media, alone achieved a combined gross advertising revenue of €7.7 billion from their television channels.

Whereas in 2008 there were almost 47,000 people working in the private broadcasting companies (almost 31,000 in television and more than 16,000 in radio), the number of people working in the public broadcasting corporations was 51,087, of whom almost 57 per cent were permanently employed. In 2006, the share of people working in the public broadcasting companies in relation to the

[3] For more on the current discussion concerning a reform of the financing of public broadcasting: P Kirchhof, *Gutachten über die Finanzierung des öffentlich-rechtlichen Rundfunks im Auftrag der ARD, des ZDF und D Radio* (Heidelberg, 2010) available online at: http://www.ard.de/intern/standpunkte/-id=1453944/property=download/nid=8236/g73vou/Kirchhof-Gutachten+zur+Rundfunkfinanzierung.pdf (last visited on 18 October 2013).

broadcasting sector as a whole was 63 per cent and 80 per cent regarding freelance workers.

The statutorily entrenched *Programmauftrag* – the programming mandate – in conjunction with the decisions of the Constitutional Court assigns the public broadcasting corporations the role of 'medium of and factor in' the process of shaping free, individual and public opinion. They have to offer an extensive overview of international, European, national and regional events in all areas of life and what they offer must serve to educate, inform, advise and entertain. According to ARD, the share of information supply (ie informative broadcasting contributions) as a part of all its programmes in 2007 was 44 per cent (excluding sports programmes).[4] ZDF even claims that information with an emphasis on political coverage makes up a total of around 50 per cent of its main programming schedule and about 40 per cent during the peak airtime period from 7pm to 11pm.[5] Despite the usual criticism regarding the level of journalism in public television,[6] the altogether high proportion of informative contributions in the two main public television channels has also been confirmed by studies. These studies show that in 2007 the share of information supply as a percentage of all programmes stood at 49 per cent whereas in 2007 RTL and Sat.1 (the main private networks) provided only 24 per cent 'information/infotainment'.[7] In 2007, the main news programme – *Tagesschau* – which is broadcast on a total of nine channels of the ARD, had on average 8.96 million viewers on a daily basis and the news programme *heute* (on ZDF and 3sat) 4.13 million, whereas the news programme which ranked third, *RTL aktuell*, only had 3.85 million viewers.[8]

III. THE STAGES IN THE DEVELOPMENT OF THE BROADCASTING CORPORATIONS IN THE FEDERAL REPUBLIC OF GERMANY

The development of broadcasting in the Federal Republic of Germany[9] can be divided into four phases, not only from a technical-economic point of view, but also from a legal point of view. The first phase encompasses the (re-)construction of broadcasting under the direction of the occupying forces up to the end of the 1950s. The second phase deals with the underpinning of the public broadcasting monopoly which stemmed from the first phase and continued until the end of the 1970s or early 1980s. The third phase, from the end of the 1970s or early 1980s,

[4] ARD-Programmdirektion, *Bericht 07/08, zugleich Leitlinien 09/10* (Ismaning, Steininger Druch, 2008) 16.

[5] ZDF (Intendant), *Erklärung zu Programm-Perspektiven des ZDF 2009-2010* (Mainz, ZDF, 2008) 3.

[6] For a critical view: S Niggemeier, 'Selbstbewusst anders sein' [2009] 9–10 *Aus Politik und Zeitgschichte* 2ff.

[7] M Gerhards and W Klingler, 'Fernseh- bzw. Bewegtbildnutzung 2007' [2008] *Media Perspektiven* 550, 556.

[8] ibid 557.

[9] For an introduction: M Eifert and W Hoffmann-Riem, 'Die Entstehung und Ausgestaltung des dualen Rundfunksystems' in D Schwarzkopf (ed), *Rundfunkpolitik in Deutschland* (Munich, dtv, 1999) 50ff.

marks an incipient phase in the licensing and accreditation of private broadcasting providers who work alongside the public broadcasters. The fourth phase is the age of digitalization, of convergence and of the internationalization of the media since the start of the new millennium.

A. (Re-)construction

The first phase in the development of the system of public broadcasting ran up until the end of the 1950s and was characterized by the (re-)construction – under the direction of the occupying forces – of the subordinated National Socialist propaganda broadcasting corporation which had existed during the Third Reich. Directly after the capitulation of Germany, the victorious allied powers had first extensively forbidden any broadcasting operations by the surviving German radio stations[10] before taking over control of them. Although from early on the medium-term repatriation of the press and broadcasting facilities back into German hands had been considered,[11] the Western Allies' initial media policy was to employ the mass medium of the radio as an instrument aimed at extensively arranging and forming social structures for the purpose of 'social engineering'.[12] In this perspective, radio appeared first and foremost as an instrument for democratizing and politically educating the people, not however as a form of plurality or freedom of expression. The Allies agreed that the aim was not only to eliminate all the National Socialist elements in the everyday life and conscience of the Germans, but also directly to exclude the possibilities of state influence once and for all.

While attempting to prepare a future structure for broadcasting, the victorious Western allied forces were particularly careful to take into consideration how to thwart and counteract the risk of a central state control over broadcasting. Such reservations regarding the establishment of a state broadcasting institution were fewer and far less strong within the Soviet occupied sector. As early as 13 May 1945, only a few days after the unconditional capitulation of the Third Reich, Berlin radio was already transmitting under the name of 'Radio Berlin'. It had the authorization of the Soviet administration in Germany and was broadcasting as a station which had previously been pioneered by communist exiles in Moscow.[13]

In the absence of any coordinated concept for the restructuring of broadcasting in all the zones, the occupying forces, when trying to re-organize the broadcasting in their respective areas of influence, oriented themselves towards the organizational

[10] Art 9 of the Declaration regarding the defeat of Germany and the assumption of supreme authority with respect to Germany by the Governments by the Allied Powers dated 05.06.1945, printed in *Official Gazette of the Control Council for Germany 1946, Supplement No. 1: Documents Relating to the Establishment of the Allied Control Authority*, doc no 4, 7ff.

[11] For more on this see General Lucius D Clay in his speech dated 17 October 1945, protocol printed in Bundesarchiv (ed), *Akten zur Vorgeschichte der Bundesrepublik Deutschland 1945–1949*, vol I (Munich, R Oldenbourg, 1976), doc no 2, 125, 127.

[12] F Kübler, *Medien, Menschenrechte und Demokratie* (Heidelberg, CF Müller, 2008) 21–22.

[13] More on this and on the monopoly of information set up in the soviet occupied zone in J Foitzik, *Sowjetische Militäradministration in Deutschland (SMAD) 1945-1949* (Berlin, Akademie, 1999) 324ff.

structures which were present in their home countries.[14] However, the political broadcasting concepts of the different occupying forces were, in part, vastly different.[15] Despite any differences and due to the primacy of the politically intended notion of *Staatsferne* – a maintaining of distance from the state – the construction and the structure of public broadcasting in the Western occupied zones finally aligned itself on the whole with the structural model of the BBC. By means of ordinances passed by the military government or by laws enacted by the *Länder*, upon which the occupying forces had considerable influence, public broadcasting institutions were established in the three Western occupied zones. They were granted the right of self-administration and were, in part, subjected to a closely delineated form of legal supervision. The basic principles of the *Programmgestaltung* – the composition and configuration of the programmes – as well as the terms of their remit, organization and economic management were all aimed at ensuring that the institutions remained independent of the state while maintaining their political neutrality. These objectives were subsequently to leave an indelible mark on the broadcasting institutions which were later established by statute or treaty without the influence of the occupying forces.

The British occupying forces bore in mind an almost continuous perception of the BBC model of self-administration which was distanced from state intervention and set within a unified and centralized broadcasting organization. A leading factor in this matter was 'to render broadcasting in the British sector – within the framework of a strongly monopolized structure – independent of any influence from government agencies or political parties'. For the purpose of this there was to be

> an independent broadcasting organization created in which freely disposed people can express their opinions on the burning issues of the day and that can be implemented as an effective expedient in order to raise awareness to the value of criticism, free speech and to elicit the clash of opposing views in a democratic society.[16]

On the basis of this, and pursuant to the military government decree No. 118 which came into force on 1 January 1948, they created 'Nordwestdeutscher Rundfunk' (NWDR), which included the *Länder* Hamburg, Lower Saxony, North Rhine-Westphalia and Schleswig-Holstein and which then, upon its gaining the status of an 'institution subject to public law', was placed in German hands. The broadcasting statute which was referred to as 'Injektion BBC' (injection BBC)[17]

[14] H Bausch, *Rundfunkpolitik nach 1945,* vol I (Berlin, de Gruyter, 1980) 20, 46.

[15] On the development of the public system of the post-war years under the influence of the Western allied occupying forces, see W Först, 'Rundfunk' in K Jeserich, H Pohl, and G-C von Unruh (eds), *Deutsche Verwaltungsgeschichte,* vol V (Stuttgart, Deutsche Verlags-Anstalt, 1987) ch XIII, § 22 paras 890ff.

[16] Statement of the British Control Commission dated 13 October 1947, printed in Bundesarchiv (ed), *Akten zur Vorgeschichte der Bundesrepublik Deutschland 1945–1949,* vol III (Munich, R Oldenbourg, 1982) doc no 42, 424, 471–72, comm 52.

[17] P von Rüden and H Wagner (eds), Die Geschichte des Nordwestdeutschen Rundfunks, vol I (Hamburg, Hoffmann und Campe, 2005) 64. For more on the NWDR as an instrument or re-education, see F Huber, Re-education *durch Rundfunk* (Hamburg, Verlag Hans-Bredow-Institut, 2005) 102ff.

contained in Article II a categorical rejection of any form of 'supervision of its operations [ie of the organs of NWDR] – pursuant to the provisions concerning the supervision of public law entities – by organs of the authorities of the State, the *Länder* or other bodies'. What is interesting is the fact that it was precisely this distance from the state which brought about the putative resistance within German politics. Alongside the criticism of the non-participation of the political parties in the composition of the NWDR main committee, it was held to be 'incompatible with the fundamental principles of democracy that the decreed public corporation was not subject to any supervision by the organs of the State, the *Länder* or any other corporations'.[18] In 1955 NWDR was, through a treaty, concluded between the *Länder* involved, divided into two separate broadcasting institutions: Norddeutscher Rundfunk (NDR) and Westdeutscher Rundfunk (WDR).

The American occupying forces, on the other hand, initially considered the model of strictly state-free and commercially organized broadcasting. However, this commercial orientation proved to be economically unfeasible owing to the absence of private capital for the broadcasting company and to the fact that the financing for advertising was quite simply hopeless during rationing.[19] A compromise which was modified by means of a strongly federalist division of the institutional landscape[20] came about with the founding of public law institutions which adopted the British model of a 'public service' establishment. Under the decisive influence of political directives of the American occupying forces, four broadcasting institutions were founded on the basis of *Länder* laws (BR, HR, Radio Bremen, SDR). By adopting the US-American system of local radio stations, this development stood in contrast to the centralized structure in the French (SWF) and British (NWDR) sectors.

There was a central concept underlying the re-organization of broadcasting in the French zone, although conveying the French system of a strong intertwining of monopolized state radio and politics over to the occupied zones was not considered owing to overriding motives. Pursuant to the decree of the military government No. 187 dated 30 October 1948 the Südwestfunk which had already gone into service in 1946 under the name of 'Südwestdeutscher Rundfunk' (SWF) was granted the status of an institution governed by public law with the right of self-administration in accordance with a formal law enacted by the occupying forces. What was different compared to the British zone was that the newly founded institution was not directly put into German hands. Until the autumn of 1949 SWF was formally deployed as a channel of the French High Command in

[18] Draft of a statement on the decree no 118, introduced on the occasion of the 18th sitting of the Zone Advisory Body in the British sector dated 14.01.1948, printed in Bundesarchiv (ed), *Akten zur Vorgeschichte der Bundesrepublik Deutschland 1945-1949*, vol IV (Munich, R Oldenbourg, 1983) doc no 10, 223, 227.

[19] B Holznagel, *Rundfunkrecht in Europa* (Tübingen, Mohr Siebeck, 1996) 11; J Sandford in J Colemann and B Rollet, *Television in Europe* (Exeter, Intellect Books, 1997) 49.

[20] R Lorimer and P Scannell, *Mass Communications: A Comparative Introduction* (Manchester, Manchester University Press, 1994) 98.

Germany without any German involvement. French broadcasting officers then took over responsibility for personnel and programme scheduling policy.[21]

With the founding of the Federal Republic of Germany on 23 May 1949 the freedom of broadcasting was enshrined in the German Constitution – the *Grundgesetz* ('GG') – pursuant to Article 5(1), sentence 2, as an independent fundamental right. Previously undertaken attempts at programming the future structure of broadcasting using a constitutional law framework had been unsuccessful.[22] Instead the dominant view in the Parliamentary Council was that the GG was not the right place to determine the broadcasting system, which had to be established under the rules of the GG. Every attempt at the constitutional 'pre-emption of a legislative (power)'[23] was repudiated and with one eye focused on the Dutch and American broadcasting structures, which were characterized by private broadcasting associations, it was deemed somewhat misguided to 'determine, once and for all, the future form of broadcasting in the Constitution'.[24]

Even after the GG had come into force, the occupying forces initially retained an extensive scope of influence. As such, pursuant to Article 3(1) of Law No. 5 of the Allied High Control Commission, new radio stations, television channels or wired radio stations were not permitted to be established without the consent of the Allied High Commission. In addition to that, pursuant to Article 1, sentence 2, the High Commission reserved the right to declare invalid or to repeal any measures taken on a political, administrative or financial basis which could threaten the freedom of broadcasting.

A lax cooperation of the institutionally organized broadcasting companies was established on 9 June 1950 when ARD was founded by the then six *Länder* broadcasting institutions BR, HR, RB, SDR, SWF and NWDR. During this phase the clear political determination favoured an organizational broadcasting model outside the bounds of the Constitution.

B. The Constitutional Underpinning of Public Monopoly Broadcasting

A second phase of development up to the end of the 1970s or early 1980s was decisively characterized by the Federal Constitutional Court's constitutional under-

[21] O Altendorfer, *Das Mediensystem der Bundesrepublik Deutschland*, vol I (Wiesbaden, Westdeutscher Verlag, 2001) ch 1, para 38c.

[22] The suggestion proposed by the MP von Mangoldt in the committee of the Parliamentary Council was to adopt as part of the Article the principle of the political independence of broadcasting and to safeguard it by way of a monopoly of broadcasting by means of 'independent public institutions', cf 32nd sitting of this committee on 11 January 1949 (Stenographisches Protokoll) 41.

[23] MP Heuss, 32nd sitting of Committee 11 January 1949 (Stenographisches Protokoll) 42.

[24] MP Süsterhenn, 32nd sitting of Committee on 11 January 1949 (Stenographisches Protokoll) 42. For criticism on the constitutional shaping of the legal framework of broadcasting, cf the defences of the MPs Heuss and Eberhard in the 25th sitting of the Committee on 24 November 1948 (Stenographisches Protokoll) 20ff. On the birth and development of Art 5(1)(2) GG, see in particular [1951] 1 *Jahrbuch des öffentlichen Rechts* 86; C Starck in C Starck (ed), *Freiheit und Institutionen* (Tübingen, Mohr Siebeck, 2002) 477, 484.

pinning of the public monopoly broadcasting which had come about in the first phase. Prior to this, there had been efforts by the federal government to establish its own federal broadcasting corporation which, after the founding of the Deutschland-Fernsehen-GmbH led to a party-political and federal 'fight for the power in the ether'[25] and which was eventually quashed by the first broadcasting judgment of the BVerfG dated 28 February 1961. During this time the Deutsche Welle and Deutschlandfunk were founded by the federation and the Zweites Deutsches Fernsehen (Second German Television – ZDF) was set up by the *Länder*.

In the 1950s the federal government had initially acknowledged the broadcasting monopoly of the *Länder* institutions and had barely shown any interest in television which, at the time, had very few viewers. However, in the course of time the government not only increasingly began to demand the establishment of federal channels for shortwave and longwave but also equal rights concerning its influence on television. Nevertheless, despite intensive negotiations with the *Länder*, which were insisting on their cultural sovereignty, agreement as to the establishment of ZDF (initially conceived on the model of the public institution of the *Länder*) within the jurisdiction of the federation could not be reached. However, when Chancellor Adenauer deemed the influence of television on the pending parliamentary election[26] decisive,[27] as well as considering the existing broadcasting institutions to be sympathetic towards the opposition, he founded Deutschland-Fernsehen-GmbH on 25 July 1960 in the name of the Federal Republic, a private company which had business headquarters in Cologne. As none of the *Länder* were prepared to take a stake in the company, the shares in the business which had been intended for the *Länder* were assigned to the federation on 25 August 1960. Henceforth, the federation functioned as the sole shareholder of Deutschland-Fernsehen-GmbH.[28]

With its decision of 28 February 1961 the BVerfG quashed the establishment of Deutschland-Fernsehen-GmbH, deeming it unconstitutional. In its judgment, the Court first seized the opportunity to resolve the open question which stemmed from the days of the Weimar Republic, the question pertaining to the distribution of competence between a central power and member state with regard to broadcasting.[29] The criticism about the style and type of approach of

[25] 'Mit beschränkter Haftung' [1960] 33 *Der Spiegel* 18, 19.

[26] Minutes of the 80th Cabinet Meeting on 30.9.1959, TOP 4, in Bundesarchiv (ed), *Kabinettsprotokolle*, vol XII (Munich, Oldenbourg, 2002) 315, 319; note 6 in the minutes of the 114th Cabinet Meeting of the Federal Government on 13.7.1960, in Bundesarchiv (ed), *Kabinettsprotokolle*, vol XIII (Munich, Oldenbourg, 2003) 266, 267; H-P Schwarz, *Adenauer: Der Staatsmann 1952–1967* (Stuttgart, Deutsche Verlags-Anstalt, 1994) 621-22.

[27] Adenauer was convinced that 'the next election would be decided through the television channels and not as a result of the speeches or what has been achieved, because with television you can really get close to the people' cited in Lars Rosumek, *Die Kanzler und die Medien* (Frankfurt am Main, Campus, 2007) 77.

[28] More on the chronology and the background to the dispute regarding the founding of Deutschland-Fernsehen-GmbH, see H Laufer, *Verfassungsgerichtsbarkeit und politischer Prozeß* (Tübingen, Mohr Siebeck, 1968) 448ff.

[29] BVerfGE 12, 205, 225ff.

the federal government was, in part, strongly formulated. Against the backdrop of tensions which existed between the government and the constitutional jurisdiction at the time, it was also possible to construe the judgment as an act of self-assertion by the constitutional judges at the peak[30] of a conflict concerning the scope of the constitutional judges' powers of scrutiny. The BVerfG emerged from this conflict to continue its characteristically emphatic style of decision-making even more strongly[31] despite – or perhaps precisely because of – Adenauer's emphatic berating of the judgment[32].

In addition to that and above all, the BVerfG outlined a concept of broadcasting freedom which was to be defining over the ensuing decades. Taking into consideration the historical development of broadcasting[33] and the legal context outside of the Constitution, the BVerfG extrapolated from the technical situation which existed at the time (lack of frequencies and high financial expenditure for running a broadcasting institution) the necessity for exceptional provisions for the realization and adherence to the guarantee of broadcasting freedom set down in Article 5 GG.[34] Article 5(1), sentence 2 GG demands that this modern instrument, which can be employed in the process of shaping public opinion, can neither be handed over to the state nor to any other group in society. What is necessary are binding guiding principles which guarantee a minimum of contentual balance, objectivity and mutual respect. That can only be securely achieved when these fundamental organizational and objective tenets are made generally binding by legislation. Article 5 GG therefore demands the enactment of such laws.[35] The BVerfG thus established an institutional-functional concept of broadcasting freedom. This in turn prioritized the functional restriction upon the guarantee of the pluralistic shaping of opinion which is inherent in the freedom of broadcasting. By doing so, the Court distanced itself from the classic-liberal defensive nature of the substance of fundamental rights which guarantee the citizens freedom from state intervention.

With its remarks, and in the light of the decisive case, the Court pursued, above all, the obvious agenda of placing constitutional obstacles in the way of any political control of broadcasting as a political or social instrument of power – and this at a time when television, owing to its technically restricted monopoly, indeed possessed a special status among the media (ie its being so current, its wide appeal and its

[30] For an interpretation of the decision as an expression, in constitutional law terms, of a determining of a particular standpoint in 'its own matter', see OW Lembcke 'Das Bundesverfassungsgericht und die Regierung Adenauer: Vom Streit um den Status zur Anerkennung der Autorität' in RC van Ooyen and HM Möllers (eds), *Das Bundesverfassungsgericht im politischen System* (Wiesbaden, Verlag für Sozialwissenschaften (VS), 2006) 151, 157–58; for more on the conflict between the BVerfG and the Adenauer government, see R Häußler, *Der Konflikt zwischen Bundesverfassungsgericht und politischer Führung* (Berlin, Duncker & Humblot, 1993) 22ff, in particular 52.

[31] Laufer, *Verfassungsgerichtsbarkeit und politischer Prozeß* (n 28) 464-65 with further evidence in fn 146; Lembcke, 'Das Bundesverfassungsgericht und die Regierung Adenauer' (n 30) 151, 158.

[32] Federal Chancellor Adenauer declared during the budget debate in the German Bundestag on 8 March 1961 that the cabinet was 'in agreement that the judgment was wrong'; cf stenographic report of the 147th sitting of 8 March 1961 (Stenographisches Protokoll, 3. Legislaturperiode) 8308 D.

[33] BVerfGE 12, 205, 208ff.

[34] BVerfGE 12, 205, 261.

[35] BVerfGE 12, 205, 262–63.

suggestive power[36]) which the BVerfG had complained about. From the point of view of the Court, and in view of this special status, the task arose of creating a constitutional basis and/or justification for an established organization which confirmed fundamental rights. Moreover, it would have to create an infrastructure outside the bounds of the Constitution, an infrastructure with which broadcasting in its existing form would be withdrawn from the access of the legislator.[37] With Deutschland-Fernsehen-GmbH, the BVerfG had at its disposal an illustrative object which was created solely on a private law basis. Within this, however, the purpose of a unilateral influencing of public opinion in the election year clearly came to the fore. The judgment, and the guiding principles which the BVerfG postulated, were thus able to be construed as the counterdraft of the business concept of Deutschland-Fernsehen-GmbH. This was, pursuant to statute, financed alone through advertising and thus required the necessary viewing figures. However, this commercial approach had already invoked the resistance of significant social and political protagonists.[38] To a great extent, the institutional significance of the freedom of broadcasting found consensus in the bodies of literature.[39]

The objective understanding, which implied the organization of the freedom of broadcasting, soon encountered rejection, finding a vent in the accusation that the BVerfG had allowed the freedom to broadcast 'to disappear in the fog of the institutional'[40] or that it 'had remodelled the element of freedom of opinion to be the sense of all broadcasting freedom and of a typical individual right [. . .] into an institutional right of broadcasting'.[41] The debate concerning the interpretation of the freedom of broadcasting as a primarily objective institutional task of formation or a classic liberal individual right[42] still continues intensively even today. In fact, it has, at times, assumed the characteristic traits of a 'war of opinions'.[43]

[36] More on this dogma which was adhered to in later decisions as well: BVerfGE 31, 314, 325; 90, 60, 87; 97, 228, 256; 103, 44, 74; 114, 371, 387.

[37] K-H Ladeur, 'Die "objektiv-rechtliche Dimension der Rundfunkfreiheit" unter den Bedingungen von Multimedia' in H Faber and G Frank (eds), *Festschrift für Ekkehart Stein* (Tübingen, Mohr Siebeck, 2002) 67, 70-71; M Cornils, *Die Ausgestaltung der Grundrechte* (Tübingen, Mohr Siebeck, 2005) 64.

[38] For more, see 'Mit beschränkter Haftung' [1960] 33 *Der Spiegel*, 18, 25; Mitteilung P/XV/222 *Sozialdemokratischer Pressedienst* (28 September 1960) 2.

[39] H Bethge, *Die verfassungsrechtliche Position des öffentlich-rechtlichen Rundfunks in der dualen Rundfunkordnung* (Baden-Baden, Nomos, 1996) 29ff; W Hoffmann-Riem, *Erosionen des Rundfunkrechts* (Munich, CH Beck, 1990) 13ff; W Hoffmann-Riem, *Rundfunkrecht neben Wirtschaftsrecht* (Baden-Baden, Nomos, 1991) 71ff; for further evidence K-E Hain, *Rundfunkfreiheit und Rundfunkordnung* (Baden-Baden, Nomos, 1993) 25, fn 71.

[40] K-A Bettermann, 'Rundfunkfreiheit und Rundfunkorganisation' [1963] *Deutsches Verwaltungsblatt* 41, 42.

[41] H Peters, *Die Rechtslage von Rundfunk und Fernsehen nach dem Urteil des Bundesverfassungsgerichtes vom 28. Februar 1961* (Gütersloh, Bertelsmann, 1961) 28.

[42] G Herrmann, *Fernsehen und Hörfunk in der Verfassung der Bundesrepublik Deutschland* (Tübingen, Mohr Siebeck, 1975) 356ff; M Bullinger, *Kommunikationsfreiheit im Strukturwandel der Telekommunikation* (Baden-Baden, Nomos, 1980) 62ff; HH Klein, 'Rundfunkrecht und Rundfunkfreiheit' [1981] 20 *Der Staat* 189ff; U Scheuner, *Grundrecht der Rundfunkfreiheit* (Berlin, Duncker & Humblot, 1982) 12ff; C-E Eberle, *Rundfunkübertragung* (Berlin, Duncker & Humblot, 1989) 27ff; Hain, *Rundfunkfreiheit und Rundfunkordnung* (n 39) 80ff.

[43] C Degenhart, 'Verfassungsrechtliche Determinanten der Rundfunkfinanzierung' in P Badura and R Scholz (eds), *Festschrift für Peter Lerche* (Munich, CH Beck, 1993) 611.

The understanding developed by the BVerfG in its judgment raised a number of questions in its wake, questions which, in part, did not manifest themselves until a later date.

What remained unanswered, for example, was the question as to whether the legislator, when executing its *Ausgestaltungsauftrag* (mandate for shaping the law) had to do so by way of a 'general law' as Article 5(2) GG requires for restrictions. It was only the judgments of the third phase[44] that expressly demarcated legislative enactments restricting the freedom to broadcast from those enactments only shaping (*ausgestalten*) it. Whereas the former call for justification and thus have to conform to the demands of Art 5(2) GG, the latter do not.[45] For them the uncertainties caused by the vastly different understandings[46] of the term,'general law' were thus avoided.

On the other hand, a dogmatic legitimization of public broadcasting ensued, but not under primary citation of the democracy principle. It was done on the basis of fundamental rights. As a result of specific aims connected to the democracy principle, the protection under fundamental rights is, however, construed as being democratic-functional. As a consequence, broadcasting is, in a non-democratic way, legitimized as being an actual functional requirement of democracy.

The decidedly far-reaching passages concerning the so-called *Ausgestaltungspflicht*[47] – the duty under material law to shape the freedom of broadcasting – led further to a constitutionalization of these provisions, with strong, binding components under constitutional law. As a result, the legislator was, to a certain extent, removed from the scene. The acceptance of a broadcasting system which was prescribed by constitutional law and formed by non-constitutional statutes was, however – particularly in its contemporaneous tendency towards de-individualization – difficult to reconcile with the historical nascence of Article 5 GG.[48]

The BVerfG also appointed itself 'parallel legislator' or even actual legislator with the dogmatic entrenchment of the administrative courts' broadcasting concept in the interpretation regarding fundamental rights. In the ensuing period this interpretation was even more strongly sought after in order to answer detailed

[44] BVerfGE 57, 295, 321; 73, 118, 166; more on this Cornils, *Die Ausgestaltung der Grundrechte* (n 37) 65-66, 159ff. Regarding the demarcation of the *Ausgestaltung* (formation) and the intervention in conjunction with broadcasting freedom, cf U Mager, *Einrichtungsgarantien* (Tübingen, Mohr Siebeck, 2003) 262-63; S Lenz, *Vorbehaltlose Freiheitsrechte: Stellung und Funktion vorbehaltloser Grundrechte* (Tübingen, Mohr Siebeck, 2006) 115.

[45] Opposed to the construction of an *Ausgestaltungsbefugnis* beyond the rules of the constitutional limits, see Lenz, *Vorbehaltlose Freiheitsrechte* (n 44) 116ff. Regarding the discussion on the inadequacy of the general law as a special legal basis for the freedom of broadcasting, see P Lerche, 'Hoheitliche Programmanforderungen für private Rundfunkveranstaltungen' in E Schreiber and others (eds), *Festschrift für Otto Roegele* (Düsseldorf, Droste, 1980) 291, 296ff.

[46] Cornils (n 37) 159ff. Regarding the relativization of the qualification substance of the 'generality' of a law, see Hain (n 39) 101.

[47] More on the content and substance of the mandate Art 5(1) GG in detail, see H Lenz, 'Rundfunkorganisation und öffentliche Meinungsbildungsfreiheit' [1963] *Juristenzeitung* 338, 339, 341, 345; M Gellermann, *Grundrechte in einfachgesetzlichem Gewande* (Tübingen, Mohr Siebeck, 2000) 186ff.

[48] Hain (n 39) 39–40.

questions, even though it is only appropriate in restricted circumstances, as for many of these questions, assessments and predictive decisions are decisive. The quasi law-making function of the BVerfG in the broadcasting sector ran the risk of there being an insufficiently considered orientation towards a barely determined notion of 'good cause' or 'good system'.[49]

Finally, it is worth considering that genuine 'freedom from state interference' is, anyway, not possible owing to the mandate of the legislator to guarantee certain contentual minimum standards. The BVerfG acknowledges that the precept of an organization of the broadcasting corporations distanced from the state is accomplished over and above the implementation of 'corporative' broadcasting councils, which are, in part, constituted under the considerable influence of the political parties. Committee members are thus inter alia delegates of groups within society and also members of forces within society which are not organized into associations. However, these people may also be nominated or elected by state authorities and are as such members of the parties or representatives of state of institutions or institutions close to the state.

C. The Continuing Development into a Dual Broadcasting System

The third incipient phase in the development of broadcasting, which began at the end of the 1970s/early 1980s, was characterized by the accreditation of private broadcasting providers who were to operate alongside the public broadcasters and thus led to the formation of a dual broadcasting system. Given the broadening of the availability of frequencies and the dismantling of the structural 'shortage situation' the fundamental reason for maintaining the monopoly position of public broadcasting no longer applied. In the so-called FRAG judgment (third broadcasting judgment) in 1981,[50] the ideal models for the internal and external pluralism of broadcasting were outlined. As a consequence of this judgment, the *Länder* passed a successive line of statutory rudiments for the accreditation of private operators.

The dual model construed by the BVerfG in the FRAG judgment assigned the public broadcasting corporations the task of *Grundversorgung* – providing the basics – (inland pluralism) while formulating correspondingly low demands on the private broadcasting companies (external pluralism).[51] Subsequently, the basic tenet of programming autonomy also became firmly established.[52]

With a view to the constitutionally decreed notion of 'distance from the state' the public programme mandate may only be broadly outlined by the legislator and the stipulating of the programmes' content and form is in the hands of the

[49] On Christoph Möller's criticism, *Staat als Argument* (Munich, CH Beck, 2000) 329ff; Ladeur, 'Die "objektiv-rechtliche Dimension der Rundfunkfreiheit"' (n 37) 69, fn 9.

[50] BVerfGE 57, 295ff.

[51] BVerfGE 57, 295, 325ff; upheld in BVerfGE 73, 118, 153ff.

[52] BVerfGE 90, 60, 96ff.

broadcasting institutions themselves. In doing so, the broadcasting institutions are only subject to a restricted form of legal supervision. During this phase a more precise set of guidelines on the forming of the committees (broadcasting councils) also ensued, in particular a demarcation only – or, initially, only – in cases of 'a grossly one-sided composition' or in the event of 'gross distortion'.[53] From 1987 onwards, in a politically concerted move by the *Länder*, broadcasting treaties gave the final shape to this dual model on a national basis.

From the standpoint of the BVerfG, the task in this phase was, by way of constitutional interpretation, to make it possible for the existing public broadcasting institutions to successfully undergo the transition from a system of a satisfactorily functioning monopoly into a system of the restricted plurality of providers.[54] In doing so it became apparent that further grounds were required for an upgrading of the existing establishments through a constitutional guarantee. This was due to the fact that the new frequencies which had become available had effectively put an end to the 'shortage situation' which had long maintained the monopoly of the public broadcasting corporations. The formation of the 'shaping' rules orientated towards a freedom of broadcasting had begun with the FRAG judgment[55] in 1981. From then on, the argument was no longer based on the technological special position which had been held, but rather on the effect, the suggestive power[56] and the ability to be current.

The corresponding judgments also led to a string of problems. On the one hand, there was the risk of overemphasizing the historical[57] and adhering too strongly to traditional institutions. On the other hand, the programming autonomy was only enabled for the benefit of the public institutions without providing any sufficient justification – which was difficult because the actual aim of this programming autonomy was to prevent or to limit an even smaller division of the channel into the category of programmes for the provision of basic needs (*grundversorgungsrelevante Sendungen*) on the one hand and, on the other, the remaining programmes.

D. Digitalization, Convergence and Internationalization

The fourth phase, which began with the new millennium, saw increasing digitalization and convergence combined with the growing access of European Community and European Union law to the German broadcasting corporations. The digitalization of media technology and the convergence of media products brought about considerable changes in the media landscape which resulted in the conventional

[53] BVerfGE 83, 238, 335.
[54] Ladeur (n 37) 70-71.
[55] BVerfGE 57, 295, 321ff.
[56] More on this dogma which was also upheld in later decisions: BVerfGE 31, 314, 325; 90, 60, 87; 97, 228, 256; 103, 44, 74; 114, 371, 387; 97, 228, 256; 103, 44, 74; 114, 371, 387.
[57] Ladeur (n 37) 71.

boundaries between the press, broadcasting and film within the meaning of Article 5(1), sentence 2 GG appearing increasingly problematic. The use and significance of the media as a whole, as well as individual ways and types of media propagation, were, in part, subjected to massive changes. The intensively regulating special regime for broadcasting and its establishment in the guarantee of a media 'basic provision' were being put under more and more pressure by the unstoppably progressive diversification of the private media in both content and form. This generated an area of tension between the constitutional law concept of broadcasting and the concept of broadcasting outside the bounds of constitutional law. The legislator saw itself confronted with the task of creating a legal infrastructure under constitutional considerations, which made it possible to make the transition from a more tightly restricted plurality of providers to a barely restricted plurality.[58]

The BVerfG was in doing so faced with the task of checking the traditional doctrine for its continuing justification. In its most recent decision from September 2007[59] it not only upheld the conventional fundamental tenets including the autonomy of the institutes, but also extended them to cover new media services. In justifying this, the BVerfG referred to the various selection criteria for the programme content of the public and the private broadcasting corporations as well as to the economic pressure in the field of the private media. The special legal doctrine surrounding broadcasting is, in the age of digitalization and convergence of the media, thereby being transferred via an allusion to the fact that the options of the public broadcasters (journalistic relevance within the meaning of being current, having a broad impact and possessing suggestive force) have gained additional significance as a result of the new technologies.[60] In addition, the BVerfG developed further tenets on the financing of broadcasting, in particular for the institutional relationship between the public institutions, the Commission for Determining the Financial Needs of the Broadcasting Institutions (Kommission zur Ermittlung des Finanzbedarfs der Rundfunkanstalten, 'KEF') and the parliaments of the *Länder*. The most recent judgment is as such by and large characterized by the adherence to the 'serving' freedom of broadcasting and the assumptions and perceptions that accompany it. The BVerfG did not take on board the stimuli to release the freedom of broadcasting – in the light of modern mass communication technology and the associated diversification of the information alternatives[61] – from its position of specialized treatment and as such to construe it as a classic liberal right to freedom like the freedom of the press.[62]

This ignited some fierce debates.[63] The court was accused of only having selectively taken on the amended factual circumstances and, when it did, only in an

[58] ibid 70–71.
[59] BVerfGE 119, 181ff.
[60] BVerfGE 119, 181, 215.
[61] C Möllers, *Das Grundgesetz: Geschichte und Inhalt* (Munich, CH Beck, 2009) 106.
[62] Regarding this point Hain (n 39) 30ff, 80ff.
[63] Comprehensive and trenchant: K-E Hain, 'Die zweite Gebührenentscheidung des Bundesverfassungsgerichts: Kontinuität in den Zeiten der Konvergenz' [2008] *Juristenzeitung* 128ff.

extremely restricted fashion. Moreover, at least in parts, it was said to have acted rather one-sidedly. The decision disclosed a tendency to accept and assert the factual prerequisites for the legal acknowledgement across the board rather than actually verifying them individually or allowing them to be verified. Major passages were based on minor real findings which, in addition, were more like obiter dicta than pivotal reasons. A scrutiny to that effect is, of course, a difficult task for the courts, but through the – self-chosen – role as 'parallel legislator' it is a conditional and, as such, unavoidable task. By isolating traditional doctrine in view of the changes in the media landscape and the possibly concomitant discontinuation of its justifying factual prerequisites, a wider leeway for the legislator only opened up.

In addition to that it has been criticized that the BVerfG does not deal with the stipulations of EC law. The Commission stayed[64] – even before any oral proceedings before the BVerfG – a test case concerning the financing of public broadcasting in Germany with particular reference to the new media services. In doing so the Commission laid down significant provisions[65] which are to be observed in future and which have almost driven to the point of conflict the relationship between the provisions of Article 5 GG (broad programming autonomy of the institution compared with the legislator) and the state aid law of the EC Treaty (a precisely defined notion of 'common good provisions' for programme content undertaken by the legislator). This gives rise to a closer examination of these questions.

IV. THE POSITION UNDER GERMAN LAW: AN INTERNATIONAL COMPARISON

Is, in international comparison, the 'serving freedom of broadcasting' a separate path and can the objectives which are linked to it also be achieved in terms of a 'serving' freedom without an appreciation of the guarantee of fundamental rights?

The idiosyncrasies of the German legal position in international comparison do not lie in the non-constitutional legal principles of the public broadcasting and the developments based upon it. A comparative law approach shows that on occasions there are different developments but, nevertheless, also parallel developments in their aims. The aim of the guarantee of pluralism and quality in broadcasting can be attested for as a broadcasting political paradigm in numerous other jurisdictions.[66] Even the derivation of a legal obligation with regard to specific guiding principles (pluralism) from a fundamental right as well as the codifying of parts of the legal system using a constitutional interpretation does not, per se, render the German legal system a loner in this regard. On the contrary, other legal systems ascribe an objective law dimension to the basic right of the freedom of broadcasting. This compels the state to legally structure the broadcasting corporations in a particular way.

[64] Commission IP/07/543 of 24 April 2007.
[65] Regarding the catalogue of demands Commission MEMO/07/150 of 24 April 2007.
[66] Cornils (n 37) 89.

The Spanish Constitutional Court grants the freedom of communication, which is established in Article 20(1), letters a. and d. of the Constitution, not only a subjective law 'defensive' character but also a democratic-pluralistically established objective-law substance.[67] In Italy, the freedom of expression of opinion, pursuant to Article 21(1) of the Constitution is enlisted to formulate the aspect pertaining to individual rights[68] alongside the objective-law demands on the formation of the broadcasting system (such as the guarantee of the diversity of information – '*pluralità di fonti di informazione*').[69] In Portugal and in the Netherlands there are also analogous structures.[70]

In Japan, too, the idea of broadcasting freedom as an 'institutional freedom' has assumed a not inconsiderable significance, particularly on the statutory but non-constitutional level.[71] The debate on broadcasting law is, in particular, influenced by the German discussion. The idea of the 'institutional freedom' taken from the German constitutional system was not directly adopted in Japan when constructing the term of broadcasting freedom. However, a similar debate recently arose, not least because of the exposed position which a few knowledgeable insiders of the German legal system assumed in the dialogue on broadcasting in Japan.[72]

In France, the freedom of audio-visual communication[73] is – in phases or even predominantly – interpreted[74] in terms of objective law and is itself not set down in the Constitutional Charter. It is acknowledged as an element of the freedom of expression under Article 11 of the Declaration on the Rights of Man and the Citizen from 26 August 1789.[75] The freedom of communication, which is predominantly

[67] Tribunal Constitucional [1981] *Jurisprudencia Constitucional* 112, 120–21; [1990] *Jurisprudencia Constitucional* 738, 757.

[68] More on this Corte Costitzionale [1974] *Giurisprudenza Costituzionale I* 1791, 1788.

[69] Corte Costitzionale [1987] *Foro Italiano I* 1965, 1972; [1988] *Foro Itialiano I* 2477, 2502.

[70] N Petersen, *Rundfunkfreiheit und EG-Vertrag* (Baden-Baden, Nomos, 1994) 234 (Portugal), 228 (Netherlands).

[71] In the Japanese broadcasting statute the emphasis lies on the reference to democracy. A serious comparison to constitutional demands of the freedom of opinion did not take place until recently: S Nishido, 'Medienkonvergenz und Meinungsfreiheit in Japan unter besonderer Berücksichtigung des Rundfunkrechts' in F Fechner (ed), *Pluralismus, Finanzierung und Konvergenz als Grundfragen des Rundfunkrechts* (Ilmenau, Ilmenau University Press, 2011) 76–77.

[72] J Hamada, 'Wettbewerb und Vermarktung in der Informationsgesellschaft' in Z Kitagawa and others (eds), *Regulierung – Deregulierung – Liberalisierung* (Tübingen, Mohr Siebeck, 2001) 103, 108. In the Constitution the freedom of broadcasting is, however, construed as a subjective legal defensive right and not an objective legal constitutional precept: H Suzuki, 'Rundfunkrecht und Internet' in K Asada and others (eds), *Das Recht vor den Herausforderungen neuer Technologien* (Tübingen, Mohr Siebeck, 2006) 83, 89–90. On the discussion as to whether the overriding criterion which is to be considered regarding the freedom of broadcasting should be the freedom of state or the reference to democracy: Nishido, 'Medienkonvergenz und Meinungsfreiheit in Japan' (n 71) 76ff.

[73] Conseil Constitutionnel [1982] *Journal Officiel de la Republique Française* 2422, 2423.

[74] B Holznagel, *Rundfunkrecht in Europa* (Tübingen, Mohr Siebek, 1996) 106; on the objective legal understanding of *libertés publiques*, see L Philip, 'La protection des droits fondamentaux en France' [1989] 38 *Jahrbuch des öffentlichen Recht* 119, 129ff; R Arnold, 'Ausgestaltung und Begrenzung von Grundrechten im französischen Verfassungsrecht' [1989] 38 *Jahrbuch des öffentlichen Recht* 197ff; M Schellenberg, 'Pluralismus: Zu einem medienrechtlichen Leitmotiv in Deutschland, Frankreich und Italien' [1994] 119 *Archiv des öffentlichen Rechts* 427, 432.

[75] 'Déclaration des Droits de l'Homme et du Citoyen' in D Willoweit and U Seif (eds), *Europäische Verfassungsgeschichte* (Munich, CH Beck, 2003) 250ff. On the incorporation of the Déclaration into

construed from the point of view of the recipient or consumer, should thereby be reconciled with the technical restrictions and with other constitutional values.[76] In doing so the Conseil Constitutionnel constantly emphasizes in its decisions that paramount significance is ascribed to the constitutional value of pluralism with regard to the shaping of the press and broadcasting systems.[77] By acknowledging an inalienable pluralistic system with regard to the press and broadcasting which is not only the effective guarantee of the fundamental rights of the broadcasting consumers but also of a functioning democracy[78] and a matter with constitutional status, the Conseil Constitutionnel reveals significant parallels not only to the prevailing institutional meaning of constitutional freedoms[79] which is in the German Constitution, but also to the role of the legislator in forming the broadcasting system.[80]

The *Regelungsauftrag* and the *Ausgestaltungsauftrag*[81] which are entrenched in Article 34 of the French Constitution, which also includes the *libertés publiques* (public rights to freedom) under Article 11 of the Declaration on the Rights of Man and the Citizen, has recently been extended by means of a constitutional amendment from 23 July 2008.[82] Alongside the existing *Ausgestaltungsauftrag* for the civic rights and the fundamental guarantees which are granted to the citizens for the awareness of their public rights of freedom, the *Gesetzgebungsauftrag* (the legislator's mandate) also comprises the freedom, the plurality and the independence of the media. The passage which was first inserted in the course of the legislative procedure at the request of the Senate is meant to introduce a legislative prerogative to safeguard pluralism in the media sector and thereby to particularly accentuate the necessity of the media for a functioning democracy.[83] What is interesting is that this addition was initially deemed adscititious not only by the National Assembly but also by the government. Thus the line was taken that the creation of a new shaping mandate for the safeguarding of pluralistic structures in the media sector was unnecessary with regard to its prior inclusion as *liberté pub-*

applicable French constitutional law via the preamble of the Constitution, see Conseil Constitutionnel [1971] *Journal Officiel de la République Française* 7114.

[76] Conseil Constitutionnel [1982] *Journal Officiel de la République Française* 2422, 2423.

[77] Conseil Constitutionnel [1986] *Journal Officiel de la République Française* 11294, 1129ff; 9393, 9394; M Herdegen, 'Pressefreiheit und Verfassungsgerichtsbarkeit in Frankreich – Die Entscheidung des Conseil constitutionnel zum neuen französischen Pressegesetz vom 10./11. Oktober 1984' [1986] *Zeitschrift für ausländisches öffentliches Recht und Völkerrecht* ff 34.

[78] On both aspects: Conseil Constitutionnel [1986] *Journal Officiel de la République Française* 11294, 11295–96.

[79] Herdegen, 'Pressefreiheit und Verfassungsgerichtsbarkeit in Frankreich' (n 77) 34, 45–46.

[80] Arnold, 'Ausgestaltung und Begrenzung von Grundrechten im französischen Verfassungsrecht' (n 74) 198ff

[81] On the interpretation of Art 34 as a so-called *Regelungsauftrag*, see M Schellenberg, 'Zu einem medienrechtlichen Leitmotiv in Frankreich und Italien' [1994] 119 *Archiv für öffentiches Recht* 427, 429.

[82] Art 11 No 2 Loi constitutionnelle N° 2008-724 dated 23 July2008 de modernisation des institutions de la Ve République [2008] *Journal Officiel de la République Française* 11890ff.

[83] Assemblée Nationale, Treizième Législature, Rapport N° 1009, 2 July 2008, sur le projet de Loi Constitutionnelle modifié par le Sénat de modernisation des institutions de la Ve République, 32, 41.

lique in the guarantee within Article 11 of the Declaration on the Rights of Man and the Citizen. Furthermore, pluralism was acknowledged as a constitutional value in the decisions of the cour constitutionnelle.[84] The fact that the newly created pluralism-specific legislative mandate was able to embrace the existing objective law substance under Article 11 of the Declaration – and as a consequence of this could emerge as a right to freedom, appears to have been excluded as a result of the decision of the Conseil based on the new constitutional position. With its decision of 3 March 2009[85] the Court upheld its pluralism-dogmatic concept based on Article 11 of the Declaration on the Rights of Man and the Citizen, that free communication of thoughts and opinions would not be actually guaranteed if the public did not have at its disposal access to the channels (of the private and public media) which guarantee the expression of diverse trends and fulfil the 'inviolable condition integrity of the information'. The listeners and viewers as most important bearers of the fundamental right under Article 11 which is entrenched in the Constitution are in the position to exercise the free choice of programmes without private interests or the state having the opportunity to replace this choice with their own decisions. Article 34 of the Constitution is, in contrast, interpreted to the effect that it is as a mere assignation of competence to the legislator as opposed to the executive. Placing materially constitutional principles in the allocation of Article 34 of the Constitution was incidentally rejected by the Conseil.[86]

The conferring of an objective legal status of the broadcasting freedom and the regulation of broadcasting does not, after all, constitute a specifically German idiosyncrasy.

V. SPECIAL PATH AND ITS PERSPECTIVES

However the German broadcasting system does possess a unique characteristic: the 'precedence of the institutional over and above the individual'[87] – which is qualified as a constitutional right – and the extensive 'repression of the right of the individual regarding the organization of broadcasting'.[88] In contrast to this, many other legal systems provide flexible assessment mechanisms for interventions in freedoms.[89]

This distinctive feature has become manifest in the decisions of the BVerfG since the third phase. From that time on the BVerfG has not seized the chance to assimilate the broadcasting model in the sense of a realignment to the actual

[84] ibid 93ff.
[85] [2009] *Journal Officiel de la République Française* 4336, 4337.
[86] Conseil Constitutionnel, 'Commentaire des décisions N° 2009-576 DC et n° 2009-577 DC' [2009] 26 *Cahiers du Conseil Constitutionnel* 109, 114.
[87] Cornils (n 37) 91-92.
[88] Schellenberg, 'Zu einem medienrechtlichen Leitmotiv in Frankreich und Italien' (n 81) 447 on the standards of the French and Italian dogmatics of pluralism.
[89] Conseil Constitutionnel [1982] *Journal Officiel de la République Française* 2422, 2423.

circumstances (ie no longer any shortage and restricted plurality) but now also pursues a replacement of the justification which was the basis of its concept of the 'serving' freedom (technical shortage and requirement of the basic provision). At the same time it is pursuing an 'impregnation' and/or 'immunization' against any later changes. The continuity of this model is not only safeguarded by the fixation of the programming autonomy – by means of its guaranteed existence and a guarantee of its development, including a claim for appropriate funding, the model has been granted a certain degree of permanence and has been uncoupled from actual changes. A comparatively minor significance for the legal boundaries of the broadcasting organization is thereby assigned to the special state of affairs which occurred owing to the restructuring of the broadcasting system after the Second World War. This was due to the fact that its effects had, at the latest, begun to disappear in the third phase of its development.

The judgment from 2007 confirms this appraisal and proves that the continuation of the decisions of the BVerfG could only be put at risk from obvious inefficiency and/or inadequacy. The proof of this would be much more difficult owing to the relative and also linguistically-related isolation of the media, for example, regarding the regulation of the telecommunications system. Increased pressure or an increased burden of justification is, on the other hand, to be expected on an 'external path' through the compacted legal ties of the EC/EU state aid regime. However, this aspect should also not be overstated: the access of European law had already sufficiently given rise to uncertainty in the framework of the 2007 judgment for the Court to react to this 'uncertainty' with reference to the requirements and/or justification of the traditional broadcasting doctrine and broadcasting regulation[90] but the BVerfG transferred this traditional approach of the freedom to broadcast in an unaltered state onto the internet.

Specific criticism in this case is directed less at the dogmatic derivation from a fundamental right of the *Ausgestaltungsregime* (the regime for shaping the broadcasting system) and more at the codification of considerable parts of the broadcasting system by way of the BVerfG's constitutional interpretation. This leads, on the one hand, to the question of the differentiation of the doctrine of other fundamental rights. The actual reason for this 'separate path' in the area of broadcasting might be the possible conflict with the limits of Article 5(2) GG, and as such a particular reason which is also intercepted by interpretation (*Ausgestaltung* – formation) in the fundamental right itself. On the other hand, the pressure to justify and/or align public broadcasting with regard to the new actual context will continue to grow. Both the regulatory problems in the area of new or electronic media, which have arisen from the dichotomy between broadcasting and the press, and the EC/EU state aid law contribute to the fact that the justification of the conventional concept of the 'serving freedom' will be frequently and increasingly scrutinized.

[90] Ladeur (n 37) 83ff.

CASES

BVerfGE 12, 205 – *1. Rundfunkentscheidung* (1961)
BVerfGE 31, 314 – *2. Rundfunkentscheidung* (1971)
BVerfGE 57, 295 – *3. Rundfunkentscheidung* (1981)
BVerfGE 73, 118 – *4. Rundfunkentscheidung* (1986)
BVerfGE 74, 297 – *5. Rundfunkentscheidung* (1987)
BVerfGE 83, 238 – *6. Rundfunkentscheidung* (1991)
BVerfGE 87, 181 – *7. Rundfunkentscheidung* (1992)
BVerfGE 90, 60 – *8. Rundfunkentscheidung* (1994)
BVerfGE 92, 203 – *9. Rundfunkentscheidung* (1995)
BVerfGE 97, 228 – *10. Rundfunkentscheidung* (1998)
BVerfGE 97, 298 – *11. Rundfunkentscheidung* (1998)
BVerfGE 119, 181 – *12. Rundfunkentscheidung* (2007)
BVerfGE 121, 30 – *12. Rundfunkentscheidung* (2008)

SELECTED LITERATURE

Bethge H, 'Die Freiheit des privaten Rundfunks' [2002] *Die Öffentliche Verwaltung* 673

—— *Die verfassungsrechtliche Position des öffentlich-rechtlichen Rundfunks in der dualen Rundfunkordnung* (Baden-Baden, Nomos, 1996)

Cornils M, *Die Ausgestaltung der Grundrechte* (Tübingen, Mohr Siebeck, 2005)

Degenhart C, 'Verfassungsrechtliche Determinanten der Rundfunkfinanzierung' in P Badura and R Scholz (eds), *Festschrift für Peter Lerche* (Munich, CH Beck, 1993) 611

Eifert M and Hoffmann-Riem W, 'Die Entstehung und Ausgestaltung des dualen Rundfunksystems' in D Schwarzkopf (ed), *Rundfunkpolitik in Deutschland* (München, Dtv, 1999) 50

Först W, 'Rundfunk' in J Jeserich, H Pohl and GC von Unruh (eds), *Deutsche Verwaltungsgeschichte*, vol V (Stuttgart, Deutsche Verlags-Anstalt, 1987) ch XIII, § 22, 890ff.

Hain KE, *Rundfunkfreiheit und Rundfunkordnung* (Baden-Baden, Nomos, 1993)

Hesse A, *Rundfunkrecht*, 3rd edn (Munich, Vahlen, 2003)

Hofmann-Riem W, *Regulierung der dualen Rundfunkordnung* (Baden-Baden, Nomos, 2000)

Klein HH, 'Rundfunkrecht und Rundfunkfreiheit' [1981] 20 *Der Staat* 189

Ladeur KH, 'Die "objektiv-rechtliche Dimension der Rundfunkfreiheit" unter den Bedingungen von Multimedia' in H Faber and G Frank (eds), *Festschrift für Ekkehart Stein* (Tübingen, Mohr Siebeck, 2002) 67

Mager U, *Einrichtungsgarantien* (Tübingen, Mohr Siebeck, 2003)

Scheuner U, *Grundrecht der Rundfunkfreiheit* (Berlin, Duncker & Humblot, 1982)

6

Rule of Law versus Welfare State

THORSTEN KINGREEN

> 'The welfare state based on the constitution can be achieved only by means of the rule of law'.[1]

I. INTRODUCTION

THE ONGOING DISCUSSION in jurisprudence on the relation between the principle of the rule of law and the welfare state is a fundamental one, but it is not a specifically German phenomenon. The constitutional state, as a state based upon the rule of law, guarantees freedom by granting fundamental rights. However, any state needs to regulate the limitations of freedom as well, and those limitations which inter alia need to be in place to facilitate the achievement of societal goals in the service of the welfare of the state's citizens. All

[1] BVerfGE 88, 203, 319.

Member States of the European Union individually and the European Union as a whole committed themselves to the fundamental rights of freedom as well as to the necessity of imposing restrictions in individual cases on those freedoms, in order to ensure security and justice within society. The relationship between a state based on the rule of law and the welfare state is thus ambivalent. On the one hand, welfare state regulation reduces constitutionally guaranteed freedom, such as in the form of compulsory insurance or in-company co-determination but, on the other hand, it creates the actual conditions to ensure that freedom can be exercised, eg through the establishment of systems of basic allowance (social assistance, housing subsidies, etc). This description might find approval and reception in similar discourses in other nations, but it is not particularly original in its universality. However, further steps to refine this description depend on the specific norms of each nation and scientific premises and decisions along the path of legal analysis and argumentation and which therefore only unfurl in a more nation-state oriented environment. Thus, more specific thoughts as to the relationship between the rule of law and the welfare state depend on national constitutions and laws. Their reference points are the respective texts of the constitutions and its body of case law; they must take into consideration the present understanding of state and constitution in its historic and intellectual history as well as the relationship between constitution and administration. Another basic reference point of those two principles is their interdependency with the democratic principle in its specific understanding and formulation in the respective nation state.

As such, two major debates have shaped the jurisprudential discussion of the topic in Germany: first, the debate in the 1930s and 1950s about the location of the welfare state in constitutional and administrative law (section II) which was largely triggered by Ernst Forsthoff, and, secondly, the discussion on the nature of fundamental rights not only as a means of protection of freedom but also as a legal foundation for claims on benefits supplied by the welfare state and the incorporation of such into the traditional German legal theories on fundamental rights, a discussion which, after an initial round in the 1970s, has recently been reopened (section III).

II. DEFINITION AND NATURE OF THE CONSTITUTIONAL WELFARE STATE[2]

The German legal debate regarding the relationship between the constitutional state and the welfare state has both a constitutional (see subsection II.A.) as well as an administrative law thread (see subsection II.B.).

Both debates have been significantly influenced by Ernst Forsthoff, each with a particular different direction of impact. This is by no means to say that such a

[2] Title of the speech by E Forsthoff and O Bachof on the Conference of the 'Staatsrechtslehrervereinigung' in Bonn 1953.

fundamental issue may be sufficiently exhausted by referring to the works of one single professor of constitutional law, especially since his works were temporarily heavily influenced by the National Socialist ideology.[3] However, for the analysis of the jurisprudential debate about the social state and its administration in the twentieth century, his works are still the most important points of reference.[4]

The history of the principle of the state in the service of the welfare of its citizens is part of the specific history of each modern nation state. Thus, terms used to denote any such state are always a reflection of the history of the state itself. Hence, the term 'welfare state' has a specific history and meaning in Germany which is partially different from the term used, for example, in the United States. As such, the term 'welfare state' is here used only in its specific German historic understanding of a certain relationship between state and subject, whereas the modern principle, which prompts a quite different understanding of state and citizen, is called the principle of the 'social state', so as to denote the difference between the two concepts.

A. The Constitutional Dimension

i. The Emergence of the Welfare State: A Sketch of its Intellectual and Factual History

The principles of rule of law and the welfare state originate from different streams of the historical development of the constitutional nation state. The rule of law emerged in the eighteenth and nineteenth century from the antagonism between the state and civil society, in the struggle of civil society to secure individual freedoms against an oppressive state. Examples of the constitutional paradigm on the relationship between state and civil society are the human rights declarations in North America and France while prominent witnesses to that development are the political philosophers John Locke and Immanuel Kant. The welfare state is younger, has a different intellectual history and is of another historical origin. The welfare state is, too, the result of opposing forces; the antipodes of state and industrial society.[5] The freedom of the individual is now endangered not by the state, but by the untamed and unrefined forces of the marketplace. But in Germany the welfare state struggles to break with the German tradition of the absolutist welfare state of the eighteenth century, a tradition disputed since the Enlightenment. This paternalistic state, and not the individual himself, claimed to have the natural

[3] See E Forsthoff, *Der totale Staat* (Hamburg, Hanseatische Verlagsanstalt, 1934), which is so to say his 'letter of application addressed at the new potentates [of the Third Reich]'; J Kaube, *Die Vorsorgemaschine,* Frankfurter Allgemeine Zeitung (Frankfurt, 14 September 2002) 34. Forsthoff distanced himself from this article.

[4] See HM Heinig, *Der Sozialstaat im Dienst der Freiheit* (Tübingen, Mohr Siebeck, 2008) 22; T Kingreen, *Das Sozialstaatsprinzip im europäischen Verfassungsverbund* (Tübingen, Mohr Siebeck, 2003) 102, 121.

[5] E-R Huber, 'Rechtsstaat und Sozialstaat in der modernen Industriegesellschaft' in E Forsthoff (ed), *Rechtsstaatlichkeit und Sozialstaatlichkeit* (Darmstadt, WBG, 1968) 589, 597–98.

prerogative to decide on the scope of the freedom of the individual.[6] Thus, the industrial revolution in Germany came about in a 'semi-feudal, state-oriented society which was never thoroughly liberalized'.[7] Even the most important German work of political philosophy on the welfare state in the nineteenth century, the *Elements of the Philosophy of Law* by Georg Wilhelm Friedrich Hegel[8] severs the philosophical ties from the absolutist welfare state somewhat imperfectly.[9] Against the background of the social and political changes brought about by industrialization, Hegel developed the essential theoretical foundation for the basic structure of the welfare state, by distinguishing civil society from the political sphere of the state. Hegel, so far dominated by the Aristotelian philosophy of the *polis*, distinguishes two forms of community: the family and the state. By nature man belongs to these institutions and, therefore, they need no further justification, and certainly not by the dubious concept of the contract, promoted by Hobbes or Locke, an instrument that implies an understanding of the individual as a subject of rights with its own will and thus arbitrariness. According to Hegel, civil society has, as a result of industrialization, pushed itself between these two original forms of community and threatens to destroy both. The family is characterized by altruism and solidarity. Owing to these inherent emotional resources, the family knows of no opposing interests that would need to be resolved by external institutions. Unity and harmony in the family are contrasted with the alienation and conflict among humans in civil society. Hegel perceives civil society not as a place of freedom, but as a hedonistic event with no moral ties between the individual and the community. Moreover, he is convinced that this tension between family and civil society can only be overcome by the state. The state represents the 'general interest', in which the conflicts between the 'special interests' within the civil society are sublated. Hegel sees it as a function of the state to mirror mechanisms of control and conflict resolution inherent in the institution of the family at the level of civil society: 'The general power will take the place of the family for the Poor'.[10]

The factual history of the German welfare state is inextricably linked to the foundation of the German national state in 1871, the Deutsche Reich. To the first German Chancellor, Otto von Bismarck, the onset of social legislation since 1881 was a significant contribution to the social integration of the workers. His political

[6] M Stolleis, 'Entwicklungsstufen der Verwaltungsrechtswissenschaft' in W Hoffmann-Riem, E Schmidt-Aßmann and A Voßkuhle (eds), *Grundlagen des Verwaltungsrechts*, vol I (Munich, CH Beck, 2006) § 2, para 26. See in particular: D Klippel, *Politische Freiheit und Freiheitsrechte im deutschen Naturrecht des 18. Jahrhunderts* (Paderborn, Schöningh, 1976); H Maier, *Die ältere deutsche Staats- und Verwaltungslehre*, 2nd edn (Dtv, 1980).

[7] M Stolleis, 'Die Entstehung des Interventionsstaates und das öffentliche Recht' (1989) 11 *Zeitschrift für Neuere Rechtsgeschichte* 129, 132–33.

[8] GFH Hegel, *Grundlinien der Philosophie des Rechts* (Berlin, 1821).

[9] See G Lübbe-Wolff, 'Über das Fehlen von Grundrechten in Hegels Rechtsphilosophie' in H-C Lucas and O Pöggeler (eds), *Hegels Rechtsphilosophie* (Stuttgart – Bad Cannstadt, Frommann Holzboog, 1986) 421.

[10] Hegel, *Grundlinien der Philosophie des Rechts* (n 8) § 241.

leitmotif was to build up a strong and inclusive state, unifying and consolidating the dispersed interests of groups within society. So to speak he wanted to fill the newly constituted formal structure of the Reich with the spirit of a common commitment throughout society. After the failure of previous attempts to lighten the plight of the workers through voluntary self-regulation, and the workers increasingly turning away from the state, he took on the social reforms with ardent zeal. His social security policy was intended to alienate the workers from the political stream of Social Democracy and to tie them to the state responsible for their welfare.[11] The social policy of Bismarck was, therefore, not a contradiction, but a necessary preventive complement of the repressive socialist law.[12]

Social insurance is hailed today as 'the most important institutional invention of the welfare state'.[13] Its basic structures have weathered the many political, economic and social upheavals of the twentieth century, remaining largely intact. As the introduction of *Pflegeversicherung* – care insurance – in 1994 in Germany demonstrates, these institutions are still considered as a model for insurance against the vicissitudes of life.

ii. Forsthoff's Incompatibility Thesis

It was not until 1949 that the social state principle became applicable constitutional law, and only since then has the relationship between the rule of law and the social state been discussed in constitutional law.

The discussion regarding social law was *the* constitutional debate of the 1950s.[14] It began with the Conference of the 'Staatsrechtslehrervereinigung' (the German association of public law professors) in 1953. Both Ernst Forsthoff and Otto Bachof gave talks about 'the concept and essence of the welfare state'. Forsthoff employed primarily the question as to

> whether the welfare state, which we have established by social security law, employment law, tenancy law, construction law and many other areas of legal life, or at least affirm in principle and strive to achieve, is part of our constitutional law.[15]

The answer to this question transpires to be succinct:

> The welfare state and the rule of law are not compatible on a constitutional level. The space which the welfare state unfolds itself in is legislation and administration. 'Social

[11] M Kaltenborn, 'Die Sozialgesetzgebung des Reichskanzlers Fürst Otto von Bismarck' [1998] *Juristenzeitung* 770, 882; G Wannagat, '100 Jahre Sozialversicherung in Deutschland: Beständigkeit und Wandel' [1981] *Die Sozialgerichtsbarkeit* 373, 374.

[12] GA Ritter, 'Bismarck und die Grundlegung des deutschen Sozialstaates' in F Ruland, B von Maydell and H-J Papier (eds), *Verfassung, Theorie und Praxis des Sozialstaates* (Heidelberg, CF Müller, 1998) 798, 819; M Stolleis, 'Die Sozialversicherung Bismarcks' in HF Zacher (ed), *Bedingungen für die Entstehung und Entwicklung der Sozialversicherung* (Berlin, Duncker & Humblot, 1979) 387, 391.

[13] GA Ritter, *Der Sozialstaat*, 2nd edn (Munich, Oldenbourg, 1991) 62.

[14] O Lepsius, 'Die Wiederentdeckung Weimars durch die bundesdeutsche Staatslehre' in C Gusy (ed), *Weimars lange Schatten: 'Weimar' als Argument nach 1945* (Baden-Baden, Nomos, 2003) 354, 378.

[15] E Forsthoff, 'Begriff und Wesen des sozialen Rechtsstaates' (1954) 12 *Veröffentlichungen der Vereinigung der Deutschen Staatsrechtslehrer* 8, 9.

> constitutional state' is the term to denote a type of a state, a term which comprises also constitution, legislation and administration. It is not a legal term.[16]

The principle of the rule of law is, according to the design of the German Constitution – the Basic Law – of 'primary value and equipped with all the judicial guarantees'.[17] Forsthoff sees the constitutional guarantees, in particular fundamental rights, as 'spaces of exclusion of the state power' and as 'thresholds', upon which state power 'comes to a stop'.[18] Only when formalized as such can the constitutional guarantees of freedom be as reliable and predictable as is necessary to comply with the rule of law.[19] Social welfare guarantees, on the other hand, are not meant to demarcate certain protected areas of freedom, but are directed at claiming a positive performance, not intended to guarantee freedom, but to enable participation.[20]

According to Forsthoff, the term 'social' refers to the process of sharing, distribution and allocation, and 'with the act of granting services or benefits it has another reference point as the protection of freedom provided by the rule of law'.[21] It is, however, according to Forsthoff, not possible to define this term in legal categories. Its specific content is only conceivable by taking into consideration non-constitutional areas and, therefore, it is not a legal term.[22] In linking the social state principle with the rule of law, Forsthoff envisages the danger that the guarantee function of the rule of law will be relativized to apply only within 'what is understood by the respective majority and its government as social'.[23]

Though Forsthoff's core thesis focuses on the welfare state as a constitutional concept, it is dependent upon his concept of the rule of law. It is based on the hypothesis that norms pertaining to the rule of law can be reformulated in an abstract and general form; norms on the social state, however, are not transformable in such a fashion. [24] The premise is an understanding of the rule of law as a formal principle directed against the absolutist welfare state with its claim of a superior morality. This understanding deprives the concept of the rule of law of any substantive content and reduces it to the claim that life in administration and society is organized through the typical formal elements of the law (proceedings, competence).[25]

The rule of law should specify the manner of governance, but without setting any material standards for its policies. This interpretation of the rule law had been fairly prevalent, in German jurisprudence since the middle of the nine-

[16] ibid thesis XV.
[17] ibid thesis IV.
[18] ibid 18.
[19] ibid 16.
[20] ibid 19.
[21] ibid 25.
[22] ibid 24.
[23] ibid 25.
[24] H Noack, *Sozialstaatsklauseln und juristische Methode* (Baden-Baden, Nomos, 1975) 144.
[25] See E Schmidt-Aßmann, 'Der Rechtsstaat' in J Isensee and P Kirchhof, *Handbuch des Staatsrechts der Bundesrepublik Deutschland*, vol II, 3rd edn (Heidelberg, CF Müller, 2004) § 26, para 18.

teenth century until the end of the Weimar Republic, though it did not go unchallenged.[26] The rule of law was understood as a system of formal legality, which was limited to the forms of exercise of state power (legality of the administration, legal remedies), which however excluded material policies such as social welfare. Its fixed point was the law, setting limits to government interference in freedom and property, an understanding perfectly befitting the spirit of Forsthoff as the rule of law as a means of 'exclusion' of the state from the societal sphere. This law, however, did not have to consider any substantive normative provisions on a higher level, nor was it considered as an instrument of promoting a certain desired societal development. The methodological basis was the constitutional positivism that separated the interpretation of positive law from non-legal, especially natural-law influences.[27]

iii. Reception and Repercussions

The radical counter-position to Forsthoff was taken by Wolfgang Abendroth at the same conference of the Staatsrechtslehrervereinigung in 1953. He tried to deduce an authorization of the state for a 'socialization' and 'democratization' of the economic order from the principle of the social state.[28] It would, however, fall short to narrow the discussion to these two extreme opposites, as was done in the 1950s and 1960s against the backdrop of the discussion as to the question of whether Germany's Constitution – the Basic Law (GG) – provides for a certain organization of the economy.[29]

In the predominantly middle-class conservative society of Germany in the 1950s, Forsthoff's position found hardly any followers.[30] One other reason was that the scientific launch of a 'broadening and deepening of the interpretive social state decision'[31] had already taken place, when H-P Ipsen presented his talk at the Conference of the Staatsrechtslehrervereinigung in 1951.[32] A few weeks later the Federal Constitutional Court acknowledged the social state principle laid down in Article 20(1) GG as a directly applicable and binding constitutional law.[33]

[26] Prominent opponents: R von Mohl, *Die Polizei-Wissenschaft nach den Grundsätzen des Rechtsstaates*, vol I, 2nd edn (Tübingen, 1844); H Heller, *Rechtsstaat oder Diktatur* (Tübingen, Mohr, 1930).

[27] On this development, see in detail W Pauly, *Der Methodenwandel im deutschen Spätkonstitutionalismus* (Tübingen, Mohr, 1993) esp 92; M Stolleis, *Geschichte des öffentlichen Rechts*, vol II (Munich, CH Beck, 1992) 331.

[28] W Abendroth in Forsthoff, 'Begriff und Wesen des sozialen Rechtsstaates' (n 15) 85–92 as well as W Abendroth, 'Zum Begriff des demokratischen und sozialen Rechtsstaats im Grundgesetz der Bundesrepublik Deutschland' in Forsthoff, *Rechtsstaatlichkeit und Sozialstaatlichkeit* (n 5) 114.

[29] E-R Huber, 'Der Streit um das Wirtschaftsverfassungsrecht' [1956] *Die öffentliche Verwaltung* 200.

[30] On the reception see K Stern, *Das Staatsrecht der Bundesrepublik Deutschland*, vol I, 2nd edn (Munich, CH Beck, 1980) 887.

[31] D Suhr, 'Rechtsstaatlichkeit und Sozialstaatlichkeit' (1970) 9 *Der Staat* 67, 69.

[32] H-P Ipsen, 'Enteignung und Sozialisierung' (1952) 10 *Veröffentlichungen der Vereinigung der Deutschen Staatsrechtslehrer* 74.

[33] BVerfGE 1, 97, 105.

Thus, Forsthoff did not succeed in resetting the discussion to zero. His understanding of the state contrasted with the constitutional guarantee of the social rule of law in Articles 20(1), (3) and 28(1) GG. He was only able to argue its irrelevance by citing the precedence of the state before the Constitution:[34]

> We understand the issue only by virtue of a point of view that is outside the written constitutional text. That does not need worry us seriously, because we no longer share the positivist narrowing of legal interpretation limited by the letter of the law.[35]

This trick by Forsthoff 'left space for a wider notion of the state', which '[contained] those basic decisions that Forsthoff did not see in the text of Constitution'.[36]

Despite the failure of his thesis of incompatibility, Forsthoff succeeded in conveying the formal concept of law to the Bonn Republic, now again at the side of his former teacher Carl Schmitt, a highly capable academic, who, however, had fallen for the Third Reich and thus had lost the respect of the jurisprudence of the Bonn Republic. He was one of the first critics of the Federal Constitutional Court's interpretation of fundamental rights as an 'objective order of values',[37] an interpretation which can be traced back to positions held by Rudolf Smend, a German legal scholar in the Weimar Republic, whose 'integration theory' was the counterposition to the decisionism of Carl Schmitt. Arguing against such a broadening understanding he profiled the 'exclusionary' function of fundamental rights – a position that later enjoyed a wide following even outside of the bourgeois-conservative constitutional theory.[38]

Essentially, it is owing to this feed-in of the debate on the 'social state of law' into the discussion of the theory and the doctrine of fundamental rights that the antediluvian controversy over the constitutional relevance of the welfare state is still paid attention to until this day. Perhaps it was only the exaggerated, almost polemical responses that have concealed the academic legitimation and the relevance of some questions.[39] The fact that there is a degree of tension between the rule of law and the welfare state which needs to be dissolved is something which is not disputed.

B. The Administrative Dimension: Services of General Interests (*Daseinsvorsorge*) as a Constitutional and Administrative Purpose

Ernst Forsthoff would not have had such a formative influence on the debate on the rule of law versus the welfare state if he had opposed the welfare state as a political concept altogether. On the contrary, as early as the 1930s – and thus a

[34] On the relation of state and constitution in Forsthoff's thinking, see C Schütte, *Progressive Verwaltungsrechtswissenschaft auf konservativer Grundlage* (Berlin, Duncker & Humblot, 2006) 27.

[35] Forsthoff (n 15) 8.

[36] Lepsius, 'Die Wiederentdeckung Weimars durch die bundesdeutsche Staatslehre' (n 14) 378.

[37] F Günther, *Denken vom Staat her* (Munich, Oldenbourg, 2004) 112.

[38] See section III.A.

[39] See also Heinig, *Der Sozialstaat im Dienst der Freiheit* (n 4) 27.

good 15 years before his talk at the Conference of the Staatsrechtslehrervereinigung in 1953 – he had attested to the contemporary administrative law, influenced by the bourgeois-conservative stream of thinking of the rule of law, a 'fatal lack of empiricism',[40] because it simply would not acknowledge the existence of a welfare-oriented administration directed at providing benefits to the population. With the term 'Services of general interests' (*Daseinsvorsorge*) he invented a key term, meaning that state and administration are responsible for social justice and which would become a 'synonym for the "*Leistungsverwaltung*"'[41], a German legal term denoting the performance-oriented and freedom-enabling – not freedom-interfering – dimension management of administration.

He laid the premises for a 'doctrine of administrative law indebted to reality'[42] a few years previously. He divided the human habitat into an accessible and a controlled area. Social change in nineteenth century, especially the expanding economic relations had, according to Forsthoff, led to the accessible space being greatly increased but the dominated space being greatly reduced and even disappearing for increasingly more parts of the whole population. Thus, existence had lost its security with the result that the individual had become dependent on 'the general conditions of a world of order'.

He maintained that it takes a large administrative apparatus to ensure the satisfaction of vital needs,[43] a satisfaction entrusted to the state by the individual.[44] The constitutional doctrine based solely on the legality of governmental functions and the rights of freedom has not taken note of these facts,

> it has failed to account for the fact that it is appropriate in the 20th century to decide first of all about how and under what conditions the people lead their simple, creaturely lives and only then to ask what the people do with these lives and which demands on freedom, order, welfare they pose.[45]

That was a rejection not only of the bourgeois-liberal idea that guaranteeing individual freedom alone would by itself lead to general prosperity and social security, but also a rejection of the German legal method which emerged under the influence of legal positivism. Under the influence of the Enlightenment until the end of the eighteenth century, the German jurisprudence on administrative law had begun to push back the welfare of the citizen as a responsibility of the state and heralded the departure of the absolutist welfare state responsible for the happiness of the individual. The separation between police and administration was the decisive the step from governmental police science towards the administrative law of

[40] E Forsthoff, *Die Verwaltung als Leistungsträger* (Stuttgart, Kohlhammer, 1938) 3.

[41] Schütte, *Progressive Verwaltungsrechtswissenschaft auf konservativer Grundlage* (n 34) 81; see also H Schulze-Fielitz, 'Grundmodi der Aufgabenwahrnehmung' in Hoffmann-Riem, Schmidt-Aßmann, and Voßkuhle, *Grundlagen des Verwaltungsrechts* (n 6) § 12, para 39.

[42] Forsthoff, *Die Verwaltung als Leistungsträger* (n 40) 14.

[43] Forsthoff uses the term 'Appropriation' by Max Weber in this context; see in detail D Scheidemann, *Der Begriff Daseinsvorsorge* (Göttingen, Muster-Schmidt, 1991) 48.

[44] E Forsthoff, 'Von den Aufgaben der Verwaltungsrechtswissenschaft' (1935) 5 *Deutsches Recht* 398.

[45] Forsthoff (n 40) 8.

the bourgeois rule of law. This administrative law distanced itself from the unbridled domination of the public authorities in the absolutist state. With an explicitly dogmatic claim they profiled the positive statutory law as a yardstick for the actions of the administration, while the formulation of non-administrative purposes by the law formulated as 'metajuridical' was discarded, and left to the practical administrative teaching and politics.[46]

With its 'semantics of the rule of law, of procedure and of subjective rights'[47] the contemporary administrative law doctrine had no room for societal goals and services by the state.[48] The law protected the civil sphere from executive interference, but was not an instrument for achieving societal goals for the benefit of everyone. Otto Mayer described the basic principle of the system he profoundly influenced with the sentence: 'The state which has no law for its administrative management or no administrative act is not a constitutional state'.[49] Although this reduction in the administrative law doctrine of administration evoked opposition as a potential danger to freedom[50] even in Mayer's lifetime, and it never corresponded to the reality of administrative action, which had long faced the problem of the 'social question'. Indeed, it speaks volumes that 40 years after the establishment of social security, Mayer was still convinced in the third edition in 1924 of his influential textbook of the era that 'nothing majorly new [. . .] can be said on that matter'.[51]

Though Ernst Forsthoff had to break with the contemporary mainstream of the bourgeois constitutional state in administrative law, he could build on an earlier historical tradition, namely the work of Lorenz von Stein,[52] whose theory of administration 'probably [would have] enabled to keep an open mind and grasp the great sociological changes, which would so crucially change the structure of society and thus the administration in the decades after [him]'.[53] In fact the purpose of *Daseinsvorsorge*,[54] which means literally 'provisioning for existence', holds a key position in von Stein's State and Public Administration theory. Von Stein's starting point is the constitutionally guaranteed freedom. According to von Stein, the rationale of the constitution of the state is it to structure the process of the formulation of the will of the state. It essentially contains the 'participation of the

[46] P Badura, 'Die Daseinsvorsorge als Verwaltungszweck der Leistungsverwaltung und der soziale Rechtsstaat' [1966] *Die öffentliche Verwaltung* 624, 625.

[47] I Mikešic, *Sozialrecht als wissenschaftliche Disziplin* (Tübingen, Mohr Siebeck, 2002) 172.

[48] It is no coincidence that Lorenz von Stein was the most important advocate of administration as a means of social design. For more on this topic see the following text.

[49] O Mayer, *Deutsches Verwaltungsrecht*, vol I (Berlin, Duncker & Humblot, 1895) 66.

[50] In detail: H Gröttrup, *Die kommunale Leistungsverwaltung* (Stuttgart, Kohlhammer, 1973) 58

[51] Preface of 3rd volume I, 1924.

[52] In detail on this relationship, see W Meyer-Hesemann, *Methodenwandel in der Verwaltungsrechtswissenschaft* (Heidelberg, CF Müller, 1981) 102; Schütte (n 34) 67.

[53] Forsthoff (n 40) 2, see esp the references to Lorenz von Stein, 11.

[54] On this predominately E-R Huber, 'Vorsorge für Dasein' in R Schnur (ed), *Festschrift für Ernst Forsthoff*, 2nd edn (Munich, CH Beck, 1974) 139, 142, who in his article gives the false impression that 'provision for existence' was a word used by von Stein and Hegel themselves. In fact the phrase as such is used by neither one of them. Its sense, however, is depicted in other words.

individual in the entire internal organism of the state, especially in the formation and determination of the will of the state'.[55]

But the transition from the constitution to their execution – *von Stein* defines it with the distinction between will and action – cannot be put into action on the level of the Constitution, but only by the *administration of the state*, governed by laws. It is the assignment of the administration 'to promote [the individual] in his real life conditions'.[56] The administration turns the abstract postulate of the constitution, the promise of free development of personality for all citizens into concrete fact. For Stein, it was the 'basic idea of our time that the administration has to be the constitution put into action'.[57]

In social administration a reasonable balance between the social antagonisms must be achieved. According to Stein,

> if administration is to be in accordance with the idea of the state and the idea of individual personality, it must essentially strive to encourage the highest development of all individuals and employ the resources of the State correspondingly. The administration of the state achieves its purest, most ideal [. . .] form when it sets the lives of *all* citizens as its only duty.[58]

Forsthoff explains the fact that Lorenz von Stein did not receive the deserved reception with the fact that his concept had been 'against the principles of the rule of law': 'For state based upon the rule of law has its point of gravity in the law. Lorenz von Stein moved that gravity point to administration, thus proving him to be a statist in the spirit of Hegel'.[59] The bourgeois-conservative understanding of administrative law, based upon the rule of law, which understands as its purpose to ensure freedom within the boundaries of the law, does not fit for an administration striving to enhance the welfare and facilitate participation. On the contrary, an essential condition of its development was the elimination of welfare as a responsibility of the state.[60]

The dichotomy of freedom-respecting and performance-oriented administration arises ultimately as an administrative reproduction of a similar indissoluble dichotomy between the rule of law and the principle of the social state in the constitution. For as the rule of law and the principle of social state find no resolution on the constitutional level, freedom-respecting administration and performance-oriented administration stand side by side, also unresolved, at the level of administrative law:

> The objective to develop a common unified system of legal rationale under which freedom-respecting administration and performance-oriented administration can be

[55] L von Stein, *Geschichte der sozialen Bewegung in Frankreich von 1789 bis auf unsere Tage*, vol I, G Salomon ed (Munich, Drei Masken, 1921) 37 – on the reception of von Stein, see in more detail Kingreen, *Das Sozialstaatsprinzip im europäischen Verfassungsverbund* (n 4) 89, 102.

[56] Lvon Stein, *Verwaltungslehre*, vol I (Cotta, 1866) 48, 60.

[57] L von Stein, *Verwaltungslehre*, vol II, 3rd edn (Cotta, 1888) 258.

[58] von Stein, *Geschichte der sozialen Bewegung in Frankreich* (n 55) 37.

[59] E Forsthoff, *Rechtsfragen der leistenden Verwaltung* (Stuttgart, Kohlhammer, 1959) 47.

[60] ibid 53.

> explained but has not yet been achieved – and perhaps because it is unachievable. Maybe it's really true that modern administrative law is and will remain dualistic not as a result of scientific incapacity, but by virtue of the logic of things.[61]

This methodological 'division of administrative law into one systematic-analytical part, based upon the rule of law, and one empirical part, based upon the social state principle'[62] frees the performance-oriented welfare administration of the ties and bonds of the rule of law which the administration in the traditional sense has to adhere to and abide by, thus evolving into a 'para-constitutional antipode'[63] of a constitutionally based principle of the social state:

> The administration appointed with the provision of services of general interests ('Daseinsvorsorge') is withdrawn as subject matter from the political decision-making in parliament. Measuring administrative law at historically idealized standards of the common good and the rule of law precludes a political influence and control by Acts of Parliament largely.[64]

Thus, Forsthoff represents a depoliticized social state, and ultimately stands in the anti-democratic tradition of the 'social monarchy' (Lorenz von Stein), which presides over the conflicting interests of society and can exist only free from democratic control.[65]

This alleged special legal nature, which the performance-oriented administration has in judicial doctrine, entails consequences in other areas, for example in the discussion about the prerogative of Parliament over the executive branch of the state to decide a rule concerning certain essential questions in form of an Act of Parliament (*Parlamentsvorbehalt*, often translated as 'parliamentary prerogative'). This naturally applies to acts regulating administrative action with freedom-endangering qualities, and whether the same prerogative applies to regulations governing the performance-oriented administration.[66] This special nature is particularly evident in German social security law, which is constitutionally required (Article 95(1) GG) to be administered by an independent judiciary, which has special laws on administrative process and procedural law (SGB X, SGG), and which has its specific struggles with legitimacy issues, presumably due to its isolation from the general administrative law.[67]

All of that questions the claim of social security law of being a part of the corpus of administrative law.[68] It is, however, not surprising against the background of the history of administrative law, in which the performance aspect of administra-

[61] Forsthoff (n 15) 14.

[62] Schütte (n 34) 108.

[63] J Kersten, 'Die Entwicklung des Konzepts der Daseinsvorsorge im Werk von Ernst Forsthoff' (2005) 44 *Der Staat* 543, 558.

[64] Lepsius (n 14) 354, 378.

[65] In detail, see Kingreen (n 4) 98.

[66] See eg H Maurer, *Allgemeines Verwaltungsrecht*, 17th edn, (Munich, CH Beck, 2009) § 6, para 19.

[67] T Kingreen, 'Governance im Gesundheitsrecht' (2009) 42 *Die Verwaltung* 339.

[68] See T Kingreen and S Rixen, 'Sozialrecht: Ein verwaltungsrechtliches Utopia? Ortsangaben zur (Wieder-)Entdeckung einer Referenzmaterie des öffentlichen Rechts' [2008] *Die öffentliche Verwaltung* 741, 742.

tion has remained a stranger. Ernst Forsthoff achieved that administrative law was a body of abstract legal theories connected with questions of practical administrative action and reality; he did, however, not succeed in leaving behind a sustainable theory of performance-oriented administrative law. The rule of law and the principle of the social state seem to remain in two separate worlds – in constitutional law as well as in administrative law.

III. THE RELATION OF THE RULE OF LAW AND THE SOCIAL STATE AGAINST THE BACKDROP OF THE GERMAN LEGAL THEORY OF FUNDAMENTAL RIGHTS

The general discussion among jurists of constitutional and administrative law on the relationship between law and social justice had already subsided in the course of the 1950s. Forsthoff's incompatibility thesis was not able to prevail if only because of the understanding of state and constitution upon which it was based. The dualism of freedom-preserving and performance-oriented administration was recognized but not processed. Nevertheless, the debate had not ended, it merely continued on a different plane: the theory of fundamental rights and its dogmatics.

A. The Principle of Distribution based upon Fundamental Rights

One of the early protagonists of this debate was the aforementioned Carl Schmitt, one of Ernst Forsthoff's academic teachers. Even during the Weimar period, Schmitt had postulated what he called the distribution principle between state and society with reference to the 'idea of the bourgeois freedom'. Individual freedom is thereby

> something not dependant on the existence of the state, but something already existing before the state did, namely the freedom of the individual is, in principle, without limit, while the power of the state to intervene with this freedom is, in principle, limited.[69]

Therefore Schmitt, as later Forsthoff did too, passionately opposed the position which was in particular promoted by Rudolf Smend. This stance advocated charging the fundamental rights with substantive material content;[70] similarly they objected to the understanding of the basic rights as an objective order of values put forth by the Federal Constitutional Court.[71] The distribution principle is based on a rigid separation between state and society, and based on the idea of the

[69] C Schmitt, *Verfassungslehre* (Berlin, Duncker & Humblot, 1928) 126.

[70] The following authors encouraged each other mutually: E Forsthoff, 'Die Umbildung des Verfassungsgesetzes' in H Barion, E Forsthoff and W Weber (eds), *Festschrift für Carl Schmitt* (Berlin, Duncker & Humblot, 1959) 35; C Schmitt, 'Die Tyrannei der Werte' in *Säkularisation und Utopie* (Stuttgart, Kohlhammer, 1967) 37.

[71] See on this topic H Goerlich, *Wertordnung und Grundgesetz* (Baden-Baden, Nomos, 1973).

rule of law in its traditional conception, ie that it will protect the citizens against the abuse of state power.[72]

The construct of an 'exclusive' space of freedom, well known from the debate on the rule of law versus welfare state, has been even far more successful in the legal field on fundamental rights and its doctrines; in fact it became the prevailing trend in the 1970s and 1980s.[73] The rationale of such a construct is that it is not the individual who has to justify its exercise of freedom, but the state which has to justify every intervention in or interference with this exclusive space and which has to have justifying grounds for every violation of fundamental rights. The Federal Constitutional Court, too, sees fundamental rights primarily as 'rights of the citizen of protection against state action',[74] which aim 'to protect certain distinctive, particularly vulnerable areas of human freedom'.[75]

The distribution principle is reflected in the widely recognized steps of the test for a basic rights violation in German legal theory. These steps are 'the scope of protected freedom' – 'the interference with freedom exercise' – 'the justification of the interference'.[76] The first step of this test is to define the protected freedom such as the right to live, the right of free religious belief or freedom of opinion, as well as stipulating the actions protected by this right. For the second step, under the term 'interference', the action of the state which encroaches upon the previously defined freedom is identified. The third step of the test, called 'justification', is to ask whether this encroachment is justified by constitutionally legitimate and reasonable ends. In this third step the interest of the state justifying the encroachment upon freedom and the value of the exercise of the affected freedom are weighed up against each other in the so-called test of proportionality. This test states that any encroachment of freedom shall not be out of proportion to the end the encroachment serves. The principle of the social state is not used as a means of defining or narrowing the protected area of freedom in the first step. It only enters the test during the third step as an example of a constitutionally legitimate and reasonable end which can justify an encroachment by the state.

The background to this sequence in which the social state only enters at the rather belated third level of the test as a counterweight to freedom, is that it would be wrong to resolve the 'irreconcilable and fundamental tension, between the protection of freedom of the individual and the requirements of the social state order'[77] by immediately narrowing the area protected by fundamental rights. This would contradict the premise that it is not the individual who has to justify its exercise of freedom, but the state which has to justify its actions in interfering

[72] E Grabitz, *Freiheit und Verfassungsrecht* (Mohr, 1976) 20.

[73] E-W Böckenförde, 'Grundrechtstheorie und Grundrechtsinterpretation' [1974] *Neue Juristische Wochenschrift* 1529, 1537; B Schlink, 'Freiheit durch Eingriffsabwehr: Rekonstruktion der klassischen Grundrechtsfunktion' [1984] *Europäische Grundrechte-Zeitschrift* 457, 467; R Wahl and J Masing, 'Schutz durch Eingriff' [1990] *Juristenzeitung* 553, 563.

[74] BVerfGE 7, 198, 204.

[75] BVerfGE 50, 290, 337.

[76] B Pieroth and B Schlink, *Staatsrecht II*, 26th edn (Heidelberg, CF Müller, 2010) para 212.

[77] BVerfGE 18, 257, 267.

with the aforesaid freedom. Thus such an approach would circumvent the specific requirement of the justification of interference.

Every welfare-state-based charging-up of the area protected by fundamental rights would lead to relativism, which gives the false impression that the freedom granted under the fundamental rights only serves certain purposes.[78] Accordingly, rejection was the overwhelming reaction against the idea of so-called 'basic social rights', ie fundamental rights granting certain rights or claims to certain performances by the state.[79] The Federal Constitutional Court decided against the assumption of such basic social rights in its rather ambitious *numerus clausus* ruling. Taken into account the concomitant burden on the community by such highly costly social rights this would lead to 'a misunderstanding of freedom, which would neglect the fact that personal freedom cannot be exercised independently of the functioning and balance of the community'. It ruled that the notion of an unlimited subjective entitlement at the expense of universality was incompatible with the notion of the welfare state.[80] This position did not prevent the Federal Constitutional Court from directly deriving under certain conditions 'a right to health care' from Article 2(1) GG in conjunction with Article 20(1) GG.[81]

B. Tendencies of Dissolution

This principle of distribution between individual freedom and the government's limited power to intervene remained largely undisputed for several decades. Nowadays, however, it has come under pressure for a variety of reasons.[82]

Over the years, the areas of protected freedom have increasingly been expanded. In particular the recognition of the general freedom of action, which guarantees the freedom to do almost anything, even trivial things such as feeding pigeons, has expanded the area of protected freedom to anything imaginable. The concept of what constitutes an encroachment in such a protected area has also been expanded. Hence, the crucial decisions are almost always made on the level of justification. Thus, they fall within the process of weighing-up in accordance with the proportionality test, which, however, does not meet the requirements of rational decision-making inherent in the distribution principle.

In addition, the relationship between state and society is changing and is becoming more and more complex through interdependence. The distribution principle sees the state rather as an adversary of freedom than as its guarantor. Thus it has its difficulties in explaining or arguing in favour of *Schutzpflichten*,

[78] See eg R Herzog in *Maunz/Dürig: Grundgesetz Kommentar*, 63rd edn (Munich, CH Beck, 2011) Art 20, section VIII, para 51: 'gigantic misinterpretation of the idea of a modern social state'.

[79] cf J Isensee, 'Verfassung ohne soziale Grundrechte' (1980) 19 *Der Staat* 367; J Lücke, 'Soziale Grundrechte als Staatszielbestimmungen und Gesetzgebungsaufträge' (1982) 107 *Archiv des öffentlichen Rechts* 15.

[80] BVerfGE 33, 303, 334.

[81] BVerfGE 115, 25, 49.

[82] U Volkmann, 'Veränderungen der Grundrechtsdogmatik' [2005] *Juristenzeitung* 261, 263.

which literally means 'duties of the state to protect', but actually means that the state is allowed and even obligated to protect the fundamental rights of its citizens by actively taking charge by providing certain existentially necessary means of living or protection against certain risks.[83]

Such fundamental rights as 'duties to protect' are of particular importance if the state does not provide services itself, but involves a third party. Then it is not the state, but the third party who is involved in the performance of public works who restricts individual rights. This entails the question of whether fundamental rights apply in such a constellation. Fundamental rights only bind the state, not the private third party. Though the state cannot escape its duty to secure and respect freedom and remains the addressee of the fundamental rights, its role changes in such a constellation. It is now its duty to guarantee the fact that the private third parties fulfil their tasks without violating the fundamental rights of the citizens.

Such changes provide an opportunity to reflect upon the impact of these amendments on a fundamental legal doctrine that represents a political and social understanding of state and society and which is deemed outdated. In times of privatization and public-private partnerships, freedom is no longer only endangered by the state but increasingly by the private third party involved in the modes of implementation of modern administration. Thus an understanding of fundamental rights simply as a means of protection against the state is too narrow for contemporary threats to freedom. The consequence is to promote an understanding of fundamental rights which emphasizes that the role of the state is to protect fundamental rights and to enable their exercise rather than to encroach upon them and endanger their exercise.[84]

Even the Federal Constitutional Court appears to have initiated a moderate course correction in its understanding of fundamental rights and shows tendencies towards narrowing the scopes of basic rights.[85] In a decision on the constitutionality of the determination of fixed prices within a tolerated price span for drugs by the health insurance companies (§ 35 SGB V) it held that 'the range of democratic rights [of Article 12 paragraph 1 GG (freedom of occupation)] are determined by the legal rules that limit and allow competition'.[86] Traditionally the German law doctrine held that the Constitution and fundamental rights are superior to statutory laws. This ruling seems to reverse the traditional normative hierarchy to interpret fundamental rights in the light of statutory law by limiting the scope of protection of the right to a free, undiscriminating market by the laws

[83] C Calliess, *Rechtsstaat und Umweltstaat* (Tübingen, Mohr Siebeck, 2001) 577; W Cremer, *Freiheitsgrundrechte* (Tübingen, Mohr Siebeck, 2003) 228; R Poscher, *Grundrechte als Abwehrrechte* (Tübingen, Mohr Siebeck, 2003) 380.

[84] W Hoffmann-Riem, 'Enge oder weite Gewährleistungsgehalte der Grundrechte?' in M Bäuerle and others (eds), *Haben wir wirklich Recht?* (Baden-Baden, Nomos, 2003) 53, 57, 71.

[85] See the collection in the work of W Kahl, 'Vom weiten Schutzbereich zum engen Gewährleistungsgehalt' (2004) 43 *Der Staat* 165, 170.

[86] BVerfGE 106, 275, 298.

regulating the same market. If the scope of the basic right is defined by statutory law, it hardly can protect freedom anymore.

Regulations on prices and fees established by public health insurance companies are actually a classic example of state intervention in the freedom of a free market and the exercise of occupation (Article 12(1) 1 GG).[87] The Court, however, sees it as a refinement of the scope of the freedom and thus the tests for a justified intervention are not applicable. The concept of a scope of a principally superior fundamental right, structured and filled with substantive content by law, is already acknowledged by certain special fundamental rights like the right of property, the content of which requires concretization by law; so far the right of occupation has not been held to be one of these rights. However, by expanding this concept beyond its original area of applicability the Court puts 'emphasis on the functions of appropriation, distribution and provision of the state as aspects of fundamental rights'.[88]

The test for the judicial review of fundamental rights violations is not constitutionally defined. Neither is there any suggestion in the Constitution that when in doubt a wide or a narrow scope of understanding generally has to be presumed.[89] There is also no rule as to which issues have to be solved in which step of the test. It is particularly hard to see why a balancing of general interests versus individual rights and freedoms on the level of the first test criterion 'scope of protection' is necessarily less rational and transparent than the same consideration under the justification test.[90]

Still it remains to be seen how and why the allegedly 'new challenges'[91] should entail a readjustment in the relationship between the concepts of 'scope of freedom' and of 'interference'.[92] An interesting question here is, for example, the following: why should the new role of the state as a guarantor of services, moderating conflicting interests within the context of privatization, entail the scopes of fundamental rights being narrowed? After all, the protective, the providing, welfare-oriented legislator is not unknown in the conventional test of proportionality which is characterized by a wide understanding of the scope of freedoms. The state which interferes with fundamental rights is thus always opposing a general or a private interest. It is a question of judicial review, especially in tests of proportionality, to what extent fundamental rights limit regulation by the legislature. On the contrary the long history of fundamental rights of the regulation on welfare issues[93] is the best example that legitimate interests and goals of society can be processed successfully using the classic test of proportionality. Why the scope of

[87] See BVerfGE 101, 331, 347.

[88] Volkmann, 'Veränderungen der Grundrechtsdogmatik' (n 82) 264.

[89] Pieroth and Schlink, *Staatsrecht II* (n 76) para 243.

[90] W Hoffmann-Riem, 'Grundrechtsanwendung unter Rationalitätsanspruch' (2004) 43 *Der Staat* 203, 209, 213.

[91] ibid 209, 226.

[92] R Martins, 'Grundrechtsdogmatik im Gewährleistungsstaat: Rationalisierung der Grundrechtsanwendung?' [2007] *Die öffentliche Verwaltung* 456, 463.

[93] For further references see Kingreen (n 4) 141, 262.

fundamental rights, however, should be subdued to the will and disposition of the whim of ever changing legislators, is unfathomable.

IV. OUTLOOK

What is left of the debates initiated by Ernst Forsthoff on the relationship between law and social state in constitutional and administrative law? His incompatibility thesis was blatantly incompatible with constitutional law; the concept of 'services of general interests' (*Daseinsvorsorge*) was, as a normative category, unable to process more complex issues. It was unproductive, especially concerning the debate as to what constitutes necessary and voluntary public and administrative tasks.[94] The distribution principle seems to have vanished from legal discussion, too.

The answers by Forsthoff may have been unsatisfactory, but public law jurists and politicians are still involved in the questions raised by him, even more so than 20 years ago. The concept of 'services in the general interests' (*Daseinsvorsorge*) and its French sister the *services publics* have been undergoing an unexpected renaissance in European Union law for some 15 years now.[95] In response to the criticism of a (supposedly) one-sided focus of European Union law on the establishment of a competition-driven single market and the associated deregulation of industry, which had been dominated almost exclusively by public companies (mail, telecommunications, transport, energy), the European Commission promoted 'services of general interest' to a 'key element of the European model of society'.[96]

In a number of individual regulations, Union law emphasizes the importance of services of general economic interest (Article 36 Charter of Fundamental Rights of the European Union), as the individual, and especially under the conditions of Europeanized and globalized markets, also requires access to and remains dependent upon basic public goods such as water, energy, transport, education and information services[97] – a topic that Forsthoff (albeit sometimes with respect to other goods) carried out as early as 70 years ago and which is now enjoying the utmost attention under the new rather fashionable term 'regulatory law'. The subject matter are new legal fields such as energy, telecommunications, transport, social and health and financial services law, but ultimately it is all about the not so new question of how competition-related activities can be organized and regu-

[94] See eg J Hellermann, *Örtliche Daseinsvorsorge und gemeindliche Selbstverwaltung* (Tübingen, Mohr Siebeck, 2000) 265; G Hermes, *Infrastrukturverantwortung* (Tübingen, Mohr Siebeck, 1998) 92; F Ossenbühl, 'Daseinsvorsorge und Verwaltungsprivatrecht' [1971] *Die öffentliche Verwaltung* 513, 516.

[95] See articles in R Hrbek and M Nettesheim (eds), *Europäische Union und mitgliedstaatliche Daseinsvorsorge* (Baden-Baden, Nomos, 2002).

[96] Commission, 'Services of General Interest in Europe' (Communication) 2001 C 17/4.

[97] More on this from the perspective of social constitutional law, see eg F Reimer, 'Der Staat als Türöffner' in A von Arnauld and A Musil (eds), *Strukturfragen des Sozialverfassungsrechts* (Tübingen, Mohr Siebeck, 2009) 223.

lated in conformity with the public interest.[98] This recent renaissance of an old debate is no surprise. On the contrary, it is rather the fading of the debate from the 1960s which is surprising, a fading which was presumably induced by a certain scientific and theoretical fatigue. The discussion on the relation between the rule of law and the social state affects the relations between government, administration, society and economy, and thus it is a key issue in public law. Therefore, this debate is actually timeless, not only in Germany.

CASES

BVerfGE 33, 1 – *Strafvollzug* (1972)
BVerfGE 33, 125 – *Facharzt* (1972)
BVerfGE 33, 303 – *Numerus Clausus* (1972)
BVerfGE 47, 46 – *Sexualkundeunterricht* (1977)
BVerfGE 49, 89 – *Kalkar I* (1978)
BVerfGE 68, 193 – *Gesetzliche Krankenversicherung* (1984)
BVerfGE 82, 60 – *Steuerfreies Existenzminimum* (1990)
BVerfGE 98, 106 – *Kommunale Verpackungssteuer* (1998)
BVerfGE 98, 219 – *Rechtschreibreform* (1998)
BVerfGE 108, 282 – *Kopftuchverbot* (2003)
BVerfGE 111, 307 – *Görgülu* (2004)
BVerfGE 115, 25 – *Gesetzliche Krankenversicherung* (2005)
BVerfGE 125, 175 – *Hartz IV* (2010)

SELECTED LITERATURE

Forsthoff E (ed), *Rechtsstaatlichkeit und Sozialstaatlichkeit* (Darmstadt, WBG, 1968)
——'Begriff und Wesen des sozialen Rechtsstaates' (1954) 12 *Veröffentlichungen der Vereinigung der Deutschen Staatsrechtslehrer* 8
Heinig HM, *Der Sozialstaat im Dienst der Freiheit* (Tübingen, Mohr Siebeck, 2008)
Kingreen T, *Das Sozialstaatsprinzip im europäischen Verfassungsverbund* (Tübingen, Mohr Siebeck, 2003)
Kunig P, *Das Rechtsstaatsprinzip* (Tübingen, Mohr, 1985)
Lücke J, 'Soziale Grundrechte als Staatszielbestimmungen und Gesetzgebungsaufträge' (1982) 107 *Archiv des öffentlichen Rechts* 15
Möllers C, *Gewaltengliederung* (Tübingen, Mohr Siebeck, 2005)
Ritter GA, *Der Sozialstaat*, 3rd edn (Munich, Oldenbourg, 2010) 62
Ruland F, von Maydell B and Papier HJ (eds), *Verfassung, Theorie und Praxis des Sozialstaates* (Heidelberg, CF Müller, 1998)
Schmidt-Aßmann E, 'Der Rechtsstaat' in J Isensee and P Kirchhof, *Handbuch des Staatsrechts der Bundesrepublik Deutschland*, vol II, 3rd edn (Heidelberg, CF Müller, 2004) § 26
Schmitt C, *Verfassungslehre* (Berlin, Duncker & Humblot, 1928)

[98] See articles in M Fehling and M Ruffert (eds), *Regulierungsrecht* (Tübingen, Mohr Siebeck, 2010).

von Stein L, *Geschichte der sozialen Bewegung in Frankreich von 1789 bis auf unsere Tage*, vol I, G Salomon ed (Munich, Drei Masken, 1921)
Suhr D, 'Rechtsstaatlichkeit und Sozialstaatlichkeit' (1970) 9 *Der Staat* 67

7

Federalism – Cooperative Federalism versus Competitive Federalism

CHRISTIAN WALDHOFF

I. INTRODUCTION

GERMANY COUNTS ITSELF among the traditionally federalist nations. This is even reflected in the nation's official name: '*Bundes*republik Deutschland' (*Federal* Republic of Germany). Each federal state is one of a kind. Nevertheless, the analysis of federal statehood and federalism lends itself well to a comparative methodology. Many debates concerning specific federalist problems have been determined by means of a comparative perspective. On the other hand, the existent federalist states are by no means mere realizations of a preset type.[1] Federalism can only be analysed inside the bounds of the precise constitutional order within which it is realized. In other words: Germany is a federalist state by means of the specifications of the German Constitution, not because of some theory about federalism.[2] It is not easy to find an equally effective way of clearly demonstrating differences than by comparison of various federalist states: the USA was founded in 1787 as the first modern federalist state, followed by Switzerland in 1848. The German federation dates back to 1867/1871 when

[1] J Isensee, 'Idee und Gestalt des Föderalismus im Grundgesetz' in J Isensee and P Kirchhof (eds), *Handbuch des Staatsrechts der Bundesrepublik Deutschland*, vol VI, 3rd edn (Heidelberg, CF Müller, 2008), § 126, para 1.

[2] J Isensee, 'Der Bundesstaat – Bestand und Entwicklung' in P Badura and H Dreier (eds), *Festschrift 50 Jahre Bundesverfassungsgericht*, vol II (Tübingen, Mohr Siebeck, 2001) 719.

Bismarck utilized the delayed development of a national state to found a republic. In all three cases, federalist states were developed from previously existing confederations. Even today, the historical context surrounding their emergence still influences the federalist provisions of the constitutions as well as theories concerning these.

In German legal doctrine, a federalist conglomeration of states is understood to be a constitutional basic decision as to state structure. In other words, it is a fundamental constitutional principle which shapes the Constitution itself and, in accordance with Article 79(3) of the German Constitution – the *Grundgesetz* ('GG') – cannot be subject to change. Federalism, therefore, describes the underlying historical principle, federalist state, the concrete constitutional occurrence. This terminological clarification is important as in English the term 'Federalism' may be used to mean opposite things. In all three classic federalist states – the USA, Switzerland and Germany – the state is structured as one central state (USA: 'Federal Government'; Switzerland: 'Bund'; Germany: 'Bund') and member states (USA: 'States'; Switzerland: 'Cantons'; Germany: 'Länder'). The member states take part in federal legislation by way of a special legislative body (USA: 'Senate'; Switzerland: 'Ständerat'; Germany: 'Bundesrat'). One of the crucial duties of the constitution of a federalist state is the division of responsibility and power between the central government and the member states. The German Constitution follows the principle – as most federalist states do – that only the enumerated powers put forth in the Constitution itself fall on the central government; all other responsibilities are, by default, given to the member states (Articles 30; 70ff; 83ff; 92ff GG). Nevertheless, there is consensus that outside of the specific distribution of powers within the Constitution, there is no general principle of subsidiarity. More than half of the Constitution deals with provisions concerning matters of the federal government. These provisions often prove to be far more technical than, say, the regulation of basic civil rights.

Within German legal scholarship, the individual member states are granted the status of true states.[3] It remains unclear, what precisely is meant by this status. Unquestionably, this does not carry the same meaning as the classification in terms of international law. Ultimately, the terminology is more likely given meaning of a symbolical nature.

As long as Germany has been a federalist state, there has been intense academic discourse regarding federalism. As far back as the Bismarck-era (1867/71 to 1918), constitutional law scholars were unable to reach a consensus regarding this legal construct. In typically German fashion, these scholars of the 'Kaiserreich' attempted to discern the question of sovereignty.[4] Today the struggles between

[3] BVerfGE 1, 14, 34; 6, 309, 346–47; 34, 9, 19–20; 36, 342, 360–61; 61, 149, 206–07; 69, 175, 207–08; 72, 330, 383, 388; Isensee, Der Bundesstaat' (n 1) para 65; fundamental criticism in C Möllers, *Staat als Argument* (Munich, CH Beck, 2000) 350.

[4] Emphasis must be placed on the controversy between the Bavarian constitutional law scholar, M von Seydel (1846–1901) and P Laband (1838–1918); cf M Stolleis, *Geschichte des öffentlichen Rechts in Deutschland*, vol II (Munich, CH Beck 1992) 365–68; also U Volkmann, 'Bundesstaat in der Krise?' [1998] *Die Öffentliche Verwaltung* 613, 614.

the European Union and its member states are often reminiscent of some of these discussions which now merely bear historical relevance.

Although the federalist nature of the German Constitution is compliant with a long-standing tradition, it was not based solely on the free decision of the German people at the time the Constitution was founded in 1948/49. In the so-called Frankfurt Documents, which initiated the process of developing a constitution in the main zones of occupation in 1948, a federalist structure was predetermined. During deliberation on the Constitution, the question of how centralized or how federal the newly created constitutional order should be proved to be one of the main points of conflict, both within the parties developing the Constitution (especially the Parliamentary Council) and also in relation to the victorious allied forces of the Second World War. To some extent, this influences the discussion, even today.

The decision for a federalist structure always demands a great deal of legitimation because, as opposed to the structure principles of democracy and the rule of law, there is a functioning alternative to federalism: centralism. This demand for legitimation escalates when dysfunctions become apparent, something which many observers believe to be the case within the current constitutional order.[5] Although the provisions dividing power and duties among the federal and state governments are fixed and cannot be altered by means of agreements or declarations, federalism is never a static entity. A substantial part of a federalist system is determined by procedural questions and arrangements concerning procedure. This tendency towards political arrangements creates a certain degree of tension in relation to the way in which federalism-related conflicts are carried out before the courts.

This chapter shall not deal with the issue that European integration is not suited for federalist nations, or as Hans Peter Ipsen wrote, it is 'blind to federalism'. Apart from Germany, only Austria and, with numerous peculiarities, Belgium may be described as federalist states. German involvement within the bodies of the European Union is hampered by the fact that a prior or simultaneous coordination between federal and state governments must occur. Article 23 GG, introduced into the Constitution in 1990, attempts to deal with this issue, but fails to provide a satisfactory solution to the problem.

II. BACKGROUND OF GERMAN FEDERALISM

When legitimizing the constitutional decision for federalism, an important contextual factor must be considered. While in the USA the founding of the nation immediately involved a federalist organization which was an expression of revolutionary democratic change, and while in Switzerland a long-standing federalist tradition existed on a local governmental basis, in Germany, federalism and a

[5] ibid 616.

federal organization of state historically represented the principles, which proved rather unsuccessful in the nineteenth century, for particularity (concerning the partitioned sovereignty of many principalities) and not for the foundation of democratic power. The German federal state was founded in 1867/71 as a league of princes whose legitimacy came not from the people, but was traditionally seen as coming from God. The main ideological movements of the nineteenth century – liberalism and nationalism – were, according to German tradition, not at all oriented towards a federal organization of the state. This burden continues to have an effect within the specific constitutional provisions themselves, as well as throughout the discussion concerning federalism and the federal state. The crucial point is that in Germany – with some regional differences (Bavaria) – federalism is met with comparatively meagre approval among the populace. Differences in legislation are often criticized in political discussions as being too partitioned and small-state-minded. The recurring passage in the German Constitution which sites the ideal of uniform or comparable living conditions among the *Länder*, the legal meaning of this passage being highly controversial, shows the desire of the populace for equality and uniformity, a fact which makes differentiation among *Länder* challenging. The traditionally weak democratic tradition within German constitutional law supplements these difficulties by inhibiting truly autonomous, independent political decisions. The 'will to autonomy' is weak within the political process as well as in constitutional discussions.

In order to understand the current debates concerning the federal organization of the state, one must know that over the course of the more than 60-year-long history of the Constitution, the general premise concerning federalism has changed. In addition, two major reforms of the federalist order – 1969 and 2006 – have brought extensive change. The federal organization is among the most often reformed portions of the Constitution.[6] In the 1960s, as a result of the economic and welfare-oriented successes after the Second World War, the desire for uniformity within the populace had become so strong – while the jurisprudence of the Federal Constitutional Court was at the same time undoubtedly unitarian[7] – that an amendment to the Constitution creating the concept of cooperative federalism was made in 1969. This applied to the constitutional rules governing public finances (Article 104a and following GG), as well as the formerly unknown communal duties given to the federal and state governments (Article 91a, 91b GG). After several decades of testing this new cooperative federalism, its drawbacks became increasingly apparent. In particular, although not only attributed to the cooperation between federal and state governments, the political responsibility for decision-making (-errors) became increasingly blurred. The citizens barely had the chance to consign responsibilities and reflect these in their electoral

[6] ibid 613.

[7] Constitutional unitary impulses emerged mainly from the jurisprudence concerning the basic civil rights, which led to standardized effects for all states, being that they derived from federal law. Moreover, social welfare law had a major influence as it was mainly governed by federal provisions which applied to all states equally.

behaviour. The pendulum therefore swung in the opposite direction, towards more autonomy and, as a consequence, towards a greater degree of responsibility of the *Länder*. Occasionally, this phenomenon has been marked with the label 'competition federalism'. This admittedly brought forth many misunderstandings, as 'competition' was transferred from the economy to constitutional matters.[8] The development of a federal senate was viewed as problematic and the desire emerged to create a greater divide between the federal and *Länder* governments. The Federalism Reform of 2006 reacted to this, although the results remain controversial.

III. TWO CURRENT POINTS OF DISCUSSION

A. Division of Responsibilities in the Legislature: Legislative Autonomy versus Uniformity of Living Conditions/Judicial versus Political Conflict Resolution

Characteristic for the federalist division of responsibilities by the Constitution which, if not otherwise ordered (Article 30 GG), presumes the competence of the *Länder*, is the fact that the state functions (the legislature, the administration, the judicature and, additionally, finance-related competences) are divided separately between the federal and *Länder* governments. While legislative responsibility is largely given to the federal government, the main administrative (particularly the execution of these laws) and judicial responsibilities are given to the *Länder*. This fact is often described using the term 'executive federalism'. The responsibilities of the member states mainly comprise the execution of federal law. This model varies in particular from the characteristic division of responsibilities in the US Constitution. There, the states possess the majority of legislative competence, including the execution of the laws and judicial supervision, while the federal government unifies legislation, administration and adjudication in the areas for which it is responsible. This division of responsibilities can best be visualized by an image of columns. According to the German Constitution, on the other hand, competences are consigned for each function of the state, without mandating for the fact that these functions conform to one another, particularly among legislation and administration.[9]

One primary difficulty in the division of legislative responsibility in Germany is that the lack of legislative capacity of the *Länder* is meant to be compensated for by their involvement in legislation on the federal level. This has been a topic of

[8] Critical in regard to any form of competition in the federalist state, H Bauer, 'Entwicklungstendenzen und Perspektiven des Föderalismus in der Bundesrepublik Deutschland – Zugleich ein Beitrag zum Wettbewerbsföderalismus' [2002] *Die Öffentliche Verwaltung* 837; more positively C Waldhoff, 'Finanzautonomie und Finanzverflechtung in gestuften Rechtsordnungen' (2007) 66 *Veröffentlichungen der Vereinigung der Deutschen Staatsrechtslehrer* 216.

[9] cf for a characterization of the various modi of division of competences, see C Waldhoff, *Verfassungsrechtliche Vorgaben für die Steuergesetzgebung im Vergleich Deutschland-Schweiz* (Munich, CH Beck, 1997) 80–81.

great discussion. Federalism can, however, only make sense if it means autonomy/difference. The participation of the states via the Bundesrat (Article 50and following GG), allows only a majority to influence legislation; differences, legislative experimentation and the like, are not possible. This form of participation proves to be a means of inhibiting federal power, but without federalist character. A legitimizing effect for a federalist structure cannot be achieved. Additionally, this model of participation of the *Länder* regarding federal legislation leads to a shift in the separation of powers. Via the federal body, the Bundesrat – the Upper House of the German Parliament – the *Länder*, particularly, the executive branches of the *Länder*, participate in policy-making on a federal level. This leads to a loss of influence and political range for the *Länder* governments/parliaments.

In this regard, an additional problem and further discussion must be addressed. As far as the notion that legislative responsibility is primarily concentrated on the federal government goes, certain prerequisites must be met in order for the federal government to utilize these competences.[10]

This leads to a fundamental question of federalist structure: who adjudicates over competency issues between federal and *Länder* government – the constitutional courts or the political process? This question is not answered sufficiently, neither in the decisions of the Federal Constitutional Court nor in academic discussions. Whereas the Constitution of 1871 – the *Reichsverfassung* – preferred a political authority to resolve such conflicts, Hans Kelsen claims that federal conflicts fall within the core responsibility of a constitutional court, whose independent judges should find a ruling in keeping with the rules of law.[11] The fundamental responsibilities of the Federal Constitutional Court refer directly or indirectly to the resolution of conflicts of a federalist nature.

The former provision in Article 72(2) GG which determined which requirements must be met in order for the federal government to apply its concurrent legislative competence was never fully taken seriously by the Federal Constitutional Court. Its content was deemed incapable of being adjudicated upon.[12] This was caused in part by the fact that the federalist structure had been, to a certain degree, forced upon the Parliamentary Council by the allied forces after World War Two, so that some were eager to see their notions of a more centralized state realized. After reunification in 1990, the legislature amended Article 72(2) in an attempt to strengthen the autonomy of the *Länder*. The intention of the legislature in doing so was clear: the Federal Constitutional Court was to be empowered to examine the need for federal legislation in a specific area.[13] Several decisions were made in

[10] Extensively C Waldhoff, 'Verfassungsrechtliche Anforderungen an die Ausübung von Gesetzgebungskompetenzen (Art. 72(2); 75(2); 125a(2) GG): materielles Kompetenzzuweisungsrecht als Element einer Föderalismusreform' in H-G Henneke (ed), *Föderalismusreform in Deutschland* (Stuttgart, Boorberg, 2005) 55.

[11] H Kelsen, 'Wesen und Entwicklung der Staatsgerichtsbarkeit' (1929) 5 *Veröffentlichungen der Vereinigung der Deutschen Staatsrechtslehrer* 30, 81.

[12] BVerfGE 13, 230.

[13] In detail Waldhoff, 'Verfassungsrechtliche Anforderungen an die Ausübung von Gesetzgebungskompetenzen' (n 10) 61.

this interest. However, the political nature of the question as to whether the federal government should legislate in a particular area or whether it should be left up to the *Länder* was finally dealt with by increasing the duty of the federal government to provide grounds for legislating in a particular area.[14] Up until the Federalism Reform of 2006 this had been the means of strengthening the individual *Länder*. The Federalism Reform then moved in another direction: the legislative competence of the federal government, for which the requirements of Article 72(2) GG must be met, were limited. In addition, the so-called 'divergence legislation' (*Abweichungsgesetzgebung*) replaced the previously existing 'framework legislation' (*Rahmengesetzgebung*) (Article 72(3) GG).

B. Public Finance: Self-Dependence versus Autonomy

The German constitutional provisions governing public finance are extremely centralized, even in international comparison. Practically all legislative competence regarding taxation is given to the federal government, leaving the *Länder* with no influence on the organization of their income. Differences in financial capacity are largely levelled out by a complex system of financial compensation between the *Länder* and the federal government, as well as among the *Länder* themselves.

It is the aim of these provisions (ie Articles 104a to 109 GG) to divide financial capacity appropriately between the federal government and the *Länder*. The experiences during the Reich Constitution of 1871 and under the Weimar Constitution had shown that the Reich and the states could only then fulfil their innate duties and obligations, if provided with appropriate funding. In other words, the party with the greater financial capacity was better able to enforce their organizational competencies. Therefore, the constitutional provisions concerning public finance in the modern German Constitution are based on the concept of providing both the federal and *Länder* governments with sufficient funding, along with the right to independently administrate and utilize these funds. The Federal Constitutional Court describes this compromise as follows: 'The federal and *Länder* governments should be enabled to administer and fulfil their constitutional duties and responsibilities'. The Court adds that 'only by this means can the independence of federation and *Länder* become realized, independence and self-sufficiency in the fulfilment of responsibilities be achieved'.[15] The constitutional provisions concerning public finance therefore prove to be 'cornerstones of the federalist order'.[16] This explains the atypical, technically complex density of provisions in this part of the Constitution.

While the acquisition and administration of funds represents a key function of the state, the classification of the constitutional provisions hereto – related as

[14] BVerfGE 106, 62; 110, 41; [2004] *Neue Juristische Wochenschrift* 2803; [2005] *Neue Juristische Wochenschrift* 493.

[15] BVerfGE 72, 330, 383.

[16] BVerfGE 55, 274, 300.

mere consequence of the federalist context within which they exist – can easily be misunderstood.[17] Nevertheless, Ferdinand Kirchhof[18] and Stefan Korioth[19] adhere to this viewpoint. Kirchhof writes that 'Art. 106 ff GG divide financial means according to a federal structure prescribed elsewhere. These provisions follow the organisational and competency-determining norms found throughout the entire Constitution'.[20] This far too one-dimensional viewpoint, however, neglects the varied interactions between federalist structure and public finance. The federal constitutional provisions concerning public finance (Articles 104a to 109 GG) are themselves a part of this order and in being so help to form it.[21] Although the acquisition of income is a central responsibility of the state which enables the fulfilment of all other governmental responsibilities, the division of financial authority between the federal and *Länder* governments results in a broad variation of effects upon, and interaction with, the 'general' activity of the state. This 'facilitative function' of state finance can only be upheld in conjunction with mandatory state responsibilities; the greater part of state responsibilities (especially in respect to finance), particularly, the financially elaborate field of community service administration and social welfare, is dependent upon the possibility of attaining funding within the framework set forth by the Constitution. Owing to the binding nature of the Constitution, even concerning public finance, the division of duties cannot solely determine the volume of funding to be achieved by the state.

When Kirchhof argues that the provisions concerning public finance can be reformed without changing the wording of the Constitution itself,[22] one must counter that the opposite is true. It would be curious to view these provisions as cornerstones of the federalist order on the one hand, but on the other hand, to view them as having no influence upon the concrete formation of the federalist state. Federalist structure in public finance and federal political structure cannot be isolated from one another. Instead, they are overlapping parts of the constitutionally founded federal system, each influencing and presupposing the other.

In summary: the depiction of the public finance provisions of the Constitution as mere consequences of the constitutional order and the claim of a facilitating function of these provisions reveals a one-sided view of the responsibilities and financial competences, which can only be seen as misleading, as it suggests that the state must acquire such funding as is needed to fulfil its constitutional duties. Beyond the mandatory responsibilities of the state, however, the political possibilities are also determined by the volumes of finance which the state is able to

[17] cf also W Heun, 'Preliminary Notes to Art. 104a–115' in *Dreier: Grundgesetz Kommentar*, vol III, 2nd edn (Tübingen, Mohr Siebeck, 2008) para 19.

[18] F Kirchhof, 'Grundsätze der Finanzverfassung des vereinten Deutschlands' (1993) 52 *Veröffentlichungen der Vereinigung der Deutschen Staatsrechtslehrer* 71.

[19] S Korioth, *Der Finanzausgleich zwischen Bund und Ländern* (Tübingen, Mohr Siebeck, 1997) 12–13, 32, 151–52 and throughout.

[20] F Kirchhof, 'Grundsätze der Finanzverfassung des vereinten Deutschlands' (n 18) 80 and throughout.

[21] cf on the contrary, Korioth, *Der Finanzausgleich zwischen Bund und Ländern* (n 19) 34 and elsewhere.

[22] Kirchhof (n 18) 80.

acquire.[23] This correlation can be described as a 'mobile system' between responsibility and funding.

As part of the Federalism Reform of 2006[24] certain forms of mixed funding were dispelled. In addition, some subject matters under sole legislative competency of the *Länder* were meant to be freed from the possibility of receiving federal funding in accordance with Article 104a(4) GG. This provision is meant to be replaced by a new Article 104b GG and taxation autonomy is meant to be created by a new Article 105(2a), sentence 2 GG. In accordance with this provision, the *Länder* will receive the power to determine the level of property taxation. The interstate EU liability[25] coupled with the national budget stability pact being raised to the level of the Constitution itself[26] complete this picture. These are, however, merely minimal corrections. A real reformation of the federalist finance structure was purposefully avoided. Even the so-called *Föderalismusreform II*[27] brought about no changes, as it was focused on national debt. The concepts and principles of the Federalism Reform of 2006 were by no means transferred to the provisions concerning public finance.

What does this question really revolve around? Peter M Huber based his 'entanglement' suggestions – designed to bring more transparency and responsibility to the German Federation – upon the democratic constitutional principle.[28] In the realm of public finance, democratic feedback and an increase in transparency mean emphasizing fiscal autonomy, as opposed to financial interdependence. The Federal Constitutional Court sees the fiscal compensation of the *Länder*, and indeed the federal financial relationships as a whole, as existing between independence, self-determination and the individuality of the *Länder* on the one hand, and the solidarity-based joint responsibility for the existence of the citizens on the other.[29] In doing so, it creates a framework of reasoning which does more than simply ease the solution of specific constitutional public finance problems;[30] it also provides a setting for reform discussion. At the same time, it establishes the foundation for a paradigm change in the understanding of the concept of federalism and federalist organization.[31] The basis for the current public finance provisions, which were mostly established in 1969, was the ideal of an active fiscal policy based on so-called global steering. This, however, presupposes

[23] C Waldhoff, 'Reformperspektiven im Finanzrecht' (2006) 39 *Die Verwaltung* 155, 156.

[24] Gesetz zur Änderung des Grundgesetzes vom 28. 8. 2006, BGBl I 2034; also Deutscher Bundestag (ed), *Dokumentation der Kommission von Bundestag und Bundesrat zur Modernisierung der bundesstaatlichen Ordnung* (Berlin, 2005) 483ff.

[25] Art 104a(6) GG after the Federalism Reform 2006.

[26] Art 109(5) GG after the Federalism Reform 2006.

[27] Gesetz zur Änderung des Grundgesetzes vom 29. 7. 2009, BGBl I 2248.

[28] PM Huber, *Klarere Verantwortungsteilung von Bund, Ländern und Kommunen? Gutachten D zum 65. Deutschen Juristentag Bonn 2004* (Munich, CH Beck, 2004) 33; PM Huber, *Deutschland in der Föderalismusfalle?* (Munich, CF Müller, 2003) 14. Huber is, however, critical of surcharge competences for acquiring funds, cf *DJT-Gutachten* 75.

[29] BVerfGE 72, 330, 398.

[30] K Vogel and C Waldhoff, *Grundlagen des Finanzverfassungsrechts* (Heidelberg, CF Müller, 1999) paras 60–61, 66.

[31] ibid para 70; critical Korioth (n 19) 93, 410.

an adequate degree of interdependence in order to ensure that the financial and fiscal policy decisions made on this basis can be enforced effectively. Economic and social control in the technocratic euphoria of the 1960s found its way into legislation with the typical delay and was then largely met with approval within the contemporary economy. The economic and fiscal malformation of this concept became apparent during its first true test, the oil crisis of 1973, and the ensuing economic situation. In the meantime, an economic paradigm change has taken place; the social sciences have analysed and described the disadvantages of cooperative federalism under the buzzword 'political entanglement trap'.[32] In light of these findings, greater emphases on the idea of autonomy of the various branches of the government as well as the strengthening of individual responsibility in financial decision-making have taken hold.

Aside from the failed concept of global steering, the rarely challenged notion of equal taxation across the nation and its connection to the demand for equal or equivalent living standards have traditionally been deciding factors in public policy provisions of the Constitution. As has been shown, this notion is, however, not a mandatory constitutional ideal but merely a single-case ruling found in various parts of the Constitution, and it is in need of interpretation within the respective context. Within a constitutional reform discussion, this notion may not block alternative viewpoints; it may not dominate the interpretation of current (fiscal) constitutional law.[33]

Even the mention of more de facto deciding factors (harmonizing effect of the federal civil rights and social welfare; federally active political parties; expectations of the populace) are subject to, as Peter Lerche said, 'the trend of creating facts, which the legal world must adjoin itself to',[34] creating the danger of a meant-to-be false conclusion.[35] The arguments revolving around equality of living standards proved to be an historical remnant of a time in which the federal German state was being developed and political unity was threatened. They have lost nearly all meaning today. The discussion is marked by factors that led to the foundation of the 'Bismarck Empire' in 1867/71 and followed its further development. During the nineteenth century, the middle classes demanded the establishment of a uniform economic realm, the abolishment of interstate customs and the freedom of internal traffic. This was compounded by the ever-increasing mobility of the populace due to industrialization. In the second half of the nineteenth century, economic issues dominated as the Kaiserreich marginalized the middle classes. Most political conciliation attempts derived from attempts at first achieving

[32] FW Scharpf, 'Die Politikverflechtungs-Falle: Europäische Integration und deutscher Föderalismus im Vergleich' (1985) 26 *Politische Vierteljahresschriften* 323.

[33] Markus Möstl indicates correctly in 'Neuordnung der Gesetzgebungskompetenzen von Bund und Ländern' [2003] *Zeitschrift für Gesetzgebung* 297, 299 the discrepancy between the demand for disentanglement of federal and *Länder* legislative competence on the one hand, and the critical view of the consequent greater disparity between the *Länder* on the other.

[34] P Lerche, 'Finanzausgleich und Einheitlichkeit der Lebensverhältnisse' in D Blumenwitz and A Randelzhofer (eds), *Festschrift für Friedrich Berber* (Munich, CH Beck, 1973) 299.

[35] HP Bull, 'Finanzausgleich im „Wettbewerbsstaat' [1999] *Die Öffentliche Verwaltung* 269, 279.

economic agreement.[36] In addition, numerous cessation movements arose at the beginning of the Weimar era as threats and repression from the outside created an atmosphere conducive to centralization and unionism. Finally, in 1948/49, the emphatically federalist viewpoints of the allied forces were pushed back as far as possible within the reconstruction of Germany. The original version of Article 72(2) GG is exemplary.[37] The interests represented during the deliberation of the Constitution were – with the exception of Bavaria – decidedly marked by centralist ideology: Hermann Höpker-Aschoff, who was a vital figure during the deliberation of the public policy provisions, lent the deliberations a clearly technocratic-centralized character, as a former high-ranking Prussian officer and minister of finance.[38] His parties – the DDP and FDP – had been centralist anyway.[39] The SPD traditionally argued for centralized financial policy as a precondition for their social policy. Thus, parts of the constitutional public finance provisions were marked by a strong drive towards uniformity. Many of these factors have, however, disappeared or have, at least, substantially lost relevance and should therefore not pollute the reform discussion.[40] The ideal of uniform or equal living conditions should serve as a non-legal factor and should be treated as a kind of pre-notion.[41]

In contrast, the reconstruction of the responsibility correlation between political decisions of the voters and fiscal policy, especially the taxation decisions of the government, should be made more visible. The unavoidable fiscal decision towards a less transparent relationship between public benefits and taxation, between taking and giving, must become apparent even at the *Länder* level and should be reflected in political competition.[42] Financial responsibility demands the freedom to make fiscal policy decisions.[43] By introducing such a correlation, a greater participation of the state citizens in the accomplishments and failures of the *Land* fiscal policy could be reached. At the very least, the transparency of public finance would be enhanced. The enormous democratic potential of competitive federalism has revealed itself.[44] The *Länder* parliaments, which have been

[36] H Abromeit, *Der verkappte Einheitsstaat* (Opladen, Leske und Budrich, 1992) 121; W Zorn, 'Wirtschafts- und sozialgeschichtliche Zusammenhänge der deutschen Reichsgründungszeit (1850–1879)' (1963) 197 *Historische Zeitschrift* 318.

[37] M Gruson, *Die Bedürfniskompetenz* (Berlin, Duncker & Humblot, 1967) 18.

[38] T Aders, *Die Utopie vom Staat über den Parteien* (Frankfurt a.M., Lang, 1983); F Spieker, *Hermann Höpker Aschoff: Vater der Finanzverfassung* (Berlin, Duncker & Humblot, 2004); similarly, the influential reporting judge at the Constitutional Convention in Herrenchiemsee, Herbert Fischer-Menshausen.

[39] Differentiated by KH Lamberty, *Die Stellung der Liberalen zum föderativen Staatsaufbau in der Entstehungsphase der Bundesrepublik Deutschland 1945–1949* (PhD thesis, University of Bonn, 1983) 116.

[40] cf also K Rennert, 'Der deutsche Föderalismus in der gegenwärtigen Debatte um eine Verfassungsreform' (1992) 31 *Der Staat* 269, 274.

[41] S Oeter, *Integration und Subsidiarität im deutschen Bundesstaatsrecht* (Tübingen, Mohr Siebeck, 1998) 13–14.

[42] HH von Arnim, *Staatslehre der Bundesrepublik Deutschland* (München, Vahlen, 1984) 486.

[43] R Grawert, 'Kommunale Finanzhoheit und Steuerhoheit' in A von Mutius (ed), *Festgabe für Georg Christoph von Unruh* (Heidelberg, v Decker, 1983) 587, 590.

[44] H Klatt, 'Parlamentarisches System und bundesstaatliche Ordnung' [1982] 32 *Aus Politik und Zeitgeschichte* 19, 22.

practically devoid of influence concerning financial intake, would be strengthened by their direct connection to the will of the voters. The 'citizen, particularly sensitive to regional differences in taxation'[45] has no opportunity to accept gaps in the tax burden within the current system, because the political correlation of responsibility and the centralized system of public benefits is not sufficiently apparent. The political pressure placed upon the fiscal policy of the federal and state governments to justify spending would increase drastically; the more burdened citizens would demand greater benefits. The argument that, because of the equal tax burden, equal benefits are expected, or that equal benefits in turn lead to the expectation of an equal tax burden,[46] is circular. This interdependency does nothing to ascertain whether the reform suggestions are politically sensible or not.

The participation of the *Länder* in taxation legislation via the Bundesrat in accordance with Article 105(3) 3 GG, cannot compensate for the lack in fiscal autonomy in generating income.[47] The loss of decision-making powers cannot be fielded by participation in a superordinate decision-making process.[48] Since the Bundesrat aims at uniformly forming political will and since only a majority can influence the legislative debate, it does not serve to uphold the decision-making power of each individual *Land*.[49] The *Länder* as a combined entity may be a counter-force to the federal government, but the lack of fiscal influence of the individual *Länder* is not counterbalanced. 'The right of each of the *Länder* to participate through the *Bundesrat* does not create a state-specific profile'.[50] The basic right to equal treatment before the law is not a concept which prevents *Länder* autonomy in matters of taxation legislation.[51]

The technical execution of the reconstruction of the democratic system of responsibility for *Länder* finances proposed here and with it, the partial disentanglement of the federal public finance provisions through the concession of autonomous means of generating income, cannot be fully discussed in this chapter. This notion exists within a context of ideas of simplification of the taxation system, which has a sound constitutional basis. The possibility of a state adjustment or supplement to the federal taxes (income and corporation taxation) under a uniform basis of assessment would fulfil the *Länder* need for influence

[45] A Dittmann, 'Gleichheitssatz und Gesetzesvollzug im Bundesstaat' in H Mauer (ed), *Festschrift für Günter Dürig* (Munich, CH Beck, 1990) 221, 239.

[46] K Tipke, *Die Steuerrechtsordnung*, vol III (Köln, Otto Schmidt, 1993) 1126.

[47] U Karpen, 'Verfassungsänderung und Föderalismus' [1995] *Zeitschrift für Gesetzgebung* 356, 359; on the function of this involvement from a comparative law standpoint see Waldhoff, *Verfassungsrechtliche Vorgaben für die Steuergesetzgebung* (n 9) 83.

[48] In general K Hesse, *Grundzüge des Verfassungsrechts der Bundesrepublik Deutschland*, 20th edn (Heidelberg, CF Müller, 1995) para 221.

[49] F Ossenbühl, 'Föderalismus und Regionalismus in Europa: Landesbericht Bundesrepublik Deutschland' in F Ossenbühl (ed), *Föderalismus und Regionalismus in Europa* (Baden-Baden, Nomos, 1990) 117, 155; K-D Henke and GF Schuppert, *Rechtliche und finanzwissenschaftliche Probleme der Neuordnung der Finanzbeziehungen von Bund und Ländern im vereinten Deutschland* (Baden-Baden, Nomos, 1993) 22.

[50] R Wendt, 'Neuorientierung der Aufgaben- und Lastenverteilung im "sozialen Bundesstaat"' [1993] *Staatswissenschaften und Staatspraxis* 56, 71.

[51] BVerfGE 10, 354, 371; 21, 54, 68.

over taxation, while upholding a scope of organization concerning the rate of taxation – the final political decision of how much tax would be collected.[52] The expert council on the assessment of the overall fiscal development made such suggestions in its report in 1992/93;[53] a report from the scientific advisory board to the Federal Ministry of Finance concerning the funding of the *Länder* compensation in the Federal Republic of Germany and the distribution of tax revenues between federal and *Länder* governments commented in this direction in 1992,[54] as did a corresponding report in 1995.[55] The Swiss taxation harmonization project serves as a functioning and tried example.[56] It is, however, important to note the limits of such concepts: the taxation harmonization on the European level must be considered and may prove to be limiting.[57] The increasingly relevant problem of differences in the financial strength of various *Länder*, which has become relevant since reunification, is a basic issue.[58] In addition, a distinct taxation competency of the *Länder* leads to an interstate double-taxation issue. This could, however, be overcome, as can be seen by considering similar solutions in Switzerland,[59] during the 'Bismarck Reich'[60] and in the area of trade taxation.[61]

CASES

BVerfGE 12, 205 – *Gesetzgebungskompetenz; Bundestreue* (1961)
BVerfGE 63, 1 – *Verbot der Mischverwaltung im Bundesstaat* (1983)
BVerfGE 72, 330 – *Bundesstaatlicher Finanzausgleich* (1986)
BVerfGE 81, 310 – *Verwaltungskompetenzen* (1990)
BVerfGE 86, 148 – *Bundesstaatlicher Finanzausgleich* (1992)
BVerfGE 101, 158 – *Bundesstaatlicher Finanzausgleich* (1999)
BverfGE 104, 249 – *Verwaltungskompetenzen* (2002)
BVerfGE 106, 62 – *Gesetzgebungskompetenz* (2002)
BVerfGE 106, 310 – *Bundesrat* (2002)
BVerfGE 109, 190 – *Gesetzgebungskompetenz* (2004)

[52] Critical Huber, *DJT-Gutachten* (n 28) 75 including the not entirely consistent argument that supplements would blur political responsibility and hinder transparency.
[53] BT-Drs 12/3774, subscript 349.
[54] Wissenschaftlicher Beirat beim Bundesministerium der Finanzen, *Einnahmeverteilung zwischen Bund und Ländern* (Bonn, 1994) 92, 99.
[55] Wissenschaftlicher Beirat beim Bundesministerium der Finanzen, *Einnahmeverteilung zwischen Bund und Ländern* (Bonn, 1995) 46–47.
[56] Waldhoff (n 9) 104–05.
[57] D Birk 'Diskussionsbeitrag' (1993) 52 *Veröffentlichungen der Vereinigung der Deutschen Staatsrechtslehrer* 169.
[58] U Häde, *Finanzausgleich* (Tübingen, Mohr Siebeck, 1996) 312–13.
[59] cf with further references Waldhoff (n 9) 201–02.
[60] *Doppelbesteuerungsgesetz* (Double Taxation Act) from 13.5.1870 (RGBl 119); replaced by *Reichsgesetz* from 22.3.1909 (RGBl 332); regarding this, P Laband, *Deutsches Reichsstaatsrecht,* 6th edn (Tübingen, Mohr, 1912) 48–49; C Schönberger, *Unionsbürger* (Tübingen, Mohr Siebeck, 2005) 234–35 with fn 384.
[61] Dismantling the unified quantification sum for business tax, cf with further references P Heine, 'Gewerbesteuer' in H-G Henneke, H Pünder and C Waldhoff (eds), *Recht der Kommunalfinanzen* (Munich, CH Beck, 2006) § 8, para 15.

BVerfGE 111, 10 – *Gesetzgebungskompetenz* (2004)
BVerfGE 111, 226 – *Gesetzgebungskompetenz* (2004)
BVerfGE 112, 226 – *Gesetzgebungskompetenz* (2005)
BVerfGE 116, 327 – *Bundesstaatlicher Finanzausgleich* (2006)
BVerfGE 119, 331 – *Verbot der Mischverwaltung im Bundesstaat* (2007)

SELECTED LITERATURE

Bauer H, *Die Bundestreue* (Tübingen, Mohr, 1992)

——'Entwicklungstendenzen und Perspektiven des Föderalismus in der Bundesrepublik Deutschland – Zugleich ein Beitrag zum Wettbewerbsföderalismus' [2002] *Die Öffentliche Verwaltung* 837–45

Baus RT, Blindenbacher R and Karpen U (eds), *Competition versus Cooperation: German Federalism in Need of Reform – A Comparative Perspective / Wettbewerb versus Kooperation: Der Reformbedarf des deutschen Föderalismus – Eine vergleichende Perspektive* (Baden-Baden, Nomos, 2007)

Hesse K, *Der unitarische Bundesstaat* (Heidelberg, CF Müller, 1962)

Huber PM, *Klarere Verantwortungsteilung von Bund, Ländern und Kommunen? Gutachten D zum 65. Deutschen Juristentag Bonn 2004* (Munich, CH Beck, 2004) D 1-D 149

Isensee J, 'Idee und Gestalt des Föderalismus im Grundgesetz' in J Isensee and P Kirchhof (eds), *Handbuch des Staatsrechts der Bundesrepublik Deutschland*, vol VI, 3rd edn (Heidelberg, CF Müller, 2008) § 126 (3–199)

——'Der Bundesstaat – Bestand und Entwicklung' in P Badura and H Dreier (eds), *Festschrift 50 Jahre Bundesverfassungsgericht*, vol II (Tübingen, Mohr Siebeck, 2001) 719-70

Jestaedt M, 'Bundesstaat als Verfassungsprinzip' in J Isensee and P Kirchhof(eds), *Handbuch des Staatsrechts der Bundesrepublik Deutschland*, vol II, 3rd edn (Heidelberg, CF Müller, 2004) § 29 (785–841)

Kirchhof P and Kommers DP (eds), *Deutschland und sein Grundgesetz. Themen einer deutsch-amerikanischen Konferenz* (Baden-Baden, Nomos, 1993) mainly part 2 'Der Föderalismus' (77–133)

Korioth S, *Integration und Bundesstaat* (Berlin, Duncker & Humblot, 1990)

Lerche P, 'Föderalismus als nationales Ordnungsprinzip' (1964) 21 *Veröffentlichungen der Vereinigung der Deutschen Staatsrechtslehrer* 66–104

Oeter S, *Integration und Subsidiarität im deutschen Bundesstaatsrecht* (Tübingen, Mohr Siebeck, 1998)

Ossenbühl F (ed), *Föderalismus und Regionalismus in Europa* (Baden-Baden, Nomos, 1990)

Volkmann U, 'Bundesstaat in der Krise?' [1998] *Die Öffentliche Verwaltung* 613–23

Waldhoff C, 'Finanzautonomie und Finanzverflechtung in gestuften Rechtsordnungen' (2007) 66 *Veröffentlichungen der Vereinigung der Deutschen Staatsrechtslehrer* 216–76

8

Financing the State – The Tax-funded State versus Multiple and Mixed Financing Strategies

HANNO KUBE

I. THE CRUCIAL QUESTION OF FINANCING THE STATE

ALMOST NO STATE action curtails the fundamental rights of the average citizen as extensively as the levying of taxes and other charges. Nonetheless, a state is only viable if it is sufficiently funded. The rules for financing the state are therefore of paramount importance for citizens as well as the state. This chapter aims to clarify the constitutional law principles governing state financing, focusing on the dichotomy between the concept of a tax-funded state on the one hand and multiple and mixed financing strategies on the other hand.

To begin, the chapter will present a brief overview of the sources of state funding expressly permitted by the German Constitution (section II). It will then address the traditional constitutional concept of the tax-funded state as well as criticisms thereof that have attempted to legitimize hybrid financing strategies on constitutional grounds (section III). Next, the chapter will evaluate recent legislative and administrative developments in the area of state financing, concluding that (particularly in light of these developments) the concept of the tax-funded state is the only funding strategy that offers long-term viability as well as constitutional conformity (section IV). The chapter then outlines the constitutional parameters that must govern German taxation regimes (section V) and concludes by embedding the concept of the tax-funded state within the framework of Germany's obligations as a member of a unified Europe (section VI.)

II. FUNDING SOURCES OF THE STATE[1]

A. Taxation

Germany funds state activity mainly through a combination of direct and indirect taxes.[2] At the federal level, more than 80 per cent of the budget is financed by taxes.[3] The term 'tax' appears in Articles 105 and following of the German Constitution, which allocate between Germany's federal and state governments the power to pass taxation legislation, receive revenues from specific assessments and administer the collection of taxes. Germany's Constitution does not define the term 'tax'. Instead, German law has accepted the definition provided in the German Fiscal Code as authoritative.[4]

Beginning in the mid-nineteenth century, German law established the 'ability to pay' (*Leistungsfähigkeit*, also translated as 'economic capacity') as the basis for taxation most consistent with constitutional principles of liberty and equality.[5] Earnings from investment activities or wages, for example, increase an individual's ability to pay and therefore increase his taxable base. Expenses necessary to secure one's existence or income may, however, be deducted from taxable income. Indirect taxation, primarily value added tax, can be justified on the grounds that consumer activity also manifests an individual's ability to pay.

B. Borrowing

In addition to taxes, the German Constitution permits state financing through borrowing. The state's ability to borrow, however, has been sharply curtailed by Germany's Federalism Reform of 2009, which was passed in light of public debt

[1] For an overview, see C Waldhoff, 'Grundzüge des Finanzrechts des Grundgesetzes' in J Isensee and P Kirchhof (eds), *Handbuch des Staatsrechts der Bundesrepublik Deutschland*, vol V, 3rd edn (Heidelberg, CF Müller, 2007) § 116, paras 82ff.

[2] For information on the volume of the taxes levied, see the website of the German Finance Ministry: www.bundesfinanzministerium.de.

[3] In 2012 the federal budget totaled about €306 billion, of which approximately €249 billion was generated by taxation.

[4] § 3(1) Abgabenordnung (Fiscal Code): 'Taxes shall mean payments of money, other than payments made in consideration of the performance of a particular activity, which are collected by a public body for the purpose of raising revenue and imposed by the body on all persons to whom the characteristics on which the law bases liability for payment apply; the raising of revenue may be a secondary objective'.

[5] BVerfGE 93, 121, 134; 99, 246, 260; 105, 73, 125; 107, 27, 45; 116, 164, 180; 117, 1, 30–31; 121, 108, 119–20; 122, 210, 230–31; 123, 111, 120; 126, 400, 417; 127, 224, 245; D Birk, *Das Leistungsfähigkeitsprinzip als Maßstab der Steuernormen* (Cologne, Deubner, 1983). Focusing on the ability to pay contrasted to other conceivable bases for calculating taxation: according to the 'doctrine of equivalence', an individual's tax burden is based on the benefits the individual received from the state during the taxable period; according to 'head tax', an individual is required to pay a specified sum to the state for each person in his household.

totalling more than €1.7 trillion at that time.[6] According to Article 109(3) of the German Constitution, German states may no longer structure debt into their financing. Instead, they may only issue debt in response to cyclical economic events. Germany's federal government retains the option to use debt as a structural component of its financing, but structural debt may not exceed 0.35 per cent of nominal gross domestic product. Any further debt issuances must be in response to extraordinary emergency circumstances.[7]

C. State-owned Companies

Germany's Constitution does not explicitly address whether and to what extent the state may establish state-owned companies whose profits could serve as a further source of state financing. Historically, however, state-owned companies have existed, and they still exist at the federal, state and also the municipal level.[8]

D. Fees and Other Charges

The German Constitution does not explicitly regulate the state's ability to demand fees and other charges from citizens.[9] In practice, such charges are levied on the basis of Articles 70 and following of the German Constitution, which allocate legislative authority between federal and state governments. The regulation of fees and other charges is therefore not treated as taxation law, but rather as an annex

[6] For decades Germany has lived beyond its means. In the early 1970s Germany's national debt was still well below €100 billion. By 1980 it had surpassed €200 billion, and by 1990 it was greater than €500 billion. Between 1990 and 1995 alone, reunification drove Germany's debt load to over €1 trillion. Currently Germany's official financial statements set the total debt of its federal and state governments at over €2 trillion – over 80% of Germany's gross domestic product. Current data on Germany's debt load may be found on the websites of the Federal Office of Statistics www.destatis.de and the German Finance Ministry www.bundesfinanzministerium.de. Despite historically low interest rates, 20% of all German state spending is devoted to nothing more than servicing the interest on this debt. Furthermore, there is additional debt beyond that reflected in Germany's official records. Germany faces substantial long-term obligations as a result of its governmental pension and social security programmes – neither of which are listed as debt in its official financial statements. Its balance sheet also fails to account for depreciation on infrastructure or reserves for infrastructure maintenance. Additionally, Germany has recently incurred liabilities up to the amount of close to €1 trillion in order to mitigate the effects of the 2008 financial crisis; these liabilities may well result in further debt in the near future. In short, Germany's debt load has become so great that it now endangers Germany's long-term viability as a functional polity. It is at this point that questions of state financing become questions of survival.

[7] According to Art 143d(1) of the German Constitution, the strict regulations just described only become effective in 2016 for the federal government and in 2020 for the states. However, the government and the states have to follow a certain path in order to be able to actually meet the new requirements in 2016 and 2020 respectively.

[8] S Storr, *Der Staat als Unternehmer* (Tübingen, Mohr Siebeck, 2001); C Waldhoff, 'Grundzüge des Finanzrechts des Grundgesetzes' (n 1) para 96.

[9] For an exception, see Art 74(1), no 22 of the German Constitution.

to general substantive law.[10] Unlike taxes, state-levied fees are assessed according to the 'doctrine of equivalence':[11] citizens must pay the state only as much as reasonably corresponds to the value they received from the service giving rise to the fee.[12]

The power to levy premiums paid to state unemployment and retirement insurance programs is also not derived from the power to tax. Instead, Germany's federal government collects social insurance premiums on the basis of its authority to establish and regulate social security programs.[13] The assessment of these premiums follows the 'doctrine of equivalence' as well as the 'ability to pay principle', as these programs are historically based on the idea of an intergenerational contract.[14]

III. THE CONCEPT OF THE TAX-FUNDED STATE AND ITS CRITICS

A. The Concept of the Tax-funded State

The German Constitution's focus on taxation provides the basis for the legal concept of the 'tax-funded state' (*Steuerstaat*).[15] Germany's Federal Constitutional Court formulated the concept as follows: the state must finance its activities 'predominantly', 'principally' and 'primarily' through 'taxation'.[16]

[10] BVerwGE 95, 188, 192–93; D Wilke, *Gebührenrecht und Grundgesetz* (Munich, CH Beck, 1973) 160; F Kirchhof, *Die Höhe der Gebühr* (Berlin, Duncker & Humblot, 1981) 37.

[11] The constitutional law foundation of the doctrine of equivalence is contested; in favor of the principle as a principle of constitutional law: BVerwGE 79, 90, 91; 80, 36, 39; 109, 272, 274; 115, 32, 44; more restrictive, however with similar results on the basis of the principle of proportionality: BVerfGE 50, 217, 227; 97, 332, 345; 108, 1, 18; A Schmehl, *Das Äquivalenzprinzip im Recht der Staatsfinanzierung* (Tübingen, Mohr Siebeck, 2004).

[12] BVerfGE 93, 319, 344; 108, 1, 17 (*Ausgleichsfunktion*).

[13] See Art 74(1), no 12 and Art 120 of the German Constitution.

[14] F Hase, *Versicherungsprinzip und sozialer Ausgleich* (Tübingen, Mohr Siebeck, 2000). These premiums are supplemented by state subsidies. As a result, state insurance programmes offer protection and services beyond what is actually covered by the premiums; see H Butzer, *Fremdlasten in der Sozialversicherung* (Tübingen, Mohr Siebeck, 2001).

[15] J Isensee, 'Steuerstaat als Staatsform' in R Stödter and W Thieme (eds), *Festschrift für Hans Peter Ipsen* (Tübingen, Mohr, 1977) 409 ('Staatstyp'); K Vogel, 'Der Finanz- und Steuerstaat' in J Isensee and P Kirchhof (eds), *Handbuch des Staatsrechts der Bundesrepublik Deutschland*, vol II, 3rd edn (Heidelberg, CF Müller, 2004) § 30, paras 69ff; K Vogel and C Waldhoff in K Vogel, K Graßhof and R Dolzer (eds), *Bonner Kommentar zum Grundgesetz*, Vorbemerkung zu Art 104a–115, paras 327ff; P Kirchhof, 'Nichtsteuerliche Abgaben' in J Isensee and P Kirchhof (eds), *Handbuch des Staatsrechts der Bundesrepublik Deutschland*, vol V, 3rd edn (Heidelberg, CF Müller, 2007) § 119, para 1; P Kirchhof, *Besteuerung im Verfassungsstaat* (Tübingen, Mohr Siebeck, 2000) 77–78; H Kube, *Finanzgewalt in der Kompetenzordnung* (Tübingen, Mohr Siebeck, 2004) 116; P Selmer and C Brodersen, 'Die Verfolgung ökonomischer, ökologischer und anderer öffentlicher Zwecke durch Instrumente des Abgaberechts' [2000] *Deutsches Verwaltungsblatt* 1153, 1164–65; historically the term 'Steuerstaat' goes back to an article by Joseph Schumpeter, 'Die Krise des Steuerstaates', from 1918; see J Schumpeter, *Aufsätze zur Soziologie* (Tübingen, Mohr Siebeck, 1953) 1.

[16] BVerfGE 78, 249, 266–67 ('predominantly'); BVerfGE 82, 159, 178 ('principally'); BVerfGE 93, 319, 342 ('primarily'); BVerfGE 101, 141, 147 ('from taxation').

Courts and commentators have traditionally justified the doctrine of the tax-funded state on several grounds. Firstly, the comprehensiveness of the tax provisions in Germany's Constitution (Articles 105 and following), when combined with its strict limits on debt (Article 109(3), Article 115(2)) and debt financing's unsustainable nature, appear to create a constitutional presumption in favour of taxation.[17]

Furthermore, although the German Constitution does not disfavour fees, tolls, duties and other special assessments, the purpose of such payments is not the generation of state revenue. Instead, they provide governmental agencies with measures for preventing legal regimes from conferring unintended economic advantages on some citizens.[18] In fact, it is for this reason that fees and special assessments are treated as general substantive law under Articles 70 and following of the German Constitution, instead of as tax provisions under Article 105.

Scholars further note that the tax-funded state – in contrast to an 'enterprise state' whose companies' profits provide its financing – is compatible with and in fact required by the fundamental individual rights contained in the German Constitution. Specifically, they argue that freedom of profession under Article 12, as well as Article 14's guarantee of private property, call for an economic order in which the factors of economic production remain predominantly subject to private ownership.[19] The state must, for its part, content itself with taxing the productive use of privately owned resources. This argument is often accompanied by what is commonly referred to as the 'market income theory' of taxation: since the state puts in place the infrastructure necessary for market activity (currency, routes of transportation, banking rules etc), it may tax the income private individuals generate through the use of that infrastructure as market participants.[20]

As a result, scholars assert that a tax-funded state guarantees the freedom of its citizens. Citizens are free to develop their economic activity as they desire. The state intervenes with taxation only when their economic activity leads to financial success. Upon paying his or her taxes, the citizen is again freed from the demands of the community that the state represents. Any further involvement that benefits greater society, be it in associations, clubs or through charitable donations, arises solely from the free decision of the citizen.[21]

Lastly, proponents of the tax-funded state argue that it is consistent with principles of democratic government. Specifically, taxation preserves an appropriate distance between the state and those that finance it.[22] As an individual's tax burden is calculated solely on the basis of the ability to pay, tax revenues are

[17] Isensee, 'Steuerstaat als Staatsform' (n 15) 409.

[18] P Kirchhof, 'Nichtsteuerliche Abgaben' (n 15) para 21; Kube, *Finanzgewalt in der Kompetenzordnung* (n 15) 117.

[19] P Kirchhof, 'Die Steuern' in J Isensee and P Kirchhof (eds), *Handbuch des Staatsrechts der Bundesrepublik Deutschland*, vol V, 3rd edn (Heidelberg, CF Müller, 2007) § 118, para 1; Kube (n 15) 118.

[20] P Kirchhof, *Besteuerung im Verfassungsstaat* (n 15) 80–81.

[21] Isensee (n 15) 409, 421.

[22] P Kirchhof, *Besteuerung im Verfassungsstaat* (n 15) 18; P Kirchhof, 'Die Steuern' (n 19) para 3.

centralized into a federal budget, and spending decisions are made on the basis of objective criteria (such as indigence in the social welfare system), the extent of any individual's tax contributions do not influence the decision-making of democratic government.

B. Scholarly Criticism

The tax-funded state has never been without its critics. Since the inception of the doctrine, critics have contended that arguments for a tax-funded state exaggerate the legal norms contained in the German Constitution.[23] When viewed under closer scrutiny, they argue, the constitutional provisions cited in support of the tax-funded state do not require the state to finance its activities primarily through taxation.

With regard to the German Constitution's division of taxation authority between state and federal governments, critics contend that such provisions simply authorize, but do not require, the state to impose taxation. The language in Articles 105 and following of Germany's Constitution evinces no constitutional preference for taxation as a means of funding the state.[24]

Instead, critics argue that the German Constitution authorizes federal and state governments to issue debt in addition to levying taxes, and states regularly borrow to fund their activities. Some economists even contend that the state's authority to issue debt should not be limited to responding to cyclical economic events.[25] Especially in light of the profit potential of credit-funded investments, the state should be permitted to integrate debt as a structural component into its financing.[26]

Moreover, critics are quick to point out that constitutional guarantees of freedom of profession (Article 12) and private property (Article 14) by no means prohibit the state from engaging in profitable market activity. The fact that individuals may participate in private markets and that profits from such activity are protected as property does not equate to a constitutional promise that the state will not compete in the same markets. In fact, the contrary appears to be the case. Article 15 of the German Constitution even allows the state to convert any 'means

[23] W Heun in H Dreier (ed), *Grundgesetz, Kommentar*, vol III, 2nd edn (Tübingen, Mohr Siebeck, 2008) Art 105, para 11; W Heun, 'Die Entwicklung des Steuerstaatskonzepts in theoretischer und tatsächlicher Hinsicht' in U Sacksofsky and J Wieland (eds), *Vom Steuerstaat zum Gebührenstaat* (Baden-Baden, Nomos, 2000) 10, 19; U Sacksofsky, *Umweltschutz durch nichtsteuerliche Abgaben* (Tübingen, Mohr Siebeck, 2000) 161; M Heintzen in I von Münch and P Kunig (eds), *Grundgesetz-Kommentar*, vol II, 6th edn (Munich, CH Beck, 2012) Art 105, para 2; H Siekmann in M Sachs (ed), *Grundgesetz, Kommentar*, 6th edn (Munich, CH Beck, 2011) vor Art 104a, paras 69–70; R Hendler, 'Umweltabgaben und Steuerstaatsdoktrin' [1990] 115 *Archiv des öffentlichen Rechts* 577, 595.

[24] Sacksofsky, *Umweltschutz durch nichtsteuerliche Abgaben* (n 23) 161; U Sacksofsky, 'Staatsfinanzierung durch Gebühren?' in U Sacksofsky and J Wieland (eds), *Vom Steuerstaat zum Gebührenstaat* (Baden-Baden, Nomos, 2000) 188, 199.

[25] See the account by W Höfling, *Staatsschuldenrecht* (Heidelberg, CF Müller, 1993) 159.

[26] W Patzig, 'Zur Problematik der Kreditfinanzierung staatlicher Haushalte' [1985] 38 *Die öffentliche Verwaltung* 293, 299; H Ruhe in D Hömig (ed), *Grundgesetz*, 8th edn (Baden-Baden, Nomos, 2007) Art 115, para 1.

of production' into state-owned property through a legislative act (a provision that has frequently been discussed in the context of efforts to 'save' failing banks during the 2008/2009 financial crisis). Additionally, as mentioned above, Germany maintains a long-standing constitutional tradition of publicly-owned companies at the federal, state and municipal levels.

With regard to fees and other charges and assessments levied by the state against specific individuals, critics of the concept of the tax-funded state argue that such payments could constitute a viable source of state funding. While traditional doctrine holds that the state may demand such payments only as compensation for 'specific' services, critics respond that the doctrine of equivalence (which is the basis on which fees are assessed) can be interpreted to create a broad class of 'specific' services. In essence, any discrete benefit the individual receives as a result of state activity could be considered subject to a fee. Subjecting a larger class of state activities to fees, the critics argue, would make the costs and benefits of state services more transparent. Greater transparency would in turn lead to more efficient allocations of resources between state and citizen.[27]

IV. RECENT LEGISLATIVE AND ADMINISTRATIVE DEVELOPMENTS IN THE AREA OF STATE FUNDING – FINDINGS, EVALUATION, CONCLUSION

While disputes surrounding the constitutional references to the tax-funded state are decades old, debates on the proper sources of state financing have recently taken on a new dynamic. The reason for this is that all levels of German federalism are increasingly employing forms of revenue generation beyond taxation in response to severe budgetary shortages. These new practices are challenging the concept of a tax-funded state in novel ways. Analysis of these new financing strategies, however, demonstrates their inconsistency with fundamental constitutional rights and confirms the necessity of taxation funding for Germany's future.

A. Charging Citizens for State Services

i. Facts

We are currently witnessing an unprecedented expansion of the fees and other charges the German state demands of its citizens.[28] German municipalities, which

[27] See most of the articles in Sacksofsky and Wieland, *Vom Steuerstaat zum Gebührenstaat* (n 23); from an economic point of view, H Grossekettler, *Steuerstaat versus Gebührenstaat* (Münster, Institut für Finanzwissenschaft, 1999); B Hansjürgens, *Die Sicht des Äquivalenzprinzips in der Finanzwissenschaft* (Stuttgart, Franz Steiner, 1999); B Hansjürgens, *Äquivalenzprinzip und Staatsfinanzierung* (Berlin, Duncker & Humblot, 2001).

[28] F Kirchhof, 'Vom Steuerstaat zum Abgabenstaat?' [1988] 21 *Die Verwaltung* 137; C Gramm, 'Vom Steuerstaat zum gebührenfinanzierten Dienstleistungsstaat?' [1997] 36 *Der Staat* 267; Kube (n 15) 347; P Kirchhof, 'Nichtsteuerliche Abgaben' (n 15) paras 2–3.

traditionally draw part of their financing through service fees, have begun to charge residents for services (in particular administrative actions) that were traditionally performed without charge. Charges for other municipal services performed for a price, such as garbage collection, utilities and cultural institutions, have risen significantly.

In addition, states, municipalities, and Germany's federal government have increasingly levied assessments against particular groups of citizens on the basis of that group's responsibility for specific actions or functions (*Sonderabgaben*). In some cases, these contributions are intended to influence behaviour. For example, when businesses fail to hire severely handicapped employees in the legally prescribed manner, they must pay.[29] Increasingly, however, such payments serve as pure financing streams. Examples include payments to a fund created to finance the clean-up of sewer sludge leaks[30] as well as premiums paid by banks to a rescue fund under Germany's recent Deposit Insurance Act.[31] Even state-sponsored advertising for the benefit of particular industries is sometimes financed through industry-specific assessments paid into a 'sales fund'.[32]

Of even greater interest are payments demanded within particular industries to finance regulatory agencies. For example, any company that offers financial services must pay fees that support Germany's Security and Exchange Commission equivalent, the Federal Financial Supervisory Authority[33] (Bundesanstalt für Finanzdienstleistungsaufsicht – 'BaFin'). The result of such payments is that the state's general regulatory supervisory activity is funded by those it regulates. In adopting this funding model, the German legislature attempted to model its agencies on the independent agencies of the United States, which are generally funded by market participants. However, a comparison between German and American agencies is difficult. Whereas America's independent agencies often resemble the self-regulatory body within an industry, German agencies exercise sovereign rights, often in an arrestingly invasive manner.

Recently, the German Parliament enacted a new law requiring financial services companies to pay premiums into a fund for the support and restructuring of failing banks.[34] Also, as compensation for extending the period in which the nuclear power industry may run nuclear power plants, the legislature obliged this industry to pay a set portion of its profits to the state in addition to the taxes it must already pay on the same profits.[35]

[29] BVerfGE 57, 139, 167.
[30] Accepted in BVerfGE 110, 370, 389.
[31] Accepted in BVerwGE 120, 311, 314; BVerfGE 124, 348.
[32] Criticized in BVerfGE 122, 316 (farming and food industry); BVerfGE 123, 132 (forestry).
[33] Accepted in BVerfGE 124, 235.
[34] Gesetz zur Restrukturierung und geordneten Abwicklung von Kreditinstituten, zur Errichtung eines Restrukturierungsfonds für Kreditinstitute und zur Verlängerung der Verjährungsfrist der aktienrechtlichen Organhaftung (*Restrukturierungsgesetz*) of 9.12.2010, Bundesgesetzblatt I 2010, 1900.
[35] Gesetz zur Errichtung eines Sondervermögens 'Energie- und Klimafonds' ('EKFG') of 8.12.2010, Bundesgesetzblatt I 2010, 1807; furthermore the industry is burdened by a new tax on the use of nuclear fuel rods: *Kernbrennstoffsteuergesetz* ('KernbrStG') of 8.12.2010, Bundesgesetzblatt I 2010, 1804.

Finally, proceeds from state auctions can also be counted among the payments to the state that are of increasing importance. In Germany, such auctions are quickly becoming the state's preferred method for allocating scarce resources.[36] The most prominent example occurred in 1999, when Germany auctioned six cellular telephone frequencies to telecommunications companies.[37] Proceeds from the auction totalled nearly €50 billion. In the abstract, such auctions may seem a reasonable approach by state administrators to the problem of finding the most efficient allocation of scarce resources. From the perspective of citizens, however, such proceeds evince a far more unsettling situation in that the state is willing to sell important rights to the highest bidder. In other words, another state service – providing and protecting important property rights – is available only upon payment.

ii. Evaluation

The ever-expanding practice of state agencies charging citizens fees, premiums and other contributions must satisfy constitutional requirements. A constitutional analysis of this practice demonstrates that the German Constitution continues to favour a predominantly tax-funded state.

Generally, federal and state legislatures are authorized to determine which state services constitute the 'specific' services for which fees may be demanded. However, this legislative prerogative is subject to constitutional limits, especially when such fees affect the exercise of fundamental rights by citizens.[38] A state that charges fees to maintain civil order with police and a court system, to educate children in public schools, or for the use of its pavements is (literally and legally) not a free state.[39] Moreover, such a state would fall far short of satisfying the German constitutional guarantee that the state will treat all citizens equally. Instead, federal and state governments would simply become another service provider to those 'citizens' able to afford its services.

Special assessments of particular groups must also accord with constitutional precepts.[40] Under constitutional guarantees of liberty, such assessments may only be levied in response to the voluntary conduct of the members of a group; where a group's voluntary conduct creates undesirable consequences, an assessment is justified. Thus, if the transactions of a specific industry result in financial risks to their customers, industry members may be required to contribute to a deposit

[36] P Naab, *Die Versteigerung knapper Ressourcen durch den Staat* (Baden-Baden, Nomos, 2010); M Martini, *Der Markt als Instrument hoheitlicher Verteilungslenkung* (Tübingen, Mohr Siebeck, 2008); F Wollenschläger, *Verteilungsverfahren* (Tübingen, Mohr Siebeck, 2010).

[37] BVerfGE 105, 185; R Petzel, *Das Versteigerungsverfahren nach dem Telekommunikationsgesetz* (Hamburg, Kovac, 2006).

[38] Kube (n 15) 365.

[39] P Kirchhof, 'Nichtsteuerliche Abgaben' (n 15) paras 28ff.

[40] See the decisions of the Federal Constitutional Court on 'Sonderabgaben': BVerfGE 55, 274, 304; 67, 256, 275; 82, 159, 180–81; 101, 141, 147–48; 108, 186, 217–18; 110, 370, 389; 113, 128, 149–50; 122, 316, 334–35; 123, 132, 142.

insurance fund.[41] However, if a specific business has engaged in no conduct that creates such a risk for its customers, an assessment against it violates its constitutionally guaranteed liberty interest. Where the assessment imposes a financial burden on the business for the actions of others ('black sheep' in the industry, for example), it further violates the constitutional guarantee of equality.[42] In light of these principles, the new premium charged on the entire financial services industry to establish a fund for supporting and restructuring failing banks poses severe problems.[43] The same can be said for the new fee-skimming of the nuclear power industry's profits.[44]

State auctions raise constitutional concerns not simply with regard to the exercise of fundamental rights. They also create perception problems for the rule of law. Under a constitution that requires the state to treat citizens equally and guarantee their liberty, the ability to award the highest bidder will only seldom constitute the correct criterion for the allocation of rights and resources.[45]

B. Delegating Public Tasks to Private Persons

i. Facts

Another novel form of revenue generation, especially popular in times demanding tight budgets, is uniquely difficult to identify. In recent years, the German state has increasingly attempted to reduce its spending by delegating the responsibility to perform administrative actions or services to the citizen.[46] More and more provisions of administrative law have commissioned citizens to perform public tasks. In most cases, citizens receive no compensation for performing such tasks. Since the alternative to transferring tasks to citizens would lie in raising administrative fees in order to finance the tasks, such transfers represent legislative shortcuts for covering administrative costs that financially burden the citizens.

A familiar example of such 'privatized' public duties can be seen in every German employer's duty to calculate and withhold the income taxes of its employees.[47] The obligation to pay taxes exists solely between the employee and the state. Nevertheless, the employer bears the financial burdens of administrating its

[41] BVerwGE 120, 311, 314; BVerfGE 124, 348.

[42] BVerfGE 113, 128, 145.

[43] The premium poses particular problems in light of the criteria employed in order to assess the individual risk contributions. For a constitutional law analysis, see W Schön, A Hellgardt and C Osterloh-Konrad, 'Bankenabgabe und Verfassungsrecht' [2010] 64 *Wertpapier-Mitteilungen* 2145, 2193; also M Martini, 'Zur Kasse bitte! Die Bankenabgabe als Antwort auf die Finanzkrise: Placebo, Heilmittel oder Gift?' [2010] 63 *Neue Juristische Wochenschrift* 2019.

[44] For a detailed analysis of the constitutionality, see C Waldhoff and H von Aswege, *Kernenergie als 'goldene Brücke'. Verfassungsrechtliche Probleme der Aushandlung von Laufzeitverlängerungen gegen Gewinnabschöpfungen* (Baden-Baden, Nomos, 2010).

[45] Kube (n 15) 418ff.

[46] See the overview in H Kube, 'Öffentliche Aufgaben in privater Hand: Sachverantwortung und Finanzierungslast' [2008] 41 *Die Verwaltung* 1.

[47] §§ 38 and following Einkommensteuergesetz ('EStG'; Income Tax Code).

employees' tax obligations. Similar in effect are the legal provisions that require telecommunications companies to install monitoring technology in their networks for the use of state agencies in criminal investigations and terrorism prevention.[48] In both cases, the state offers citizens no compensation for the performance of duties having a distinctly public character.

An especially controversial form of the imposition of public duties on private citizens occurs when the state intervenes in markets in order to subsidize individual market participants.[49] By distorting price formation, the state essentially enlists one contractual partner to bear the costs of the public task of subsidizing. One example is what is referred to in German legal circles as 'high-price maintenance' for green electricity. Owners of electrical grids must allow electricity produced in an environmentally sustainable manner to interconnect to their networks; in addition, they are obligated to purchase such electricity at prices significantly above market rates.[50] As a result, the expense of subsidizing green electricity is effectively transferred to the owners of electrical grids, who will eventually pass on the burden to their customers.

An inverse example with identical results can be seen in the 'low-price maintenance' in Germany's pharmaceutical industry. German law obligates pharmacists as well as pharmaceutical companies to sell medicines at reduced prices to Germany's state-run health insurance system.[51] The goal of such mandated low prices is to stabilize the costs of Germany's health care system. Nevertheless, when the law requires pharmaceutical companies to engage in such 'low-price maintenance', it effectively transfers the costs of stable health care to the pharmaceutical industry, which, of course, promptly passes such costs on to its other customers.

Lastly, the minimum wage regulations, which have begun sprouting within various branches of Germany's economy,[52] result in citizens indirectly subsidizing other citizens. Where employers are obligated to pay employees a minimum wage that is greater than market wages, the state has effectively transferred the responsibility for holding the employee above the poverty level to the employer. According to German constitutional law, the duty to provide all citizens with the minimum income needed to exist is a responsibility of the state.[53] However, a minimum wage transfers the duty of securing one citizen's existence to another citizen – again without compensation.

ii. Evaluation

As with the increase in state-levied fees, the increasing commissioning of citizens to perform public services is often of questionable constitutionality. The difficulty

[48] § 110 Telekommunikationsgesetz ('TKG').

[49] C von Stockhausen, *Gesetzliche Preisintervention zur Finanzierung öffentlicher Aufgaben* (Berlin, Duncker & Humblot, 2007).

[50] §§ 16 and following Erneuerbare-Energien-Gesetz ('EEG').

[51] §§ 130, 130a Sozialgesetzbuch V ('SGB V').

[52] An important normative basis is the *Arbeitnehmer-Entsendegesetz* ('AEntG').

[53] Art 1(1), Art 20(1) of the German Constitution.

of squaring this novel means of state financing with constitutional principles again demonstrates that the German Constitution supports a primarily tax-funded state.

To the extent that the state can show some nexus between a citizen's voluntary conduct and a public task, it can justify delegating the responsibility to perform that task as a reasonable response to harmful consequences of the citizen's conduct.[54] However, when the state transfers public tasks to citizens whose conduct stands in no relation to those tasks, it likely violates constitutional guarantees. Drafting citizens into government service without compensation substantially impairs their ability to exercise fundamental constitutional liberties – especially under a constitution that requires justification for any curtailment of personal liberty.

Against this background, German jurisprudence is in need of an open and substantive discussion as to whether, for example, the German Constitution permits the state to require employers to administer, without compensation, the tax obligations of their employees.[55] An even more pressing question relates to minimum wages. Does the German Constitution allow the state to commission employers with the task of holding their employees above the poverty level?[56] German jurisprudence must also evaluate whether the German Constitution permits the state to place the burden of subsidizing one industry on another. For example, it is not clear whether the owners of power grids should bear any responsibility for the survival of the green power industry.[57] Similarly, the reasons for charging the pharmaceutical industry with supporting the stability of Germany's system of health care remain in need of clarification.[58]

[54] Kube, 'Öffentliche Aufgaben in privater Hand' (n 46) 1; H Kube, 'Der eingriffsrechtfertigende Konnex: Zu Inhalt und Grenzen freiheitsbegleitender Verantwortung' [2010] 65 *Juristenzeitung* 265.

[55] See M Burgi, 'Finanzieller Ausgleich für Bürokratielasten: ein Verfassungsgebot!' [1999] 45 *Gewerbearchiv* 393; G Kirchhof, *Die Erfüllungspflichten des Arbeitgebers im Lohnsteuerverfahren* (Berlin, Duncker & Humblot, 2005); see also BVerfGE 22, 380, 382.

[56] With regard to Art 9(3) of the German Constitution, see H Sodan and M Zimmermann, 'Tarifvorrangige Mindestlöhne versus Koalitionsfreiheit' [2009] 54 *Neue Juristische Wochenschrift* 2001; F Bayreuther, 'Einige Anmerkungen zur Verfassungsmäßigkeit des Arbeitnehmer-Entsendegesetzes und des Mindestarbeitsbedingungengesetzes 2009' [2009] 62 *Neue Juristische Wochenschrift* 2006.

[57] von Stockhausen, *Gesetzliche Preisintervention zur Finanzierung öffentlicher Aufgaben* (n 49) 482, 753; M Altrock, *'Subventionierende' Preisregelungen. Die Förderung erneuerbarer Energieträger durch das EEG* (Munich, CH Beck, 2002). The Federal Constitutional Court has – up to now – been reluctant to deal with the problem; see BVerfG [1997] 50 *Neue Juristische Wochenschrift* 573; BVerfG [2002] 15 *Neue Zeitschrift für Verwaltungsrecht-Rechtsprechungsreport* 321.

[58] The Federal Constitutional Court considers this burden to be constitutional; BVerfGE 114, 196, 249–50; see also BVerfG [2000] 53 *Neue Juristische Wochenschrift* 1781; BVerfGE 106, 351; 106, 359; 106, 369; also U Becker, 'Arzneimittelrabatte und Verfassungsrecht: Zur Zulässigkeit der Preisabschläge nach dem Beitragssatzsicherungsgesetz' [2003] 12 *Neue Zeitschrift für Sozialrecht* 561, 564; more critical: FE Schnapp, 'Der Apothekenrabatt: Eine Sonderabgabe sui generis?' [2003] 21 *Vierteljahresschrift für Sozialrecht* 343, 357; von Stockhausen (n 49) 505–06, 782–83.

C. Concealed Borrowing

i. Facts

Germany's 'Federalism Reform' of 2009[59] subjected the state's ability to borrow to strict limitations. Since borrowing constituted a primary cause of the financial problems that gave rise to the reform, such limitations make sense. The reform largely eliminates the danger that unlimited borrowing posed to the state and its future. In doing so, the reform – to the extent that future law-makers respect its limitations – effectively forces the German state to fulfil current obligations with 'current financing', ie with financing not accompanied by servicing and a maturity date. In other words, the reform appears to favour financing through taxation.

Nevertheless, two important considerations remain. First, the borrowing restrictions of the reform do not apply to 'legally independent assets'. Thus, if the state forms a legally independent juridical person (be it a foundation, institution, limited liability company, corporation, or other similar organizational form), it may borrow money through the independent entity without regard to constitutional debt restrictions.[60] The ability to engage in unlimited borrowing through such shell organizations offers substantial potential for abuse, the dangers of which have been demonstrated on countless occasions.

Secondly, the German state has increasingly employed methods of financing that, while not categorized as 'borrowing' or 'debt', are identical in effect to the assumption of new credit. Examples include capital leases, sale-and-lease-backs and public-private partnerships. In such transactions, the state often binds itself to long-term obligations that pose risks to budgetary security almost identical to those created by credit transactions.[61]

ii. Evaluation

The danger of abusing shell corporations to circumvent the debt restrictions in Articles 109(3) and 115(2) of Germany's Constitution renders the intent of these articles all the more clear. They represent a fundamental decision to require the state to meet its current obligations primarily with current revenue streams that create no future liabilities – in other words, through taxation – in order to protect the constitutionally guaranteed freedoms of future citizens. Taking this principle seriously requires imputing the debts of legally independent entities to the state

[59] A combination of constitutional amendments as well as Acts of Parliament.

[60] H Kube in T Maunz, G Dürig and others (eds), *Grundgesetz, Kommentar* (Munich, CH Beck, 2013) Art 115, para 60.

[61] C Kaeser, *Alternative Finanzierungsmodelle der öffentlichen Hand und Kreditschranken des Art. 115 GG* (Frankfurt/Berlin/Bern/Bruxelles/New York/Oxford/Wien, P Lang, 2002); C Jahndorf, *Grundlagen der Staatsfinanzierung durch Kredite und alternative Finanzierungsformen im Finanzverfassungs- und Europarecht* (Heidelberg, CF Müller, 2003); Kube (n 60) Art 115, para 71.

where the state owns a substantial interest in the entity, where it services the debt itself, or where it guarantees repayment of the debt.[62]

The same mistrust applies to all novel forms of state financing to the extent that they demonstrate a potential for circumventing constitutional borrowing restrictions. As a general rule, any transaction whose results are substantially similar to borrowing should be presumed to be governed by the constitutional debt restrictions. An example of a transaction substantially similar to borrowing can be found wherever an agreement conveys equitable title to property to the state – for example, in capital leases. In such leases, the state's beneficial ownership allows it to treat the leased premises as its property – even against the holder of legal title – in exchange for a (usually long-term) stream of payments.[63] Such a transaction, which in substance appears identical to a loan, should be considered a constructive borrowing by the state and subjected to constitutional debt limits.[64]

D. Conclusion: The Constitutional Command to Fund State Activity Primarily through Taxation

Traditional debates between supporters and critics of the tax-funded state generally consisted of vague arguments carried on in the abstract. The above analysis of the German government's newer financing strategies, however, clearly confirms that taxation offers the only means of substantial state financing consistent with constitutional guarantees of liberty and equality. It is this specific focus on the individual's ability to exercise fundamental constitutional rights that differentiates the 'modern' from the 'traditional' debate on the tax-funded state.[65]

In a tax-funded state, individuals are free to decide whether and how they will generate income. The state provides the infrastructure necessary for income generation, then does nothing more than participate in the economic success of voluntary market participants.[66] In calculating taxes on the basis of ability to pay (or economic capacity), the state remains neutral regarding the specific income-generating activity as well as the individual it taxes. The result is a

[62] ibid para 61.

[63] cf § 39 (II) (2) Abgabenordnung (Fiscal Code).

[64] E Reimer in *Beck'scher Onlinekommentar zum Grundgesetz,* Art 115, para 16; Kube (n 60) Art 115, para 71.

[65] As the citations above show, the 'modern' debate on the tax-funded state largely consists of occasional, isolated responses to particular aspects of the modern funding practices. One reason for this may be that newer financing practices have been difficult to fit into the paradigms and terms that governed the older discussions. Another may lie in the fact that novel financing strategies often involve hidden, off-balance-sheet transactions or administrative law riders in larger bills that only a small clique of observers are likely to notice. As a result, few have registered that such actions constitute new forms of state financing. After all, novel financing strategies often 'creep' into their full form over the course of years, thereby leaving many observers with snapshots (but not a complete picture) of the state's evolving tactics. In light of the lack of attention they have received, it is especially imperative to subject these novel forms of financing to thorough constitutional analysis.

[66] P Kirchhof (n 19) para 1.

non-discriminatory levy on income consistent with constitutional rights guaranteeing liberty and equality.

Furthermore, all taxes flow into a central treasury that pays all state expenses pursuant to democratic governance. As a result, citizens can be assured that democratic process alone (not their ability to pay more than others) determines how the funds are being used.[67]

Fees, special assessments, the issuance of debt and state participation in private markets, on the contrary, cannot create financing processes that protect constitutional rights of freedom and equality. Such methods of financing must therefore be subject to strict limitations.

V. CONSTITUTIONAL PARAMETERS FOR TAXATION – SETTLED AND NON-SETTLED LAW

The constitutional guarantees of freedom and equality not only call for a tax-funded state. They also provide the constitutional parameters that the taxation regime is subject to. Some of these parameters can be found in the constitutional restraints generally applicable to all state action. Additionally, the past decades have seen a rapid increase in decisions of the Federal Constitutional Court creating and interpreting specific constitutional taxation law.[68] The following section will discuss the settled and non-settled elements of the constitutional jurisprudence relevant to taxation.

A. Taxation as 'Invasive Law'

Under German law, state action that constitutes an 'invasion' (*Eingriff*) of the liberty or property of an individual is subject to enhanced constitutional scrutiny. Such action must be conducted pursuant to sufficiently definite parliamentary regulations that have democratic legitimacy and render the invasive action legally foreseeable.[69] Since taxation constitutes a palpably clear state invasion into the liberty and especially into the property of individuals, it is subject to these stricter constitutional standards. As a result, the simplification of the incredibly complex German tax code to render its application more foreseeable – a topic of legal discussions for decades – is nothing less than a constitutional mandate.[70]

[67] ibid para 3.

[68] For a general introduction, see Kirchhof, *Besteuerung im Verfassungsstaat* (n 15); D Birk (ed), *Steuerrecht und Verfassungsrecht: Zur Rolle der Rechtsprechung bei der verfassungskonformen Gestaltung der Steuerrechtsordnung* (Aachen, Shaker, 2009).

[69] Doctrine of the *Gesetzesvorbehalt*; see J Ipsen, *Staatsrecht II*, 24th edn (Munich, Vahlen, 2013) 223.

[70] cf K Vogel, 'Der Verlust des Rechtsgedankens im Steuerrecht als Herausforderung an das Verfassungsrecht' in KH Friauf (ed), *Steuerrecht und Verfassungsrecht*, Deutsche Steuerjuristische Gesellschaft (DStJG), vol XII (Cologne, Dr. Otto Schmidt, 1989) 123ff.

Retroactive changes in taxation law – a relic of traditional tax legislation that continues today – raise the question of whether the 'invasion' that such backward-looking taxation constitutes is constitutional. Countless scholars have challenged the constitutionality of retroactive changes to tax regulations.[71] The state contends that retroactive changes that affect only the current taxable year do generally not violate the rule of law principle because an individual's tax obligation does not arise until the end of the taxable year.[72] Thus, it argues, the point for determining the foreseeability of an individual's tax burden is at the year's end, and at the year's end the retroactive tax regulations affecting the individual's burden are already in place. Such contentions are misplaced. Foreseeability is instead intended to protect individuals who – in reliance on tax regulations in existence at the time they engage in a transaction – irreversibly dispose of assets.[73] In July 2010, Germany's Federal Constitutional Court ruled on the matter.[74] It held that although retroactive changes to tax laws are not per se unconstitutional, even those affecting only the current tax year must satisfy a balancing test.

B. Types of Taxes

Taxation based on the 'ability to pay principle' requires different types of taxes that take account of the multiple indications of an individual's ability to pay.[75] German law therefore taxes different 'increases to wealth', such as individual or corporate income, gifts and inheritance. It also taxes the holding of assets, as is the case with property taxes. Finally, it taxes consumption by various taxes, such as the real estate transfer tax, the value added tax, excise taxes and the motor vehicle tax. The sum of all taxes levied upon an individual must correspond to the totality of his or her manifested ability to pay.

C. Determining the Taxable Base

Every single tax assessed against an individual must be calculated on the basis of his or her actual ability to pay.

[71] D Birk in W Hübschmann and others (eds), *Abgabenordnung/Finanzgerichtsordnung, Kommentar*, § 4 AO, para 739; KH Friauf, 'Gesetzesankündigung und rückwirkende Gesetzgebung im Steuer- und Wirtschaftsrecht' [1972] 27 *Betriebs-Berater* 669, 675–76; J Hey, *Steuerplanungssicherheit als Rechtsproblem* (Köln, Dr. Otto Schmidt, 2002) 259; J Hey in K Tipke and J Lang (eds), *Steuerrecht*, 21st edn (Köln, Dr. Otto Schmidt, 2012), § 3, para 260 and followings.

[72] § 36 (1) Einkommensteuergesetz (Income Tax Code).

[73] cf the jurisdiction of the Federal Constitutional Court on the protection of expectations surrounding the irrevocable disposition of assets in connection with 'steering taxes': BVerfGE 97, 67; 105, 17; 114, 258.

[74] BVerfGE 127, 1; 127, 31; 127, 61; see D Birk, 'Der Schutz vermögenswerter Positionen bei der Änderung von Steuergesetzen' [2011] 93 *Finanz-Rundschau* 1.

[75] For an overview, see D Birk, *Steuerrecht*, 15th edn (Heidelberg, CF Müller, 2012) 21.

The value added tax, which is calculated solely on the basis of an independently set purchase price,[76] reflects at most a mere conjecture as to the purchaser's actual ability to pay. Increasing efforts to shift the primary revenue streams of the tax system to indirect taxes – especially to the value added tax – should therefore be viewed with a critical eye.

Income taxes provide a much more precise correlation between taxation and individual ability to pay. In determining a business' taxable base, German governmental agencies apply what is known as the 'objective netting principle'. According to this principle, any expense related to earning activity that lessens the business' assets or disposable income is an allowable deduction. An expense is related to earning activity when its purpose is to preserve the business' capacity to earn. A substantial percentage of scholars argue that the 'objective netting principle' is constitutionally required under constitutional guarantees of equality and freedom.[77] However, the Federal Constitutional Court recently refused to decide whether Germany's Constitution demands such 'objective netting' in calculating a business' tax burden.[78]

In contrast, practically all courts and scholars agree that the German Constitution requires the deduction of expenses necessary to 'secure one's existence' from taxable income ('subjective netting principle'). The constitutional basis for such deductions is provided in Article 1's guarantee of human dignity, which the Federal Constitutional Court has interpreted in connection with Article 20's provision of a welfare state and Article 6's guarantee of marriage and family. In a series of cases, the Court has repeatedly required German tax laws to guarantee that families retain the minimum income required for their subsistence in German society.[79] Specifically, the Court held that the German Constitution requires that personal exemptions, child credits and deductible children's educational and care expenses must be calculated to guarantee a family's minimum subsistence. However, the extent of any deductions and credits beyond those needed to ensure subsistence lies in the discretion of the legislature.[80] Especially with regard to expenses necessary for subsistence, constitutional decisions of the last two decades have resulted in more realistic assessments that better harmonize taxation law with Germany's system of social welfare.[81] Nevertheless, some problems remain to be resolved in this context, with perhaps the most pressing need being a coherent structuring of deductions for expenses arising from long-term retirement accounts.

[76] § 10 Umsatzsteuergesetz (Value Added Tax Code).

[77] M Lehner, 'Die verfassungsrechtliche Verankerung des objektiven Nettoprinzips' [2009] 47 *Deutsches Steuerrecht* 185; see the articles from the '2. Steuerwissenschaftliches Symposium im Bundesfinanzhof: Zulässigkeit und Grenzen der Durchbrechung des objektiven Nettoprinzips im Einkommen- und Körperschaftsteuerrecht' [2009] 47 *Deutsches Steuerrecht* Supplement to no 34.

[78] BVerfGE 122, 210, 234; 123, 111, 121.

[79] BVerfGE 82, 60, 85–86; 87, 153, 169–70; 99, 246, 259; 120, 125, 154–55.

[80] See §§ 10 and following, §§ 33 and following Einkommensteuergesetz (Income Tax Code).

[81] See the articles in R Mellinghoff (ed), *Steuern im Sozialstaat*, Deutsche Steuerjuristische Gesellschaft ('DStJG'), vol XXIX (Cologne, Dr. Otto Schmidt, 2006).

D. Rates of Taxation

To determine an individual's tax burden, the applicable tax rate is applied to the individual's taxable income. Despite the attention that tax rates (in particular personal and corporate income tax rates) receive whenever tax reform is the object of public attention, the German Constitution offers little guidance as to how tax rates should be set. The German Constitution requires only that personal tax credits[82] guarantee individuals the minimum income required for subsistence. Beyond the mere guarantee of subsistence, it is entirely within the discretion of the legislature to decide how rules that determine the tax rates will assess the ability to pay of each individual in a manner consistent with Germany's social welfare system. Thus, the German Constitution is indifferent as to whether the legislature taxes income under a progressive or 'flat tax' model.

The German Constitution is not, however, indifferent to tax rate provisions that treat some types of income more favourably than others. Specifically, conflict exists regarding the tax rates applicable to capital gains, which are lower than rates applicable to (other) business or trade income.[83] Preferential treatment of capital gains is typically justified by noting that capital can easily be moved out of the reach of the German tax authorities (through legal and illegal means) whereas relocating brick-and-mortar businesses requires substantially more effort. Thus, preferential capital gains rates offer incentives to repatriate capital or to leave it within German borders, which, especially in the case of direct investments, can benefit Germany's employment rate and economy.

Under governing constitutional interpretations, however, any deviation from taxation based on ability to pay, such as preferential tax rates, must be narrowly tailored to further an important state policy objective. Therefore, the argument that preferential capital gains rates incentivize tax evaders to return to legality carries no weight. In any society governed by the rule of law, obedience of the law is demanded of every citizen, and the mere fact that a class of persons regularly breaks the law should not result in the state 'incentivizing' them not to do so. The argument that preferential capital gains rates result in job creation is also untenable. Preferential tax rates for capital gains are not a 'narrowly tailored' mechanism for increasing employment. They offer disparate treatment not only to capital in danger of being spirited to foreign markets, but also to a substantial amount of purely domestic capital with little chance of leaving Germany.

Preferential capital gains rates also raise wider constitutional concerns. The constitutional rule-of-law principle requires that all laws are 'clear' and

[82] § 32a Einkommensteuergesetz (Income Tax Code) (*Grundfreibetrag*).

[83] See the detailed analysis in C Wagner, *Steuergleichheit unter Standortvorbehalt? Verfassungsrechtliche Grenzen einer ungleichen Einkommensbesteuerung von Kapital und Arbeit* (Frankfurt/Berlin/Bern/Bruxelles/New York/Oxford/Wien, P Lang, 2010); also N Meyer-Sandberg, *Die Duale Einkommensteuer als Modell ungleicher Besteuerung von Arbeit und Kapital* (Frankfurt/Berlin/Bern/Bruxelles/New York/Oxford/Wien, P Lang, 2008).

'understandable' to those they govern – requirements that are not met by the complex provisions differentiating capital gains from business or trade income. Moreover, the German Constitution guarantees each citizen the right to freely develop his personality. Since applying preferable tax rates to some types of income influences a person's vocational choices, such tax rates must be subjected to heightened constitutional scrutiny. Given the lack of any substantial argument that would satisfy such heightened scrutiny, the constitutionality of lowered tax rates for capital gains is very questionable.

Thus, constitutional considerations clearly argue in favour of treating all income equally, for example by extending the preferential tax rate treatment offered to capital gains to all forms of income.

E. The Tax Burden

The German Constitution provides only rudimentary guidance as to the total tax burden that may be placed on an individual. Specifically, it only sets the extremes beyond which an individual may not be taxed. German constitutional jurisprudence places state spending within the purview of the legislative branch, thus permitting the legislature to institute a greater or lesser amount of state programs and to finance these programs with a greater or lesser tax burden on individuals.

Historically, a tax is not permitted if it 'strangles' the activity that provides the basis for taxation.[84] In other words, if a tax is so burdensome that it effectively bans persons from engaging in the activity giving rise to the tax, it is unconstitutional. As German law views excessively burdensome taxes as indirect restraints on economic activity, such taxes are not even classified as 'taxes' under the German tax statutes, but rather as 'regulatory prohibitions' within the purview of administrative law.

In 1995, the Federal Constitutional Court set a further limit on taxation in a case evaluating the constitutionality of Germany's tax on net worth. Article 14 of Germany's Constitution guarantees property owners the freedom to use their property as they wish, but equally requires that the use of property serve the public good. As a result, the Court concluded that Article 14 guarantees property owners, 'in most cases', a right to retain 'roughly half' of the proceeds generated by their assets.[85] Thus, any tax that demands greater than half of such proceeds limits the owner's freedom of property to an unconstitutional degree. In German legal language, the Court's holding was quickly dubbed the 'halving principle'.

In a later case, however, the Court refused to declare the 'halving principle' a general constitutional limitation applicable to all taxes. Specifically, it stated that locally assessed business taxes were constitutional even though the resulting

[84] Preußisches OVG, [1916/17] 38 *Preußisches Verwaltungsblatt* 116; BVerwGE 6, 247, 267–68; BVerfGE 16, 147, 161; 29, 327, 331; 38, 61, 81; 98, 106, 118.

[85] BVerfGE 93, 121, 138.

aggregate tax burden exceeded half of the income generated by local businesses.[86] Nevertheless, the Court's decision on the net worth tax remains a constant reminder to the political branches that 'overtaxation' violates individual constitutional rights. If money is 'minted freedom', the taking of money constitutes the deprivation of liberty. An individual's total tax burden (comprised of both direct and indirect taxes) must therefore correspond to the totality of that individual's ability to pay.

F. Legislative Discretion and 'Internal Consistency'

Despite the constitutional requirements and limits on taxation discussed above, the German legislature maintains wide discretion in determining what activities provide the basis for imposing direct or indirect tax burdens as well as the extent of the tax burden that will be imposed.[87] However, when the legislature has determined that a specific activity will serve as the basis for imposing a tax burden, newer jurisprudence requires that it embody its decision in a set of 'internally consistent' regulations.[88] This requirement of 'internal consistency' arises from the German Constitution's guarantees of equality and the rule of law, and takes on more teeth the more complex and detailed a taxation provision becomes.

For example, the Federal Constitutional Court recently applied the internal consistency requirement to declare unconstitutional a law that repealed tax deductions for commuting expenses.[89] The Court looked at the relevant area of taxation law – income tax regulations – and found that the new law left other, similar expenses 'related to earning activity' deductible, despite treating commuting expenses as non-deductible. As a result, eliminating the deductibility of commuting expenses was not 'internally consistent' with the remainder of income tax law and was therefore unconstitutional.

'Internal consistency' is a judicially-created constitutional requirement for tax regulations that is not without criticism.[90] Some authors complain it constitutionalizes – and thereby cements – what should be more flexible legislative determinations as to how the tax system should allocate the total tax burden among citizens. Others point out the difficulty of differentiating an 'internally consistent' from an 'internally inconsistent' regulation. Lastly, critics argue that 'internal consistency' places unrealistic demands on the political branches. Since legislators must almost

[86] BVerfGE 115, 97; also BFH [1999] Bundessteuerblatt II 771; [2004] 17; [2005] 398.

[87] BVerfGE 117, 1, 30.

[88] BVerfGE 84, 239, 271; 93, 121, 136; 99, 88, 95; 99, 280, 290; 101, 132, 138; 101, 151, 155; 105, 73, 126; 116, 164, 180; 117, 1, 31; 120, 1, 29; 121, 108, 119–20; 122, 210, 231; 123, 111, 120–21; 126, 268, 278; 126, 400, 417; 127, 224, 245; P Kirchhof, *Besteuerung im Verfassungsstaat* (n 15) 43.

[89] BVerfGE 122, 210.

[90] U Kischel, 'Systembindung des Gesetzgebers und Gleichheitssatz' [1999] 124 *Archiv des öffentlichen Rechts* 174; U Kischel, 'Gleichheitssatz und Steuerrecht: Gefahren eines dogmatischen Sonderweges' in R Mellinghoff and U Palm (eds), *Gleichheit im Verfassungsstaat* (Heidelberg, CF Müller, 2008) 175, 183; O Lepsius, 'Erwerbsaufwendungen im Einkommensteuerrecht' [2009] 64 *Juristenzeitung* 260.

always compromise in passing legislation, they can often only regulate changes to tax regimes in incremental steps. 'Internal consistency' requirements, however, demand that legislators either implement systemic changes to entire bodies of tax law or face constitutional challenges.

As justified as criticism of the 'internal consistency' requirement is, demanding 'internal consistency' of taxation regulations avoids the kinds of societal harms that German constitutional guarantees are intended to prevent.[91] If tax regulations are not internally consistent, they necessarily discriminate against some citizens without a basis for doing so, thus violating Germany's constitutional guarantee of equality among citizens. Thus, while an 'internal consistency' requirement may have its practical problems, its proper mooring in the German Constitution cannot be denied.

As a result, the appropriate response to critics is a reasonable and careful application of the 'internal consistency' requirement. In fact, when the Federal Constitutional Court's decisions are examined more closely, it becomes clear that the Court does not require legislators to pass sweeping systemic changes to entire bodies of law to avoid 'internal consistency' challenges. Instead, it merely requires evidence that any challenged legislation (even if passed in isolation) is part of a larger legislative action that, on the whole, would be internally consistent.[92] Unfortunately, however, tax regulations often cannot be connected to a larger, more sweeping legislative project.

G. Simplification, Typification and General Terms in Taxation Rules

Administering the tax system necessarily involves processing incredible masses of information. As a result, taxation law must create simplified and general categories and classifications that, while they may apply without objection in the great majority of cases, result in harm to some taxpayers. Such harm does not violate the German Constitution's guarantee of equality as long as the generalized categories are designed to address the most common cases and are in that sense 'reality-oriented'.[93] Additionally, the harm that generalizations cause to atypical taxpayers must stand in reasonable proportion to the administrative efficiency benefits that such generalizations create.

In fact, the tendency to create generalized tax categories has further constitutional support. German courts have interpreted the German Constitution as granting individuals the right to freely determine what personal information about themselves is disclosed to the public.[94] In that they eliminate the need to

[91] K-D Drüen, 'Anmerkung zum Gebot der steuerrechtlichen Folgerichtigkeit' [2010] 65 *Juristenzeitung* 91.

[92] BVerfGE 122, 210, 242.

[93] BVerfGE 99, 280, 290; 105, 73, 127; 117, 1, 31; 122, 210, 232–33; 123, 111, 121.

[94] First in BVerfGE 65, 1 (*informationelles Selbstbestimmungsrecht*).

collect personal information from taxpayers, generalized tax classifications help protect this right.[95]

H. Actual Equality in Allocating the Tax Burden

General and simplified taxation categories do not merely enable the state to process the masses of information involved in tax administration. They also ensure that the total tax burden is allocated in a manner consistent with constitutional guarantees of equality before the law.

German constitutional law requires that all laws treat all citizens equally in the manner they are actually applied. If the particular application of a law results in unequal treatment (for example, if a lack of personnel requires arbitrarily selecting only a subset of suspicious tax returns for auditing), the underlying tax law is unconstitutional as applied. Nevertheless, the law itself suffers from no constitutional deficiencies; the responsibility for corrective action lies with the agency applying the law, not with the legislature.

If, however, a prima facie reading of a law shows that its provisions are structured in a manner that will tend to result in unequal treatment (often the case where procedural protocols do not accompany substantive guarantees), the legislation itself is unconstitutional. Based on such reasoning, the Federal Constitutional Court has already declared two pieces of taxation legislation unconstitutional. Firstly, it held that legislation taxing interest was unconstitutional because it did not provide adequate mechanisms for addressing all cases that fell under its provisions.[96] Also, the court declared legislation taxing profits made by 'speculation' as unconstitutional, again pointing to the structure of the law that tends to result in unequal treatment.[97]

I. 'Steering Taxes'

Despite the prohibition of discriminatory taxation, one subgroup of taxes is designed to discriminate intentionally against specific groups of people. The main aim of these taxes is not to raise revenue, but rather to influence the behaviour of the persons taxed by increasing or decreasing the costs of an activity. As such, they are imposed not on the basis of the taxpayer's ability to pay, but rather as incentives to the taxpayer to engage in or refrain from the activity giving rise to the tax. German jurisprudence refers to such taxes as *Lenkungsteuern*, literally translated as 'steering taxes', a term that does justice to the purpose of the taxes to modify behaviour.[98]

[95] BVerfGE 120, 351, 359; P Kirchhof, *Besteuerung im Verfassungsstaat* (n 15) 68–69.

[96] BVerfGE 84, 239.

[97] BVerfGE 110, 94.

[98] American theory often refers to such taxes as 'regulatory taxes' because they are commonly employed (and tend to generate more controversy) as regulatory tools. This chapter will use the German term 'steering taxes' because it more accurately describes the broad range of taxes, many of which are imposed outside of industry regulation, whose ostensible purpose is to influence citizens' behaviour.

In some cases, such 'steering taxes' can lead taxpayers to economically sensible, efficient decision-making. Their dangers, however, are manifold.[99] Steering taxes that burden the taxpayer beyond his or her ability to pay act as a hidden command regarding certain behaviours – a command that richer citizens can afford to disobey, but which poorer citizens are forced to accept. Tax credits (for example, for the manufacturing industry, intended to ease the economic burdens of 'energy-intensive' fabricating processes and thus encourage local production) result in the equivalent of state expenditures, the exact extent of which no one knows.

More importantly, steering taxes often result in policy confusion. If the goal of taxation is revenue generation, the main goal of a steering tax is the opposite. The better a tax actually 'steers' citizens' behaviour, the less revenue it generates. Yet it is often the 'unsuccessful' (and therefore lucrative) steering taxes that the government chooses to retain perpetually in the ostensible effort to influence citizens' behaviour. Generating revenue under the guise of preventing socially harmful behaviour damages the state's credibility. Germany's tax on energy provides a paradigmatic example. Although described as a tax to steer citizens away from environmentally damaging energy consumption habits, energy tax revenue was – and still is – used to finance Germany's various social welfare programs.[100] In other words, an important state interest often lies in the steering tax not steering citizens' consumption habits.

VI. THE TAX-FUNDED STATE EMBEDDED IN THE EUROPEAN UNION

In addition to the limits that the German Constitution places on the tax-funded state, German tax law is subject to the ever-growing demands of European Union law. While the European Union has no power to levy taxes, law-making instances within the European Union are steadily edging towards unifying the Member States' law of taxation.[101] The European Union primarily influences the tax law of Member States through one of two means. On the one hand, it engages in what is referred to as 'positive integration', which it accomplishes through regulations and directives that ensure that certain principles of substantive tax law are

[99] P Selmer, *Steuerinterventionismus und Verfassungsrecht* (Frankfurt/M, Athenäum, 1972); P Kirchhof, *Besteuerung im Verfassungsstaat* (n 15) 70; Kube, *Finanzgewalt in der Kompetenzordnung* (n 15) 216; R Wernsmann, *Verhaltenslenkung in einem rationalen Steuersystem* (Tübingen, Mohr Siebeck, 2005).

[100] The link is not legally binding.

[101] For an overview, see D Williams, *EC Tax Law* (New York, Longman, 2001); P Farmer and R Lyal, *EC Tax Law* (Oxford, Clarendon Press, 2003); B Terra and P Wattel, *European Tax Law*, 4th edn (The Hague, Kluwer, 2005); L Gormley, *EU Taxation Law* (Oxford, OUP, 2005); in German: D Birk (ed), *Handbuch des Europäischen Steuer- und Abgabenrechts* (Herne/Berlin, Neue Wirtschaftsbriefe, 1995); D Kellersmann and C Treisch, *Europäische Unternehmensbesteuerung* (Wiesbaden, Gabler, 2002); H Weber-Grellet, *Europäisches Steuerrecht* (Munich, CH Beck, 2005); J Sedemund, *Europäisches Ertragsteuerrecht* (Baden-Baden, Nomos, 2008); H Rehm and J Nagler, *Europäisches Steuerrecht* (Wiesbaden, Springer Gabler, 2013).

harmonized throughout the Member States. On the other hand, the decisions of the European Court of Justice often result in 'negative integration'. By issuing judgments regarding fundamental freedoms under the Treaty on the Functioning of the European Union, Member States uniformly know the kinds of provisions their tax systems may not include.

A. Harmonizing the Tax Law of Member States

A series of European Union directives has determined the manner in which European Union Member States may indirectly tax their citizens through value added taxes and other consumption taxes.[102] Thus, Member States are left with little discretion in drafting appropriate implementing legislation. For example, in implementing the value added tax directives, Member States are essentially limited to setting the rate of the tax and to defining when relief from the tax is available.

In contrast, European Union directives have left Member States' rights to directly tax their citizens mostly untouched. Although several isolated directives ensure that direct taxes on businesses do not injure entrepreneurial liberty within the European market,[103] the great body of direct taxation legislation has been left to the competence of Member States.

B. Decisions of the European Court of Justice

While the European Union law-making instances have generally not regulated the direct taxation measures of Member States, the European Court of Justice has issued numerous decisions with far-reaching effects on direct taxation regimes throughout the European Union. The European Court of Justice has applied the fundamental freedoms contained in the Treaty on the Functioning of the European Union[104] to strike down numerous Member States regulations' in the area of direct tax law as inconsistent with EU standards.[105]

[102] For an overview, see the website of the European Union http://europa.eu/legislation_summaries/taxation/index_en.htm. The most important directive in this area is the Council Directive 2006/112/EC of 28 November 2006 on the common system of value added tax, [2006] OJ L347/1.

[103] For an overview, see the website of the European Union http://europa.eu/legislation_summaries/taxation/index_en.htm. Here the most important directives are: Council Directive 90/435/EEC of 23 July 1990 on the common system of taxation applicable in the case of parent companies and subsidiaries of different Member States, [1990] OJ L 225/6; Council Directive 90/434/EEC of 23 July 1990 on the common system of taxation applicable to mergers, divisions, transfers of assets and exchanges of shares concerning companies of different Member States, [1990] OJ L 225/1; Council Directive 2003/49/EC of 3 June 2003 on a common system of taxation applicable to interest and royalty payments made between associated companies of different Member States, [2003] OJ L 157/49; Council Directive 2003/48/EC of 3 June 2003 on taxation of savings income in the form of interest payments, [2003] OJ L 157/38.

[104] Fundamental freedoms: Art 34, 45, 49, 56, 63 TFEU; see also: prohibition on state aid, Art 107 TFEU.

[105] For an overview, see Weber-Grellet, *Europäisches Steuerrecht* (n 101); Sedemund, *Europäisches Ertragsteuerrecht* (n 101); also MJ Graetz and AC Warren, 'Income Tax Discrimination and the Political

The European Court of Justice's approach involves a paradigm which is new to international tax law. Traditionally, the law of international taxation assumed that each state in which a business operates rightfully maintains an independent tax regime. As a result, internationally active business persons must assume that they would face a series of independently calculated obligations arising from different nations' direct taxation regimes. The possible burden of double taxation is then mitigated through bilateral double taxation conventions or unilateral measures of the tax-levying states.[106] In its decisions, however, the European Court of Justice has assumed a different perspective. On the grounds of the fundamental freedoms, the European Court of Justice evaluates the legality of a direct tax from the perspective of an internationally active business person who wishes to be treated no differently from purely domestic businesses. From this perspective, the European Court of Justice often discovers restrictions on or discrimination against internationally active business persons within Member States' direct taxation regimes. It then declares such restrictions or discrimination contrary to European Union law, thus indirectly regulating the direct taxation regimes of all Member States.

C. The Future of European Taxation Law

European Union law has yet to achieve the proper balance between the Member States' interest in their direct taxation regimes and the European Union's interest in guaranteeing a European market free from discrimination against foreign competitors. Finding this balance will be among the most important tasks for scholars and practitioners of taxation law in the coming years.

As an alternative to balancing Member States' and European Union interests gradually, some have suggested creating uniform European regulations for determining the assessment basis of direct company taxation[107] and, going further, for the apportionment of tax returns between the Member States.[108] The European Commission has even developed the idea of creating a new, independent European Union tax to generate returns that are directly allocated to the budget of the European Union. The downfall of both plans lies in the political process. Although the political will of the Member States to support such plans may materialize in the future, it does not exist at present.

What remains beyond question is that taxation provides the only means of financing public expenses that is consistent with fundamental guarantees of indi-

and Economic Integration of Europe' [2006] 115 *Yale Law Journal* 1186; MJ Graetz and AC Warren, 'Dividend Taxation in Europe: When the ECJ Makes Tax Policy' [2007] 44 *Common Market Law Review* 1577.

[106] See Art 23 of the OECD-Model Tax Convention on Income and Capital.

[107] See the work of the Common Consolidated Corporate Tax Base Working Group (CCCTB Working Group); http://ec.europa.eu/taxation_customs/taxation/company_tax/common_tax_base/index_en.htm.

[108] It is interesting to compare developments in Europe with current practice in the US in this regard (relationship between the federal government and the States).

vidual liberty and equality, irrespective of whether the basis is the Member State's tax law embedded in European Union law or a genuine European Union tax law.

CASES

BVerfGE 55, 274 – *Berufsausbildungsabgabe* (1980)
BVerfGE 82, 60 – *Steuerfreies Existenzminimum* (1990)
BVerfGE 93, 121 – *Einheitswerte* (1995)
BVerfGE 93, 319 – *Wasserpfennig* (1995)
BVerfGE 98, 106 – *Kommunale Verpackungsteuer* (1998)
BVerfGE 99, 216 – *Familienleistungsausgleich* (1998)
BVerfGE 105, 185 – *UMTS-Erlöse* (2002)
BVerfGE 122, 210 – *Entfernungspauschale* (2008)
BVerfGE 122, 316 – *Abgabe an den Absatzfonds der Land- und Ernährungswirtschaft* (2009)
BVerfGE 124, 235 – *Finanzierung der Bundesanstalt für Finanzdienstleistungsaufsicht* (2009)
BVerfGE 127, 1 – *Rückwirkung im Steuerrecht* (2010)

SELECTED LITERATURE

Birk D (ed), *Steuerrecht und Verfassungsrecht: Zur Rolle der Rechtsprechung bei der verfassungskonformen Gestaltung der Steuerrechtsordnung* (Aachen, Shaker, 2009)

Gramm C, 'Vom Steuerstaat zum gebührenfinanzierten Dienstleistungsstaat?' [1997] 36 *Der Staat* 267

Hendler R, 'Umweltabgaben und Steuerstaatsdoktrin' [1990] 115 *Archiv des öffentlichen Rechts* 577

Isensee J, 'Steuerstaat als Staatsform' in R Stödter and W Thieme (eds), *Festschrift für Hans Peter Ipsen* (Tübingen, Mohr, 1977) 409

Kirchhof F, 'Vom Steuerstaat zum Abgabenstaat?' [1988] 21 *Die Verwaltung* 137

Kirchhof P, *Besteuerung im Verfassungsstaat* (Tübingen, Mohr Siebeck, 2000)

——'Die Steuern' in J Isensee and P Kirchhof (eds), *Handbuch des Staatsrechts der Bundesrepublik Deutschland*, vol V, 3rd edn (Heidelberg, CF Müller, 2007) § 118

Kube H, *Finanzgewalt in der Kompetenzordnung* (Tübingen, Mohr Siebeck, 2004)

Sacksofsky U and Wieland J (eds), *Vom Steuerstaat zum Gebührenstaat* (Baden-Baden, Nomos, 2000)

Schmehl A, *Das Äquivalenzprinzip im Recht der Staatsfinanzierung* (Tübingen, Mohr Siebeck, 2004)

Vogel K, 'Der Verlust des Rechtsgedankens im Steuerrecht als Herausforderung an das Verfassungsrecht' in KH Friauf (ed), *Steuerrecht und Verfassungsrecht*, Deutsche Steuerjuristische Gesellschaft, vol XII (Cologne, Dr. Otto Schmidt, 1989) 123

——'Der Finanz- und Steuerstaat' in J Isensee and P Kirchhof (eds), *Handbuch des Staatsrechts der Bundesrepublik Deutschland*, vol II, 3rd edn (Heidelberg, CF Müller, 2004) § 30

Waldhoff C, 'Grundzüge des Finanzrechts des Grundgesetzes' in J Isensee and P Kirchhof (eds), *Handbuch des Staatsrechts der Bundesrepublik Deutschland*, vol V, 3rd edn (Heidelberg, CF Müller, 2007) § 116

9

Relationship between State and Church – Public Church Law versus Religious Constitutional Law

STEFAN MÜCKL

I. PROBLEM

STAATSKIRCHENRECHT, OR 'public church law', is the traditional term used to describe the legal relationship between state and church within Germany and many other European legal systems.[1] The term has

[1] In Italy and Spain the terms *diritto ecclesiastico* and *derecho eclesiástico del Estado* respectively are universally accepted. The French legal system summarizes the state-church-relationship in the term *droit (civil) ecclésiastique*, although on the whole, the term *droit des cultes* prevails. In England, the term *ecclesiastical law* is commonly used, although the line between ecclesiastical law and the internal law of the Church of England is often blurred.

been generally understood in a broad, comprehensive sense to include the state's relationship to all churches and religious bodies.

This traditional understanding of public church law still prevails within scholarly discourse, as well as in judicial and political practice, though it has not remained unchallenged. The points of criticism expressed over the past 30 years essentially derive from three fundamental arguments. The first is that there can be no public church law because the German Constitution (*Grundgesetz* – 'GG') forbids the existence of a national or state church (Article 140 GG in conjunction with Article 137(1) of the Weimar Constitution (*Weimarer Reichsverfassung* – 'WRV')). Secondly, the term, which refers equally to state and church, implies an antiquated understanding of the subject, whereby church and state stand on a par with one another, which in turn implies that the practical consequences can be seen as being outside the competence of the Constitution. Lastly, the term is unilaterally tailored to Christian religious bodies, thereby insufficiently including other religious bodies and, in consequence, discriminating against them.[2]

The suggested alternatives for a term to summarize the subject matter are presented below (section II). Following this, the content of the corresponding terms will be highlighted (section III). These different approaches will then be illustrated with the help of various constitutional references to the subject (section IV). There is in particular, considerable disagreement as to whether and to what extent Muslim religious bodies can participate in the constitutional guarantees given in this area (section V). This will lead to the broader question of the legal significance of the subject matter within the Constitution (VI).

II. ALTERNATIVE TERMINOLOGY

The criticism of the traditional terminology of 'public church law' has generated a number of suggested alternatives.[3] The term *Religionsrecht* – 'religious law' – is the oldest among these suggestions; however, the term *Religionsverfassungsrecht* – 'religious constitutional law' – is not only the one with the most followers but, more importantly, contains what is at least to some extent a different material concept of the subject matter.

[2] A compendium of concerns can be found in M Morlok, *Die korporative Religionsfreiheit und das Selbstbestimmungsrecht nach Art. 140 GG/Art. 137 Abs. 3 WRV einschließlich ihrer Schranken* in HM Heinig and C Walter (eds), *Staatskirchenrecht oder Religionsverfassungsrecht?* (Tübingen, Mohr Siebeck, 2007) 185, 187–88.

[3] For a detailed study of the history of the terminology, see A Hollerbach, *Staatskirchenrecht oder Religionsrecht? Begriffs- und problemgeschichtliche Notizen* in W Aymans and KT Geringer (eds), *Festschrift für Heribert Schmitz zum 65. Geburtstag* (Regensburg, Pustet, 1994) 869; A Hense, *Staatskirchenrecht oder Religionsverfassungsrecht: mehr als ein Streit um Begriffe?* in A Haratsch and others (eds), *Religion und Weltanschauung im säkularen Staat* (Stuttgart, Boorberg, 2001) 9.

A. Religious Law

Paul Mikat introduced the term 'religious law' into scholarly discourse in the early 1970s.[4] It was his aim to include not only public church law in a narrow sense, but also the entirety of statutory provisions concerning religious interests.[5] This objective itself proves that Mikat did not want to create an antithesis to the term 'public church law', as he has often pointed out. In so far as this did in fact happen, the cause must be sought in the work of other authors, who cite Mikat without adopting his approach with regard to the content of the term.

Basically, the term 'religious law', as Mikat intended it, complements the term 'public church law' rather than replacing it. Probably as result of its negative historical connotations relating to unconstitutional political contexts,[6] acceptance of the term has remained limited.[7]

B. Religious Constitutional Law

The term *Religionsverfassungsrecht*, or 'religious constitutional law', as coined by Peter Häberle, on the other hand, has grown to have considerable influence.[8] Over the last 10 years it has enjoyed increasing use in academic literature, albeit with widely diverging orientation, as far as content is concerned.[9] As a result of the variances in content, it finds itself in a more conflicting relationship to the term 'public church law' than the term 'religious law' does.

Häberle's primary aim was simply to replace a term which was, in his opinion, no longer appropriate, while other authors combine the renaming with an at least partial realignment or accentuation of the content. This explains why the more distinguished advocates of this term belong to the younger generation of scholars, who have discussed the subject at great length and often use it as the topic of their dissertations.[10]

[4] P Mikat, *Zur rechtlichen Bedeutung religiöser Interessen* (Düsseldorf, Rheinisch-Bergische Druckerei- und Verlagsgesellschaft, 1973).

[5] ibid 65.

[6] As detailed in Hollerbach, *Staatskirchenrecht oder Religionsrecht?* (n 3), 869, 875–76; see also J Winter, *Die Wissenschaft vom Staatskirchenrecht im Dritten Reich* (Frankfurt et al, Lang, 1979).

[7] CD Classen, *Religionsrecht* (Tübingen, Mohr Siebeck, 2006)

[8] P Häberle, '"Staatskirchenrecht" als Religionsrecht der verfaßten Gesellschaft' [1976] *Die Öffentliche Verwaltung* 73, 79–80.

[9] See section III.

[10] See eg C Walter, *Religionsverfassungsrecht in vergleichender und internationaler Perspektive* (Tübingen, Mohr Siebeck, 2006); HM Heinig, *Öffentlich-rechtliche Religionsgesellschaften* (Berlin, Duncker & Humblot, 2003); also CD Classen, *Religionsfreiheit und Staatskirchenrecht in der Grundrechtsordnung* (Tübingen, Mohr Siebeck, 2003).

C. Others

As a result of fundamentally diverging ideas concerning the applicable constitutional norms, a small number of authors have also developed alternative terminologies, mostly corresponding to political positions consistently critical of religion as such. Among these are terms such as *Bekenntnisverfassungsrecht*[11] ('law of denominations') or *Religions- und Weltanschauungsrecht*[12] ('religious and ideological law'). These terms have not, however, been subject to substantial endorsement, but remain within a limited circle of users.

III. CONCEPT REGARDING CONTENT

In the following, focus will be placed on the two most influential and prominent concepts, *Staatskirchenrecht* and *Religionsverfassungsrecht*. In the first place, their main conclusions and assertions will be presented in a general manner. By doing so, it will become evident that the matter does not revolve merely around a terminological debate, but that behind these terms stand specific ideologies concerning the relationship between church and state.[13]

A. *Staatskirchenrecht*

The traditional term *Staatskirchenrecht* – 'public church law' –, introduced in the nineteenth century, is based on the idea that the subject defines the legal relationship between the state (*Staat*) and the church (*Kirche*).[14] The set phrase 'institutional law' (*institutionelles Recht*) is meant to highlight the fact that legal guarantees in this area must be seen as independent of, and sometimes even more far-reaching than, the constitutional system of guarantees (specifically that of freedom of organized religion).

There can be no doubt that the provisions governing the complex relationship between state and church do indeed contain a constitutional element. Yet this constitutional element should not be viewed as standing independently of the

[11] L Renck, 'Zum Stand des Bekenntnisverfassungsrechts in der Bundesrepublik' [1999] 45 *Bayerische Verwaltungsblätter* 70.

[12] G Czermak, *Religions- und Weltanschauungsrecht* (Berlin, Springer, 2008).

[13] See hereto the convention notes cited in Heinig and Walter, *Staatskirchenrecht oder Religionsverfassungsrecht?* (n 2) (publication of lectures held in November 2005, regarding the meeting of the various viewpoints). For a comprehensive assessment: M Heckel, 'Zur Zukunftsfähigkeit des deutschen "Staatskirchenrechts" oder "Religionsverfassungsrechts"' (2009) 134 *Archiv des öffentlichen Rechts* 309; for a topical legal and political survey: C Waldhoff, *Neue Religionskonflikte und staatliche Neutralität – Erfordern weltanschauliche und religiöse Entwicklungen Antworten des Staates? Gutachten D für den 68. Deutschen Juristentag* (Munich, CH Beck, 2010).

[14] As well as other religious and (owing to the equation set forth in Art 140 GG in conjunction with Art 137(7) WRV) ideological communities respectively.

institutional aspect; the two are closely linked.[15] Public church law is grounded in the constitutional right to freedom of religion. At the same time, the relationship between the state and the various churches also influences the content of this constitutional guarantee.[16] In addition, the institutional aspects are meant, at least in part, to facilitate the realization of freedom of religion. This institutional aspect of public church law reflects the need to differentiate between the constitutional aspect, on the one hand, and the institutional, on the other; however this *differentiation* does not necessarily correspond to a *separation* of the two. The reason lies in the fact that these aspects emerged from different sources. Constitutional rights are the expression of a general notion of human rights that are ubiquitous and therefore must be applied to *all* religions. In contrast, public church law is concerned with the specific religious, historical and cultural factors of a given state that shape it and make it different from others;[17] as such, it is indigenous law.[18]

In addition to these fundamental considerations, there is the precise interpretation of prevailing constitutional law: as such, the institutional aspect suggests that the provisions which define the relationship between the state and churches greatly surpass that to which the churches are entitled under constitutional law. Rights such as the right of self-determination of churches (Article 140 GG in conjunction with Article 137(3) WRV),[19] their status as public-law corporations (Article 140 GG in conjunction with Article 137(5) WRV) or the right of taxation (Article 140 GG in conjunction with Article 137(6) WRV), as well as the content of concordats and church agreements, are not products of constitutional guarantees.

B. *Religionsverfassungsrecht*

To begin with, it must be made clear that the term *Religionsverfassungsrecht* – 'religious constitutional law' – is not understood by all authors to mean the same thing. Those who use the expression include, on the one hand, a movement of legal policy, which aims towards an amendment of the current provisions; and on the other, legal scholarship, which is based on current provisions although it aims to develop and modify these.

[15] Summarized in S Mückl, 'Grundlagen des Staatskirchenrechts' in J Isensee and P Kirchhof (eds), *Handbuch des Staatsrechts der Bundesrepublik Deutschland*, vol VII, 3rd edn (Heidelberg, CF Müller, 2009) § 159, para 2.

[16] More specifically, regarding these interdependeces: S Mückl, *Religions- und Weltanschauungsfreiheit im Europarecht* (Heidelberg, Universitätsverlag Winter, 2002) 32.

[17] For a detailed study, see A Uhle, *Freiheitlicher Verfassungsstaat und kulturelle Identität* (Tübingen, Mohr Siebeck, 2004) 269, 458, 484.

[18] J Isensee, *Die Zukunftsfähigkeit des deutschen Staatskirchenrechts* in J Isensee, W Rees and W Rüfner (eds), *Festschrift für Joseph Listl zum 70. Geburtstag* (Berlin, Duncker & Humblot, 1999) 67, 72.

[19] Dealt with exhaustively in B Grzeszick, 'Staatlicher Rechtsschutz und kirchliches Selbstbestimmungsrecht' (2004) 168 *Archiv des öffentlichen Rechts* 168, 195. Previously, W Hassemer and D Hömig, 'Die Rechtsprechung des Bundesverfassungsgerichts im Bereich der Bekenntnisfreiheit' [1999] *Europäische Grundrechte-Zeitschrift* 525, 531 had emphasized that this right bears protection beyond that of freedom of organized religion (Art 140 GG in conjunction with Art 137(3) WRV, SM) From the cited decisions: BVerfGE 53, 366, 401; 57, 220, 244; 66, 1, 20.

i. Legal Policy: Amendment of Current Provisions

The group of academics who view the term 'religious constitutional law' as code for a desired legal policy ideal is small but highly active. At the forefront of this movement are Ludwig Renck and Gerhard Czermak,[20] both retired administrative court judges from Bavaria, who are continuing the path laid down by the Attorney Erwin Fischer of Ulm in the 1960s. In his *Trennung von Staat und Kirche* ('Division of Church and State') of 1964, he argued that by incorporating Article 137(1) WRV into the Constitution, the founders did not achieve a true separation of church and state; instead they created a wealth of mechanisms which uphold the cooperation between church and state and must therefore be viewed as unconstitutional elements within the Constitution itself.[21] This thesis is still argued by his followers today.

Renck and Czermak began their campaign with rhetoric against the use of the term 'public church law'[22] and later replaced it with the term 'religious constitutional law' as it gained a broader following from the late 1990s. As will be shown in the following, the term was merely borrowed by Renck and Czermak, as their concept differed greatly from that of its creators.[23] Even their basic principle is an example of begging the question.[24] It goes on to set up the straw horse of a supposedly prevailing opinion, apparently unaware that the notions against which it is aimed have long since ceased to be argued.[25] This is achieved by using a notably introverted vein of argumentation: both Renck and (to a lesser degree) Czermak

[20] G Czermak, 'Religionsverfassungsrecht im Wandel' [2000] 19 *Neue Zeitschrift für Verwaltungsrecht* 896; G Czermak, 'Das System der Religionsverfassung des Grundgesetzes' [2000] 33 *Kritische Justiz* 229; G Czermak, 'Das Religionsverfassungsrecht im Spiegel der Tatsachen' [2001] 34 *Zeitschrift für Rechtspolitik* 565.

[21] G Schmidt-Eichstaedt, *Kirchen als Körperschaften des öffentlichen Rechts?* (Cologne, Heymanns, 1975) 107; M Kleine, *Institutionalisierte Verfassungswidrigkeiten im Verhältnis von Staat und Kirchen unter dem Grundgesetz* (Baden-Baden, Nomos, 1993) 212.

[22] While L Renck, 'Die Trennung von Staat und Kirche' [1988] 34 *Bayerische Verwaltungsblätter* 225, 230 postulated a 'republican Staatskirchenrecht', Czermak polemicized against 'the so-called Staatskirchenrecht'. The expression was first used in: *Bewegung ins Staatskirchenrecht!* [1990] 34 *Zeitschrift für Rechtspolitik* 475–76; later: *Staat und Weltanschauung: Eine Auswahlbiographie. Mit einer Abhandlung zu Entwicklung und Gegenwartslage des sogenannten Staatskirchenrechts* (Aschaffenburg, Alibri, 1994).

[23] Hans Michael Heinig references this in: *Kritik und Selbstkritik* in Heinig and Walter (n 2) 357, 360.

[24] The premise of these authors is in itself incorrect: the Constitution does not lay down 'the' commandment of separation of church and state. There is no such ubiquitous separation principle within the bounds of constitutional law (which can be seen by perusing the opposing systems of separation to be found in France and the United States). Rather, the Constitution contains *a* (but not *the*) principle of separation of church and state. Wholly inaccurate is the presumption that one solitary provision (that of separation of church and state) be classified as the 'norm', thereby superseding any number of other provisions expressly stipulating the cooperation of the church and state.

[25] For an extremely clear statement of the case, see M Germann, *Die Staatskirchenverträge der neuen Bundesländer* in S Mückl (ed), *Das Recht der Staatskirchenverträge* (Berlin, Duncker & Humblot, 2007) 91, 104 vis-à-vis Renck: 'Those who are shooting from this corner, are most likely still lying in the trenches of the battle against the theoretical excesses of the coordination doctrine in the time up to the early 1960s . . . They overlook, however, the fact that these trenches are no longer where the battle is taking place'.

argue their positions in a profusion of mostly identical papers, none of which respond to the various criticisms and objections made by others.

Within politics, these groups may have had a certain impact.[26] Within academic discourse, however, they must be viewed as largely irrelevant. In light of this, their ideas can be discounted in the following accounts.

ii. Legal Scholarship: Development of Current Law

Since the latter part of the 1990s, various authors have started to use the terminology proposed by Peter Häberle, but have imbued it with a specific understanding of the underlying subject. In stark contrast to the traditional institutional understanding of the relationship between church and state, they aimed to 'reconstruct' the term in order to provide it with a meaning closer to the Constitution.[27] As one of the protagonists of this movement stated, 'public church law, as it was formerly marked by metaphors of the religious institutions, can no longer escape a redefining in terms of constitutional basic rights'.[28] This pinpoints the central theme in the discussion regarding terminology: a closer tie to basic constitutional rights. The provisions that define the relationship between church and state, almost all of them to be found in parts of the Constitution distinct from guarantees of fundamental rights, are to be understood as emanating from the right to religious freedom. It must be the aim of religious constitutional law to provide a constitutional paradigm that contains both a boundary to, and also an overlap with, public church law.[29]

The central theme of this approach is the status of the church as a public law corporation (Article 140 GG in conjunction with Article 137(5) WRV).[30] In a decision of December 2000 regarding Jehovah's Witnesses, the Federal Constitutional Court was inspired by the idea of a closer relationship to the basic rights guaranteed in the Constitution: 'In the context of the Constitution', the Court argued that the corporation status is 'a means to realize religious freedom', which is meant to 'encourage the autonomy and independence of the various religious communities'.[31] Meanwhile, attempts were made to identify a constitutional foundation for further

[26] In Germany, various organizations exist that aim at achieving these political goals (Humanistische Union, Internationaler Bund der Konfessionslosen und Atheisten). In some cases the authors cited can be associated with these organizations. Particularly in Berlin, these groups have become influential. For an overview of the religious policy there, see HM Heinig, 'Ordnung der Freiheit – das Staatskirchenrecht vor neuen Herausforderungen' (2008) 53 *Zeitschrift für evangelisches Kirchenrecht* 235, 240. In autumn 2010, an organization was formed as a substructure of the Social Democratic Party (SPD), with the aim of integrating the question into the political process.

[27] Specifically those mentioned in n 10.

[28] Heinig, *Öffentlich-rechtliche Religionsgesellschaften* (n 10) 497.

[29] HM Heinig, 'Art. 13 EGV und die korporative Religionsfreiheit nach dem Grundgesetz' in Haratsch and others, *Religion und Weltanschauung im säkularen Staat* (n 3) 215, 222, fn 28.

[30] Apart from Heinig (n 10), see also S Magen, *Körperschaftsstatus und Religionsfreiheit: Zur Bedeutung des Art. 137 Art. 5 WRV im Kontext des Grundgesetzes* (Tübingen, Mohr Siebeck, 2004).

[31] BVerfGE 102, 370, 389. It may be useful to note the combination (not unusal in Germany) of the academic and the practical (not necessarily at the same time): Magen (see n 30), at the time of the decision in the case of Jehovah's Witnesses, was assistant to the reporting judge, Winfried Hassemer.

church-related phenomena, such as church tax[32] and the safeguarding of church property.[33]

The advocates of this idea view it as their intention, in terms of constitutional policy, to strengthen public church law.[34] They claim that it is not their goal to advance 'razing the bastions',[35] but instead to change the legal circumstances surrounding the subject, in order to strengthen the democratic legitimatization of the relationship between church and state, thereby securing this relationship in the face of challenges.[36] These authors have, in fact, argued against such ideas and expectations in the past.[37]

IV. INDIVIDUAL LEGAL INSTITUTIONS IN THE SCOPE OF BOTH INTERPRETATIONAL METHODS

A. Status as a Public Corporation

One aspect upon which the two interpretational methods can be compared is the status of churches as public corporations, as set down in Article 140 GG in conjunction with Article 137(5) WRV. According to this provision, this legal status is maintained for those religious bodies which possessed it prior to 1919.[38] All others are entitled to be granted the status, providing their organization and strength (as regards membership) provide a guarantee of the permanence of their existence.

Until early in the 1990s, the status of public corporations did not pose a cause for conflict. Then, the request made by the Jehovah's Witnesses to acquire the same status led to a drawn-out legal process, which was met with animated discussion among academics, culminating in the only decision of the Federal Administrative

[32] Heinig (n 10) 311.

[33] E Ost, *Kirchengut und Religionsverfassungsrecht*, Freiburg, 2008 (accessible online at: www.freidok.uni-freiburg.de). The observation remarked in n 31 applies also here: The author was involved as assistant judge in the case of *St Salvator* BVerfGE 99, 100, up to now the only decision of the Federal Constitutional Court concering the safeguarding of church property.

[34] Heinig, *Kritik und Selbstkritik* (n 23) 357, 360; Heinig, 'Ordnung der Freiheit' (n 26) 250.

[35] Title of the famous work by H Urs von Balthasar, *Schleifung der Bastionen* (Einsiedeln, Johannes, 1952).

[36] H Weber, *Der öffentlich-rechtliche Körperschaftsstatus der Religionsgemeinschaften nach Art. 137 Abs. 5 WRV* in Heinig and Walter (n 2) 230, 246–47.

[37] At the convention of the Association of German Constitutional Law Teachers in 2008, Ute Sacksofsky argued for the abolition of the public corporation status, 'Religiöse Freiheit als Gefahr?' (2009) 68 *Veröffentlichungen der Vereinigung der Deutschen Staatsrechtslehrer* 7–46, 28. In the ensuing discussion, Hans Michael Heinig (101–02), Christian Walter and Claus Dieter Classen opposed this position (108–09 and 110).

[38] Practically speaking, this applies only to the various organizational elements of the Catholic Church and the protestant state churches (specifically, the Catholic dioceses and the protestant state churches, as well as their subdivisions, such as parishes and congregations) and Jewish religious communities. Contrary to popular belief, 'the church' is an ecclesiastical term, with no per se legal status whatsoever.

Court on the subject to date.[39] After the lower administrative courts had granted recognition as a public corporation, the Federal Administrative Court denied the Jehovah's Witnesses this status, citing the group's lack of 'state loyalty' as the reason.[40]

The Federal Constitutional Court, however, did not accept this decision and seized the opportunity to take a fundamental stance regarding the very institution of the public corporation status. To some extent affirming the views held by legal scholars,[41] the Court interpreted the status in terms of constitutional basic rights, thereby fanning the flames of an already lively debate.[42]

The Federal Constitutional Court found that the public corporation status was designed to facilitate the realization of the basic freedom of religion as laid down by the Constitution itself. Its justification was to be seen in its ability to strengthen that constitutional freedom.[43] Previously, the court had emphasized that the public corporation status was intended to affirm the autonomy and independence of the church from the state, as well as to reinforce the church's own powers[44] – a formula which should establish a consensus within legal academia. The concept put forward in the Jehovah's Witnesses decision, however, proves to be largely inconsistent when looked at more closely.[45]

According to the unambiguous wording of the Constitution, only established religious bodies may attain this special status (Article 140 GG in conjunction with Article 137(5), sentence 2 WRV: *Gewähr der Dauer* – guarantee of constancy). If

[39] Stages of Appeal: VG Berlin [1994] *Neue Zeitschrift für Verwaltungsrecht* 609; OVG Berlin [1996] *Neue Zeitschrift für Verwaltungsrecht* 478; BVerwGE 105, 117. Following the decision of the Federal Constitutional Court (BVerfGE 102, 370), the Federal Administrative Court sent the case back to the Higher Administrative Court of Berlin for further appraisal of the facts (BVerwG [2001] *Neue Zeitschrift für Verwaltungsrecht* 924), which finally (after a failed attempt at settlement) mandated the state of Berlin to bestow public corporation status (OVG Berlin [2005] *Neue Zeitschrift für Verwaltungsrecht* 1450); the non-admission complaint was turned down (BVerwG [2006] *Neue Juristische Wochenschrift* 3156).

[40] BVerwGE 105, 117, 125–26; the background for the decision was the fact that the Jehovah's Witnesses forbade their members under threat of punishment from taking part in government elections.

[41] S Korioth, *Loyalität im Staatskirchenrecht* in W Erbguth, F Müller and V Neumann (eds), *Rechtstheorie und Rechtsdogmatik im Austausch: Gedächtnisschrift für Bernd Jeand'Heur* (Berlin, Duncker & Humblot, 1999) 221; M Morlok and HM Heinig, 'Parität im Leistungsstaat – Körperschaftsstatus nur bei Staatsloyalität?' [1999] *Neue Zeitschrift für Verwaltungsrecht* 697; see on the other hand the sentence review of A Hollerbach [1997] *Juristenzeitung* 117; S Muckel, 'Religionsgemeinschaften als Körperschaften des öffentlichen Rechts' (1999) 38 *Der Staat* 569.

[42] Following the same line as the Federal Constitutional Court were Walter, *Religionsverfassungsrecht in vergleichender und internationaler Perspektive* (n 10) 546; Heinig (n 10) especially 265; Classen, *Religionsfreiheit und Staatskirchenrecht in der Grundrechtsordnung* (n 10) 6; and Magen, *Körperschaftsstatus und Religionsfreiheit: Zur Bedeutung des Art. 137 Art. 5 WRV im Kontext des Grundgesetzes* (n 30) 197; very different, C Hillgruber, 'Der Körperschaftsstatus von Religionsgemeinschaften' [2001] *Neue Zeitschrift für Verwaltungsrecht* 1347; A Uhle, 'Ein "rätselhafter Ehrentitel"?' in O Depenheuer and others (eds), *Festschrift für Josef Isensee* (Heidelberg, CF Müller, 2007) 1033.

[43] BVerfGE 102, 370, 387 – with an inaccuarate citation of BVerfGE 42, 312, 322 –, 390.

[44] BVerfGE 30, 415, 428.

[45] Pros and cons of the decision can be found in the papers of Christian Hillgruber and Hermann Weber entitled *Der öffentlich-rechtliche Körperschaftsstatus nach Art. 137 Abs. 5 WRV* in Heinig and Walter (n 2) 213, 229.

the public corporation status is viewed as one building block in a complex relationship between church and state, based on their inherent institutions, it becomes clear that this requirement is meant to secure and enable a long-term collaboration between the two entities. The basic rights interpretation, on the other hand, presents considerable difficulties. Freedom of religion is not dependent upon the previous establishment of a religious organization. Indeed, it would be a singular concept within the Constitution to provide constitutional protection only on the basis of 'tried and tested'.[46] In addition, the right to taxation (Article 140 GG in conjunction with Article 137(6) WRV), the only constitutional power derived from the public corporation status, cannot be understood to be an exercise of freedom of religion.[47] Furthermore, according to unanimous perception, all religious and ideological organizations are meant to participate equally in the constitutional guarantee of religious freedom.[48] Consequently, the question must arise as to what additional constitutional yield can be drawn from the status of public corporation, as opposed to that granted to any civil law corporation. It is not clear why the level of organization stipulated in the criteria for constancy, should be relevant for the realization of basic constitutional rights, for these points are classic examples of internal questions of the church itself, which the state should not influence.[49] The prerequisites implicitly postulated by the Federal Constitutional Court for attaining the public corporation status are irreconcilable with basic constitutional principles: why should a religious organization that is a public corporation have to take measures to guarantee that its future behaviour will not endanger the constitutional principles stipulated in Article 79(3) GG, the basic constitutional rights of third parties as well as the basic principles of freedom of religion?[50] In the words of Rudolf Smend,[51] this is simply puzzling.[52] The claim that public corporation religious groups have a greater obligation to protect the basic constitutional rights of third parties because of their greater influence[53] cannot be substantiated, and demonstrates the argumentative confusion of fact and law.

[46] See Hillgruber, 'Der Körperschaftsstatus von Religionsgemeinschaften' (n 42) 1349; Uhle, 'Ein "rätselhafter Ehrentitel"?' (n 42) 1039.

[47] Examined in detail in R Tillmanns, *Kirchensteuer kein Mittel zur Entfaltung grundrechtlicher Religionsfreiheit* in S Muckel (ed), *Festschrift für Wolfgang Rüfner* (Berlin, Duncker & Humblot, 2003) 919.

[48] See instead M Heckel, 'Die religionsrechtliche Parität' in J Listl and D Pirson (eds), *Handbuch des Staatskirchenrechts der Bundesrepublik Deutschland*, vol I, 2nd edn (Berlin, Duncker & Humblot, 1994) 589, 605.

[49] Art 140 GG in conjunction with Art 137(3) WRV.

[50] BVerfGE 102, 370, 392.

[51] According to the famous phrase of the distinguished public church law scholar R Smend, *Staat und Kirche nach dem Bonner Grundgesetz* (1951) 1 *Zeitschrift für evangelisches Kirchenrecht* 4, 9, the public corporation status is a 'somewhat puzzling honorary title'.

[52] See the critique in S Muckel, 'Körperschaftsstatus für die Zeugen Jehovas?' [2001] 23 *Juristische Ausbildung* 456, 458; and Uhle (n 42) 1045.

[53] BVerfGE 102, 370, 393.

B. Religious Organizations and the Right of Self-determination

One of the pillars of the constitutional provisions concerning the relationship between church and state is the right of self-determination, as found in Article 140 GG in conjunction with Article 137(3) WRV.[54] According to this principle, each religious organization may order its own affairs as it sees fit within the confines of the laws pertaining to all subjects. It may appoint all officials, without influence from the state or the civil community. Johannes Heckel describes the extraordinary importance of this position for religious bodies using the term *lex regia*.[55] Essentially, the provision in Article 137(3) WRV is merely the logical consequence of the structural ideals of secularity and neutrality:[56] if the constitutional order stipulates that church and state are separate entities and that the state may not interfere in internal church affairs, then logically it must be the duty of the church itself to structure its own affairs, in matters of administration as well as regulation. This recognition of the inherent[57] independence of the church merely shows one dimension of the constitutional provision: had the founders of the Constitution intended the provision merely to prevent state involvement in internal church affairs, it would have been a mere declaratory reiteration of what Article 140 GG in conjunction with Article 137(1) WRV and Article 9(1) GG already states. Presuming therefore, that the provision must contain some meaning beyond this,[58] this meaning can be found most obviously in the acknowledgement of the relevance of organized religious groups and churches for the entire community.[59]

It is apparent that not only are the rights of self-determination and freedom of religion closely associated with one another, but in many cases they coincide and overlap. Traditionally the Federal Constitutional Court, supported by various leading authors, viewed the relationship between the two legal positions as complementary and supplementary:

> The guarantee of freedom of administration and organization of internal affairs is a necessary, albeit legally distinct, guarantee, *adjoined* to the freedom of religious life and

[54] Occasionally, the term 'self-administration' is used. However, the constitutional guarantee is not limited to administration, making the term 'self-determination' a more appropriate choice. Seminal: K Hesse, *Das Selbstbestimmungsrecht der Kirchen und Religionsgemeinschaften* in Listl and Pirson, *Handbuch des Staatskirchenrechts der Bundesrepublik Deutschland* (n 48) 521.

[55] J Heckel, *Melanchthon und das heutige deutsche Staatskirchenrecht* in *Um Recht und Gerechtigkeit: Festgabe für Erich Kaufmann* (Stuttgart, Kohlhammer, 1950) 83, 85. The phrase is occasionally and erroneously attributed to his son, Martin, as seen in M Morlok, *Dreier: Grundgesetz Kommentar*, vol III, 2nd edn (Tübingen, Mohr Siebeck, 2008) Art 137 WRV, para 43, fn 109.

[56] On these principles, see Mückl, 'Grundlagen des Staatskirchenrechts' (n 15) § 159, paras 61–66, 67–72.

[57] eg A Frhr von Campenhausen and Heinrich de Wall, *Staatskirchenrecht*, 4th edn (Munich, CH Beck, 2006) 102.

[58] Hesse, *Das Selbstbestimmungsrecht der Kirchen und Religionsgemeinschaften* (n 54) 523.

[59] BVerfGE 42, 312, 330; 46, 73, 85; Hesse (n 54) 531.

operation, and provides for the necessary freedom to create statutes and organizational and administrative structures, in order to realize these freedoms.[60]

Authors favouring a more basic rights-oriented approach go much further. In agreement with notions from earlier literature – such as Joseph Listl's idea of a complete overlap between corporative religious freedom and the right to self-determination[61] – they view both legal positions as equal in strength:[62] thus whenever a church or religious entity exercises its right to self-determination, it is, at the same time, realizing its freedom of religion.

Attractive as this interpretation may be, it clashes with the wording and recognized interpretation of both constitutional provisions: 'freedom of religion and conscience' and 'unhindered exercise of religion' (Article 4(1) and (2) GG) cannot truly be understood to be congruent with the right of religious organizations to determine their internal affairs independently (Article 137(3) WRV). Of course, it can be said that the core of the right to self-determination is indeed also protected as part of the freedom of religion:[63] but the relationship between the two provisions is much more complex. Fundamental elements of the right of self-determination[64] – such as fiscal, economic and estate administration or free enterprise activities – cannot be understood to be part of religious freedom.[65] Therefore, it is better to keep separate the guarantees made by the two provisions, while bearing in mind the reciprocal nature of their relationship to one another.[66]

V. TREATMENT OF MUSLIM COMMUNITIES

As a kind of test case for the various concepts of public church law and religious constitutional law, the question is often posed as to what extent these ideas concerning the relationship between church and state can be applied to Muslim religious groups. Admittedly, the larger and more strongly perceptible (as well as decidedly more assertive) presence of Muslim religious groups when compared to

[60] BVerfGE 42, 312, 332 – emphasis added; BVerfGE 53, 366, 401; 72, 278, 289; affirming, Frhr von Campenhausen and de Wall, *Staatskirchenrecht* (n 57) 100; S Korioth, *Vom institutionellen Staatskirchenrecht zum grundrechtlichen Religionsverfassungsrecht?* in M Brenner, PM Huber and M Möstl (eds), *Festschrift für Peter Badura* (Tübingen, Mohr Siebeck, 2004) 727, 740–41.

[61] J Listl, *Das Grundrecht der Religionsfreiheit in der Rechtsprechung der Gerichte der Bundesrepublik Deutschland* (Berlin, Duncker & Humblot, 1971) 372.

[62] Heinig (n 10) 150–51; Walter (n 10) 540–41; Morlok, *Die korporative Religionsfreiheit* (n 2) 185, 190, 201.

[63] BVerfGE 42, 312, 322; 66, 1, 22; S Mückl in *Bonner Kommentar zum Grundgesetz*, Art 4 GG, para 177.

[64] For an overview of the scope of the guarantee see Mückl (n 15) § 159, para 82.

[65] Advocated, even today, by the Federal Constitutional Court, see BVerfGE 24, 236, 246; 35, 366, 376.

[66] This is the approach of PM Huber, *Die korporative Religionsfreiheit und das Selbstbestimmungsrecht nach Art. 137 Abs. 3 WRV einschließlich ihrer Schranken* in Heinig and Walter (n 2), 155, 164, 167 – 'concentric system'.

earlier eras, poses a great challenge both in Germany[67] and in other European countries.[68]

A substantial number of advocates of the traditional institution-based perception show a decided reluctance to afford Muslim religious groups access to the legal guarantees of public church law: they emphasize the historical context of the subject matter and the continuing functional logic for the democratic constitutional state. Public church law, which can only be understood in the historical context from which it emerged, is reliant upon the willingness and capacity of all the parties concerned (the state as well as religious organizations) to cooperate in the interests of public welfare. Therefore, the state may only afford a position going beyond that of basic constitutional guarantees of freedom of religion and extending as far as allowing a certain participation in sovereign power, to such groups from which a lasting cooperation can be expected. In accordance with this theory, the prerequisite for this is that any religious group wishing to be afforded these extended positions must have a culture compatible with the democratic and constitutional order, born of a certain historical and cultural context.[69] The so-called 'culture caveat' is to be seen as a functional provision, a point that should be emphasized in the light of various misunderstandings and misconstructions. It is not the culture from which a religion emerged that is the relevant factor, but rather the stance of the religion towards the modern legal order.[70] It cannot be disputed that approaches based on historical tradition are not sustainable when viewed in the light of the modern, secular constitutional text. These approaches present a merely retrospective privilege, not possessing any power for change in the present and entirely without illumination for the future. The theory of the 'culture caveat' aims to get away from the largely fruitless constitutional positivism, without falling into a realm of theoretical desires detached from statutory rules. Its aim is to emphasize the idea that any right is the result of specific cultural facts, not subject to opportunistic disposition, and that this applies to public

[67] Summarized in S Muckel (ed), *Der Islam im öffentlichen Recht des säkularen Verfassungsstaates* (Berlin, Duncker & Humblot, 2008).

[68] U Khaliq, *The Accomodation and Regulation of Islam and Muslim Practices in English Law* (2002) 6 *Ecclesiastical Law Journal* 332; S Poulter, *Muslim Headscarves in School: Constrasting Legal Approaches in England and France* (1997) 17 *Oxford Journal of Legal Studies* 43; in French literature, F Frégosi, *Les problèmes liés à l'organisation de la religion musulmane en France* (1996) 46 *Revue de Droit Canonique* 215; also Consortium Européen pour l'étude des relations Églises-État/European Consortium for Church-State Research (ed), *European Union and Islam: Proceeding of the Meeting, Vienna, November 15–17 2001* (Leuven, Peeters, 2004).

[69] Explored at length in: A Uhle, *Staat – Kirche – Kultur* (Berlin, Duncker & Humblot, 2004) 139; Uhle, *Freiheitlicher Verfassungsstaat und kulturelle Identität* (n 17) 454; similar view in J Isensee, *Tabu im freiheitlichen Staat* (Paderborn, Schöningh, 2003) 80–81; P Kirchhof, *Die Freiheit der Religionen und ihr unterschiedlicher Beitrag zu einem freien Gemeinwesen* in B Kämper and H-W Thönnes (eds), *Essener Gespräche zum Thema Staat und Kirche*, vol XXXIX (Münster, Aschendorff, 2005) 105; P Kirchhof, *Die Kirchen und Religionsgemeinschaften als Körperschaften des öffentlichen Rechts* in Listl and Pirson (n 49) 651, 667, 682; C Hillgruber, *Der deutsche Kulturstaat und der muslimische Kulturimport* [1999] *Juristenzeitung* 538; see also K-H Ladeur and I Augsberg, *Toleranz – Religion – Recht* (Tübingen, Mohr Siebeck, 2007) 70.

[70] As clarified in A Uhle, *Die Integration des Islam in das Staatskirchenrecht des Grundgesetzes* in Heinig and Walter (n 2) 299, 321 and fn 86, 323 and fn 93.

church law as much as to any other subject. Ultimately, it is the attempt to transfer the 'ideals and convictions conveyed through culture and rooted in history', as indicated by the Federal Constitutional Court in its 'Crucifix Ruling' of 1995,[71] into practical constitutional interpretation.

For obvious reasons, the 'religious constitutional law' approach opposes this stance. Its proponents emphasize the 'open constructional government' set down in the Constitution, which cannot be trumped by 'hermetic religious cultural concepts'.[72] The state referred to in the Constitution is, therefore, no longer a 'Christian' one – and this fact should not be glossed over by blurring the line between the emergence of legal statutes and their current application.[73]

These voices choose instead to emphasize the stipulation of equal treatment and the rule of parity.[74] In a religiously and ideologically neutral state whose Constitution forbids the existence of a state church (Article 140 GG in conjunction with Article 137(1) WRV), there can be no room to treat established churches 'more equally' than newly founded churches or religious communities originating in other countries: in so far as the demands of a statute conveying a certain legal right are met, that legal right must be granted. Further culturally founded or unwritten specifications are viewed as inadmissible.

This view does not fail to recognize that existing law does not always 'fit' Muslim religious groups. Even the term 'religious group' (which can be the only subject of the right in question) cannot always be applied with certainty to Muslim groups.[75] However, calling into question the very existence of these legal institutions, as the only fair way to establish equality, is only rarely seen as the solution.[76] For the most part, emphasis is placed on using the legal instruments available to facilitate the integration of Muslim communities and individuals.

The idea of 'integration through law'[77] is generally acknowledged.[78] Even though a certain degree of liberality is possible in this area,[79] care must be taken to ensure

[71] BVerfGE 93, 1, 22 – 'Even a state which copiously protects the right of freedom of religion and thereby obligates itself to be religiously and ideologically neutral, cannot fully strip away the culturally and historically rooted convictions and values upon which societal solidarity is based and upon which the fulfilment of its own duties is dependant. The Christian faith and the Christian churches have had a tremendous influence upon these convictions and values, regardless of how their legacy is viewed today. The state cannot ignore the traditional ideas, experiences and behavioural patterns resulting from these'.

[72] Morlok (n 55) para 102 with fn 317.

[73] Heinig (n 26) 245.

[74] For meaning and relevancy in public church law, see Mückl (n 15) paras 73–79.

[75] For the development of Muslim religious schooling, BVerwGE 123, 49.

[76] Sacksofsky, 'Religiöse Freiheit als Gefahr?' (n 37); see similarly, G Britz, 'Der Einfluß christlicher Tradition auf die Rechtsauslegung als verfassungsrechtliches Gleichheitsproblem?' [2000] *Juristenzeitung* 1127, who intend to analyse the entire legal system, in order to find 'hidden' cases of Christian grounding and question. Counter to such tendencies, Waldhoff, *Neue Religionskonflikte und staatliche Neutralität* (n 13), 51.

[77] For terminology and development, see M Cappelletti, M Seccombe and JHH Weiler (eds), *Integration Through Law* (Berlin, de Gruyter, 1986); E Schmidt-Aßmann, *Das Allgemeine Verwaltungsrecht als Ordnungsidee*, 2nd edn (Berlin, Springer, 2004) 390.

[78] Dealt with in more detail in S Mückl, *Europäisierung des Staatskirchenrechts* (Baden-Baden, Nomos, 2005) 407–08.

[79] M Brenner, 'Staat und Religion' (2000) 59 *Veröffentlichungen der Vereinigung der Deutschen Staatsrechtslehrer* 264, 287.

that this integration occurs within the confines of the law and is not made its substitute. Whether the hope of creating a western, 'enlightened' and constitutionally compatible 'Euro-Islam' (as it is often called by both political scientists[80] and legal scholars[81]) associated with this strategy can be fulfilled should not be viewed too optimistically. The practical experiences of other European countries warrant caution.[82]

From a legal perspective, the question arises whether a secular state, religiously and ideologically neutral may intervene in the process of clarifying the core values of a religion or religious group and thereby promote those groups whose compatibility with constitutional values it recognizes. The same question arises when the state creates or activates previously non-existent legal structures with the aim of fostering cooperation with churches and religious groups, in cases when these groups (often Muslim groups) have failed to produce tangible organizational structures themselves.[83] That which, from a constitutional standpoint, might appear to be merely state aid towards realizing basic constitutional rights,[84] can be viewed from a public church law perspective as an excessive anti-secular paternalism foreign to the Constitution.[85] It is in any case necessary (and in Germany so far not achieved) to attempt to get to know the representative ideology of western Muslim groups from the inside.[86]

These distinctly differing concepts should not, however, alter our perception to the point of overlooking the extensive overlaps and similarities between them.

There is no doubt that in a secular and neutral constitutional state, people of Muslim faith – and indeed Muslim communities themselves – have the same freedom of religion guaranteed by the Constitution as all other religious groups.[87] In keeping with this notion, occasional pleas (usually within the political arena), arguing that in many Muslim states freedom of religion is limited or in some cases

[80] C Leggewie, *Alhambra: Der Islam im Westen* (Hamburg, Rowohlt, 1993) 169; C Leggewie, *Auf dem Weg zum Euro-Islam?* (Bad Homburg v.d. Höhe, Herbert-Quandt-Stiftung, 2002) throughout; B Tibi, *Im Schatten Allahs* (Berlin, Ullstein, 2003) 491.

[81] M Rohe, *Rechtliche Perspektiven eines deutschen und europäischen Islam* (2000) 64 *RabelsZ* 256, 294; similarly, Brenner, 'Staat und Religion' (n 79) 287: 'in the medium term our concern should be to germanize the robes of the Prophet'.

[82] Initiated in France – arising from such integration ideas – the then Interior Minister (and later President) Nicolas Sarkozy advocated the creation of a *Conseil français du culte musulman* (National Muslim Council). The first election in April 2003 led to a crippling defeat for its initiator.

[83] Some German states have replaced traditional religion classes in school, which are supported by the Constitution (Art 7(3) GG), with the subject 'Muslim Instruction', whose constitutionality is at least contested. In 2005, the state of Hesse integrated into its Protestant Studies Department at the University of Frankfurt a Chair for Muslim Religious Studies, supported by the Turkish Agency for Religious Affairs ('Diyanet').

[84] Classen (n 10) 82.

[85] Mückl (n 15) para 66; lucidly explained, Uhle, *Staat – Kirche – Kultur* (n 69) 165: 'hothouse cultivation of a post-Enlightenment liberal Euro-Islam'. See also the important concerns voiced by Waldhoff (n 13) 75.

[86] Fundamental, but also available only in the original Arabic, L Wick, *Islam und Verfassungsstaat* (Würzburg, Ergon, 2009).

[87] Emphasized by supporters of the *Staatskirchenrecht* interpretation: see Uhle, *Die Integration des Islam in das Staatskirchenrecht des Grundgesetzes* (n 70) 300; Hillgruber, *Der deutsche Kulturstaat und der muslimische Kulturimport* (n 69) 541.

entirely lacking or that the inherent discrepancy between the Muslim faith and the 'values system' of the German Constitution cannot be overcome, can be easily quashed as legally insubstantial.[88]

On the other hand, there is general agreement that for Muslim groups to have access to the pertinent legal institutions discussed in this chapter, several questions still need to be clarified. This applies especially to the internal organization of such groups. If these groups wish to participate in institutions which require long-term cooperation with the state, they must first provide for executive bodies which can make binding decisions concerning organization and doctrine and can mandate the execution of these decisions within the community. Whether or not this is practically possible is viewed differently by the various proponents of the religious constitutional law perspective.[89]

VI. MEANING OF THE SUBJECT FOR THE WHOLE OF THE CONSTITUTION

The debate about the continuation of a 'public church law' versus a paradigm change towards the formation of a 'religious constitutional law' must be viewed within the context of a changing social and legal framework. German society of the twenty-first century is no longer a homogenous structure, but a secular, religiously indifferent, and at the same time pluralistic one. These tendencies, contrary in part, present new challenges for existing law. It is evident that public church law is marked by an inherent historic and cultural character. In Germany, public church law has been characterized by cooperative mechanisms based on Christianity since the religious divide of the sixteenth century, first between the various religious parties themselves and later between these and the state.[90] One of the definitive questions of the twenty-first century for Germany and Europe as a whole is whether, and to what extent, the developed church-law systems can react to changes in their non-legal contexts. Arguably the prevalent concept in Germany is not ill-suited to handle these challenges.[91] It offers the necessary statutory potential, while at the same time providing an atmosphere in which religious plurality may exist without returning to the battles of the nineteenth and twentieth

[88] Uhle (n 70) 303–04, is correct in noting that international law and its principle of reciprocity in regard to basic civil rights cannot be applied here; E Riedel, *Religionsfreiheit und völkerrechtliche Reziprozität* in J Schwartländer (ed), *Freiheit der Religion* (Mainz, Grünewald, 1993) 436.

[89] W Heun, *Integration des Islam* in Heinig and Walter (n 2) 339, views the public corporation status as virtually unattainable for Muslim groups, owing to their organizational structure (341) and doubts, too, the possibility of religious schooling (350–51). Heinig (n 10) 258, is more optimistic about religious schooling: 'it's a matter of time'. Waldhoff (n 13) 107–08 on the other hand, is highly sceptical.

[90] Uhle (n 69) throughout; Mückl, *Europäisierung des Staatskirchenrechts* (n 78) 403–05.

[91] See S Korioth and I Augsberg, 'Religion and the Secular State' in J Basedow, U Kischel and U Sieber (eds), *German National Reports to the 18th International Congress of Comparative Law* (Tübingen, Mohr Siebeck, 2010) 1, 18, which emphasize the 'productive role' of the 'German model' and its 'future possibilities': 'even in the modern pluralist society a merely individualistic conception of religion is insufficient'.

centuries;[92] but on the other hand, it also exhibits the necessary stability, so that no doubts can arise as to the decisiveness of governmental rule in the face of a pluralist arena of religious authority.

The fundamental requirement for the achievement of this level of constitutional development is that, in Germany and Europe as a whole, the leading protagonists – church and state – have drastically modified their theoretical assumptions concerning their mutual relationship: the state no longer views itself as omnipotent so it can focus on carrying out secular duties and responsibilities without perceiving the church as a rival for sovereign power. On the other hand, the churches have greatly limited their desire to rely upon governmental power in order to achieve religious or internal church goals. In this, however, lies the constitutionally relevant division: the state no longer tries to play pope nor the church the emperor. As a result of this bilateral limitation of power their fundamental roles, both parties are free to interact and collaborate in areas where secular matters and matters of a clerical or religious nature meet. The division thereby facilitates cooperation.

The concept of public church law describes this cooperation in a way that is especially appropriate to the developed historical and cultural requirements of a constitutional democracy. The activities of the churches are not limited to questions of cult, but instead manifest themselves in multifaceted forms in daily life. Over the course of history, the state has assumed many responsibilities previously belonging to the churches – taking care of the impoverished and involvement in school and university education, to name but two – without usurping the churches' competence in this area (or even intending to, for that matter). The churches have always produced benefits for public welfare, as well as for the state itself, by performing functions which the state cannot perform, either because it is legally obliged to refrain from doing so, owing to the doctrine of neutrality and secularity, or because its resources would be entirely swallowed up if it did. The purpose of public church law must, therefore, be that the secular state may participate in the public welfare achievements of the churches *for its own benefit*. It is for precisely this reason that the state creates the legal atmosphere in which institutionalized church activities are protected and safeguarded, in the form of public church law, so that these may make their contribution to secular public welfare. In short: the primary beneficiary of public church law is not the *churches* (which are already comprehensively protected by the guarantee of basic rights in the Constitution), but the *state*. It is the state that can cultivate but not establish its own roots.[93] This interdependence could never be explained or secured by a system based solely upon the basic rights guarantees of the Constitution.

[92] Examples of French law in Mückl (n 78) 167–69, 216, 406–07.

[93] In this context, the classic phrase by Ernst-Wolfgang Böckenförde must be included: 'The freedom-oriented secular state thrives from requirements which it cannot guarantee', first published in *Die Entstehung des Staats als Vorgang der Säkularisation* in *Säkularisation und Utopie* (Stuttgart, Kohlhammer, 1967) 75, 93.

If the state meets the phenomenon of 'religion' in this spirit – on the one hand being aware of its own relative nature,[94] and on the other being resolute in the fulfilment of the secular functions of the law – then even the changing factual base of the law should provide no cause to perceive religious freedom or its exercise as dangerous.[95] Nevertheless, it remains the duty of the state to ensure that the exercise of constitutional rights – be they individual or institutional – should not undermine the Constitution itself. As such, the appeal to the prevalent (albeit somewhat inane) term 'tolerance' should be materially affirmed.[96]

Ensuring this is the duty not only of the state, but also of those powers which have enjoyed constitutionally guaranteed legal positions, partnering them with the state for nearly one hundred years.

CASES

BVerfGE 42, 312 – *Inkompatibilität; Kirchliches Amt* (1976)
BVerfGE 53, 366 – *Konfessionelle Krankenhäuser* (1980)
BVerfGE 57, 220 – *Volmarstein* (1981)
BVerfGE 66, 1 – *Konkursausfallgeld* (1983)
BVerfGE 102, 370 – *Zeugen Jehovas I* (2000)
BVerwGE 105, 17 – *Zeugen Jehovas II* (2002)

SELECTED LITERATURE

Classen CD, *Religionsfreiheit und Staatskirchenrecht in der Grundrechtsordnung* (Tübingen, Mohr Siebeck, 2003)

Heckel M, 'Zur Zukunftsfähigkeit des deutschen "Staatskirchenrechts" oder "Religionsverfassungsrechts"' (2009) 134 *Archiv des öffentlichen Rechts* 309

Heinig HM, *Öffentlich-rechtliche Religionsgesellschaften* (Berlin, Duncker & Humblot, 2003)

——'Ordnung der Freiheit – das Staatskirchenrecht vor neuen Herausforderungen' (2008) 53 *Zeitschrift für evangelisches Kirchenrecht* 235

[94] It must be emphasized that, contrary to the powerful philosophical and theoretical magnification of the state (as seen especially in Hegel), the state is not an end in itself. Instead, it is, in the words of Josef Isensee, 'a sectoral state', *Staat und Verfassung* in J Isensee and P Kirchhof (eds), *Handbuch des Staatsrechts der Bundesrepublik Deutschland*, vol I, 3rd edn (Heidelberg, CF Müller, 2003) § 15, paras 69, 75.

[95] Such was the first topic at the convention of the Association of German Constitutional Law Teachers in 2008 (*Religiöse Freiheit als Gefahr*), which Heinig (n 26) 248 with fn 56, comments sceptically: 'the selection of topics is lurid and worthy of a tabloid magazine'. See the noteworthy, and balanced, presentation of C Möllers, 'Religiöse Freiheit als Gefahr?' (2009) 68 *Veröffentlichungen der Vereinigung der Deutschen Staatsrechtslehrer* 47–93.

[96] A sharp critique towards the 'tolerance' model prevalent in literature and adjudication is made by Ladeur and Augsberg, *Toleranz – Religion – Recht* (n 69) esp 133. See also Ladeur and Augsberg, *The Myth of the Neutral State: The Relationship between State and Religion in the Face of New Challenges* (2007) 8 *German Law Journal* 143.

—— and Walter C (eds), *Staatskirchenrecht oder Religionsverfassungsrecht?* (Tübingen, Mohr Siebeck, 2007)
Kirchhof P, 'Die Freiheit der Religionen und ihr unterschiedlicher Beitrag zu einem freien Gemeinwesen' in B Kämper and H-W Thönnes (eds), *Essener Gespräche zum Thema Staat und Kirche*, vol XXXIX (Münster, Aschendorff, 2005) 105
Ladeur KH and Augsberg I, *Toleranz – Religion – Recht* (Tübingen, Mohr Siebeck, 2007)
Mückl S, *Europäisierung des Staatskirchenrechts* (Baden-Baden, Nomos, 2005)
—— *Grundlagen des Staatskirchenrechts* in J Isensee and P Kirchhof (eds), *Handbuch des Staatsrechts der Bundesrepublik Deutschland*, vol VII (Heidelberg, CF Müller, 2009) § 159
Uhle A, *Staat – Kirche – Kultur* (Berlin, Duncker & Humblot, 2004)
Walter C, *Religionsverfassungsrecht in vergleichender und internationaler Perspektive* (Tübingen, Mohr Siebeck, 2006)

Part II

Administrative Law

10

Democratic Legitimization of the Administrative Power – Exclusive versus Inclusive Democracy

MATTHIAS JESTAEDT

I. THE SIGNIFICANCE OF THE DEBATE ABOUT DEMOCRATIC LEGITIMIZATION

A. Democratic Legitimization and Democratic Legitimacy

IN HIS FAMOUS Gettysburg address, Abraham Lincoln used a three-dimensional description of democracy: 'government of the people, by the people, for the people'.[1] In each of the three elements of democracy, the focus is placed firmly upon the relationship between exercise of power by the state and the people of the state: sovereign power must be legitimized before the people. Although these three aspects of the relationship between state power and the people are dissimilar, they dovetail extremely well in the double maxim: first, state power requires the justification by the people and secondly, although this justification can be supplemented and enriched by measures put in place by the state under the rule of law (*Rechtsstaat*) or the welfare state (*Sozialstaat*), it can never be replaced. The concept can therefore be couched in the following terms: with the victory of the western constitutional model, the theory of democratic monistic legitimization was laid down. In light of the dignity, freedom and equality of each citizen, viewed as original and inalienable, the state – or more generally, the public authority – requires justification for the exercise of state authority – in other words for the external determination of the free and equal citizens, and this justification can only exist if the public authority, acting heteronomously on behalf of the individual, can be traced back to an act of self-determination by the people: if the public authority can be identified as an emanation of the sovereignty of the people. Competing forms of legitimization – such as monarchist-dynastic ones – can no longer be afforded credence. This 'claim to exclusivity' of democracy is formulated as constitutional law by the German Constitution, the *Grundgesetz* ('GG'), in Article 20(2), clause 1, as follows: 'All authority of the state emanates from the people'.

In light of the constitutionally defined link between democracy and popular sovereignty, Lincoln's triad poses two questions which must be considered separately under legal auspices: the question of democratic legitimization (*Legitimation*) and that of democratic legitimacy (*Legitimität*). While legitimacy poses the question as to whether there is an inner material justification which creates actual acceptance or at least acceptability, legitimization is framed rather more formally. It depends on the observance of prescribed forms and procedures of substantiation of governance and is consequently a type of justification which is bound by procedure, form, institutions and competence. State authority is democratically legitimate if it can prove itself to be 'government *for* the people'. However, it can be said to be democratically 'legitimized' only if it is 'government *by* the people'. Article 20(2), clause 1 GG does

[1] A Lincoln, 'Address at the Dedication of the Gettysburg National Cemetery (November 11, 1863)' in P van Doren Stern (ed), *The Life and Writings of Abraham Lincoln* (New York, The Modern Library, 1940) 788. In accordance with Art 2(5) of the Constitution of the Fifth Republic of France (1958) the *principe* of the *Rėpublique* is the 'gouvernement du peuple, par le peuple et pour le peuple'.

not (or at least not directly) speak of fleeting democratic legitimacy, which is, anyway, difficult to put into effect, even with the help of the law. Instead it deals with its formal-procedural alter ego, democratic legitimization.

B. Two Ways of Interpreting Democratic Legitimization

Along with the guarantee of human dignity (*Menschenwürdegarantie*) set out in Article 1(1), clause 1 GG ('Human dignity is inviolable'), the guarantee of sovereignty of the people (*Volkssouveränität*) is considered most important in the framework of the constitutional order. Both, human dignity and sovereignty of the people form the basis of the liberal-democratic constitutional order. As a result of the National Socialist reign of terror, this guarantee has been made immune to any legal challenge by the *Grundgesetz*. Any amendment to the Constitution which would affect the guarantee is impermissible. In other words, the *Grundgesetz* stipulates that the principle of democracy is inalterable (see Article 79(3) GG). Only a revolution which overturned the constitutional order of the *Grundgesetz* would be capable of changing this state of affairs.

The legal principle of democratic legitimization, therefore, may be regarded as one of the two fundamental norms contained in the German Constitution. The matter of the legal claims and the effects given rise to by this provision, however, is not resolved by this finding. To this extent, there are two possibilities: the precept of legitimization could, on the one hand, be regarded as an 'image of self' codified in the Constitution, the factual legal identity of the legal order upon which the *Grundgesetz* is based. If this were taken to be the case, the precept of democratic legitimization contained in Article 20(1) GG would already be fulfilled by the parliamentarian democracy provided for in the *Grundgesetz*. In the everyday business of legislating and the application of the law, this point would no longer be relevant and it would no longer require discussion. This corresponds to the knowledge that, for more than six decades, the Federal Republic of Germany has been a democratic state to exactly the same extent as the USA or the United Kingdom. From a legal perspective, democratic legitimization would be primarily a matter for the drafters of the Constitution (and Constitution-changing legislator) on the one hand, and constitutional theory and constitutional policy on the other. The practical branch of jurisprudence, known as *Rechtsdogmatik* (legal doctrine) in Germany, would not have to concern itself any further with democratic legitimization – given and guaranteed, as it is *per constitutionem* – but would also be unable to extract any autonomous guidelines from Article 20(2), clause 1 GG.

A second and completely different way of interpreting the precept which requires all state power to emanate from the people is also possible, albeit more challenging. According to this interpretation, it is not sufficient that Germany is, more or less, a democratic state owing to the fact that the people and their representatives are accorded an essential function in the exercise of state power but rather the precept of democratic legitimization demands specific evidence in each individual case that state power – ranking below the Constitution – is traced back to an act of determination of the people. The legal principle of democratic legitimization would, therefore, be regarded as an independent, feasible requirement to create and exercise state power which would need to be honoured anew every time – indeed this condition requires fleshing out in each case but is operationable.

Most constitutional states – such as the USA, the United Kingdom or France – and the European Union adhere to the first alternative of the precept of democratic legitimization, even if this is not expressly stated. As such, matters of democratic legitimization play no part in legislating and applying the law. It would, in any case, be of no avail to seek to employ an elaborate doctrine of democratic legitimization there, as it would be superfluous. In Germany, however, this is not the case. Irrespective of any differences in opinion which are directed at the precept of democratic legitimization, it is unanimously accepted that the precept of democratic legitimization set out in Article 20(2) GG is to be interpreted in the second reading. This may be due to the fact that the Federal Republic is organized as a parliamentarian democracy and that, consequently, there is a greater need to guarantee the role of the sole federal organ which is directly legitimized by the people. In any case, the decision to answer the matter in the second way explains why the precept of democratic legitimization, as a legal rule, plays no role in western democracy – with the additional exception of Austria, perhaps – and why its meaning and requirements are so often and so strongly disputed within Germany. In this sense, the legal doctrine of democratic legitimization is a *querelle allemande*.

C. Democracy and Administration

As Article 20(2), clause 1 is by its legal nature not descriptive but rather contains a norm intended to steer behaviour, there can no longer be any doubt as to the situation in Germany. There is, however, no consensus regarding the matter of which concrete behavioural obligations are caused by the requirement of democratic legitimization. This difference of opinion is linked to the public administrative power in particular: what are the democratic-legitimizing requirements for the executive or, more specifically, the administrative exercise of state power? How can adherence to these requirements be guaranteed against the multifaceted and pluralist administration that is opened to non-state private actors as well as to the supra-state European Union? Depending on the circumstances, matters of justification and the limits of independent entities of administration are discussed and the problems associated therewith are expounded upon, but this generally occurs without having recourse to the principle of democracy. The pertinent question is, therefore, not specifically a German one; the manner in which the answer is sought, on the other hand, is.

The matter of which standards must be met by the public administration in order to satisfy the principle of democracy is today still as much a controversial question in the intersection between constitutional and administrative law. The significance attached to this dispute and the gravity with which it is conducted cannot be ascribed solely to the particular weight of the principle of democratic legitimization within the area of constitutional law. Rather it can be to the fact that the matter of democratic legitimization leads to questions regarding the relationship between democracy and (constitutional) law, ideality and positivity of the law, law and 'reality', legal and non-legal steering and justification and, finally, the reach and the 'steering power' of law. To the extent that democraticity becomes an element of the concept of law, any answer to the questions regarding the requirements of democratic legitimization also becomes an avowal of juridical *Weltanschauung*.

The following will provide a brief outline of the historical development concerning the significance which was – and is – accorded to the matter of democratic legitimization of the administrative power in the *Grundgesetz* (section II). In the main body of the essay, the connected matter of the two competing fundamental concepts of democratic legitimization will be presented and discussed (section III). This will give rise to a number of remarks relating to the relationship between a juridical *Weltanschauung* and the concept of legitimization (section IV).

II. FLUCTUATIONS IN THE DEVELOPMENT OF THE MEANING OF THE PRINCIPLE OF DEMOCRACY

A. The Beginnings

For most of the first 40 years of the *Grundgesetz*'s existence, ie from 1948/49 until the 1980s, the principle of democracy – interpreted as the legal principle of democratic legitimization within the meaning of Article 20(2), clause 1 GG – had more or less no part to play in the jurisdiction of the Bundesverfassungsgericht ('BVerfG' – Federal Constitutional Court, 'FCC') or in the area of constitutional law academia. Even the emancipatory socio-political understanding of democracy – employed by the then Chancellor, Willy Brandt (1969–74) in the formula *mehr Demokratie wagen* ('dare more democracy'),[2] which was as catchy as it was politically effective, demanded, in the 1970s, a response to the 'democratization of the administrative power' – with which it went hand in hand – from constitutional law, jurisdiction and jurisprudence.[3] However, the conflict concerning the essentially democratically designed opening-up of the administration – which had been perceived as being bureaucratic and hierarchical – under the headings of 'co-determination in public service'[4] and 'participation of those affected in the

[2] Federal Chancellor Willy Brandt, 'Erklärung der Bundesregierung' (Declaration of the Federal Government) of 28 October 1969 (Stenographische Protokolle, 6. Legislaturperiode) 20 C.

[3] Pars pro toto: W Hennis, 'Demokratisierung. Zur Problematik eines Begriffs' in M Greiffenhagen (ed), *Demokratisierung in Staat und Gesellschaft* (Munich, Piper, 1973) 47.

[4] eg F Ossenbühl, *Grenzen der Mitbestimmung im öffentlichen Dienst* (Baden-Baden, Nomos, 1986).

execution of administrative tasks'[5] was initially – and above all – contested in the language of fundamental rights. The prevailing opinion in the constitutional law of the time strove to achieve the principle of democracy in order to demonstrate that the demands relating to democracy could not be supported by the constitutional principle laid down in Article 20 GG, but rather, was completely the opposite; an unauthorized infringement in the area of the democratic state.[6]

At the same time, the principle of democracy, along with the principle of the *Rechtsstaat*, aimed at curbing the independence of the administration so that in order to make a decision of material importance, a parliamentary statute conferring the authority for it is needed (the so-called *Vorbehalt des Gesetzes*).[7] However, recourse to the principle of democracy remained general and non-specific and an independent system of legitimization for the different state functions (legislative, governing, administrative, judicial) was not developed. The additional discourse regarding the extent and the character of the independence of the administrative power – in particular, the administration's own areas of control which had to be respected by the legislator (so-called *Verwaltungsvorbehalt*),[8] on the one hand, and, on the other, areas of discretion of the administration[9] which were kept outside the purview of the judiciary – focused rather on the separation of powers and the density of judicial review. Arguments which were specifically democratic-legitimatory in nature were seldom employed, if at all.

B. Taking Democratic Legitimization Seriously

It was only in the second half of the 1980s, after the foundations had been laid in the previous decade,[10] that Article 20(2), clause 1 GG was accepted as being a constitutional norm the purpose of which was to steer behaviour in all state exercise of power. It was only then, too, that an intensive jurisprudential gauging and preparation was undertaken. The seminal research of Ernst-Wolfgang Böckenförde was particularly pioneering and formative to the discourse. In 1987, he set out a system of democratic legitimization within the meaning of the *Grundgesetz* which was as

[5] cf W Schmitt Glaeser, 'Partizipation an Verwaltungsentscheidungen' (1973) 31 *Veröffentlichungen der Vereinigung der Deutschen Staatsrechtslehrer* 178.

[6] ibid 209, 214, 221.

[7] From the decisions of the Federal Constitutional Court see BVerfGE 47, 46, 78 – *Sex Education* (1977).

[8] cf H Maurer, 'Der Verwaltungsvorbehalt' (1985) 43 *Veröffentlichungen der Vereinigung der Deutschen Staatsrechtslehrer* 135; FE Schnapp, 'Der Verwaltungsvorbehalt' (1985) 43 *Veröffentlichungen der Vereinigung der Deutschen Staatsrechtslehrer* 172.

[9] A representative view on this topic is provided by E Pache, *Tatbestandliche Abwägung und Beurteilungsspielraum* (Tübingen, Mohr Siebeck, 2001).

[10] cf F Ossenbühl, *Verwaltungsvorschriften und Grundgesetz* (Bad Homburg, Gehlen, 1968); R Herzog, *Allgemeine Staatslehre* (Frankfurt am Main, Athenäum, 1971); E-W Böckenförde, *Verfassungsfragen der Richterwahl: Dargestellt anhand der Gesetzentwürfe zur Einführung der Richterwahl in Nordrhein-Westfalen* (Berlin, Duncker & Humblot, 1974).

elaborate as it was consistent.[11] He interpreted Article 20(2), clause 1 GG in the sense of the precept of '[E]ffective democratic legitimization of the exercise of state power'.[12] Consequently, he distinguished between the basic components of the legitimization relationship: the subject of legitimization (ie the people) and the object of legitimization (ie the exercise of state power).[13] The tracing back of the object of democratic legitimization to its subject, ie the 'emanation' of state power from the people, takes place by means of three forms of democratic legitimization – functional-institutional, organizational-personal as well as a material-substantial. In order to be effective in the manner that is demanded by the Constitution, a certain level of legitimization must be reached which differentiates according to function (discussed in greater detail in subsection III.A.i). If it is unpacked in this sense, the precept of democratic legitimization, which was previously practically without function, becomes a serious hurdle for tendencies of a more pluralist and independent administration.

This interpretation of democratic legitimization passed its first test as early as 1990. With the cooperation of the constitutional judge Böckenförde, the Federal Constitutional Court declared the granting of the right to vote on a municipal level to foreigners to be contrary to the fundamental rights. As in the case of representatives of the people on federal and regional levels, municipal parliaments are to be chosen by the citizens alone (in this case, within each municipal parcel of land); foreigners did not belong to this category.[14] The court reduced the political scope of its verdict by pointing out a route for the constitutional legislator to the right to vote within municipalities for citizens of European Union.[15] Two years later, this route was adopted by the constitutional legislator in connection with the additional amendments to the *Grundgesetz* which were deemed necessary by the Maastricht Treaty in 1992. Among these were two amendments which were of significance for the matter of democratic legitimization: the first in relation to European integration (Article 23 GG) and the second concerning the German Central Bank (*Bundesbank*; Article 88(2) GG).[16] This meant the establishment of an understanding of democratic legitimization which was shortly after labelled as a monistic or as the classic legitimization model – NB from an opposing point of view –; focused on the people, aimed at the state, a concept of constitutional rank in all of its material elements. However, even from the outset, this concept was the

[11] E-W Böckenförde, 'Demokratie als Verfassungsprinzip' in J Isensee and P Kirchhof (eds), *Handbuch des Staatsrechts der Bundesrepublik Deutschland*, vol I (Heidelberg, CF Müller, 1987) § 22; latest version in vol II, 3rd edn (Heidelberg, CF Müller, 2004) § 24; in addition, see E-T Emde, *Die demokratische Legitimation der funktionalen Selbstverwaltung* (Berlin, Duncker & Humblot, 1991) 26, 49; M Jestaedt, *Demokratieprinzip und Kondominialverwaltung* (Berlin, Duncker & Humblot, 1993) 204, 265.

[12] Böckenförde, 'Demokratie als Verfassungsprinzip' (n 11) § 24, before para 11.

[13] ibid para 10. In addition, see E Schmidt-Aßmann, 'Verwaltungslegitimation als Rechtsbegriff' (1991) 116 *Archiv des öffentlichen Rechts* 329, 338, 348, 351, 355, 366.

[14] BVerfGE 83, 37, 50 – *Suffrage of Foreigners for Local Elections in Schleswig-Holstein* (1990); BVerfGE 83, 60, 71 – *Suffrage of Foreigners for the District Assemblies of Hamburg* (1990).

[15] BVerfGE 83, 37, 50 – *Suffrage of Foreigners for Local Elections in Schleswig*-Holstein (1990).

[16] 38. Gesetz zur Änderung des Grundgesetzes vom 21. December 1992, BGBl I 2086.

subject of strong academic criticism,[17] which would be dealt with by the Federal Constitutional Court in the following decade (see subsection II.E).

C. The Touchstone: Functional Self-government

Self-government provided a visible touchstone for the principle of democratic legitimization, in particular, self-government in its functional variation – in other words, administration by persons affected by a particular field of activity such as, for example, associations of doctors, lawyers or craftspeople.[18] Here, it was generally the rationale for a particular result rather than the result itself – the conformity of functional self-government with the Constitution – which was controversial. The significance attached to this conceptual question can be adduced from the pluralism and heterogeneity of its answers. On the one hand, supporters of a 'monistic' model do not acknowledge legitimization by those affected as being democratic and, consequently, demand a specific justification which would lie in strict material- and task-oriented aspects,[19] in an explicit constitutional acknowledgement[20] or in the collective-personal legitimization of the 'corporate people' (*Verbandsvolk*) by acknowledgement of the legislator.[21] On the other hand, supporters of a 'pluralist' model regard legitimization by the 'corporate members' as being a type of autonomous democratic legitimization which exists in addition to legitimization provided by the people of the state[22] and/or supplement the usual input-oriented approach to legitimization with output-oriented approaches. These hold that shortcomings in legitimatory inputs can be compensated for by the quality of the accomplishment of tasks (output).[23]

[17] See eg B-O Bryde, 'Die bundesrepublikanische Volksdemokratie als Irrweg der Demokratietheorie' (1994) 5 *Staatswissenschaften und Staatspraxis* 305.

[18] In Germany, one distinguishes between local self-government and such functional self-government. In opposition to local self-government, it is not the territorial aspect which determines the extent of the self-government, but rather the functional aspect. Those parties which are concerned with carrying out particular task, eg a defined professional field, make up the members who carry out the common regulatory tasks independently. For example, doctors form doctors' associations.

[19] Böckenförde (n 11) § 24, paras 33–34.

[20] Jestaedt, *Demokratieprinzip und Kondominialverwaltung* (n 11) 490, 537.

[21] W Kluth, *Funktionale Selbstverwaltung: Verfassungsrechtlicher Status – verfassungsrechtlicher Schutz* (Tübingen, Mohr Siebeck, 1997) 376.

[22] J Oebbecke, *Weisungs- und unterrichtungsfreie Räume in der Verwaltung* (Cologne & Stuttgart, Deutscher Gemeindeverlag & Kohlhammer, 1986); Emde, *Die demokratische Legitimation der funktionalen Selbstverwaltung* (n 11) 363, 382.

[23] H-H Trute, 'Die demokratische Legitimation der Verwaltung' in W Hoffmann-Riem, E Schmidt-Aßmann and A Voßkuhle (eds), *Grundlagen des Verwaltungsrechts*, vol I, 2nd edn (Munich, CH Beck, 2012) § 6, paras 53, 82.

D. Further Problems in the Area of Democratic Legitimization of the Administrative Power

In addition to (functional) self-government, further instances of the administration's transition to independence and entities of administration which had become independent respectively, are in the focus of the precept of democratic legitimization. In this way, a lively and controversial discourse has developed, specifically regarding the question of whether democratic legitimization is sufficient in certain areas and how it can be achieved:

- by administrative committees which are excluded from the instructional – typically ministerial – hierarchy (so-called ministry-independent areas);[24]
- by administrative decision-making committees which are pluralist in nature and comprised of various groups;[25]
- regarding co-determination by administrative personnel in the accomplishment of administrative tasks;[26]
- by private economic enterprises which are completely or partly state-owned (so-called public enterprises);[27]
- regarding the independence of the German Central Bank (*Bundesbank*);[28]
- regarding the 'New Public Management' which has been adopted within the administration.[29]

E. The Jurisdiction of the Federal Constitutional Court in a State of Flux

The development of jurisprudential discourse is also reflected in the jurisdiction of the BVerfG. After the court received its first opportunity in the late 1970s to comment on democratic legitimization within the municipal authorities,[30] it opted, at the beginning of the 1990s, to support the 'monists' in the – then politically very delicate – matter of municipal voting rights for foreigners. In arriving at its decision, it extracted an input-oriented concept of legitimization from the *Grundgesetz*, in accordance with which all state power – federal or *Land* power, as

[24] The ministerial-free areas (*ministerialfreie Räume*) constitute state administration units which conduct administration tasks but are independent of steering and control by a minister, who is responsible to Parliament. Thereto, H Dreier, *Hierarchische Verwaltung im demokratischen Staat* (Tübingen, Mohr Siebeck, 1991) 134.

[25] The committees are administrative councils in which the agents of the represented groups of society exercise sovereign power without directive. See for detail Jestaedt (n 11) 41, 120, 369.

[26] eg U Battis and J Kersten, 'Demokratieprinzip und Mitbestimmung im öffentlichen Dienst' [1996] *Die öffentliche Verwaltung* 584.

[27] In detail and to the point H Gersdorf, *Öffentliche Unternehmen im Spannungsfeld zwischen Demokratie- und Wirtschaftlichkeitsprinzip* (Berlin, Duncker & Humblot, 2000).

[28] F Brosius-Gersdorf, *Deutsche Bundesbank und Demokratieprinzip* (Berlin, Duncker & Humblot, 1997).

[29] V Mehde, *Neues Steuerungsmodell und Demokratieprinzip* (Berlin, Duncker & Humblot, 2000).

[30] BVerfGE 47, 253 – *District Assemblies of North Rhine-Westphalia* (1978).

the case may be – had to be capable of being traced back to the people, meaning all citizens.[31] Barely five years later, the same Second Senate of the BVerfG, in its judgment regarding the Law concerning Co-determination in the Land of Schleswig-Holstein, extended the concept of legitimization to cover co-determination by staff council. Generally it held that, in light of the precept of democratic legitimization, there was no room for an autonomy of the public service. However, the less decisions under involvement of the staff council were part of the responsible observance of the administrative mandate, and the more strongly they affected the interests of the employees, the more the participation of councils can be regarded as compatible with the requirements of democratic legitimization.[32] A further significant step forward was made by the court in its 2002 decision concerning two water associations. While the establishment of self-administrating bodies requires a statute which adequately sets out tasks and requirements in order to take action, the democratic principle, which was understood as being open to development, was supplemented and strengthened by functional self-government. Moreover, the legislator is permitted to grant a right of co-determination in the exercise of state power to those affected, as well as to external experts, in order to achieve its aims and objectives more effectively.[33] This decision was the final step in transforming the originally 'monistic' model into a hybrid model of democratic legitimization, combining elements of the 'monistic' and 'pluralist' models.

III. MONISTIC VERSUS PLURALISTIC CONCEPT OF DEMOCRATIC LEGITIMIZATION

At this point, having already touched lightly on their strengths and weaknesses, both concepts will be examined more closely. It should first be mentioned that both the 'monistic' and 'pluralist' models of legitimization are basic models from which, in recent times, a multitude of variations and even combinations have developed.

A. The Monistic Concept of Legitimization: Exclusive Democracy

i. The Concept

Although each individual variation contains its own nuances and/or differences, the 'monistic' concept is comprised of three basic elements which correspond to the three questions posed by Article 20(2), clause 1 GG ('All power of the state

[31] BVerfGE 83, 37 – *Suffrage of Foreigners for Local Elections in Schleswig-Holstein* (1990); BVerfGE 83, 60 – *Suffrage of Foreigners for the District Assemblies of Hamburg* (1990).

[32] BVerfGE 93, 37 – *Law on Co-determination in Schleswig-Holstein* (1995).

[33] BVerfGE 107, 59 – *Lippeverband and Emschergenossenschaft* (2002); see additionally BVerfGE 111, 191 – *Chamber of Notaries* (2004).

emanates from the people'). These three questions are: Who legitimizes? What must be legitimized? How should such legitimization take place? The three fundamental elements of the legitimization model set out in the *Grundgesetz* are the people (of the state), the citizenship as sole legitimization subject, the exercise of state power as the object of legitimization which keeps the precept of legitimization current and, finally, the tracing back of state power to the people as a medium of legitimization or relationship of legitimization between the subject and the object. The final element requires definition on two levels. First, how is legitimization implemented in the order of the *Grundgesetz*? Which instruments are recognized or permitted by the *Grundgesetz* in order to put legitimization between the subject and object into action? The questions here relates to the means or modes of democratic legitimization. Secondly, a question arises as to the level of immediacy or density of the democratic legitimization required by the Constitution in a particular context. This matter relates to the so-called level of legitimization (*Legitimationsniveau*), which is not uniform in all instances of exercise of state power, but rather is decided depending on which individual function is being performed. A differentiation between levels of legitimization is, in any case, suggested by Article 20(2), clause 2 GG in its separation of powers which is placed in a democratic context. The various effects of legitimization – be they material effects or effects upon personnel, or even of a functional-institutional type – are not all individually required in order to reach the required level of legitimization. Rather, their effects are to be combined and summarized; in their entirety, the sum of these effects must guarantee that the density of connection provided for in the Constitution is reached. The manner in which the level of legitimization that is to be achieved is actually ascertained arises from the constitutional provisions devoted to regulating the exercise of state power (and, insofar as the exercise of power by the *Länder* is concerned, the corresponding provisions within the constitutions of the *Länder*) rather than from Article 20(2) GG itself. The blueprint of democratic legitimization is to be read into the organizational model of the state at both federal and *Länder* level.

The administration is characterized by – in personnel terms – the so-called unbroken chain of legitimization (*ununterbrochene Legitimationskette*) which extends from the top of administration and the government (and, possibly, the head of state) and which can be traced indirectly back to the parliament and the people. From a material content perspective, the obligation to abide by statutes and the subordination of administrative employees to the administrative power of those with parliamentary responsibility, ie the departmental ministers, determine the administrative exercise of power. The *Grundgesetz*, as well as the constitutions of the *Länder*, recognize an array of more or less systematic deviations from the general administrative-legitimatory model. These include some deviations which involve a lowered level of legitimization as well as others which do not. The most important example of the exercise of state power which involves a deviation in the elements of legitimization involved, but no lowering in the level of legitimization, is that which occurs within the parameters of local self-government. In addition to the personnel and material (as well as institutional) tracing-back to the people of the Federal Republic and those of the *Länder*, there is a tracing-back to the respective citizens of the particular local district which is partly substitutionary. The people of a particular locality, however – with the constitutional modification of Article 28(1), clause 3 GG for citizens of the European Union – represent nothing more than a territorial section of the people of the state within the meaning of Article 20(2), clause 1 GG. Functional self-government is, however, a different matter. Its 'corporate people' (*Verbandsvolk*) are not linked to one another by their nationality and citizenship but rather they constitute a group of people who are associated with each other by virtue of their social functions, for example, by reason of their profession. Accordingly, it cannot act as an agent of democratic legitimization in the sense of Article 20(2), clause 1 GG. The lowering of the level of legitimization, which goes hand in hand with this, requires justification through the Constitution of the Federal Republic or by the respective *Land* which is usually bound by statutory provisions that are stipulated in abstract or concrete terms.

ii. The Criticism

Note, first of all, that the elements of the input-oriented model of legitimization which concern its individual components as well as its entire composition have found wide recognition within legal scholarly writings and jurisprudence. However, the 'monistic' model of legitimization described above attracts criticism, which is – in part – quite severe, because of its demand of exclusivity, on the one hand, and, on the other, its – so goes the criticism – one-sidedness in relation to the determination of almost all elements of legitimization.

In this way, the concept of the centrality of the people is met with the criticism that democracy '[a]s an organisational consequence of human dignity'[34] – ie the legitimization monism which is directed at the people – is open to plurality and pluralism of legitimization subjects. In addition to the legitimization which can be traced back to the people (of the Federal Republic, *Länder* or other localities), the 'autonomous' legitimization which can be traced back to a so-called 'corporate people' (*Verbandsvolk*) must also be recognized as being democratic within the meaning of the *Grundgesetz*. In relation to the modes and the means of democratic legitimization, critics of the 'monistic' concept deem that it concentrates one-sidedly on the personnel and material aspects of legitimization; other modes of legitimization are not employed – or are not sufficiently recognized. The fixation upon steering methods – which are important but not in the least all-encompassing and/or completely exclusive – such as statutes and directives, is just as reductionist. Other instruments employed to implement democratic legiti-

[34] Trute, 'Die demokratische Legitimation der Verwaltung' (n 23) para 19, subsequent to P Häberle, 'Die Menschenwürde als Grundlage der staatlichen Gemeinschaft' in J Isensee and P Kirchhof, *Handbuch des Staatsrechts der Bundesrepublik Deutschland*, vol II, 3rd edn (Heidelberg, CF Müller, 2004) § 22, para 67.

mization in this 'parliament-focused steering optimism'[35] are wantonly ignored. Legitimatory super-elevation of ministerial administration is a counterpart of this: it is erroneously declared to be a rule from which deviations are possible only if justifications of varying levels of severity are employed. Differentiation and pluralization which already exist within the administration are rather misunderstood, as concepts of unity and homogeneity of the administration are projected upon past times in a historically incorrect manner.

The criticism may be summarized as follows: the 'monistic' concept is not complex enough in its composition and unrealistic in its consequences. It has a formal(istic) and static approach. In light of the differentiation, the pluralization and the Europeanization of the administrative power, such a normative idealization can be accorded only minor explanatory value.

B. The Pluralistic Concept of Legitimization: Inclusive Democracy

i. The Concept

The legitimization model which calls itself 'pluralistic' responds to the criticism of the alleged one-sidedness of the 'monistic' model. Its character as an alternative plan does not arise out of the negation of the input-oriented concept of legitimization, but rather out of the fact that it enriches this concept on all levels by adding further elements of legitimization – in this sense, it pluralizes the concept.

This begins at the level of the subject of legitimization. The people are not defined exclusively as a group of state nationals or citizens, but rather autonomy and self-determination of the individual, as products of human dignity, are to be acknowledged as the basis of all democracy which leads to a plurality of subjects of democratic legitimization that are in tension amongst themselves. It is primarily a matter for the legislator to determine the exact meaning of this 'open definition of the people'[36] in a manner which does justice to the particular circumstances and which is free of discrimination. In this sense, 'autonomous legitimization'[37] is also equipped by statute to be a repository of fully valid democratic legitimization.

The 'classic' model of democratic legitimization must also be supplemented on the level of the object of legitimization. Not only the decision-making ability of the state requires democratic legitimization, which gives rise to the enactment of law; rather, each act capable of being ascribed to the state – even in particular, the mere act of consultation – elicits the need for legitimization. Furthermore, the responsibility of the state for legitimization is not limited to its own organizational area but stretches to the area of cooperation with private persons, though this is, admittedly, a weaker form.

[35] Trute (n 23) para 32.
[36] ibid para 25.
[37] Emde (n 11) 383; thereto Trute (n 23) paras 54–55.

The strongest modifications to the 'classic model' are to be found in the area of the actual ways of legitimization. The decisive point of reference of the 'pluralist' approach is that the democratic nexus of attribution must be verifiable in concreto and effective in practice.[38] This, however, calls for the steering instrument and various instances of interaction responsible for the achievement of a sufficient level of legitimization to be recorded in a realistic manner. Accordingly, organizational and procedural democratic legitimization must be regarded as being on equal terms with the usual modes of democratic legitimization. The formal input view, which is based upon the so-called legitimization chain, is to be supplemented by a material output legitimization. It is not only the formal input view which is decisive; an effective performance of function is a supplement and, in part, a substitution.[39] The achievement of a legitimate goal for the benefit of all justifies (or compensates for) the possible reduction of input-legitimization. The decisive matter is that in the institutional-procedural-material-personnel arrangement which has actually been set out, there exists a sufficiently democratic nexus of attribution which can continue to be achieved 'under realistic conditions' and not just in a normative fictitious manner.[40] The task of establishing a structure assigned to the legislator plays a central role. In its performance of this task, the legislator possesses a considerable margin of appreciation in the areas of ascertainment, estimation and design.

As a result of administrative bodies establishing themselves as independent entities and becoming more pluralized, the matter of constitutional justification of a democratic legitimization deficit – which is a matter for concern under the 'monistic' model – is no longer the main focus. In its place, a question which is more all-encompassing must be determined, ie whether the concrete arrangement of organizational, personnel, material and procedural steering effects as well as input- and output-oriented legitimization can guarantee a sufficiently effective nexus of attribution between the people and the exercise of state power. First and foremost, it obliges the legislator to achieve an arrangement, differentiated according to the concrete task and organization, of de-coupling and re-integration for the exercise of administrative state power. In the case of the integration of those parties concerned in the execution of administrative tasks, the matter of 'sufficient responsiveness to the interests of those affected'[41] in relation to autonomous democratic legitimization must be taken into account. Moreover, in the case of cooperation with private parties, a guarantee that the 'requirement to perform tasks in a proper way and to certify sufficient neutrality in the overall institutional arrangement'[42] is respected must be brought to the fore.

[38] cf BVerfGE 107, 59, 91 – *Lippeverband and Emschergenossenschaft* (2002). Accordingly, Trute (n 23) paras 2, 34, 56 and throughout.

[39] This approach is – on a basis of a legitimatory aligned contract theory of James M Buchanan – particularly stressed by S Bredt, *Die demokratische Legitimation unabhängiger Institutionen* (Tübingen, Mohr Siebeck, 2006) 173, 280.

[40] Trute (n 23) para 56.

[41] ibid para 88.

[42] ibid para 96.

ii. The Criticism

There are four central objections to the 'pluralistic' concept of legitimization. First, the objection that there is an insufficient link between this concept and current constitutional law, or rather, that this link cannot exist (1), secondly, the objection that it has no critical value to speak of (2), thirdly, the objection that it does not live up to its own claims (3), and finally, the objection that the output-legitimization of which it boasts is expertocratic and not of democratic origin (4).

(1) The bulk of schemes which aim to enrich legitimization by making it more pluralist are rolled out without having first made clear the constitutional provisions from which these addenda originate. This is clearest in the theory of the pluralism of legitimization subjects on the one hand, and, on the other, the determination of the level of legitimization.

The 'open definition of the people' – beyond the differentiation of the people of the state into federal, *Länder* and regional people (Article 20(2) and Article 28(1) GG) which, in whole and in part, are interrelated – is substantiated by the fact that democracy is an organizational consequence of human dignity, autonomy and self-determination of the individual. The connection between democracy and human dignity can certainly not be denied, but is so vague that the 'open definition of people' (*offener Volksbegriff*) cannot be seen as being a necessary consequence. According to the system of regulation in the *Grundgesetz*, it would be much more pertinent to differentiate in this case: the self-determination of the individual is primarily and directly protected by the *Rechtsstaat* and the fundamental rights, while democracy can be seen as the collective self-determination of the people in which the individual plays a part 'only' as a 'member' of this group (a German citizen). This second form of autonomy, which is substantiated by human dignity, is bound by two conditions for the individual. First, it is not the quality of being a person which grants democratic autonomy, but rather the fact of belonging to a democratic association of self-determination, ie the fact of being a citizen. Secondly, linked with this first condition is the fact that the right to self-determination within the collective people is mutated to the right to collective determination. Finally, as is documented by numerous provisions in the *Grundgesetz*, although the constitutional connection between democracy and nation continues to exist (see in particular the preamble, Article 1(2), Article 20(2), Article 23(1), Article 28(1), Article 33, Article 38(1), Article 56, Article 64(2), Article 146 GG), this does not mean that democracy can only exist within national borders.

Similarly, proponents of the 'pluralist' concept of legitimization tend to quote no constitutional provisions whatsoever where the level of legitimization and its determination are concerned. They do, however, also emphasize that a sufficient legitimatory nexus of attribution must be verified. However, constitutional norms are generally not used to determine how exactly 'sufficient' should be defined when referring to any function-differentiated requirements upon legitimization. How, then, can the level of legitimization be asserted to be a measure of ensuring the nexus of attribution which is demanded by the Constitution? The mistaken presumption under positive law in relation to the determination of the required level of democratic legitimization continues in the question which arises as a consequence; which measures should be used and with which methods should it be ascertained whether or not the institutional arrangement of an independent administrative body successfully reaches or falls short of the level of legitimization required by the Constitution? This is a particularly pressing question in light of the plurality and heterogony of the effects of legitimization. What relation do the different effects of legitimization bear to one another in the areas of allocation and commensurability? And with which of the methods and units of measurement which are available to legal scholars and lawyers should one *measure* the concrete tangibility and the actual effectiveness of a legitimatory nexus of attribution?

(2) On the one hand, the requirements of legitimization enumerated by 'pluralists' appear, on the whole, to be so vague and so general, so dependent upon their configuration and upon further determination that neither exact nor concrete measures can be taken as being required by the Constitution. On the other hand, for each instance of pluralization of or each instance of gaining of independence by the administration in its actions, an exorbitant number of (at least potential) effects of legitimization which must be taken into account can be enumerated so that the achievement of a sufficient nexus of attribution should not be too difficult. The legitimatory repertoire of the 'pluralistic' concept is so varied, so rich and so vast in its possibilities of application and combination that there is a justification for any institutional-organizational form conceivable and/or desired. The only constitutional principle which is really easily understood is the requirement that every independent act of the administration requires a parliamentary statute which is framed in sufficiently definite terms. This principle, however, arises out of the generally acknowledged institutional reserve (*institutioneller Gesetzesvorbehalt*), which, in addition to its democratic roots also originates out of the principle of *Rechtsstaat* and that of the Federal State (*Bundesstaatsprinzip*). Thus in order to substantiate the requirement of the existence of a statute, no immense democratic-legitimatory superstructure is required.

(3) One can certainly not accuse the 'pluralistic' model of having named too few and too little different effects of legitimization in comparison to its 'monistic' competitors. But it is imperative that the model remains under-complex where actual tangibility and effectiveness in each individual case of the exercise of state power are to be taken seriously as the reference figures of legitimization. It is true that this concept may not be spared the reproach that it does not (and, under realistic expectations, cannot) achieve the requirements which it itself defines. This is because the particular measure which was decisive in relation to the way in which a particular act of state power occurred may rarely be stated with certainty. If it depends upon the actual currents of influence, the actual tangible and effective relationships of attribution, then one may not limit one's survey to influences which are capable of being observed from the exterior, those which can be generalized or formalized. The inclusion of psychological, individual and informal factors,

however, leads to hypercomplexity which does not allow a model of legitimization to operate or to appear operational, and that problem is not just one in theory, but also one in practice. When one takes *all* of the real steering effects in each individual case into account, those who must apply the law, who already inescapably and intentionally operate in a manner which aims to reduce complexity, are hopelessly overstretched. This is also the case in relation to the law itself. Talk of the actual tangibility and effectiveness of democratic legitimization – ie the incursion of 'reality' into law – should, then, not be taken very seriously.

(4) The 'pluralist' concept has a considerable asset, namely its supplementing of input-legitimization with output-legitimization. However, the question arises as to what exactly remains specifically democratic in relation to this form of justification of leadership. In this, it is really of no importance whether or not the output-legitimization can be traced back to a material necessity which is openly political or functional-practical. For in both cases, the matter is one not of a democratic – and therefore voluntaristic – argument, but rather a genuinely expertocratic – and therefore idealistic – one. In the case of output-legitimization, the decisive matter is not the tracing back to the will of the people, but rather the quality with which tasks are carried out, which is often achieved more capably by experts than by representatives of the people. The basic democratic-relativist proposition *stat pro ratione voluntas* is here, idealistically, overturned: *stat pro voluntate ratio*. The fact that certain public tasks are achieved more effectively, efficiently and adequately by independent experts or by other societal elites than they would be by a parliamentary-controlled power – here, the task of controlling currency carried out by an independent bank of issue springs to mind – may be the case. At this juncture, however, it is contended that there are boundaries upon the ability of democratic leadership to act. There are some good arguments for this point of view – as in the case of the independent bank of issue. Equally, one can discuss whether or not, in light of the existence of pluralist and fragmented societies, and in light of the demands of a globalized economy, the democratic legitimization of leadership can be complemented and even partially replaced by expertocratic legitimization. The former, however, can be best served by the requirement of 'government for the people'. It is not 'government by the people', being democratic within the meaning of the *Grundgesetz*. Consequently, output-legitimization cannot act as a substitute for input-legitimization in the area of the principle of democracy, but is rather incommensurable.

IV. BEYOND 'MONISM' AND 'PLURALISM'

A. A Matter of Positivization

The discussion relating to what the precept of democratic legitimization within the meaning of the *Grundgesetz* means and demands has two faults. The first is to be found in the 'everything must be democratic' dilemma: nowadays, democracy as a form of state has no alternative which can really be taken seriously. Consequently, there is a struggle, as well as an expectation, that every form of exercise of power which is legally provided for in a political system need be proven to be democratic. Undemocratic or not democratic amounts to being unconstitutional and illegal. Democraticity and legality are implicitly regarded as being congruent. A certain extent of democratic legitimization is easily understood to be a certain extent of legality. Levels of legality are, however, difficult to imagine. Under these conditions, it is difficult to remain unbiased as one investigates the question of whether, and if yes, to what extent applicable German constitutional law contains contrary principles which can justify any exceptions to the principle of democratic legitimization. Furthermore, the discussion is complicated by the fact that it is dominated by the juxtaposition of both models – the 'monistic' and 'pluralistic'. In the foreground stands the alternative as to whether one supports 'monism' or 'pluralism'. Here, however, the concepts threaten to assume an independent reality. Under the auspices of state theory, the 'monists' are the statists who, as ever, insist upon the national state while the 'pluralists' assume the role of anti-statists who regard concentration upon a national state to be obsolete and misguided. The decision is really a matter of one's own personal *Weltanschauung*.

Conversely, it must be remembered that the question of how democratic legitimization – *within the meaning of the Grundgesetz* – should be designed is not one concerning one's own preferred world-view (for or against one of the two concepts), nor is it one of a preference for criteria outside of law. *To this extent*, it cannot be a matter of which concept of legitimization is more ethical for society, which of the prevailing socio-political circumstances is more reasonable, which accommodates the conditions of state exercise of power in pluralist and fragmented, economy-centred and media-determined societies more convincingly or which promises the most efficiency under the auspices of (institutional-)economic allocation of resources. To this end, the sole decisive matter is how valid positive constitutional law answers the question of the form and manner of democratic legitimization. If the democratic principle in its guise as a norm of valid positive constitutional law is the central point of focus, then the matter is not (primarily) one of the character or the intrinsic logic of democracy under political theory, institutional economics, jurisprudence, theory of state, constitutional theory or constitutional sociology, but rather under constitutional dogmatics (*Verfassungsdogmatik*).[43] This question is linked to a specific normative viewpoint according to which democratic legitimization is classified as a nexus of attribution qualified by certain norms of positive law. As a result of this, if and insofar as the Constitution which is in force qualifies a nexus of attribution and the steering media which constitute this relationship as being normatively relevant (ie neces-

[43] In Germany, legal dogmatics (*Rechtsdogmatik*) is understood as practical or practice-oriented jurisprudence, ie any (sub-)discipline of jurisprudence which prepares the law in a scientific manner – primarily – for the party who applies the law. To this extent, valid positive law defines the borders of legal dogmatics. Inasmuch as the position of legal dogmatics in relation to the valid positive law is structurally affirmative, the party applying the law has little power to question valid positive law.

sary and/or sufficient), evidence to the effect that steering performance expected of the instruments in question by the Constitution cannot be empirically verified or negated. It is as untrue to claim that the linguistic philosophy can unmask the concept of the law's binding force as far from reality or that the recent findings of brain research can debunk the normative construct of human free will as obsolete, as it is to rebuke the positive law's concept of legitimization under the auspices of social science solely because of the fact that it does not encompass or acknowledge the actual steering and interaction influences in the exercise of state power. The so-called 'reality' – which, when seen in the cold light of day is nothing more than an interpretive construct itself – cannot refute 'the norm'. In this regard, it is not decisive for the principle of democracy *as a norm of valid positive law* how the steering influences in a particular institutional arrangement can be described. The decisive matter is if and to what extent steering effects have been distinguished as being relevant by the constitutional legislator.

If, however, the matter is that of with which concept the legal position is better described and explained by the *Grundgesetz*, then the 'monistic' concept may have the upper hand on the 'pluralistic' – as has already been implied above – requiring, as it does, less toil to harmonize its assumptions and consequences with the *Grundgesetz*.[44]

B. The Democratic Legitimization of the European Union at a Glance

The fact that the choice of judicial ideology (*Weltanschauung*) does not necessarily coincide with a monistic or pluralistic understanding of legitimization can best be seen in the example of the democratic legitimization of the European Union.[45] On the basis of a state-related model of democracy, the monistic view recognizes deficits of legitimization on the part of the European Union. The BVerfG has broadly adopted this point of view in its *Maastricht*[46] and *Lisbon*[47] decisions. At the same time, the pluralistic view should have no difficulty – as often – in attesting to the fact that the European Union has achieved a sufficient level of legitimization.

An approach based on strict positivity, in that sense positivistic approach, might tend towards a point of view that lies across the 'battle lines' described above: sovereign acts of the European Union (NB: under German constitutional law only) do not lack democraticity on the grounds that they would not comply with the monistic interpretation of the *Grundgesetz*'s requirements for exercising sovereignty. However, the mere ability to find an institutional arrangement for those sovereign acts that make the context of attribution tangible and truly

[44] Regarding the majority of relevant interpretation matters, see in detail Jestaedt (n 11) 138, 178, 265, 301, 369, 425.

[45] For a very detailed overview, A von Komorowski, *Demokratieprinzip und Europäische Union: Staatsverfassungsrechtliche Anforderungen an die demokratische Legitimation der EG-Normsetzung* (Berlin, Duncker & Humblot, 2010).

[46] BVerfGE 89, 155, 171–72, 182 – *Treaty of Maastricht* (1993).

[47] BVerfGE 123, 267, 330, 340 – *Treaty of Lisbon* (2009).

effective does not mean that there were no democratic-legitimatory concerns. Instead this question was answered by the constitutional legislator on the occasion of the ratification of the Treaty of Maastricht in 1992. The concept of legitimization specifically designed for the European Union was included and positivized in Article 23(1) GG (see, in particular, clause 1 referring to 'basic democratic principles'). As long as the European Union stays within the (pluralistic) track of legitimization laid down by the Treaty of Maastricht when exercising sovereignty, its actions will not be classified by the *Grundgesetz* as lacking of democratic legitimization.

V. THE PARADOX OF THE DEMOCRATIC PRINCIPLE

The different conjunctures characterizing the democratic legitimization of the administrative power under the *Grundgesetz* show what can be regarded as the paradox of the democratic principle. This principle ironically receives practical legal effectiveness solely on the condition that its scope and mode of operation are not overstretched. Instead it is one of many constitutional principles and, as such, is interpreted and applied just as all constitutional principles are. Hot-wiring law and 'reality' – and thereby regarding everything as being democratically legitimated – will not only devalue the practical effectiveness of the democratic principle, but may even lead to creeping de-democratization of the state's authority under democratic auspices. This will turn the opaque constitutional principle into a toothless tiger.

CASES

BVerfGE 47, 253 – *District Assemblies of North Rhine-Westphalia* (1978)
BVerfGE 83, 37 – *Suffrage of Foreigners for Local Elections in Schleswig-Holstein* (1990)
BVerfGE 83, 60 – *Suffrage of Foreigners for the District Assemblies of Hamburg* (1990)
BVerfGE 93, 37 – *Law on Co-determination in Schleswig-Holstein* (1995)
BVerfGE 107, 59 – *Lippeverband and Emschergenossenschaft* (2002)
BVerfGE 111, 191 – *Chamber of Notaries* (2004)
BVerfGE 123, 267 – *Treaty of Lisbon* (2009)
BVerfGE 130, 76 – *Execution of Measures of Correction and Prevention by a Private Entity* (2012)

SELECTED LITERATURE

Bauer H, Huber PM, and Sommermann KP (eds), *Demokratie in Europa* (Tübingen, Mohr Siebeck, 2005)

Böckenförde EW, 'Demokratie als Verfassungsprinzip' in J Isensee and P Kirchhof (eds), *Handbuch des Staatsrechts der Bundesrepublik Deutschland*, vol II, 2nd edn (Heidelberg, CF Müller, 2004) § 24, 429–96

Bredt S, *Die demokratische Legitimation unabhängiger Institutionen: Vom funktionalen zum politikfeldbezogenen Demokratieprinzip* (Tübingen, Mohr Siebeck, 2006)
Bryde BO, 'Die bundesrepublikanische Volksdemokratie als Irrweg der Demokratietheorie' (1994) 5 *Staatswissenschaften und Staatspraxis* 305–30
Classen CD, *Demokratische Legitimation im offenen Rechtsstaat: Zur Beeinflussung des Demokratieprinzips durch Rechtsstaatlichkeit und internationale Offenheit* (Tübingen, Mohr Siebeck, 2009)
Dreier H, *Hierarchische Verwaltung im demokratischen Staat: Genese, aktuelle Bedeutung und funktionelle Grenzen eines Bauprinzips der Exekutive* (Tübingen, Mohr Siebeck, 1991)
Emde ET, *Die demokratische Legitimation der funktionalen Selbstverwaltung: Eine verfassungsrechtliche Studie anhand der Kammern, der Sozialversicherungsträger und der Bundesanstalt für Arbeit* (Berlin, Duncker & Humblot, 1991)
Gersdorf H, *Öffentliche Unternehmen im Spannungsfeld von Demokratie- und Wirtschaftlichkeitsprinzip: Eine Studie zur verfassungsrechtlichen Legitimation der wirtschaftlichen Betätigung der öffentlichen Hand* (Berlin, Duncker & Humblot, 2000)
Groß T, *Das Kollegialprinzip in der Verwaltungsorganisation* (Tübingen, Mohr Siebeck, 1999)
Hanebeck A, 'Bundesverfassungsgericht und Demokratieprinzip. Zwischen monistischem und pluralistischem Demokratieverständnis' (2004) *Die öffentliche Verwaltung* 901–09
Jestaedt M, *Demokratieprinzip und Kondominialverwaltung: Entscheidungsteilhabe Privater an der öffentlichen Verwaltung auf dem Prüfstand des Verfassungsprinzips Demokratie* (Berlin, Duncker & Humblot, 1993)
Kluth W, *Funktionale Selbstverwaltung: Verfassungsrechtlicher Status – verfassungsrechtlicher Schutz* (Tübingen, Mohr Siebeck, 1997)
Köller S, *Funktionale Selbstverwaltung und ihre demokratische Legitimation: Eine Untersuchung am Beispiel der Wasserverbände Lippeverband und Emschergenossenschaft* (Berlin, Duncker & Humblot, 2009)
Komorowski A von, *Demokratieprinzip und Europäische Union: Staatsverfassungsrechtliche Anforderungen an die demokratische Legitimation der EG-Normsetzung* (Berlin, Duncker & Humblot, 2010)
Mehde V, *Neues Steuerungsmodell und Demokratieprinzip* (Berlin, Duncker & Humblot, 2000)
Möllers C, *Demokratie – Zumutungen und Versprechen* (Berlin, Verlag Klaus Wagenbach, 2008)
Oebbecke J, *Weisungs- und unterrichtungsfreie Räume in der Verwaltung* (Cologne & Stuttgart, Deutscher Gemeindeverlag & Kohlhammer, 1986)
Ossenbühl F, 'Gedanken zur demokratischen Legitimation der Verwaltung' in HD Horn(ed), *Festschrift für Walter Schmitt Glaeser* (Berlin, Duncker & Humblot, 2003) 103–18
Schliesky U, *Souveränität und Legitimität von Herrschaftsgewalt* (Tübingen, Mohr Siebeck, 2004)
Schmidt J, *Die demokratische Legitimationsfunktion der parlamentarischen Kontrolle: Eine verfassungsrechtliche Untersuchung über Grundlage, Gegenstand und Grenzen der parlamentarischen Kontrolle unter besonderer Berücksichtigung der ministerialfreien Räume und der Privatisierung* (Berlin, Duncker & Humblot, 2007)
Schmidt-Aßmann E, 'Verwaltungslegitimation als Rechtsbegriff' (1991) 116 *Archiv des öffentlichen Rechts* 329–90

Trute HH, 'Die demokratische Legitimation der Verwaltung' in W Hoffmann-Riem, E Schmidt-Aßmann and Voßkuhle A (eds), *Grundlagen des Verwaltungsrechts*, vol I, 2nd edn (Munich, CH Beck, 2012) § 6, 341–435

Unger S, *Das Verfassungsprinzip der Demokratie: Normstruktur und Norminhalt des grundgesetzlichen Demokratieprinzips* (Tübingen, Mohr Siebeck, 2008)

Waechter K, *Geminderte demokratische Legitimation staatlicher Institutionen im parlamentarischen Regierungssystem: Zur Wirkung von Verfassungsprinzipien und Grundrechten auf institutionelle und kompetenzielle Ausgestaltungen* (Berlin, Duncker & Humblot, 1994)

11

Conceptualizing Administrative Law – Legal Protection versus Regulatory Approach

MARTIN EIFERT

I. INTRODUCTION

WHAT PURPOSE DOES the study of administrative law serve and what methods should be used in its pursuit? Over the past few decades, these questions have developed into a field of intensive, sustained academic debate. The debate has focused on the main ideas of administrative law, its fundamental categories and concepts and the role of jurisprudence in the legal system with respect to administrative law – in short, on the self-concept of that part of legal scholarship that focuses on administrative law.

The following portrayal of the debate is divided into four sections. In section II, the origins of the recent debates regarding administrative law and the different conceptual starting points will be sketched out. Section III will summarize the competing schools of thought, and section IV will illustrate the partial discourses which have fed the broader debate. Section V will survey the contemporary treatment of this discussion in the relevant literature, and will conclude with a look at the future. Each section will necessarily take a woodcut-like schematic form, and citations will be intermittent.

II. THE JURISPRUDENTIAL SELF-CONCEPT OF ADMINISTRATIVE LAW AND ITS TRANSFORMATIONS

A. Development of the Dominance of Formal Concepts and a Rights-protection Perspective

An oft-cited *bon mot* expresses the consensus view of German legal science's self-concept: 'Legal science is either systematic or it does not exist at all'.[1] From its very beginnings, the systematic ordering of legal concepts has been a central aim of German legal science in general and jurisprudential analysis of administrative law in particular.[2] This systematization is depicted in the distinction between a 'General Part' (setting forth broad definitions and basic categories) and a 'Special Part' (containing specific rules) for administrative law, as well as in the customary division of many sub-categories of administrative law itself into general and special parts.[3] The self-imposed goal of establishing a systematic ordering brings in its wake an approach which places special emphasis on the criteria of the systematization and the development of a system of concepts.

[1] H-J Wolff, 'Typen im Recht und in der Rechtswissenschaft' (1952) 5 *Studium Generale* 195, 205.

[2] cf C Bumke, *Relative Rechtswidrigkeit* (Tübingen, Mohr Siebeck, 2004) 249, 255. As a current cornerstone, see E Schmidt-Aßmann, *Das Allgemeine Verwaltungsrecht als Ordnungsidee*, 2nd edn (Berlin, Springer, 2004); cf for an analysis of the problems entailed, C Möllers, 'Methodische Zugänge zum Verwaltungsrecht' in W Hoffmann-Riem, E Schmidt-Aßmann and A Voßkuhle (eds), *Grundlagen des Verwaltungsrechts*, vol 1 (Munich, CH Beck, 2006) § 3, paras 35.

[3] cf T Groß, 'Die Beziehungen zwischen dem Allgemeinen und dem Besonderen Verwaltungsrecht' (1999) 32 *Die Verwaltung* supplement 2, 57; J Kersten and S-C Lenski, 'Die Entwicklungsfunktion des Allgemeinen Verwaltungsrechts' (2009) 42 *Die Verwaltung* 501.

This basic understanding initially provides only a formal methodical framework. The actual substance depends on which perspective drives the academic approach, which criteria are selected for the system and what role the concepts play. This is where administrative law has found itself in a state of continuous tension. On the one hand, scholars were dealing with abstractions which permitted general legal differentiation, for instance, when a certain activity could be linked to a typical legal consequence. The typical example of this construct was the 'administrative act', which bound action to legal consequence particularly effectively. This approach was in marked contrast to the merely cumulative presentation that characterized the former attempts of the so-called *Staatswissenschaften*.[4] On the other hand, administrative law also needs to study the ordinary administrative tasks that shape the practice and goals of public administration. Public safety and fiscal administration, and also later benefits administration, are different tasks that must be fulfilled in varying ways according to the specific area of activity. All of the major early attempts to systematize administrative law[5] – from Otto Mayer to Walter Jellinek, from Hans Peters to Ernst Forsthoff – reflected and addressed this tension between formal abstraction and task-orientation.[6] It was, however, the doctrine of *forms of action*, as a formal abstraction that developed the clearest contours and thus became a central focus of the study of administrative law and the pivotal point of its General Part.[7] The principal legal construct in this doctrine, which was initially shaped by Otto Mayer, was the *administrative act*.

The orientation towards forms of action was from Otto Mayer onwards organically linked to a rights-protection perspective. The guarantee of protection of the subject's legal rights before administrative courts was, for a long time, conditioned on the presence of an administrative act – that is, a certain form of legal action. To this day, the concrete contours of legal protection in administrative law are linked to the existence of an administrative act. The rights-protection perspective was also strengthened by the comprehensive recognition of and emphasis on the individual as a legal subject in the early days of the post-war Federal Republic of Germany since the protection of rights in the German system is directly linked to whether the law accords subjective rights.[8]

[4] For an analysis and history of the approach which is linked to, among others, R von Mohl (early attempt) and L von Stein, see M Stolleis, *Geschichte des öffentlichen Rechts in Deutschland*, vol II (Munich, CH Beck, 1992) 258, 385; H Peukert, *Das tradierte Konzept der Staatswissenschaft* (Berlin, de Gruyter, 2005).

[5] cf for a clearer picture O Mayer, *Deutsches Verwaltungsrecht*, vol II, 3rd edn (Berlin, Duncker & Humblot, 1924); W Jellinek, *Verwaltungsrecht*, 3rd edn (Berlin, Julius Springer, 1931); H Peters, *Lehrbuch der Verwltung* (Berlin, Springer, 1949); E Forsthoff, *Lehrbuch des Verwaltungsrechts*, vol I, 10th edn (Munich, CH Beck, 1973).

[6] Concise overview in C Bumke, 'Die Entwicklung der verwaltungsrechtswissenschaftlichen Methodik in der Bundesrepublik Deutschland' in E Schmidt-Aßmann and W Hoffmann-Riem (eds), *Methoden der Verwaltungsrechtswissenschaft* (Baden-Baden, Nomos, 2004) 73, 85.

[7] A Hueber, *Otto Mayer: Die 'juristische Methode' im Verwaltungsrecht* (Berlin, Duncker & Humblot, 1981); W Meyer-Hesemann, *Methodenwandel in der Verwaltungsrechtswissenschaft* (Heidelberg, CF Müller, 1981) 15.

[8] R Wahl, *Herausforderungen und Antworten: Das Öffentliche Recht der letzten fünf Jahrzehnte* (Berlin, de Gruyter, 2006) 22.

Until well into the 1970s, it can be said (in a somewhat oversimplified fashion) that the study of administrative law was marked by a primary (albeit somewhat unstable, given the hidden tension) focus on forms of action and legal protection.

B. The Reform Discussion since the 1990s: The Regulatory Role of Administrative Law as a Conceptual Centrepiece

The legal-protection perspective of administrative law studies has never been exclusive.[9] However, it was increasingly questioned in the 1990s and challenged by the emergence of a new concept.[10] At the heart of this new concept was the realization of the goals that administrative law was intended to achieve.

i. Reaction to the Social-engineering Aspirations of the Modern Welfare State and its 'Crisis'

A central trigger for this change in perspective was the recognition by sociologists that the modern welfare state, with its ambition of social engineering through law, had led to a significant 'legalization' of social life. However, the actual effect of legal regulations was insufficient to achieve these aims. The discourses on legalization,[11] the change in the state's function[12] and the lack of effectiveness of traditional sanctions and remedies[13] brought new phenomena and new fields of action to the fore and called into question the relevance of traditional approaches to administrative law.

This was an era of political reform, and social science posed the question of the possibilities and limits of social engineering. This tendency found an echo in the study of administrative law: an increased demand to see administrative law as a means of social regulation, and to see law as a means of solving problems by furnishing appropriate instruments for the task. In the following decades, there was a corresponding call for a reform of administrative law. The reform was predomin-

[9] cf Meyer-Hesemann, *Methodenwandel in der Verwaltungsrechtswissenschaft* (n 7) 15; for a critical assessment in the 1960s, see P Badura, *Verwaltungsrecht im liberalen und im sozialen Rechtsstaat* (Tübingen, Mohr, 1966).

[10] Initially there were merely innovative academic questions and analysis. The approach used for these was first presented as a challenge to the traditional method by W Hoffmann-Riem, 'Reform des Allgemeinen Verwaltungsrecht' (1985) 110 *Archiv des Öffentlichen Rechts* 400; the following development was described as a fundamental conflict by C Möllers, 'Braucht das öffentliche Recht einen neuen Methoden- und Richtungsstreit?' (1999) 90 *Verwaltungsarchiv* 187; for a historical outline from the point of view of the new concept, see W Hoffmann-Riem, 'Zwischenschritte zur Modernisierung der Rechtswissenschaft' (2007) *Juristenzeitung* 645.

[11] F Kübler and HF Zacher, *Verrechtlichung von Wirtschaft, Arbeit und sozialer Solidarität* (Frankfurt am Main, Suhrkamp, 1985).

[12] D Grimm (ed), *Wachsende Staatsaufgaben – sinkende Steuerungsfähigkeit des Rechts* (Baden-Baden, Nomos, 1990); D Grimm (ed), *Staatsaufgaben* (Baden-Baden, Nomos, 1994).

[13] R Mayntz and others (eds), *Vollzugsprobleme der Umweltpolitik: empirische Untersuchung der Implementation von Gesetzen im Bereich der Luftreinhaltung und des Gewässerschutzes* (Stuttgart, Kohlhammer, 1978).

antly – although not exclusively – driven by discussions that Wolfgang Hoffmann-Riem and Eberhard Schmidt-Aßmann had fostered by means of annual conferences held over the course of a decade.[14] It resulted in a three-volume handbook on the fundamental structures of administrative law.[15]

ii. From a Legal-protection Focus to a Regulatory Focus

Administrative law's new focus entailed a fundamental change of perspective. Formerly, the focus had been on citizens seeking to protect their rights. Now, administrative law studies adopted the perspective of the bureaucracy and the legislator who had passed administrative laws, and sought to implement the norms and political goals contained in those enactments.[16]

Areas of research were thus created to address these new problems in context. Early on, environmental protection was a particular focus, and with it the special field of risk regulation, which has always been difficult for the legal system to deal with.[17] All major government reforms – including the re-organization of public administration in accordance with the principles of 'New Public Management', deregulation and privatization and the increased use of information and communications technology in electronic government – were also monitored by administrative law scholars.[18]

This orientation to specific problems expanded the scope of administrative law scholarship in two ways. The first expansion came in the form of an assessment of the variety of governing instruments, including their functional equivalents and questions of regulatory choice. This expansion brought into focus various phenomena that, despite their real importance, had until then been ignored or underrated: informal administrative action; neglected forms of action such as the public-private

[14] W Hoffmann-Riem, E Schmidt-Aßmann and GF Schuppert (eds), *Reform des Allgemeinen Verwaltungsrechts* (Baden-Baden, Nomos, 1993); W Hoffmann-Riem, E Schmidt-Aßmann (eds) *Innovation und Flexibilität des Verwaltungshandelns* (Baden-Baden, Nomos, 1994); W Hoffmann-Riem, Schmidt-Aßmann (eds), *Öffentliches Recht und Privatrecht als wechselseitige Auffangordnungen* (Baden-Baden, Nomos, 1996); W Hoffmann-Riem, E Schmidt-Aßmann (eds), *Effizienz als Herausforderung an das Verwaltungshandeln* (Baden-Baden, Nomos, 1998); W Hoffmann-Riem, E Schmidt-Aßmann (eds), *Verwaltungsrecht in der Informationsgesellschaft* (Baden-Baden, Nomos, 2000); W Hoffmann-Riem, E Schmidt-Aßmann (eds), *Verwaltungsverfahren und Verwaltungsverfahrensgesetz* (Baden-Baden, Nomos, 2002); E Schmidt-Aßmann and W Hoffmann-Riem (eds), *Verwaltungsorganisationsrecht als Steuerungsressource* (Baden-Baden, Nomos, 1997); E Schmidt-Aßmann and W Hoffmann-Riem (eds), *Strukturen des Europäischen Verwaltungsrechts* (Baden-Baden, Nomos, 1999); E Schmidt-Aßmann and W Hoffmann-Riem (eds), *Verwaltungskontrolle* (Baden-Baden, Nomos, 2001); E Schmidt-Aßmann and W Hoffmann-Riem (eds), *Methoden der Verwaltungsrechtswissenschaft* (Baden-Baden, Nomos, 2004).

[15] W Hoffmann-Riem, E Schmidt-Aßmann and A Voßkuhle (eds), *Grundlagen des Verwaltungsrechts*, vol I–III (Munich, CH Beck, 2006-09).

[16] Concise analysis by Bumke, 'Die Entwicklung der verwaltungsrechtswissenschaftlichen Methodik' (n 6) 73, 105. For a critical view on the change of perspective, see O Lepsius, *Steuerungsdiskussion, Systemtheorie und Parlamentarismuskritik* (Tübingen, Mohr Siebeck, 1999).

[17] cf among others R Wahl (ed), *Prävention und Vorsorge* (Bonn, Economica, 1995); A Scherzberg, 'Risikosteuerung durch Verwaltungsrecht, Ermöglichung oder Begrenzung von Innovationen?' (2004) 63 *Vereinigung der Deutschen Staatsrechtslehrer* 214–63.

[18] cf for a brief overview A Voßkuhle, 'Neue Verwaltungsrechtswissenschaft' in Hoffmann-Riem, Schmidt-Aßmann and Voßkuhle, *Grundlagen des Verwaltungsrechts* (n 2) § 1, para 49.

contract; new ideas such as mediation and statements of agreed goals; economic instruments such as internal markets, fees, and certificates; or the alternative relationship between state activity and state-regulated private activity as a means of realizing the public interest.[19]

The second expansion in the focus of administrative law was a more in-depth exploration, not only of the final decisions of the bureaucracy, but also of the conditions under which those decisions were made.[20] The importance of the organization of public administration and its procedures was highlighted by the perceived granting of more discretion to government agencies by the legislator, by the realization of the importance of information and knowledge for administrative activity in complex regulatory fields and by the search for the appropriate treatment of the remaining uncertainties.[21] The term 'proceduralization' was used to characterize those areas in which the law adapted the control of administrative action itself by substantive prescriptions into a structuring of decision-making procedures primarily by means of procedural forms.[22]

The general disappointment with the effectiveness of command and control legislation, as well as the increased focus on the legal instruments and the central role of information and knowledge, made the cooperation of the bureaucracy with private actors a main focus of research.[23] The concretization of the general welfare was seen as the result of a process of the division of labour in which governmental and private actors could contribute in all phases of implementation. Examples included private contributions to fact investigation; the private-sector creation of standards in social, environmental and technological law; private oversight of product safety;

[19] cf eg E Bohne, *Der informale Rechtsstaat* (Berlin, Duncker & Humblot, 1981) (for informal administrative action); H Bauer, 'Anpassungsflexibilität im öffentlich-rechtlichen Vertrag' in Hoffmann-Riem and Schmidt-Aßmann (eds), *Innovation und Flexibilität* (n 14), 245 (for new aspects of the public-private contract); W Hoffmann-Riem, *Konfliktmittler in Verwaltungsverhandlungen* (Heidelberg, CF Müller, 1989) (for mediation); G Lübbe-Wolff, 'Instrumente des Umweltrecht: Leistungsfähigkeit und Leistungsgrenzen' in Gesellschaft für Umweltrecht (ed), *Dokumentation zur 24. wissenschaftlichen Fachtagung der Gesellschaft für Umweltrecht e.V.* (2001) 29; T Vesting, 'Zur Entwicklung einer 'Informationsordnung' in P Badura and H Dreier (eds), *Festschrift 50 Jahre Bundesverfassungsgericht*, vol II (Tübingen, Mohr Siebeck, 2001) 219–24 (for an outline of the discussion on instruments in environmental law).

[20] cf Schmidt-Aßmann, *Das Allgemeine Verwaltungsrecht als Ordnungsidee* (n 2), 239; and the references in n 21. For contrary approaches to the legal analysis of organizations in the field of science, see H-H Trute, *Die Forschung zwischen grundrechtlicher Freiheit und staatlicher Institutionalisierung* (Tübingen, Mohr Siebeck, 1994), on the one hand, and KF Gärditz, *Hochschulorganisation und verwaltungsrechtliche Systembildung* (Tübingen, Mohr Siebeck, 2009) on the other.

[21] cf as an early example in the field of environmental law, K-H Ladeur, *Das Umweltrecht in der Wissensgesellschaft* (Berlin, Duncker & Humblot, 1995); as an example for the regulation of telecommunications, H-H Trute, 'Regulierung – am Beispiel des Telekommunikationsrechts' in CF Eberle (ed), *Festschrift für Winfried Brohm* (Munich, CH Beck, 2002); general approach, A Scherzberg, 'Die Öffentliche Verwaltung als informationelle Organisation' in Hoffmann-Riem and Schmidt-Aßmann (eds), *Verwaltungsrecht in der Informationsgesellschaft* (n 14) 195.

[22] cf the colourful description of the tendency by E Hagenah, *Prozeduraler Umweltschutz* (Baden-Baden, Nomos, 1996); for a theoretical underpinning K-H Ladeur, *Postmoderne Rechtstheorie* (Berlin, Duncker & Humblot, 1992).

[23] cf E-H Ritter, 'Der kooperative Staat: Bemerkungen zum Verhältnis von Staat und Wirtschaft' (1979) 104 *Archiv des Öffentlichen Rechts* 389; GF Schuppert (ed), *Jenseits von Privatisierung und 'schlankem' Staat* (Baden-Baden, Nomos, 1999).

and the creation of private organizational structures to achieve government goals, such as the recycling of reusables in the waste-disposal industry, or private contributions to infrastructure maintenance. From an administrative law perspective, a central task then became the regulation of private contributions in collaborative structures in ensuring an overall outcome that promotes the general welfare. The term used for the field was *Gewährleistungsverwaltungsrecht*.[24]

The focus on problematic areas and the emphasis on procedure, organization and knowledge also led to an emphasis on the temporal dimension in administrative law. Important themes included the dynamic adaption of legal demands on technical developments and environmental changes, the need for opportunities to review and/or revise decisions made under conditions of uncertainty as well as the importance of a legally structured information system to ensure the state's learning capacity.

iii. Methodological Opening to Other Disciplines

When the realization of goals and the formation of a problem-solving capacity of law became conceptual centres, the law was linked much more closely to reality than in the previous formal approach under the rights-protection perspective. Since legal scholars had few of their own methods for assessing reality, they became dependent on knowledge from other disciplines. Attempts to reform administrative law and its study therefore also brought in its wake openings towards other fields, in particular the social sciences.[25]

Conceptually, drawing on empirical data collection is the obvious first step. Empirical methods, in the form of studies of implementation deficits, helped trigger reform and these studies also provided direct information about the effects and effect-conditions of legal rules. The demand for more empirical research was, therefore, raised early,[26] although it remained largely unfulfilled. The research agendas of social sciences are (necessarily) too independent of jurisprudence to deliver precisely tailored answers to the questions posed by the latter. Furthermore, there are too many administrative law questions to permit them all to be answered by dint of empirical studies. The interface with social science was therefore driven primarily by ideas about the possibilities and limits of social engineering – some empirical, some theoretical – that intermeshed well with questions raised in administrative law debates. The work of the Max Planck Institute for Social

[24] A Voßkuhle, 'Beteiligung Privater an der Wahrnehmung öffentlicher Aufgaben und staatliche Verantwortung' (2003) 62 *Vereinigung der Deutschen Staatsrechtslehrer* 266; C Franzius, *Gewährleistung im Recht* (Tübingen, Mohr Siebeck, 2009).

[25] Hoffmann-Riem, *Zwischenschritte zur Modernisierung der Rechtswiss*enschaft (n 10); H-H Trute, 'Die Wissenschaft vom Verwaltungsrecht' (1999) 32 *Die Verwaltung* supplement 2, 9; for a detailed analysis concerning the key word 'Responsibility', see JH Klement, *Verantwortung* (Tübingen, Mohr Siebeck, 2006); for an integration of findings of social science in administrative law, see GF Schuppert, *Verwaltungswissenschaft* (Baden-Baden, Nomos, 2000).

[26] A Voßkuhle, 'Verwaltungsdogmatik und Rechtstatsachenforschung' (1994) 85 *Verwaltungsarchiv* 567.

Research under the directorship of Renate Mayntz and Fritz Scharpf with the approach of actor-centred institutionalism[27] was particularly relevant. The debate was also drawing (within certain limits) on the systemic theoretical work by Niklas Luhmann, Helmut Willke and Gunther Teubner, in particular on the approach of contextual control[28] and reflexive law.[29] More recently, new institutional economics, with its analyses of incentive structures and their effects, has increased in importance and the debate has been linked to the interdisciplinary discussion of governance.[30]

III. REGULATORY APPROACH AND TRADITIONAL METHOD AS DIFFERENT ORIENTATIONS: A SYNOPSIS

Neither the traditional approach nor the regulatory approach which had been developed during the reform discussion created a comprehensive methodical concept which could have resulted in a canonization. They are, rather, vague summaries of approaches that each differ in detail. They differ at least in their basic perspectives, the focus of their attention, their main criteria and their conversational context. Consequently, a conceptual distinction has emerged. The traditional approach has in accordance with the respective method in Private Law been called the 'juristic method' (*Juristische Methode*),[31] while the new approach, generated by the reform discussion, is known as the 'regulatory approach' (*Steuerungswissenschaftlicher Ansatz*) or, more recently, as the 'New Science of Administrative Law' (*Neue Verwaltungsrechtswissenschaft*).[32] Before the current debate over these approaches is analysed more closely, the main components of the methods, as represented by their primary orientations, will be summarized in a condensed form.[33]

[27] R Mayntz and FW Scharpf, 'Der Ansatz des akteurszentrierten Institutionalismus' in R Mayntz and FW Scharpf (eds), *Gesellschaftliche Selbstregelung und politische Steuerung* (Frankfurt am Main, Campus, 1995).

[28] H Willke, *Ironie des Staates: Grundlinien einer Theorie des Staates in polyzentrischer Gesellschaft* (Frankfurt am Main, Suhrkamp, 1992) 335.

[29] G Teubner, 'Reflexives Recht' (1982) 68 *Archiv für Rechts- und Sozialphilosophie* 14.

[30] GF Schuppert, 'Governance im Spiegel der Wissenschaftsdisziplinen' in GF Schuppert (ed), *Governance-Forschung*, 2nd edn (Baden-Baden, Nomos, 2006) 371.

[31] cf M Stolleis, *Geschichte des öffentlichen Rechts*, vol II (Munich, CH Beck, 1992) 330.

[32] Voßkuhle, 'Neue Verwaltungsrechtswissenschaft' (n 18).

[33] cf for more detailed summaries A Voßkuhle, 'Die Reform des Verwaltungsrechts als Projekt der Wissenschaft' (1999) 32 *Die Verwaltung* 545; W Krebs, 'Die Juristische Methode im Verwaltungsrecht' in W Hoffmann-Riem and E Schmidt-Aßmann (eds), *Methoden der Verwaltungsrechtswissenschaft* (Baden-Baden, Nomos, 2004) 209; M Ruffert (ed), *The Transformation of Administrative Law in Europe* (Munich, Sellier, 2004); M Eifert, 'Das Verwaltungsrecht zwischen klassischem dogmatischen Verständnis und steuerungswissenschaftlichem Anspruch' (2008) 67 *Vereinigung der Deutschen Staatsrechtslehrer* 286; I Appel, 'Das Verwaltungsrecht zwischen klassischem dogmatischen Verständnis und steuerungswissenschaftlichem Anspruch' (2008) 67 *Vereinigung der Deutschen Staatsrechtslehrer* 226.

A. The Regulatory Approach: Administrative Law as a Legal Framework for a Governmental Pursuit of the General Welfare

The regulatory approach focuses on goals established by the law. The law is seen as a means of behavioural regulation and as a medium for accomplishing context-appropriate tasks marked by questions of organization and procedure, and which is aware of its dependence on the cognitive dimension. In the cooperative state, private action is incorporated into the analysis and the goal is a comprehensive framework for problem-solving and government action in securing the general welfare. The primary interest under this approach is developing an appropriate governance structure, and the primary dialogue partners are the bureaucracy and the legislator.

B. The Juristic Method: Administrative Law as a Means of Disciplining State Authority in Order to Secure Freedom

The juristic method concentrates on the final state decision, the legal act, which is classified abstractly as a form of action which entails specific legal consequences. Legal acts and their consequences are ordered into a formal, consistent system. The main goal of this approach is to discipline the bureaucracy in the name of the rule of law, as seen from the external perspective of the citizen's legal position. The goal is creating satisfactory legal protections for citizens. Thus, the primary dialogue partners are the courts.

IV. THE 'DEBATE' AS A CROSSFIRE OF VARYING DISCOURSES

The contrasting compilation of working methods in the concepts listed above is an expression of uncertainty and conflict, but also a precondition for reflection among scholars of administrative law. In the current debate over the various approaches, however, methodological questions are mixed with other discussions in which the personal lines of conflict are likely to run in similar directions. The crossfire thus has the potential to contribute to an unproductive formation of camps instead of discursive clarity. To avoid this effect, the component parts of the debate should be considered separately.

A. Different Conceptions of the Role of Administrative Law

On a very general level, the administrative law studies show different conceptions of the primary role of administrative law. Some approaches stress limits on state power and judicial control,[34] while others focus on social engineering. These standpoints grow out of political positions and ideologies, but they also influence legal scholarship as they focus their attention on the subject of administrative law and its presumed functions. By bearing in mind that administrative law is a multi-layered field, we can avoid rushing into judgments concerning the value of these various scholarly approaches.

B. Different Attitudes to the Growing Independence of the Bureaucracy

On a different – albeit related – level are contrasting attitudes towards the growing independence of the bureaucracy. In many areas of modern administrative law, fundamental questions of practice are no longer resolved by parliamentary law, but rather by rule-making and individual decisions of the bureaucracy. This is true of environmental and social-welfare law, as well as for the regulation of the network industries or the various kinds of interest reconciliation implemented by means of planning. The desire for a decision supported by as much expertise as possible regularly forms the backdrop for this approach, a factor which also spurs the creation of independent units within administrative organizations dedicated to the enrichment or evaluation of expert knowledge. Both developments, especially when combined, raise questions concerning the appropriate democratic legitimation of these decisions (see Jestaedt in this volume for an extended version of this argument). One line of argument is extremely critical of this development, particularly concerning independent agencies from a legitimation standpoint[35] and demands that the legislator be required once again to take a more active role in regulation. The other approach builds on a transformation of the concept of legitimacy, paving the way for problem-solving techniques that are seen to be based on reliable expert knowledge. This dispute relates, first and foremost, to a central question of public law. However, it also resonates in debates concerning administrative law insofar as subjects such as organization, procedure and information systems become all the more important as the bureaucracy's scope of action expands, and as the legislator resorts to such guidelines to structure the bureaucracy's discretionary powers. Nevertheless, normative preliminary

[34] cf inter alia Gärditz, *Hochschulorganisation und verwaltungsrechtliche Systembildung* (n 20) 263; J Lege, 'Diskussionsbeitrag' (2008) 67 *Veröffentlichungen der Vereinigung der Deutschen Staatsrechtslehrer* 344–45.

[35] A very intense discussion, which is paradigmatic, deals with the degree of independence of the agency which regulates the network industries (Bundesnetzagentur) and the margin of discretion for its regulatory measures, cf K Oertel, *Die Unabhängigkeit der Regulierungsbehörde nach §§ 66. TKG* (Berlin, Duncker & Humblot, 2000) 397, 411; J-P Schneider, 'Flexible Wirtschaftsregulierung durch unabhängige Behörden im deutschen und britischen Telekommunikationsrecht' (2000) 164 *Zeitschrift für das gesamte Handelsrecht* 513, 535; J Masing, *Soll das Recht der Regulierungsverwaltung übergreifend geregelt warden? Gutachten D zum 66. Deutschen Juristentag 2006* (Munich, CH Beck 2006) 73, 152, 180; more restrictive T Mayen, 'Verwaltung durch unabhängige Einrichtungen' (2004) *Die öffentliche Verwaltung* 45; J Kersten, 'Herstellung von Wettbewerb als Verwaltungsaufgabe' (2010) 69 *Veröffentlichungen der Vereinigung der Deutschen Staatsrechtslehrer* 288, 328.

questions should be held apart from practical consequences, just as constitutional law theories, in turn, should be kept separate from actual conditions within the administrative bureaucracy.

C. Questions Concerning the Identity and Independence of Legal Science

The two discourses explored above manifest divergent political and constitutional background assumptions. They would, in themselves, furnish adequate grounds for an intensive discussion of the appropriate conceptual approach to administrative law. The discussion is marked by a particular quality, though, in that its fundamental methodical components also implicate the self-concept of the entire discipline of legal science.[36]

i. New Criteria for System-building and the Functions of Concepts

This deeper aspect becomes particularly clear when one views the construction of systems and systems of concepts as central tasks of the study of administrative law. In contrast to the juristic method, the regulatory approach has changed both the criteria of system-building as well as the function of concepts.

In the juristic method, concepts serve the function of differentiation – in particular, the differentiation of legal consequences. Regulatory approaches, by contrast, use concepts primarily to formulate problems. Concepts serve under this theory as heuristic instruments. They organize, for instance, the opening towards the social sciences, in that concepts are specifically chosen that are used in several disciplines (for example, 'control' or 'responsibility'). This choice of concepts creates a structured correspondence between different specialties ('key concepts'; 'bridge concepts').[37] From the perspective of the juristic method, this deployment of concepts would be seen as blurring essential borders and sacrificing rationality.

With regard to the criteria for system-building, a similar situation prevails on several levels.[38] The juristic method builds its system primarily by means of a relational sorting of concepts derived by means of formal abstraction. This basically creates a system of forms of action in which an administrative act is differentiated from a legal ordinance, or in which administrative acts themselves are divided into fact-finding, law-shaping, provisional etc and thus linked with specific legal

[36] cf in search for a sound self-concept C Engel and W Schön (eds), *Das Proprium der Rechtswissenschaft* (Tübingen, Mohr Siebeck, 2007); H Schulze-Fielitz (ed), 'Staatsrechtslehre als Wissenschaft' (2007) *Die Verwaltung* supplement 7.

[37] cf H-H Trute, 'Verantwortungsteilung als Schlüsselbegriff eines sich verändernden Verhältnisses von öffentlichem und privatem Sektor' in Schuppert (ed), *Jenseits von Privatisierung und 'schlankem' Staat* (n 23) 13; A Voßkuhle, '"Schlüsselbegriffe" der Verwaltungsrechtsreform' (2002) 93 *Verwaltungsarchiv* 184.

[38] C Möllers, 'Methodische Zugänge zum Verwaltungsrecht' in Hoffmann-Riem, Schmidt-Aßmann and Voßkuhle (n 2) § 3, paras 38–39.

consequences. A regulatory approach, by contrast, forms its conceptual system by determining links between overall administrative tasks and legal instruments. These scholars speak, for instance, of legal arrangements as 'building blocks' or of 'elements' of *Gewährleistungsverwaltungsrecht*.[39] The regulatory approach may also systematize on the basis of operative mechanisms and their connections, so that regulation stands beside sovereign self-regulation, and the latter is differentiated in regard to enterprise-related organizational tasks, created markets, etc. This approach is thus based on rule-patterns, not directly on legal consequences.

An easing of the direct links with legal consequences is also expressed by the standards which form the basis for systematic observations. The goal of ensuring the fulfilment of specialized tasks correspondingly highlights the importance of 'soft' evaluative criteria such as functionally appropriate organization and extends the relevant categories beyond legality to measures of 'correctness' which also comprise acceptance, feasibility, etc.[40] While the juristic method's system was primarily concerned with the distinction legal/illegal, the control-theory system pursued optimal problem-solving in which legality is 'only' one criterion, albeit a mandatory one.

ii. Relationship to 'Dogmatics' as a Defining Feature of the Discipline

The heuristic concepts used by the regulatory approach bring with them broader and less precise standards. As a result of this approach, the border between normative and descriptive content – as well as between illegality and functional inappropriateness – becomes unclear. This lack of clarity can be avoided by more transparent argumentation, but still it relates to the core of the approach's self-identity: the fact that it is centred on dogmatic work.

The notion of dogmatics is itself rather blurred.[41] It is related to the application of laws, but goes beyond the interpretation of individual norms. Ultimately, it attempts to build a layer of legal constructs and styles of arguments between legal norms and their application in an individual case which ensures the operationalization of the legal norms as well as the coherence of the legal system.[42] Because of its orientation towards the application of legal rules, dogmatics focuses on the difference between legality and illegality. The regulatory approach, with its somewhat different orientation, is soon confronted with the objection that it is not

[39] cf Voßkuhle (n 24) 266.

[40] cf W Hoffmann-Riem, 'Eigenständigkeit der Verwaltung' in Hoffmann-Riem, Schmidt-Aßmann and Voßkuhle (n 2) § 10, para 11; Schmidt-Aßmann (n 2) ch 6, para 57; for a detailed discussion: M Fehling, 'Das Verhältnis von Recht und außerrechtlichen Maßstäben' in H-H Trute and others (eds), *Allgemeines Verwaltungsrecht – zur Tragfähigkeit eines Konzepts* (Tübingen, Mohr Siebeck, 2008) 461.

[41] cf for an analysis A Scherzberg, 'Das Allgemeine Verwaltungsrecht zwischen Praxis und Reflexion – Theoretische Grundlagen der modernen Verwaltungsrechtswissenschaft' in Trute and others, *Allgemeines Verwaltungsrecht* (n 40) 837, 849; R Alexy, *Theorie der juristischen Argumentation* (Frankfurt am Main, Suhrkamp, 1983) 307.

[42] cf the widely accepted description by W Brohm, 'Die Dogmatik des Verwaltungsrechts vor den Gegenwartsaufgaben der Verwaltung' (1972) 30 *Veröffentlichungen der Vereinigung der Deutschen Staatsrechtslehrer* 193, 245–46.

dogmatic, and thus driven by 'mere' policy. This discussion thus necessarily implicates the authority to determine the (apparent) core meaning of the discipline. Such apparently high stakes contribute to a harshness of the discussion which, I will argue below, is not justified.

iii. Existing Law as Orientation Point and the Question of Policy

The focus on legal dogmatics entails a focus on existing law. Discussion of policy questions were, as a rhetorical matter, always a recognized aspect of jurisprudence. From a reputational standpoint, however, they were considered to have less dignity than dogmatic analyses of existing law. The acceptance of legal policy studies is not derived from scientific criteria, but from proximity to political power. From an academic standpoint, therefore, there is uncertainty about the methodological tools and the location of the discipline.[43] This hinders the adoption of the more affirmative attitude of the well-fitting[44] regulatory approach. It should nevertheless be noted that – in light of the openness of constitutional discourse and law-making within a multi-level system – both law-making and the application of law are much more routinely interlinked than the self-regard of the profession might prefer to acknowledge.

V. BETWEEN PRODUCTIVE DIALOGUE AND POLEMICAL POLARIZATION

Even within this very crude differentiation between the various strands of the debate, it has become clear that the sensibilities of the participants in the discussion fuel a perceived need for clear borders. In fact, such sharp distinctions hardly seem necessary.

A. Conceptual-Substantive Compatibility of the Approaches

When judged soberly, the difference between the approaches is less than the debate might lead one to believe. Both approaches are, conceptually and substantively, fairly compatible. The juristic method has for quite some time accepted the meaning and purpose of legal norms as valid interpretive criteria. With this step, consideration of a norm's real-world effects became inevitable, both in individual arguments and in dogmatic systems. These layers of argument thus parallel those in the regulatory approach. Conversely, the primarily heuristic systematizations of the regulatory approach can lead to normative concretizations in the form of dogmatic constructs. Systematic analysis, for example, of the various statutes that require specialist officers at establishment level (*Betriebsbeauftragte*) have led

[43] R Wahl, *Herausforderungen und Antworten* (n 8) 90.
[44] cf A Voßkuhle, 'Methode und Pragmatik im Öffentlichen Recht' in H Bauer and others (eds), *Umwelt, Wirtschaft und Recht* (Tübingen, Mohr Siebeck, 2002) 171.

some scholars to assume that those are to be deemed a legal institution so that incomplete legal regulations in one field are to be complemented by recourse to its general rules.[45] This kind of argument is typical for legal dogmatics.

Independent of these converging tendencies, the borders of the disciplines also dissolve with regard to the areas to which the regulatory approach devoted increasing attention. Investigations of, for example, procedural and organizational law were often driven by the regulatory approach, although the actual exploration of these areas was very much aided by the formal conceptual apparatus of the juristic method.[46] The adaptation of legal requirements and permits to technical developments affects the form of action called an administrative act – and its effects – in the face of dynamic developments. To meet these challenges in a comprehensible manner, the best approach transparently combines both methods. Which method is given the credit for particular advances may, in fact, be assigned somewhat arbitrarily.

Most authors who occupy themselves with both approaches as such assume that, because of their differing emphases, they either complement one another or, in concrete applications, productively limit one another,[47] and, in fact, both approaches have been successfully integrated in any number of academic books and articles.

B. Unproductive Rhetorical Polarization and its Causes

Nevertheless, the debate continues to be characterized by rhetorical polarization, showing that both sides continue to feel threatened by one another. Each side repeatedly makes claims to exclusivity which, upon closer inspection, must be rejected on the grounds that neither side can boast a complete methodical system. A root of this misunderstanding is most certainly the denominations used by each approach. Both denominations claim to embrace the entire discipline. As a conceptual matter, the 'juristic method' equates its method to jurisprudence. The moniker 'new administrative law' – intended as an expression of something more than gradual differentiation – covers the entire area of administrative law, implying that competing ideas should be thought of as relatively unattractive 'old' approaches. Further factors include the discrepancy between theoretical acceptance of a plurality of legal sciences, on the one hand, and a narrow institutional

[45] J Junker, *Gewährleistungsaufsicht über Wertpapierdienstleistungsunternehmen* (Berlin, Duncker & Humblot, 2003) 177.

[46] cf eg M Burgi, *Funktionale Privatisierung und Verwaltungshilfe* (Tübingen, Mohr Siebeck, 1999); T Groß, *Das Kollegialprinzip in der Verwaltungsorganisation* (Tübingen, Mohr Siebeck, 1999); M Fehling, *Verwaltung zwischen Unparteilichkeit und Gestaltungsaufgabe* (Tübingen, Mohr Siebeck, 2001); and more recently B Wollenschläger, Wissensgenerierung im Verfahren (Tübingen, Mohr Siebeck, 2009); Gärditz (n 20).

[47] cf Appel, 'Das Verwaltungsrecht zwischen klassischem dogmatischen Verständnis und steuerungswissenschaftlichem Anspruch' (n 33); Eifert (n 33); Kersten and Lenski (n 3); W Kahl, 'Über einige Pfade und Tendenzen in Verwaltungsrecht und Verwaltungsrechtswissenschaft: Ein Zwischenbericht' (2009) 42 *Die Verwaltung* 463.

focus on legal dogmatics, on the other. One might also discern elements of a generational conflict that keeps the pendulum swinging between tradition and reform and different perceptions about the degree of openness of the discussion on the reform of administrative law.

In the final analysis, the regulatory approach also necessarily implicates a certain challenge which hinders its relaxed acceptance. If applied conscientiously, the regulatory approach would add considerable complexity to legal scholarship. To many, the difficulties seem as insurmountable as they are unavoidable. Against this background, a pointed debate over (apparent) fundamentals may allow some deferral.

C. Overview: The Plurality of Administrative Law Studies

From a distance, the debate regarding the appropriate conceptual approach to administrative law may appear heated. However, it can also be seen as a completely normal contest over differentiation within an academic discipline. Nevertheless, precisely this sort of differentiation poses difficulties for administrative law. By virtue of the fact that it deals with normative questions, it regards itself generally as a normative discipline and, as a result, tends to apply an overhasty determination of what is permissible and what is impermissible, also with regard to internal methodological questions. A methodical plurality which permits each approach to be measured by its ability to generate insight, far from being capricious, is actually quite appropriate to a modern, multi-layered approach to the study of administrative law.

SELECTED LITERATURE

Appel I, 'Das Verwaltungsrecht zwischen klassischem dogmatischen Verständnis und steuerungswissenschaftlichem Anspruch' (2008) 67 *Veröffentlichungen der Vereinigung der Deutschen Staatsrechtslehrer* 226–77.

Badura P, *Verwaltungsrecht im liberalen und im sozialen Rechtsstaat* (Tübungen, Mohr, 1966)

Bumke C, 'Die Entwicklung der verwaltungsrechtswissenschaftlichen Methodik in der Bundesrepublik Deutschland' in E Schmidt-Aßmann and W Hoffmann-Riem (eds), *Methoden der Verwaltungsrechtswissenschaft* (Baden-Baden, Nomos, 2004)

Eifert M, 'Das Verwaltungsrecht zwischen klassischem dogmatischen Verständnis und steuerungswissenschaftlichem Anspruch' (2008) 67 *Veröffentlichungen der Vereinigung der Deutschen Staatsrechtslehrer* 286–329.

Franzius C, *Gewährleistung im Recht* (Tübingen, Mohr Siebeck, 2009)

Gärditz KF, *Hochschulorganisation und verwaltungsrechtliche Systembildung* (Tübingen, Mohr Siebeck, 2009)

Grimm D (ed), *Wachsende Staatsaufgaben – sinkende Steuerungsfähigkeit des Rechts* (Baden-Baden, Nomos, 1990)

Grimm D (ed), *Staatsaufgaben* (Baden-Baden, Nomos, 1994)

Hoffmann-Riem W, 'Reform des Allgemeinen Verwaltungsrechts' (1985) 110 *Archiv des öffentlichen Rechts* 400–47.

——, Schmidt-Aßmann E and Schuppert GF (eds), *Reform des Allgemeinen Verwaltungsrechts* (Baden-Baden, Nomos, 1993)

——, Schmidt-Aßmann E and Voßkuhle A (eds), *Grundlagen des Verwaltungsrechts*, vol I–III (Munich, CH Beck, 2006–09)

Hueber A, *Otto Mayer: 'Die juristische Methode' im Verwaltungsrecht* (Berlin, Duncker & Humblot, 1981)

Lepsius O, *Steuerungsdiskussion, Systemtheorie und Parlamentarismuskritik* (Tübingen, Mohr Siebeck, 1999)

Meyer-Hesemann W, *Methodenwandel in der Verwaltungsrechtswiss*enschaft (Heidelberg, Müller, 1981)

Möllers C, 'Braucht das öffentliche Recht einen neuen Methoden- und Richtungsstreit?' (1999) 90 *Verwaltungsarchiv* 187–207.

——'Methodische Zugänge zum Verwaltungsrecht' in W Hoffmann-Riem, E Schmidt-Aßmann E and A Voßkuhle (eds) *Grundlagen des Verwaltungsrechts*, vol I (Munich, CH Beck, 2006) § 3

Scherzberg A, (2008): 'Das Allgemeine Verwaltungsrecht zwischen Praxis und Reflexion – Theoretische Grundlagen der modernen Verwaltungsrechtswissenschaft' in H-H Trute and others (eds), *Allgemeines Verwaltungsrecht – zur Tragfähigkeit eines Konzepts* (Tübingen, Mohr Siebeck, 2008) 837–68

Schmidt-Aßmann E, *Das Allgemeine Verwaltungsrecht als Ordnungsidee: Grundlagen und Aufgaben der verwaltungsrechtlichen Systembildung*, 2nd edn (Berlin, Springer, 2006)

——and Hoffmann-Riem W (eds), *Methoden der Verwaltungsrechtswissenschaft* (Baden-Baden, Nomos, 2004)

Stolleis M, *Geschichte des öffentlichen Rechts in Deutschland*, vol II (Munich, CH Beck, 1992)

Schuppert GF, *Verwaltungswissenschaft* (Baden-Baden, Nomos, 2000)

Voßkuhle A, 'Die Reform des Verwaltungsrechts als Projekt der Wissenschaft' (1999) 32 *Die Verwaltung* 545–54.

——'Neue Verwaltungsrechtswissenschaft' in W Hoffmann-Riem, E Schmidt-Aßmann and A Voßkuhle A (eds), *Grundlagen des Verwaltungsrechts*, vol I (Munich, CH Beck, 2006) § 1

Wahl R, *Herausforderungen und Antworten: Das Öffentliche Recht der letzten fünf Jahrzehnte* (Berlin, de Gruyter, 2006)

12

Subjective Public Rights – Historical Roots versus European and Democratic Challenges

BERNHARD W WEGENER

I. INTRODUCTION

'SUBJECTIVE PUBLIC RIGHT' (*subjektives öffentliches Recht*) describes a fundamental category and a fundamental orientation within German public law. It is often described as being the very 'crux' and 'cornerstone' of the entire system of public law because, by dint of subjective public rights, a subset of the more extensive objective public law is assigned to the individual.[1]

Even today the determining doctrines of subjective public rights are still of central importance with regard to the question of defending collective, supra-individual interests before the (administrative) courts. This is where the so-called *Verletztenklage* – the aggrieved party claim – serves to protect subjective public rights. The German model of (administrative) legal redress thereby differs from the so-called *Interessentenklage* – the interested party claim – which can be found in other European jurisdictions and jurisdictions with a distinctly European

[1] E Schmidt-Aßmann in *Maunz/Dürig: Grundgesetz Kommentar*, 63rd edn (Munich, CH Beck, 2011) Art 19(4), para 117.

character.[2] This *Interessentenklage* orientates itself towards the interest of the claimant and endeavours to safeguard the objective legitimacy of the administration.

The *Schutznormtheorie* – the theory of protective norms – provides for the identification of the judicially enforceable subjective public rights pertaining to the *Verletztenklage.* Pursuant to this theory, individual rights can only be established by those norms which do not merely serve to protect the general public, but at least, in some way, intend to protect the individual as well. The *Verletztenklage* and *Schutznormtheorie* are, in principle, detrimental to the implementation of collective and supra-individual interests before the courts, and this is precisely their aim. The implementation of interests beneficial to the *Gemeinwohl* – the general welfare of the public – is, pursuant to the underlying *Staatsverständnis* – the conception of the relationship between the state and the citizen –, a matter for the administration alone and not for individuals or any non-state association founded by individuals (see section II).

In its historical origins the doctrine of subjective public rights goes back in particular to Hegel's categorical differentiation between the perceived general public welfare to be secured by the state on one hand and the individual interests of the citizen on the other hand.[3] This differentiation, established in its prevailing form in the nineteenth century, is a product of the historical compromise between the bourgeoisie and the monarchy in the period of late constitutionalism (see section III).

Under the impact of the growing threat to common goods such as the natural environment,[4] and in view of an alleged or actual (partial) failure on the part of executive to deal with these dangers, the legislature and the judiciary have strengthened the means by which these supra-individual interests can be defended before the courts. The keywords in this context are the liberalization of the concepts of subjective public rights and of the *Klagebefugnis* – the locus standi or the right to instigate legal proceedings – as well as the admission of actions brought by associations, pressure groups or non-governmental organizations (NGOs). This development is partially indebted to obligatory European and international guidelines and provisions. As the German legal system is still attempting to distance itself from these guidelines, and to the extent that it is trying to do so, it finds itself taking an increasingly problematic separate path (see section IV).

The defensive stance of the determining doctrines of subjective public rights also appears precarious because they hinder legal relief orientated towards the benefit of the general public as a whole which may be characterized as democratically deficient (see section V).

[2] For the theoretical formation and the contrasting difference between the models: V Skouris, *Verletztenklagen und Interessentenklagen im Verwaltungsprozeß* (Cologne, Heymann, 1979).

[3] GWF Hegel, *Grundlinien der Philosophie des Rechts* (Berlin, Nicolai, 1820/21) §§ 182ff.

[4] cf M Ruffert, *Subjektive Rechte im Umweltrecht der EG* (Heidelberg, v Decker, 1996) 101ff regarding the numerous attacks against the *Schutznormtheorie* from an environmental-political point of view.

II. THE RESTRICTIVE EFFECT OF SUBJECTIVE PUBLIC RIGHTS ON THE RIGHT OF ACTION

Article 19(4) of the German Constitution – *Grundgesetz* ('GG') – guarantees recourse to legal action in the event of someone's 'rights' being violated by a public power or authority. The central guarantee of legal redress in the German Constitution is thereby already linked to the violation of subjective rights.[5] In terms of public law, this link is firmly established in the *Verwaltungsgerichtsordnung* ('VwGO') – the Regulations Governing the Administrative Courts. Pursuant to § 42(2) VwGO, the *Anfechtungsklage* – the rescissory action/action of voidance – and the *Verpflichtungsklage* – the action for the issue of an administrative act – are only admissible if the claimant is able to assert that one of 'his rights' has been violated. Moreover, the respective claims pursuant to § 113(1), sentence 1 VwGO are only then justified, if the claimant is actually violated in 'his rights'. The corresponding prerequisites for the admissibility and the reasonable justification of the claim are, by analogy, also valid for the majority of other types of claims which German administrative procedural law has at its disposal. The *Normenkontrollklage* – an action for judicial review of administrative acts of a more general nature – pursuant to § 47 VwGO, which originally required no link to subjective public rights, now, after a corresponding amendment, links the locus standi to the violation of one's own rights.

To date the question as to what subjective public rights for the purpose of administrative procedural law actually are, and/or from which norm and under which prerequisites they arise, has not been entirely clarified and remains the subject of continual and gradual change. In order to answer these questions, it is generally necessary to revert to the so-called *Schutznormtheorie*[6] postulated by Ottmar Bühler.[7] Pursuant to this theory, only such norms which, at the very

[5] Schmidt-Aßmann in *Maunz/Dürig: Grundgesetz Kommentar* (n 1) paras 116ff.

[6] cf the abundance of literature: H Bauer, *Geschichtliche Grundlagen der Lehre vom subjektiven öffentlichen Recht* (Berlin, Duncker & Humblot, 1986); H Bauer, 'Altes und Neues zur Schutznormtheorie' (1988) 113 *Archiv des öffentlichen Rechts* 582ff; W Krebs, 'Subjektiver Rechtsschutz und objective Rechtskontrolle' in H-U Erichsen and others (eds), *Festschrift für Christian-Friedrich Menger* (Köln, Heymann, 1985) 191ff; P Preu, *Subjektivrechtliche Grundlagen des öffentlichrechtlichen Drittschutzes* (Berlin, Duncker & Humblot, 1992); D Ehlers, 'Die Klagebefugnis nach deutschem, europäischem Gemeinschafts- und U.S.-amerikanischem Recht' [1993] *Verwaltungsarchiv* 139ff; M Schmidt-Preuß, *Kollidierende Privatinteressen im Verwaltungsrecht: Die subjektiven öffentlichen Rechte im multipolaren Rechtsverhältnis* (Berlin, Duncker & Humblot, 1992); A Scherzberg, 'Grundlagen und Typologie des subjektiv-öffentlichen Rechts' [1998] *Deutsches Verwaltungsblatt* 129ff. Regarding the particularly intensely debated discussion with regard to environmental law: A Blankenagel, 'Klagefähige Rechtspositionen im Umweltrecht: Vom subjektiven Recht eines Individuums zum Recht eines individualisierten Subjekts' [1993] *Die Verwaltung* 1ff; M Zuleeg, 'Hat das subjektive öffentliche Recht noch eine Daseinsberechtigung?' [1976] *Deutsches Verwaltungsblatt* 509ff; S König, *Drittschutz: Der Rechtsschutz Drittbetroffener gegen Bau- und Anlagegenehmigungen im öffentlichen Baurecht, Immissionsschutzrecht und Atomrecht* (Berlin, Duncker & Humblot, 1993) 101ff; also from a comparative law perspective: Ruffert, *Subjektive Rechte im Umweltrecht der EG* (n 4) 90ff.

[7] O Bühler, *Die subjektiven öffentlichen Rechte und ihr Schutz in der deutschen Verwaltungsrechtsprechung* (Berlin, Kohlhammer, 1914) in particular 21.

least, aim to achieve the protection of the individual are capable of establishing subjective rights. On the other hand, the individual should obtain no subjective rights from norms which first and foremost serve to protect the interests of the public.

These formulae provided by the *Schutznormtheorie* are per se not particularly convincing and they have made it possible for the judiciary to successively extend the scope of legal norms which allow the individual to instigate proceedings. The remaining significance of the restricted right to legal recourse which is derived from the *Schutznormtheorie* is best illustrated by the important group of legal norms which even today, in accordance with the judgments of the Federal Administrative Court (Bundesverwaltungsgericht, 'BVerwG'), can still not be assigned any subjective legal quality.

This refers specifically to the precautionary setting of threshold values in environmental law and health protection law. These precautionary threshold values are not directed towards warding off immediate dangers, but rather towards estimated long-term risks. The precautions taken against these risks should, for their part, be solely for the benefit of the general public and, as such, not for the benefit of a specifically identifiable group of people affected.

Therefore, the legal procedures pertaining to administrative law should not, as a matter of principle, allow individuals to enforce compliance with these precautionary threshold values under German environmental law.[8] This restriction is of considerable importance as the precautionary threshold values are more stringent than those determining threshold values which solely serve to protect from danger. As such, the potentially most protective and relevant norms are, to a great extent, withdrawn from the courts' scrutiny.

The same is true of regulations which, in substance, do not aim at protecting individual but rather supra-individual legal interests. This applies in the case of norms concerning nature conservation. Nature conservation is, in this respect, regarded as a supra-individual matter, the implementation of which is assigned to the authorities alone. Individuals should not be able to make the courts' scrutiny of the compliance with and the application of conservation regulations their business, even if – as a resident or a nature lover – they have a particularly close relationship to the protected area or the protected object concerned.[9] For similar reasons, the implementation by individuals of norms relating to the protection of listed and landmarked buildings was, until recently, considerably restricted. In accordance with cases decided by numerous Higher Regional Administrative Appeal Courts (Oberverwaltungsgerichte), even the owners of protected cultural monuments should have no claim before the courts regarding how the protection of historical monuments was implemented, as this was supposedly a matter

[8] cf more recently VGH Kassel [2009] *Zeitschrift für Umweltrecht* 504 with reference to BVerwGE 119, 329, 333.

[9] cf BVerwG [2007] *Natur und Recht* 546. Similar previously OVG Hamburg [2006] *Neue Zeitschrift für Verwaltungsrecht-Rechtsprechungsreport* 97ff.

decreed solely for the interest of the general public.[10] It was not until recently that the Federal Administrative Court introduced a certain degree of subjectivization in favour of the owners of listed and landmarked buildings in relation to the norms for the protection of historical monuments.[11]

What is also considerably restricted is the legal redress with regard to such legal norms which merely oblige the administration to undertake a supra-individual, planning-related and, as such, a normatively insufficiently individualized course of action. This is exemplified by the norms which, in the event of particular environmental quality standards being contravened, compel the administration to propose plans of action which, when implemented, should ensure future compliance with the standards. This also applies if the quality standards as such are aimed at protecting people's health. Indeed the aim of the planning is to create standards which inherently protect the individual. However, the *Planungsverpflichtung* – the duty to plan – which is linked to this, is, in respect of the affected individual, considered to be too vague and indeterminate for the individual to be entitled to a corresponding claim which could be enforced by the courts.[12]

The scope of subjective public law rights which are enforceable by the courts is also restricted by the fact that German law attributes relatively little significance to administrative proceedings. German law does recognize individual claims for the compliance with procedural law guidelines, for instance in licensing procedures (*Genehmigungsverfahren*). The significance of procedural law guidelines are, however, dramatically reduced by a myriad of remedial options (*Heilungsoptionen*) and insignificancy rules (*Unbeachtlichkeitsvorschriften*). It is often possible for the administrative authority to make up for omissions in the procedural steps, right up into the administrative court proceedings themselves. Even in a situation where a remedy for procedural errors on factual grounds or for reasons of time can no longer be considered, the administrative act which has erroneously come about will not automatically be deemed null and void. A procedural error is routinely to be treated as insignificant if the court is convinced that even if the course of proceedings had been carried out entirely in accordance with the regulations, no other decision would have been issued in the case.[13] Behind these relativizations lies the notion of the one sole imaginable correct decision which is merely to be determined by the proceedings, but which can be identified even without these

[10] VGH Kassel [1986] *Neue Zeitschrift für Verwaltungsrecht* 680; OVG Münster [1991] *Natur und Recht* 89; OVG Frankfurt (Oder) [1998] *LKV* 72; OVG Berlin [2001] *Neue Zeitschrift für Verwaltungsrecht-Rechtsprechungsreport* 722; OVG Lüneburg [2007] *Niedersächsisches Verwaltungsblatt* 49, 171; OVG Münster, decision of 20 February 2008 – 7 A 966/07 – paras 28ff to § 47(2) VwGO; OVG Lüneburg [2009] *Zeitschrift für Umweltrecht* 503; VGH Mannheim, judgment of 27 September 2007 – 3 882/06 – paras 21ff.

[11] BVerwG [2009] *Zeitschrift für Baurecht* 580ff.

[12] BVerwG [2007] *Neue Zeitschrift für Verwaltungsrecht* 695ff.

[13] On the significance of administrative proceedings in German and in European law: E Bülow, *Die Relativierung von Verfahrensfehlern im Europäischen Verwaltungsverfahren und nach §§ 45, 46 VwVfG* (Baden-Baden, Nomos, 2007).

proceedings. In this respect, the proceedings are not assigned a legitimizing effect but rather just an ancillary character.[14]

The determining doctrines of subjective public rights also ultimately play a role in the law pertaining to state liability, ie the liability of public bodies and officials. The central claim based on public liability pursuant to § 839 of the German Civil Code (*Bürgerliches Gesetzbuch*, 'BGB') and Article 34 of the German Constitution, requires the breach of an official duty which is 'aimed at the individual'. In this sense duties 'aimed at the individual' should only be those official duties which are not solely intended for the protection of the general public as a whole, but rather those which at least serve to protect the rights of individuals. This differentiation is particularly relevant with regard to the exclusion of liability due to legislative injustice. By virtue of the fact that (constitutional and faultless) legislation is already deemed a matter indebted to the general public by virtue of the universality of the law, any corresponding omissions or oversights should not inherently be able to give rise to claims by individuals on the grounds of public liability.[15] The exclusion of liability on the grounds of legislative injustice has, however, during the process of implementation by (European) Union law, been relativized as well – if the Member States wrongly implement EU directives, they are, in principal, obliged to pay damages.[16]

III. HISTORIC ROOTS OF SUBJECTIVE PUBLIC RIGHTS

Even modern accounts of the system of legal redress afforded under German administrative law cannot do without detailed references to the seminal works of Gerber,[17] Jellinek[18] and Bühler.[19] Legal redress under administrative law in Germany – along with it the doctrine of subjective public rights – have, even up to the present day, more than just their roots in the nineteenth century. The authoritative differentiation between the general public/the common good on the one

[14] M Kment, 'Planerhaltung auf dem Prüfstand: Die Neuerungen der §§ 214, 215 BauGB 2007 europarechtlich betrachtet' [2007] *Deutsches Verwaltungsblatt* 1275; R Wahl, 'Das Verhältnis von Verwaltungsverfahren und Verwaltungsprozessrecht in europäischer Sicht' [2003] *Deutsches Verwaltungsblatt* 1285, 1287; CD Classen, 'Strukturunterschiede zwischen deutschem und europäischem Verwaltungsrecht' [1995] *Neue Juristische Wochenschrift* 2457–58.

[15] cf B Grzeszick, 'Staatshaftungsrecht' in H-Uwe Erichsen and D Ehlers (eds), *Allgemeines Verwaltungsrecht*, 14th edn (Berlin, de Gruyter, 2010) § 44, para 27 with further evidence in particular on the relevant decisions of the German Federal Court of Justice.

[16] Joined Cases C-46 and C-48/93 *Brasserie du Pecheur Factortame III* [1996] ECR I-1029.

[17] C Friedrich von Gerber, *Über öffentliche Rechte* (Tübingen, H Laupp, 1852). Only in a very restricted sense can Gerber be seen as the precursor of the doctrines of subjective public rights. His considerations stand too much under the influence and comprehension of the absolutist conquest of the *jura quaesita* of the *Ständestaat*; cf G Lübbe-Wolff, 'Das wohlerworbene Recht als Grenze der Gesetzgebung im neunzehnten Jahrhundert' (1986) 103 *Zeitschrift der Savigny-Stiftung für Rechtsgeschichte, Germanistische Abteilung* 103ff.

[18] G Jellinek, *System der subjektiven öffentlichen Rechte* (Mohr, 1892).

[19] Bühler, *Die subjektiven öffentlichen Rechte und ihr Schutz in der deutschen Verwaltungsrechtsprechung* (n 7).

hand and the individual, civic-bourgeoisie interests of the individual on the other ties in with Hegel's fundamental differentiation between state and society.[20] From the very outset, Hegel was, for his part, significantly influenced in this by Rousseau's concept of the common good as an objectively recognizable quantity.[21] Hegel considered that only the constitutional-monarchic state was qualified to recognize, formulate and realize itself as the 'reality of the moral idea'.[22] In this respect, it appeared to him that the civil servants of this state formed a body of public officials which, for the purpose of fulfilling its duties, was to be extracted from civic society, a society which itself was solely bound to satisfying the needs of individual interests – the 'system of needs'.[23]

The notion of the separation of state and society, which had already been theoretically developed, as well as the restriction of the individual citizen in defending its own rights, became firmly and permanently established when, in the wake of the failure of the revolution in 1848, the struggle of the aspiring bourgeoisie to assume state power was lost. The defeat was, in this respect, a 'mild' one since it led to the historical compromise of German constitutionalism. Indeed, an assumption of state power – or even just a substantial participation – was no longer open to the bourgeoisie. However, what became all the more important for this socially defining stratum was the much adjured 'freedom from the state' – the liberal right, to be able to now make unhindered, unrestricted use of 'freedom and property', as the established wording was at the time. As Dieter Grimm formulated it:

> Endeavouring to take the state into one's own hands and to constitute it according to the needs of society was a notion which, for the time being, had been given up. The monarchist principle that ensures the state's distinct right to govern was accepted. The *quid pro quo* existed within a state-approved sphere for the pursuit of civil interests which found its mode of legal expression in private law – private law founded on the basis of private autonomy – and the civil effort was now concentrated upon safeguarding this pursuit of civil interests; citizen and bourgeois separated.[24]

Just as on a constitutional level the parliamentary involvement consequently concentrated on reserving statutory powers for interventions into freedom and

[20] Hegel, *Grundlinien der Philosophie des Rechts* (n 3) §§ 182ff.

[21] J-J Rousseau, 'Gesellschaftsvertrag' in J-J Rousseau, *Politische Schriften*, vol I (Paderborn, Schöningh, 1977).

[22] Hegel (n 3) § 257.

[23] ibid §§ 182ff, 189ff.

[24] D Grimm, 'Die Entwicklung der Grundrechtstheorie in der deutschen Staatslehre' in G Birtsch (ed), *Grund- und Freiheitsrechte von der ständischen zur spätbürgerlichen Gesellschaft* (Göttingen, Vandenhoeck & Ruprecht, 1987) 235, 249 (translation by myself). For details on the criticism directed at this historical situation, see R Smend, *Bürger und Bourgeois im deutschen Staatsrecht* (Berlin, Preußische Druckerei und Verlags-AG, 1933), also in R Smend, *Staatsrechtliche Abhandlungen*, 2nd edn (Berlin, Duncker & Humblot, 1968) 306, 314. With hindsight, this must be considered rather an incantation of an idealized past in the face of the impending catastrophe. For more on the difference between the terms citizen and bourgeois, see also C Schmitt, *Verfassungslehre* (Berlin, Duncker & Humblot, 1928) 258.

property, the newly created[25] administrative courts had to restrict themselves – in line with the vast consensus of opinion – to safeguarding individual rights.

However, there were also – particularly in Prussia – completely opposing trends towards an objective legal control of the public administration. At the meeting of the Association of German Jurists in 1875, an influential expert in constitutional and administrative law, Rudolf von Gneist, lamented somewhat the German general tendency which 'only ever enthuses over and warms to "own rights"'.[26] Within the framework of the objective legal system of administrative law which is 'administered for the sake of public law and well-being', '*all* scrutinizing controls of the state administration' are thus 'intended for the protection of the totality as well as the individual concurrently'.[27] Even Otto Mayer,[28] the 'actual creator and classical portrayer of modern administrative law methods',[29] as he is not unjustifiably referred to, was of the opinion that the judicial control of administrative law should

> serve the *objective rights*, the legal system – which needs to be upheld and sustained – and thereby indirectly the interests which are protected by this very legal system but which in themselves do not necessarily possess the dedicated form of subjective rights.[30]

Nevertheless, the notion that the 'subservient'[31] was able to set the courts in motion, even when it was not a matter concerned with his own personal or economic freedom, must have appeared to the majority of contemporary constitutional and administrative law experts to be contradictory to the distinctively dualistic fundamental structure of constitutionalism. Furthermore, it must also have appeared to be an inadmissible infringement of the royal responsibility towards both state and public welfare, a responsibility which needed to be safeguarded from any form of popular government. Moreover, for as long as they referred to and confined the implementation of the applicable law, the demand

[25] For more on this process, see G--C von Unruh, *Verwaltungsgerichtsbarkeit im Verfassungsstaat* (Herford, Maximilian Verlag, 1984); A Görlitz, *Verwaltungsgerichtsbarkeit in Deutschland* (Neuwied, Luchterhand, 1970) 15ff.

[26] *Verhandlungen des 12. Deutschen Juristentages 1875*, vol III (Berlin, 1875) 221, 231.

[27] R von Gneist, *Der Rechtsstaat*, 2nd edn (Berlin, Verlag von Julius Springer, 1879) 270 (italics in the original).

[28] E Forsthoff, *Lehrbuch des Verwaltungsrechts*, vol I, 10th edn (Munich, CH Beck, 1973) 51. cf W Meyer-Hesemann, 'Die paradigmatische Bedeutung Otto Mayers für die Entwicklung der deutschen Verwaltungsrechtswissenschaft' (1982) 13 *Rechtstheorie* 496ff.

[29] For more on Mayer, see M Stolleis, *Geschichte des öffentlichen Rechts in Deutschland*, vol II (Munich, CH Beck, 1992) 403ff.

[30] O Mayer, *Deutsches Verwaltungsrecht*, vol I, 3rd edn (Berlin, Duncker & Humblot, 1924) 132 (italics in the original).

[31] This was the typical description of the individual at the time. The description was still commonplace in the constitutional and administrative law literature of the Weimar Republic. Even in 1955 O Bühler, 'Altes und Neues über Begriff und Bedeutung der subjektiven öffentlichen Rechte' in O Bachof and others (eds), *Gedenkschrift für Walter Jellinek* (München, Isar Verlag, 1955) 269, 274 still defined the term and meaning of subjective public rights as 'the position of the subject to the state'. For more on the post-war social acceptance which was achieved by switching the labels from 'subject' to 'citizen', see Bauer, 'Altes und Neues zur Schutznormtheorie' (n 6) 134.

for an objective legal scrutiny aimed at the common good was, against the backdrop of the newly achieved constitutional satisfaction, deemed an expression of illegitimate mistrust towards the monarch.[32] Confining legal protection to cover individual legal rights became a significant element in the constitutional arrangement which, particularly after the foundation of the Reich in 1871, was supported and approved of by large swathes of the civil population.[33]

The acceptance of this restriction was rendered all the more easy since it bore not only a democratically functional loss but also – on the other hand – the opportunity to secure a special capacity and effectiveness for the subjective public law rights which had been wrested from absolutism. Concentrating merely on the protection of individual rights made, to some extent, the legal protection afforded by administrative law undisputable, thereby allowing it to be developed and extended up to the point where, at least at the time, it was unreservedly accepted and admired in terms of 'perfection'. The bourgeoisie were fully satisfied with these results of the 'struggle for subjective rights'.[34]

In terms of the determining doctrines of subjective public rights and the model of legal protection purely for the individual, the demise of the monarchy in the November Revolution of 1918 and the transition to the democratic republic brought consolidation rather than change in its wake.[35] Here – like almost nowhere else – Otto Mayer's famous statement: 'Constitutional law passes, administrative law remains' rang true.[36] The state under the rule of law, the legal protection of administrative law and of subjective public rights all appeared as central achievements of the bourgeoisie. Their principal restrictions – given that considerations of the theoretical underpinning of the young democracy were, anyhow, underdeveloped – could not be challenged. Furthermore, the Republic's obvious difficulties did not

[32] O von Sarwey, *Das öffentliche Recht und die Verwaltungsrechtspflege* (Tübingen, Laupp, 1880) 132ff.

[33] Correspondingly, in one of its early decisions the Prussian Higher Administrative Court turned away from the Gneistian concept of an objective legal scrutiny and turned towards a subjective-based understanding of legal protection afforded by administrative law; cf PrOVGE 2, 351, 353–54 (neighbourly dispute concerning a building – 1877). Pursuant to this judgment it was stated that 'the task of Administrative litigation proceedings – just like any other litigation proceedings before the courts – is restricted and determined to serving to protect those interests which when violated also occasion a violation of subjective rights'. The justification that this restriction 'stems from the existing term of the "jurisdiction of administrative litigation"' was somewhat tenuous, cf J Masing, *Die Mobilisierung des Bürgers für die Durchsetzung des Rechts* (Berlin, Duncker & Humblot, 1997) 82.

[34] To precisely what extent this satisfaction among civic society was regarded as being freedom from responsibility for society as a whole – and approved of as such – is emphasized by G Mann, *Erinnerungen und Gedanken: Lehrjahre in Frankreich* (Frankfurt am Main, S Fischer Verlag, 1999) 28, after his father, Thomas Mann, had perceived the late Imperial Era (*Kaiserzeit*) as being so 'happy and free' because 'he did not have to concern himself with politics at all' and that the 'authoritarian state' took this onerosity from him. Contrary to Peter Sloterdijk, *Im selben Boot* (Frankfurt am Main, Suhrkamp, 1995) 74, democracy is not the form of society which 'does not make it possible to think of the state and the art of belonging together'. German constitutionalism at least liberated people from the former burden on a much wider scale.

[35] For a detailed critical view from the standpoint of the legal relationship: Bauer (n 6) 84ff.

[36] Mayer, *Deutsches Verwaltungsrecht* (n 30) VI.

generally inspire a strengthening of pluralist tendencies leading to increased participation and civic responsibility.[37]

What appeared yet more attractive was the promise of prevailing over the much lamented social turmoil within – as it soon transpired – an anti-democratic, dictatorial community ideology. From the right-wing, there was no lack of criticism regarding the 'liberal-individual' conception of subjective public rights. However, for the approaching spirit of the times and the subsequently implemented National Socialist 'legal renewal', it had nothing to do with a democratically motivated expansion of the rights of the individual but rather meant the suppression and destruction of these rights. The aim and the very purpose of this was the practical and theoretical deprivation of the rights of the individual as well as the individual's integration into – or, for certain others, their exclusion[38] from – the 'national community'. Even at an early stage, there was a call to arms by the 'renewers of the law' and later by the 'custodians of the law', a call to a 'fight' and a 'campaign against subjective rights', an 'eradication'[39] and thereby an appeal to throw them 'overboard in one bold, decisive fell swoop'.[40] Despite certain delays and restrictions – caused by the necessities of executing everyday legal business as well as an initial reticence on the part of sections of the legal authorities – this fight was essentially successful and its ramifications were palpable.[41] As such, the announcement proclaiming the 'end of the subjective public right' – as Theodor Maunz headlined it[42] – was news which was celebrated as an expeditious victory for the National Socialist community ideology. The totality of the established National Socialist formulations 'You are nothing, the people is everything' (*Du bist nichts, Dein Volk ist alles*) and 'the common good takes precedence over self-interest' (*Gemeinnutz geht vor Eigennutz*) found their legal equivalents in phrases such as those which referred to 'people's community instead of subjective rights' (*Volksgemeinschaft statt subjektiver Rechte*),[43] the 'cog in the community' (*Gliedstellung in der Gemeinschaft*),[44] the 'national comrade legal status' (*volksgenössische Rechtsstellung*)[45] – a community-centric status which was not duty

[37] For more on the criticism of pluralism in the Weimar Republic and its continued effect: JH Kaiser, *Die Repräsentation organisierter Interessen* (Berlin, Duncker & Humblot, 1956) 314ff.

[38] C Schmitt, *Die geistesgeschichtliche Lage des heutigen Parlamentarismus*, 2nd edn (Berlin, Duncker & Humblot, 1926) 14 spoke as early as 1926 of the 'national homogenity' and, should it be deemed necessary, the requisite 'expulsion or annihilation of heterogeny'. The ensuing link to one of Schmitt's democracy terms which, in itself, was somewhat exaggerated, later became dispensible.

[39] W Schönfeld, 'Der Kampf wider das subjektive Recht' [1937] *Zeitschrift der Akademie für Deutsches Recht* 107.

[40] ibid 107, 110.

[41] cf on the expeditious suspension of central fundamental rights pursuant to the *Reichstagsbrandverordnung* (Reichstag Fire Enactment): Bauer (n 6) 113.

[42] T Maunz, 'Das Ende des subjektiven öffentlichen Rechts' (1936) 96 *Zeitschrift für die gesamte Staatswissenschaft* 71ff.

[43] The title of a contribution by H Krüger [1937] *Deutsche Verwaltung* 37ff.

[44] K Larenz, 'Rechtsperson' in K Larenz (ed), *Grundfragen der neuen Rechtswissenschaft* (Berlin, Junker & Dünnhaupt, 1935) 225, 240.

[45] ER Huber, 'Die Rechtsstellung des Volksgenossen' (1936) 96 *Zeitschrift für die gesamte Staatswissenschaft* 438, 446–47.

bound to the individual, but established for the sake of the community. Moreover, these terms substantiated the rejection of the 'isolated individual' that 'lives its own interests free from nationalistic commitment' (*das isolierte Individuum, das frei von völkischer Bindung nur seinen eigenen Interessen lebt*)[46] and promoted 'the natural acknowledgement of the absolute precedence of the people as a whole, the community and their demands over and above the interests of the individual' (*die selbstverständliche Anerkennung des unbedingten Vorrangs des Volksganzen, der Gemeinschaft und ihrer Forderungen vor den Interessen des Einzelnen*).[47]

The dreadfully real consequences of this negatively charged concept of community ideology, which was aimed both at excluding people and depriving them of their legal rights, and the implications for its legal practices, traumatized the German democrats and moulded the immediate post-war period. Even today, these still have an effect, as is clearly evinced by the continuing reluctance towards using the term *Gemeinwohlbegriff*[48] – 'for the good of the community'. With its guarantee for the protection of individual rights set down in Article 19(4) GG and with its emphasis on the basic rights of the individual – rights which had previously been discarded on the 'rubbish heap of history'[49] by the 'legal renewers' in a characteristic over-estimation of their own historical significance, the German Constitution contained the answers to the reign of terror which had been directed towards the individual in the name of the people or the people's community. Against this backdrop, it was no surprise that the very same Ottmar Bühler who, in the days of the German Empire, had already laid considerable foundations for the public law protection of the individual by means of the *Schutznormtheorie*, evoked, in conjunction with Article 19(4) GG, the revitalized continuity of this doctrine and predicted its impending development.[50] Under democratic auspices, an altogether conceivable and fundamental opening-up of the legal protection afforded by administrative law which would also allow for the defence of statutorily protected public welfare interests – an idea which had not become taboo as a result of the terminology of NationalSocialism[51]

[46] U Scheuner, 'Die Rechtsstellung der Persönlichkeit' [1937] *Deutsches Verwaltungsrecht* 82.

[47] ibid.

[48] cf only E-W Böckenförde, 'Demokratie als Verfassungsprinzip' in J Isensee and P Kirchhof (eds), *Handbuch des Staatsrechts der Bundesrepublik Deutschland*, vol II, 2nd edn (Heidelberg, CF Müller, 2004) § 24, para 78. Fundamental regarding the whole matter: M Stolleis, *Gemeinwohlformeln im nationalsozialistischen Recht* (Berlin, Schweitzer, 1974). Defending the term: HH von Arnim, *Gemeinwohl und Gruppeninteressen* (Frankfurt am Main, Metzner, 1977) 5ff.

[49] E Forsthoff, *Die Verwaltung als Leistungsträger* (Stuttgart, Kohlhammer, 1938) 1: 'Fundamental rights are a part of the past'. Similarly, Huber, 'Die Rechtsstellung des Volksgenossen' (n 45) 438, 440: 'eradicated once and for all'.

[50] Bühler, 'Altes und Neues über Begriff und Bedeutung der subjektiven öffentlichen Rechte' (n 31) 269ff; in the interwar years Bühler continued to use his term of subjective public law, cf 'Zur Theorie des subjektiven öffentlichen Rechts' in *Festgabe für Fritz Fleiner* (Tübingen, Mohr, 1927) 26, 27, 36.

[51] In this sense KA Bettermann, 'Wesen und Streitgegenstand der verwaltungsgerichtlichen Anfechtungsklage' [1953] *Deutsches Verwaltungsblatt* 163, 164: 'The idea that the notion of administrative jurisdiction as an institution which serves to provide a qualified and neutral scrutiny of the state can only have its place in an authoritarian or totalitarian system cannot, however, be supported on historical and dogmatic grounds'. More than 20 years later, F Weyreuther, *Verwaltungskontrolle durch*

– was evidently not considered at all at the time,[52] perhaps in part owing to a lack of a sense of necessity to do so.

IV. SUBJECTIVE PUBLIC RIGHTS IN THE PROCESS OF EUROPEANIZATION AND INTERNATIONALIZATION

The German model of the *Verletztenklage* (the aggrieved party action) and the accompanying link to a restricted scope of subjective public rights has, in recent years, been exposed to the increasing influence of European law. Furthermore, in some areas the influence of international law is also making itself felt. Tendentially, Europeanization and internationalization both work towards widening the scope of the actionable legal positions, particularly in environmental law.[53] The German Federal Administrative Court and, in particular, the federal legislator have, in the past, tended to assume a rather defensive stance in the light of these stimuli.

A. The Legal Protection of the Individual in the Decisions of the European Court of Justice

Up to now the most considerable stimuli towards a European transformation of the German model of the *Verletztenklage* have stemmed from the decisions of the European Court of Justice ('ECJ').[54] The guidelines developed from the case law of the Court apply directly to the extensive area of law determined by the European Union. Furthermore, they influence the traditional legal concepts, even in areas which are not directly subject to the mandatory requirements of EU law.

The determining doctrine of the ECJ with regard to the legal protection of the individual is, however, still not clearly discernible. The judicial practice up to now, however, has displayed a considerable extension of the scope of actionable

Verbände? (Düsseldorf, Werner, 1975) 83 was of the opinion that the constitutional restriction of subjective legal protection was 'doubtful and not permitted [sic] because at the same time there was a rejection of the legal concept of the National Socialist era in this decision, a rejection which was known to have characterized the Basic Law in other places'.

[52] Bauer (n 6) 128ff. His new approaches, which were given in his lecture, remain largely insignificant and firmly fixed to the reference to the individual of the traditional conception. Critical view to the latter, Masing, *Die Mobilisierung des Bürgers für die Durchsetzung des Rechts* (n 33) 111ff.

[53] For more detail on these developments: BW Wegener, 'Rechtsschutz im europäischen (Umwelt-) Recht: Sekundär- und richterrechtliche Bausteine einer gemeinschaftlichen Dogmatik' in R Hendler and others (eds), *Jahrbuch des Umwelt- und Technikrechts* (Berlin, Erich Schmidt Verlag, 2008) 319ff.

[54] cf in particular the works of Ruffert (n 4); BW Wegener, *Rechte des Einzelnen* (Baden-Baden, Nomos, 1998); C Calliess, 'Kohärenz und Konvergenz beim europäischen Individualrechtsschutz – Der Zugang zum Gericht im Lichte des Grundrechts auf effektiven Rechtsschutz' [2002] *Neue Juristische Wochenschrift* 3577ff; for subsequent treatment, cf only U Baumgartner, *Die Klagebefugnis nach deutschem Recht vor dem Hintergrund der Einwirkungen des Gemeinschaftsrechts* (Berlin, Rhombos, 2005); C Klöver, *Klagefähige Individualrechtspositionen im deutschen Umweltverwaltungsrecht und nach Maßgabe von Umweltrichtlinien der Europäischen Gemeinschaft* (PhD thesis, University of Münster, 2005).

legal norms when contrasted with the traditional German notion. According to the widespread belief of many, the ECJ is, in this respect pursuing – in collaboration with the EU legislative body – a determined policy of 'mobilizing the citizens'.[55] It must, however, first be noted that European Union law compels the Member States to guarantee effective legal protection under Union law. This obligation emanates from ECJ case law which, in the meantime, has been incorporated into Article 19(1) sub-paragraph 2 TEU. The detailed demands which derive from this basic rule are being continually further developed by the ECJ with reference to the precepts of non-discriminatory and effective legal protection.[56] In this respect, the Member States' remaining creative leeway to develop and formulate specific national concepts is becoming noticeably more constricted.

Pivotal examples for this judicial transformation of the German model of the *Verletztenklage* into the conception of something corresponding to the *Interessentenklage* are the decisions of the ECJ on the establishment of individually actionable rights emanating from the setting of EU threshold values for the protection of the environment and health protection, from EU regulations on the development of plans and programmes, from EU regulations on national administrative proceedings and from EU provisions on conservation. With regard to the conferring of individually actionable rights, the ECJ, in all cases, goes beyond that which is customary under German law. Thus, such threshold values – like those for the protection of groundwater – are to be assigned a constitutive, right-creating effect which they would not acquire under conventional German law owing to their precautionary nature.[57] Furthermore, pursuant to a decision of the ECJ – and contrary to what the German Federal Administrative Court had assumed – the individual is, when the relevant EU quality threshold values have been exceeded, entitled to a claim for the development of a plan of action to maintain clean air.[58] In addition to this, it should be possible to start legal action for the failure to carry out an environmental impact assessment without it thereby depending on any insignificance of this omission.[59] With regard to conservation it also appears that the ECJ is open-mindedly addressing the idea of individual

[55] cf in detail: Masing (n 33).

[56] cf recently, Case C-240/09 *Zoskupenie v Ministerstvo životného prostredia Slovenskej republiky* (ECJ, 8 March 2011) para 48 with further evidence.

[57] cf Case 131/88 *Commission v Germany* [1991] ECR I-825, 867; Case C-59/89 *Commission v Germany* [1991] ECR I-2607, 2631; Case 361/88 *Commission v Germany* [1991] ECR I-2567, 2601.

[58] cf Case C-237/07 *Janecek v Freistaat Bayern – Aktionsplan Luftreinhaltung* [2008] ECR I-6221; critical towards the unspecific demands of the ECJ with regard to trade stipulated by the authorities: K Faßbender, 'Neues zum Anspruch des Bürgers auf Einhaltung des europäischen Umweltrechts' [2009] *Europarecht* 400, 405ff. The German Federal Constitutional Court ('BVerwG') had, at best, previously considered a claim to decree specific measures as pre-existing, cf BVerwG *Neue Zeitschrift für Verwaltungsrecht* 2007, 1425ff; cf T Streppel, 'Subjektive Rechte im Luftqualitätsrecht – Grundsatzentscheidungen des BVerwG' [2008] *Zeitschrift für Umweltrecht* 23ff; J Hentschel and G Wurzel, 'Nochmals Feinstaub' [2008] *Neue Zeitschrift für Verwaltungsrecht* 165ff.

[59] Case C-201/02 *R (on the application of Wells) v Secretary of State for Transport* [2004] ECR I-7237; cf aforementioned Case C-435/97 *WWF v Autonome Provinz Bozen* [1999] ECR I-5613, paras 68ff. The German legislator has in the meantime implemented this provision into s 4(1) of its *Umweltrechtsbehelfsgesetz* (Environmental Legal Remedy Act).

rights emanating from the relevant norms pertaining to the European protection of species and biotopes.[60]

B. Legal Protection of the Individual in Accordance with the Aarhus Convention and EU Legislation

The decisions of the ECJ pertaining to the rights of the individual which derive from EU law, and which have been outlined here, were supplemented – and still are supplemented – by the Union legislator which also places the citizen in the role of an agent of implementation of Union law. The corresponding concept of legal protection which can be achieved and safeguarded before the national courts far exceeds environmental law. An example of this is the forced subjectivization of public procurement by EU law.[61] The EU legislators have also strongly consolidated the significance of administrative proceedings. Numerous EU provisions call on the Member States to develop licensing procedures (*Genehmigungsverfahren*) and thereby to establish the rights of the individual and the public to obtain information and to participate in the proceedings. The rights of information are, moreover, also guaranteed independently of any ongoing proceedings.[62]

In contrast, the EU legislator failed for a long time to formulate express provisions pertaining to subjective legal protection before national courts. The development of the dogmatics of the protection of the individual, which was linked to the objective provisions of EU law, was thus left entirely in the hands the ECJ. In terms of environmental law, corresponding provisions have recently emerged in new versions of the directives on the Environmental Impact Assessment Directive[63] and on the Integrated Pollution Prevention and Control Directive.[64] Both directives have been amended by the so-called Remedies Directive.[65] For their part, the regulations introduced here concerning legal protection before the national courts date back to the guidelines pertaining to international law contained in the so-called Aarhus Convention.[66] In principle, they open up a choice to the Member

[60] cf recently, *Zoskupenie* (n 56). See also Case C-115/09 *BUND v Bezirksregierung Arnsberg* (ECJ, 12 May 2011).

[61] see also H Pünder, 'Vergaberecht' in D Ehlers, M Fehling and H Pünder (eds), *Besonderes Verwaltungsrecht*, 3rd edn (Heidelberg, CF Müller, 2011); M Fehling in H Pünder and M Schellenberg (eds), *HK-Vergaberecht* (Baden-Baden, Nomos, 2011) § 97 GWB, paras 7ff.

[62] cf in particular Council Directive 2003/4/EC on public access to environmental information and on the repeal of Council Directive 90/313/EEC [2003] OJ L41/26.

[63] Council Directive 85/337/EEC on the Environmental Impact Assessment Directive regarding specific public and private undertakings [1985] OJ L175/40.

[64] Council Directive 96/61/EC on the Integrated Pollution Prevention and Control [1996] OJ L257/26.

[65] Directive 2003/35/EC of the European Parliament and of the Council providing for public participation in respect of the drawing up of certain plans and programmes relating to the environment and amending with regard to public participation and access to justice Council Directives 85/337/EEC and 96/61/EC [2003] OJ L156/17.

[66] cf the law dated 9.12.2006 pertaining to the Convention of 25 June 1998 on the access to information, the public participation in decision proceedings and the access to the courts in environmental matters (Aarhus Convention), BGBl II 2006, 1251.

States, the choice between the legal protection of the individual based on a breach of subjective public rights and legal protection of the individual linked to the defending of interests. The *Verletztenklage* and the *Interessentenklage* are, as such, declared to be equally legitimate models of legal protection. However, not only the Aarhus Convention but also the EU directives which implement it contain a duty to provide 'broad access to the courts'. The possible repercussions of this regulation on the decisions of the ECJ are to date still not entirely discernible.[67]

Moreover, the Aarhus Convention and the EU directives legally compel the Contracting States and the Member States respectively to establish an additional legal action instigated by an association, pressure group or NGO in the field of environmental law. This is discernibly conceived as compensation for the potential deficits in legal protection which arise from the acceptance of the *Verletztenklage.*

However, with regard to the German Environmental Legal Remedy Act (*Umwelt-Rechtsbehelfsgesetz*), the German legislator initially decided upon a markedly restrictive implementation of these provisions. By doing so, it linked the class action to the existence of individual rights and, as such, confined it to some extent to a form of protection of individual rights which is to be restrictively interpreted. This transformation is not compatible with either the provisions under international law nor is it compatible with those pertaining to European law.[68] The ECJ has recently decided upon this in the so called 'BUND-judgment'. According to the ECJ, the restrictions in the German Environmental Legal Remedy Act do not conform with the EU Remedies Directive. Environmental NGOs thus have a directly applicable right to challenge the decisions of public environmental protection authorities.[69] In the meantime, the German legislator has adapted the Environmental Legal Remedy Act.[70]

[67] More on these problems and possible friction between remedial provisions of the Union legislator and the corresponding determining doctrines of the ECJ: Wegener, 'Rechtsschutz im europäischen (Umwelt-) Recht' (n 53) 319, 347ff.

[68] Prevailing opinion, cf inter alia: Rat von Sachverständigen für Umweltfragen, *Rechtsschutz für die Umwelt – die altruistische Verbandsklage ist unverzichtbar* (2005) 7ff; H-J Koch, 'Die Verbandsklage im Umweltrecht' [2007] *Neue Zeitschrift für Verwaltungsrecht* 369, 376ff; A Epiney and K Sollberger, *Zugang zu Gerichten und gerichtliche Kontrolle im Umweltrecht: Rechtsvergleich, völker- und europarechtliche Vorgaben und Perspektiven für das deutsche Recht* (Berlin, Erich Schmidt Verlag, 2002) 328; J Ziekow, 'Das Umwelt-Rechtsbehelfsgesetz im System des deutschen Rechtsschutzes' [2007] *Neue Zeitschrift für Verwaltungsrecht*259, 260; S Schlacke, 'Das Umwelt-Rechtsbehelfsgesetz' [2007] *Natur und Recht* 8, 14; C Walter, 'Internationalisierung des deutschen und europäischen Verwaltungsverfahrens- und Verwaltungsprozeßrechts – am Beispiel der Århus-Konvention' [2005] *Europarecht* 302, 318ff; Wegener (n 53) 319, 339ff; M Genth, 'Ist das neue Umwelt-Rechtsbehelfsgesetz europarechtskonform?' [2008] *Natur und Recht* 28ff; W Ewer, 'Ausgewählte Rechtsanwendungsfragen des Entwurfs für ein Umwelt-Rechtsbehelfsgesetz' [2007] *Neue Zeitschrift für Verwaltungsrecht* 267, 272; for a different opinion, see T von Danwitz, *Zur Ausgestaltungsfreiheit der Mitgliedstaaten bei Einführung der Verbandsklage anerkannter Umweltschutzvereine nach den Vorgaben der Richtlinie 2003/35/EG und der sog. Århus-Konvention* (specialist report for the VDEW, 2005).

[69] Case C-115/09 *BUND v Bezirksregierung Arnsberg* (ECJ, 12 May 2011); cf also Advocate General Sharpston [2011] *Zeitschrift für Umweltrecht* 79ff; also BW Wegener, 'Ein Ferrari mit verschlossenen Türen' [2011] *Zeitschrift für Umweltrecht* 84-85; BW Wegener, 'Die europäische Umweltverbandsklage' [2011] *Zeitschrift für Umweltrecht* 362ff.

[70] Environmental Legal Remedy Act (*Umwelt-Rechtsbehelfsgesetz*) of 7 December 2006 (BGBl. I, 2816), adapted in Art 1 of the law of 21 January 2013 (BGBl. I, 95); cf S Schlacke, 'Der Referentenentwurf

V. DEMOCRATIC CRITICISM OF THE THEORY OF SUBJECTIVE PUBLIC RIGHTS

In order to overcome the specific restrictions in the right to instigate legal proceedings which the doctrine of subjective public rights inherently brings in its wake, democracy theory must be considered. The recognition of the individual in administrative procedures and – under the conditions of the mass democracy – the recognition of the organized interest in public welfare, corresponds in particular to the traditional democratic model of the 'citizen' or '*citoyen*'. This democratic model does not discriminate against civic interests vis-à-vis private interests. The right of each and every citizen to be actively involved in promoting the benefit of the public is commonly recognized in democracy theory.[71] It is part of the widespread democratic ideal and sentiment which deems any commitment aimed at benefiting the public interest as a whole as being more worthwhile than the pursuit of one's own interests or those of a particular group. As Josef Isensee stresses: 'In a liberal democracy it is deemed honourable, to be actively committed to serving the good of the community'.[72]

It is apparent just how tension-wrought the relationship between the German model of the protection of the legal rights of the individual appears when compared to this image of the democratic citizen.[73] Accordingly, the citizen's interest in the welfare of the community does not find a sympathetic ear or recognition before the courts. On the contrary, anyone who seeks to advance anything more than his subjective rights will be reproached for seeking to place himself on a pedestal, assuming the position of an unappointed custodian of the public welfare and, thereby, arrogating to himself a role to which he is not entitled.

On the other hand, anyone who has specifically come to defend his very own interests against the impertinence and unreasonable demands of the putative community welfare – putative because it has already been described as such by the

zur unionsrechtskonformen Anpassung des UmwRG: neue Hürden für Verbandsklagen' [2012] *Zeitschrift für Umweltrecht* 393.

[71] In this respect there was, despite the polarity of the views, evidently agreement among the speakers and participants of the Vienna Constitutional Law Experts Conference on the subject of 'Civic responsibility in the democratic, constitutional state' (1996) 55 *Veröffentlichungen der Vereinigung der Deutschen Staatsrechtslehrer*. M Jestaedt, *Demokratieprinzip und Kondominalverwaltung* (Berlin, Duncker & Humblot, 1993) 188 speaks of 'the free resolution of individuals affected by governance to political social activity'. The question, which Jestaedt answers in the negative, regarding the 'competence establishing' significance of these rights, does not play any role in the question which is being considered here because the exercise of the merely appellatory rights of action is, upon closer consideration, not an exercise of state power which requires competence.

[72] J Isensee, 'Grundrecht auf Ehre' in B Ziemske (ed), *Festschrift für Martin Kriele* (Munich, CH Beck 1997) 5, 37–38. When Isensee criticizes directly that Rudolf Smend, *Bürger und Bourgeois im deutschen Staatsrecht* (n 24) 306, 311 for his part was, in an anti-liberal tradition, playing off 'the wretched, pitiful bourgeois against the state-projecting democracy-constituting citoyen', it was meant purely in a way to oppose the alleged defamation of the former but not the estimation of the latter.

[73] Similarly under aspects of the common good, von Arnim, *Gemeinwohl und Gruppeninteressen* (n 48) 303.

legislature and/or the executive – will be welcomed with open arms and possibly also protected.

From the perspective of the theory of democracy, this contrast appears all the less convincing for the simple reason that in line with current general consensus,[74] the function of the protection of individual rights by administrative courts is also the scrutinizing of both the application and the implementation of objective law. Even Rudolf von Ihering was already of the opinion – albeit restricted to private law – that everyone is 'Custodian and executor of the law within their own sphere'. The specific right which 'He possesses is nothing more than delegated power, inspired by his own interests to enter the lists on behalf of the law and to ward off injustice'. By maintaining his right, the individual upholds the law 'within the confined space which he occupies. The interest and the implications of this, his conduct, go well beyond him as a person'.[75] Ottmar Bühler, one of the fathers of the *Schutznormtheorie*, admitted 'that every norm which serves to protect the interests of the individual, simultaneously but indirectly serves the public interest as a whole'.[76]

This objective function of the legal protection of individual rights becomes particularly evident and, at the same time, particularly problematic in the example of the (land)owner. The owner may only be dispossessed pursuant to Article 14(3), sentence 1 GG 'for the well-being of the general public'. According to prevailing opinion, the owner can, therefore, also start an action before the administrative courts to fight state measures which are aimed at his dispossession or even measures which, at the very least, directly prepare for this dispossession, even though the law being violated is a law which was – pursuing the logic of the *Schutznormtheorie* – discernibly not created to protect him or any other individual, just like the laws of nature conservation or the laws pertaining to the protection of historical buildings and monuments. Neither the conservationalist in general nor the architectural conservationist specifically are, in accordance with this, allowed to make a defence of the interests of the community as a whole their business before the courts; the landowner on the contrary may do so. Against the backdrop of the postulate of democratic equality, it is difficult to justify this privilege.

Contrary to that, the right to show an interest in the development of the community and to influence it in accordance with the postulate of the equality of all

[74] On the objective function of the constitutional complaint as well BVerfG [1998] *Europäische Grundrechte-Zeitschrift* 395ff assenting thereto: BW Wegener, 'Rechtschreibreform und Verfassungsrecht' [1999] *Jura* 185, 186; dissenting: V Wagner, 'Einzelfallentscheidung oder Paradigmenwechsel?' [1998] *Neue Juristische Wochenschrift* 2638ff.

[75] R von Jhering, *Der Kampf ums Recht* (Vienna, Manz, 1874) 49; cf for public law: Krebs, 'Subjektiver Rechtsschutz und objective Rechtskontrolle' (n 6) 191ff; cf as well HD Jarass, 'Drittschutz im Umweltrecht' in H Lessmann and others (eds), *Festschrift für Rudolf Lukes* (Köln, Heymann, 1989) 57, 63 on the function of the individual action as an important stimulus to the effective implementation of environmental standards and the risks which are linked to it owing to its restriction under German law.

[76] Bühler (n 7) 44. cf as well the assessment of Giese, *Die Grundrechte* (Tübingen, Mohr, 1905) 71, pursuant to which 'a strong separation of the state and the interests of the individual is not possible – one always indirectly benefits the other'.

citizens, which is itself inherent in the democracy principle, may neither be monopolized nor oligopolized through state measures. As Michael Sachs formulated: any rule is 'irreconcilable [with the democracy principle] which grants sections of the population an increased influence on state and government authority for the pursuit of the interests of the public welfare'.[77]

In contrast, a system of the bare legal protection of individual rights reduces the individual to its role as 'bourgeois' and the courts to institutions for defending private interests. Nevertheless, in the case of Germany it proves to be a product of the anti-democratic elements of late constitutionalism and as a relic of an extreme but partly surviving division of state and society.

A system of legal protection which makes it possible to defend collective rights before the courts, serves to implement objective law and thereby to strengthen the power of the directly democratically legitimized legislator in the system of the separation of powers. As a result of this, the frequently evoked danger of excessively overstating the power of the courts – courts which, in comparison and in democratic terms are weakly legitimized – must be put into perspective. Incidentally, this danger will be confronted with stringent restrictions in the application of the law.

The executive's own responsibility which is democratically legitimized does not justify any fundamental, wholesale exclusion of a more generous objective judicial control of its actions. Nevertheless, it does allow a pragmatically differentiated organizational framework for the courts' assertion of the interests of the public welfare initiated by individuals or associations. In this respect, precautionary measures taken against a merely arrogated or misused defence of the public good raised by an individual or an association, are compatible with the democratic principle.

VI. CONCLUSION

To this day the doctrine of subjective public rights and, in particular, the restrictions to the legal protection for defending supra-individual interests which came about with its conception, are still being defended, particularly with reference to the quality of the legal protection of the individual under public law. Less is more, as the maxim goes.[78] However, it remains incomprehensible how and why the implementation of individual rights will have to suffer restrictions by the procedural recognition of altruistic motives. The motive for this tenacious defence of the traditional model of the *Verletztenklage* is a significantly political one: it serves to maintain not only privileges to specific economically powerful special interests, but also the partial exemption of the administration from judicial scrutiny. From

[77] Michael Sachs in M Sachs, *Grundgesetz Kommentar* 3rd edn (Munich, CH Beck 2003) Art 20, para 19.

[78] Schmidt-Aßmann (n 1) para 117.

a European law perspective, and from the perspective of the democracy theory, there is no longer any sufficient legitimization for these functions of the determining doctrines of subjective public rights. In this respect, at least, it does indeed prove to be an *Auslaufmodell* – a model which is on the verge of being phased out.[79]

CASES

PrOVGE 2, 351, 353 – *Nachbarstreit* (1877)
BVerwGE 119, 329 – *Nanopartikel* (2001)
ECJ C-237/07 – *Janecek v Freistaat Bayern – Aktionsplan Luftreinhaltung* (2008)
ECJ C-240/09 – *Zoskupenie v Ministerstvo životného prostredia Slovenskej republiky* (2011)
ECJ C-115/09 – *BUND v Bezirksregierung Arnsberg* (2011)

SELECTED LITERATURE

Bauer H, Geschichtliche Grundlagen der Lehre vom subjektiven öffentlichen Recht (Berlin, Duncker & Humblot, 1986)
Bühler O, *Die subjektiven öffentlichen Rechte und ihr Schutz in der deutschen Verwaltungsrechtsprechung* (Berlin, Kohlhammer, 1914)
Ehlers D, 'Die Klagebefugnis nach deutschem, europäischem Gemeinschafts- und U.S.-amerikanischem Recht' [1993] *Verwaltungsarchiv* 139
von Gerber CF, *Über öffentliche Rechte* (Tübingen, H Laupp, 1852)
Giese F, *Die Grundrechte* (Tübingen, Mohr, 1905)
Grimm D, 'Die Entwicklung der Grundrechtstheorie in der deutschen Staatslehre' in G Birtsch (ed), *Grund- und Freiheitsrechte von der ständischen zur spätbürgerlichen Gesellschaft* (Göttingen, Vandenhoeck & Ruprecht, 1987) 235
Jellinek G, *System der subjektiven öffentlichen Rechte* (Freiburg, Mohr, 1892)
Krebs W, 'Subjektiver Rechtsschutz und objective Rechtskontrolle' in HU Erichsen and others (eds), *Festschrift für Christian-Friedrich Menger* (Köln, Berlin, Bonn, München, Heymann, 1985) 191
Preu P, *Subjektivrechtliche Grundlagen des öffentlichrechtlichen Drittschutzes* (Berlin, Duncker & Humblot ,1992)
Scherzberg A, 'Grundlagen und Typologie des subjektiv-öffentlichen Rechts' [1998] *Deutsches Verwaltungsblatt* 129
Schmidt-Preuß M, *Kollidierende Privatinteressen im Verwaltungsrecht: Die subjektiven öffentlichen Rechte im multipolaren Rechtsverhältnis* (Berlin, Duncker & Humblot 1992)
Wegener BW, *Rechte des Einzelnen* (Baden-Baden, Nomos, 1998)
Zuleeg M, 'Hat das subjektive öffentliche Recht noch eine Daseinsberechtigung?' [1976] *Deutsches Verwaltungsblatt* 509

[79] From a European law perspective and sceptical in this respect E Schmidt-Aßmann, *Das allgemeine Verwaltungsrecht als Ordnungsidee* (Berlin, Springer, 1998) 199ff.

13

Administrative Procedure – Mere Facilitator of Material Law versus Cooperative Realization of Common Welfare

HERMANN PÜNDER

C. Consideration of Comparative Law
i. Administrative Procedure in England and France
ii. Administrative Procedure in European Law
V. Concluding Remarks

I. INTRODUCTION

ADMINISTRATIVE PROCEDURE LAW regulates the decision-making process within the administration – from the preparation of activities all the way through to the final decision and its enforcement. In Germany, this field is designated as part of 'formal' administrative law (*formelles Verwaltungsrecht*) and is thus separated from substantive or 'material' administrative law (*materielles Verwaltungsrecht*), which regulates the substance of the legal relations between administrative bodies and citizens. This division has led to a depreciation of procedural law. Traditionally, administrative procedure is viewed merely as a facilitator of material law (section II).[1] The constitutional perspective, however, shows that the method by which administrative decisions are reached is not only relevant for the efficient and effective fulfilment of administrative duties, but is also crucial for the legal protection of those affected and for the democratic legitimacy of the administrative decision. To establish an adequate equilibrium between these constitutional principles is the legislator's duty (section III). The true conflict emerges regarding the question as to which consequences ought to be imposed upon procedural mistakes (section IV). There is a myriad of rules concerning the correction or irrelevance of such mistakes and the comparative perspective reveals that Germany does not stand alone in Europe in downplaying the role of administrative procedure to a certain extent. However, the debate over the importance of administrative procedure is anything but concluded in all countries that adhere to the idea that the public administration is bound by the rule of law and needs legitimation by the people. A path to a transnational *ius commune proceduralis* in administrative law has been entered.[2] In

[1] cf BT-Drs 7/910, 65; 13/1445; BVerwGE 92, 258, 261; J Pietzcker, 'Verwaltungsverfahren zwischen Verwaltungseffizienz und Rechtsschutzauftrag' (1983) 41 *Veröffentlichungen der Vereinigung der Deutschen Staatsrechtslehrer* 193, 221; HA Wolff, 'Die dienende Funktion der Verfahrensrechte – eine dogmatische Figur mit Aussagekraft und Entwicklungspotential' in R Pitschas and A Uhle (eds), *Festschrift für Rupert Scholz* (Berlin, Duncker & Humblot, 2007) 977. Extensive critique by F Hufen and T Siegel, *Fehler im Verwaltungsverfahren*, 5th edn (Baden-Baden, Nomos, 2013) para 31, 918. See for a summary of the discussion: C Möllers, 'Materielles Recht – Verfahrensrecht – Organisationsrecht' in H-H Trute and others (eds), *Allgemeines Verwaltungsrecht – zur Tragfähigkeit eines Konzepts* (Tübingen, Mohr Siebeck 2008) 525; M Fehling, 'Der Eigenwert des Verfahrens im Verwaltungsrecht' (2011) 70 *Veröffentlichungen der Vereinigung der Deutschen Staatsrechtslehrer* 278; H Pünder, 'German Administrative Procedure in a Comparative Perspective – Observations on the Path to a Transnational "Ius Commune Proceduralis" in Administrative Law' (2013) 11 *International Journal of Constitutional Law* (no. 4, forthcoming).

[2] see Pünder, 'German Administrative Procedure in a Comparative Perspective' (n 1).

closing, it is therefore essential to stress that administrative procedure is in fact an independently significant instrument to achieve a cooperative realization of common welfare (section V).

II. ADMINISTRATIVE PROCEDURE LAW IN HISTORIC PERSPECTIVE

A. Administrative Procedure in the Shadow of Material Law and Court Procedure

For a long time, the importance of administrative procedure has been underestimated. During the nineteenth century, as the so-called 'juristic method' (*juristische Methode*) began unfolding in Germany,[3] administrative procedure stood in the shadow of 'material law' (*materielles Recht*) in the development of general rules of administrative law. Scholars of 'public law' (*öffentliches Recht*) were eager to bind administrative activities to the constitutional rule of law in the newly established 'legal state' (*Rechtsstaat*) by creating the institution of the *Verwaltungsakt* ('administrative act'). Seminal in this development was the work of Otto Mayer (1846–1924).[4] He coined the phrase '*Justizförmigkeit der Verwaltung*', which refers to the notion that the administration must be bound to the ideals of court justice. Meyer's analogy, however, was not focused upon the procedure followed by the administration, but upon the legally binding decisions being a just solution to each individual case. The idea of codifying administrative law faced hardship. Neither during the 'Kaiserreich' (1871–1919) nor during the Weimar Republic (1919–33) were the fruits of liberal administrative doctrine inscribed into general codifications. Even the *Grundgesetz* ('GG'), the modern German Constitution enacted in 1949, contains no provisions for administrative procedure. The mistrust toward the executive branch, which rose out of the ashes of the Hitler dictatorship (1933–45), is reflected only in the constitutional guarantees concerning court protection. Examples can be seen in the right to judicial review of administrative actions (Article 19(3)GG), rules regarding the independence of the judiciary (Article 97 GG), and in the right to be heard before a court (Article 103(1)GG). Thus, the codification of administrative law was focused primarily on the judiciary, not on administrative procedure. The Administrative Court Procedures Code (*Verwaltungsgerichtsordnung*, 'VwGO') was enacted in 1960.[5]

[3] cf M Stolleis, *Geschichte des öffentlichen Rechts*, vol II (Munich, CH Beck, 1992) 330; M Pauly, 'Wissenschaft vom Verwaltungsrecht' in A von Bodgandy, S Cassese and PM Huber (eds), *Handbuch Ius Publicum Europaeum*, Vol IV – *Verwaltungsrecht in Europa: Wissenschaft* (Heidelberg, CF Müller, 2011) 41, 44.

[4] O Mayer, *Deutsches Verwaltungsrecht* (1895/96), 3rd edn (Berlin, Duncker & Humblot, 1924).

[5] See also the Social Court Procedures Code (*Sozialgerichtsgesetz*) of 1953 and the Tax Court Procedures Code (*Finanzgerichtsordnung*) of 1965.

B. Codification of Administrative Procedure Law

i. Obstacles on the Road to Codification

In comparison to the development of administrative court procedure, the procedure of administrative agencies experienced far less progress. The administrative decision-making was governed primarily by unwritten legal principles. In spite of encouraging comparative legal research (above all in respect to US law),[6] there was a great deal of scepticism as to whether or not it would be possible to produce a uniform procedural code which would satisfy practical necessities. While the famous 'Staatsrechtslehrervereinigung' (the German association of public law professors) maintained this scepticism toward codification in 1959,[7] the 'Deutscher Juristentag' (the traditional 'Assembly of German Jurists') voted in favour of a codification of administrative procedure in 1960.[8] Nevertheless, it took 17 more years before the project reached completion. In 1977 the federal Administrative Procedure Act (*Verwaltungsverfahrensgesetz*, 'VwVfG') came into force. The German federal states (*Bundesländer*) – with the exception of Schleswig-Holstein, which had enacted its own administrative procedure act in 1967 – followed suit and passed state Administrative Procedure Acts based on the same draft law as the federal code, fully assuming most policies.[9]

ii. Constrained Scope of Application of the Administrative Procedure Acts

Contrary to their titles, the German Administrative Procedure Acts do not comprise the entire administrative procedure. In fact, they address only 'the activity of authorities having an external effect and directed to the examination of basic requirements, the preparation and adoption of an administrative act or to the conclusion of an administrative agreement under public law' (§ 9 VwVfG). All

[6] cf F Becker, *Das Allgemeine Verwaltungsverfahren in Theorie und Praxis* (Stuttgart, Kohlhammer, 1960); FO Kopp, *Verfassungsrecht und Verwaltungsverfahrensrecht* (Munich, CH Beck, 1971); G Langrod, *La doctrine allemande et la procédure administrative non contentieuse* (Brussels, Institut International des Sciences Administratives 1961); CH Ule and F Becker, *Verwaltungsverfahren im Rechtsstaat* (Cologne, Grote, 1964). For an actual comparison see Pünder, 'German Administrative Procedure in a Comparative Perspective' (n 1).

[7] cf CA Bettermann, 'Das Verwaltungsverfahren' (1959) 17 *Veröffentlichungen der Vereinigung der Deutschen Staatsrechtslehrer* 11; more optimistically, E Melichar, 'Das Verwaltungsverfahren' (1959) 17 *Veröffentlichungen der Vereinigung der Deutschen Staatsrechtslehrer* 183. During the discussion, many of the speakers expressed their rejection of the idea of codification (219).

[8] See for the background CH Ule in K Jeserich and others (eds), *Deutsche Verwaltungsgeschichte*, vol V (Stuttgart, Deutsche Verlags-Anstalt, 1987) 1162, 1170.

[9] In Lower Saxony the cross-reference to the federal code is 'static', while Berlin, Rhineland-Palatinate and Saxony chose a 'dynamic' reference, which means that the current version is always referenced, while a static reference refers only to the version in force at the time of enactment. The remaining states enacted so-called *Vollgesetze* (fully fledged codes), in which the provisions of the federal code are, to a large degree, assumed, word for word. Schleswig-Holstein, however, remains true to the system previously developed before the federal code came into force.

other forms of administrative action – the enactment of *Rechtsverordnungen* (executive rules)[10] and *Satzungen* (charters), the decision-making process in regard to 'informal' actions as well as the procedure merely leading to internal decisions – were not included. In addition, the codices refer only to administrative activities within the realm of public law (§ 1(1) VwVfG) and omit the fact that administrative bodies can also take action within the confines of civil law. To fill these voids, it is necessary to revert to the use of analogies, general legal principles and directly to constitutional law.[11] Finally, more specific procedural provisions take priority over the general rules (§ 1 VwVfG).[12] This fragmentation of administrative procedure leads to a severe loss in predictability which is often lamented.

C. Procedural Euphoria and Subsequent Disenchantment

i. Adjudication of the Federal Constitutional Court

Decisions reached by the Federal Constitutional Court (Bundesverfassungsgericht) since the late 1970s have been of greater significance than the codification of administrative procedure law. The Court applied the prerequisites for effective court protection to administrative procedure. In 1977, the justices emphasized that 'the necessity for a dialogue between the administration and the citizens corresponds to the constitutional appreciation of the position of the citizens within the state'.[13] Thus, the administrative decision-making gained relevance in its own right, separated from court procedure and material law. In light of only limited control through material law and the correspondingly large scope of administrative discretion, it was established by the Court in 1979 that

> the protection of the constitutional fundamental rights must also be a concern of administrative procedure, and that these fundamental constitutional rights shall influence not only material law, but also procedure, in as far as this is required to adequately protect these rights.[14]

[10] cf in a comparative perspective, H Pünder 'Democratic Legitimation of Delegated Legislation – A Comparative View on the American, British and German Law' (2009) 58 *International and Comparative Law Quarterly* 353.

[11] See the explanatory notes of the legislature in BT-Drs 7/910, 42.

[12] While some statutes constrict themselves to certain points, others – such as the *Bundesimmissionsschutzgesetz* (Federal Control of Pollution Act) – contain an almost complete set of procedural regulations. Some areas of administration are excluded completely from the application of the general administrative procedure codes (§ 2 VwVfG). This applies namely to the Financial and Social Services Administration (§ 1, para 1 and 4 VwVfG). However, the regulations governing procedure in these fields (*Abgabenordnung*, Tax Code, and *Sozialgesetzbuch*, Social Code, volume X), correspond almost entirely with the general rules.

[13] cf BVerfGE 45, 297, 335: 'Die Notwendigkeit des Gesprächs zwischen Verwaltung und Bürger entspricht dem grundgesetzlichen Verständnis der Stellung des Bürgers im Staat' (translation by the author).

[14] BVerfGE 53, 30, 65 (translation by the author). cf also the decisions cited in n 32.

In academia, these decisions were greeted with great approval, as they fitted in with the *Zeitgeist* of an era determined by a changing relationship between the public administration and the citizens. At the Congress of the 'Staatsrechtslehrervereinigung' in Regensburg in 1971, Peter Häberle had already developed the concept of a *status activus processualis.*[15] Ferdinand Kopp had studied the constitutional foundation of administrative procedure from a comparative legal perspective.[16] The judicature of the Federal Constitutional Court led to a procedural euphoria. Administrative procedure was perceived as the very 'concept of cooperative common welfare'.[17]

ii. Measures Towards Expediting Administrative Procedure

Over time, however, disenchantment has taken the place of euphoria. In the midst of intensive discussions concerning the role of Germany in global economics, administrative procedure law is viewed as a burden (although empirical studies have not affirmed this perception[18]). During the 1990s, the legislature reacted to this growing perception. In the interest of creating procedural law more in tune with the high demand confronting administrative bodies, provisions were enacted which broadened the irrelevance of procedural errors (see section IV). The legislation in this area has met with fierce criticism in academia. It has been asserted that with it comes the decline of the procedure.[19] It is feared that the new rules might lead the administration to take on a lax cavalier approach to procedure. Some have said that in light of the irrelevancy of certain procedural errors, some administrative bodies purposefully deny citizens the possibility to state their arguments, knowing that it is unlikely the citizen will seek legal remedy before a court.[20] The legislature, however, remained unimpressed by these critiques. The newest statutes concerning the expedition of administrative procedure came into force in 2006/07.[21]

[15] P Häberle, 'Grundrechte im Leistungsstaat' (1972) 30 *Veröffentlichungen der Vereinigung der Deutschen Staatsrechtslehrer* 43, 80, 86, 121.

[16] Kopp, *Verfassungsrecht und Verwaltungsverfahrensrecht* (n 6). For a recent comparative view see Pünder, 'German Administrative Procedure in a Comparative Perspective' (n 1).

[17] cf W Schmitt Glaeser, 'Die Position der Bürger als Beteiligte im Entscheidungsverfahren gestaltender Verwaltung' in P Lerche, W Schmitt Glaeser and E Schmidt-Aßmann, *Verfahren als staats- und verwaltungsrechtliche Kategorie* (Heidelberg, CF Müller, 1984) 37, 53; E Schmidt-Aßmann, 'Verwaltungsverfahren' in J Isensee and P Kirchhof (eds), *Handbuch des Staatsrechts der Bundesrepublik Deutschland*, vol V, 3rd edn (Heidelberg, CF Müller, 2007) § 109, para 2. Generally to the concept of 'proceduralization', G-P Calliess, *Prozedurales Recht* (Baden-Baden, Nomos, 1999); A Tschentscher, *Prozedurale Theorien der Gerechtigkeit* (Baden-Baden, Nomos, 1999).

[18] cf A Fisahn, *Demokratie und Öffentlichkeitsbeteiligung* (Tübingen, Mohr Siebeck, 2002) 34; M Martin, *Heilung von Verfahrensfehlern* (Berlin, Berliner Wissenschafts-Verlag, 2004) 165; C Wölki, *Verwaltungsverfahrensgesetz im Wertewandel* (Frankfurt am Main, Peter Lang, 2004) 98, 105; J Ziekow, A Windoffer and M-P Oertel, 'Evaluation von Regelungen zur Beschleunigung von Genehmigungsverfahren: Ein Ansatz zur Schließung einer Forschungslücke' (2006) *Deutsches Verwaltungsblatt* 1469.

[19] GF Schuppert, *Verwaltungswissenschaft* (Baden-Baden, Nomos, 2000) 780ff; F Schoch, 'Der Verfahrensgedanke im allgemeinen Verwaltungsrecht' (1992) 25 *Die Verwaltung* 21, 41.

[20] cf H Sendler, 'Guter Rechtsschutz und Verfahrensbeschleunigung' (1982) *Deutsches Verwaltungsblatt* 812, 818.

[21] See for examples W Erbguth, 'Abbau des Verwaltungsrechtsschutzes' (2009) *Die öffentliche Verwaltung* 921, 927.

III. CONSTITUTIONAL BASIS OF ADMINISTRATIVE PROCEDURE LAW

The discussion concerning the importance of administrative procedure draws attention to the constitutional requirements, which the legislature must observe when stipulating such provisions and which the administrative body itself must follow when interpreting and applying these provisions.[22] Since the German Constitution lays down no explicit rules regarding administrative procedure, constitutional guidelines can only be found in general 'constitutional principles' (*Verfassungsprinzipien*).[23] This, however, must be done with great care. The demands of constitutional law must be separated from political ambitions. The legislator is granted discretion (*Gestaltungsspielraum*) when creating law and not every form of administrative law can be seen as 'concretized constitutional law' (*konkretisiertes Verfassungsrecht*).[24]

A. Efficacy by Procedure

Traditionally, administrative procedure was designed to merely facilitate the completion of administrative duties.[25] The idea of efficacy within the administration means that the 'output' of an administrative body must meet the demands of the factual circumstances while fulfilling all legal requirements of such an action in accordance with Article 20(3) GG.[26] Administrative procedure is actually a means of realizing administrative material law.[27] One aspect which serves to effectively fulfil administrative duties is the inquisitorial system (*Untersuchungsgrundsatz*, as it is specified in § 24 VwVfG). The rules concerning the impartiality (*Unparteilichkeit*) of the acting administrative officer (§§ 20, 21 VwVfG) are also relevant. Furthermore, the obligation to state the grounds (*Begründungspflicht*) for administrative decisions (§ 39 VwVfG) forces the administrative body to assess carefully both the legal and factual conditions before reaching any conclusion.

However, the 'bureaucratic mechanism', as put forth by Max Weber, does not always represent the 'most rational form in which to exercise power'.[28] Information asymmetries between the administration and the affected parties are a frequent

[22] See for more details H Pünder, 'Verwaltungsverfahren' in H-U Erichsen and D Ehlers (eds), *Allgemeines Verwaltungsrecht*, 14th edn (Berlin, de Gruyter, 2010) § 13, paras 9–16.

[23] General theories differentiate between 'legal rules', which can only be either met or not met, and 'legal principles', which can be fulfilled to different degrees. See eg R Alexy, *Theorie der juristischen Argumentation* (Frankfurt am Main, Suhrkamp, 2001) 21, 229, 319.

[24] This famous saying derives from F Werner, 'Verwaltungsrecht als konkretisiertes Verfassungsrecht' (1959) *Deutsches Verwaltungsblatt* 527 (translation by the author).

[25] cf eg BVerfGE 46, 325, 333; 53, 30, 74.

[26] H Pünder, *Haushaltsrecht im Umbruch* (Stuttgart, Kohlhammer, 2003) 57.

[27] R Wahl, 'Verwaltungsverfahren zwischen Verwaltungseffizienz und Rechtsschutzauftrag' (1983) 41 *Veröffentlichungen der Vereinigung der Deutschen Staatsrechtslehrer* 151.

[28] M Weber, *Wirtschaft und Gesellschaft*, 5th edn (Tübingen, Mohr Siebeck 1976) 56 (translation by the author).

obstacle in public decision-making. Therefore, it can be helpful to involve those who are confronted with the problem first-hand. Procedural rights given to the individuals involved can play a crucial role in fulfilling administrative duties effectively.[29] In particular, the right to a hearing (*Anhörungsrecht*, as set by § 28 VwVfG) is a 'prerequisite to a correct administrative decision'.[30] As such, it is in the parties' own interest to assist the administrative body in ascertaining the specifics of the circumstances at hand (§ 26(2) VwVfG). Cooperative solutions will frequently suit problems better than the exercise of administrative authority will.[31] The right of access to the agency's records (*Akteneinsicht* according to § 29 VwVfG) can disclose an undue '*agency capture*'. Finally, efficient cooperation between citizens and administration demands an atmosphere of mutual trust. The obligation to counsel and advise the party involved (*Beratungspflicht* pursuant to § 25 VwVfG) and the inadmissibility of undue disclosure of the ascertained information to third parties (*Geheimhaltung* as demanded by § 30 VwVfG) facilitate this goal.

B. Legal Protection by Procedure

Furthermore, it is a constitutionally rooted aim of administrative procedure to provide the parties involved with effective pre-judicial legal protection. As mentioned earlier, the Federal Constitutional Court has emphasized repeatedly that the constitutional fundamental rights (*Grundrechte*) contain not only a guarantee as to the application of material law, but for procedural law as well.[32] Administrative procedure plays an important role in the realization of the constitutional fundamental rights, especially when statutes offer a large scope of administrative discretion (*Ermessen*), leaving the courts with only limited means of judicial review.[33] Being that legal protection can be attained far more quickly through administrative procedure than in court proceedings, it can often be the more effective form of legal remedy. Nevertheless, administrative procedure cannot fully replace legal protection by courts.[34] It can only be used to supplement the judicial form of legal remedy.[35]

[29] cf in a comparative perspective Pünder 'Democratic Legitimation of Delegated Legislation' (n 10).

[30] BVerfGE 9, 89, 95 (translation by the author).

[31] cf Pünder, 'Verwaltungsverfahren' (n 22) § 16, para 8.

[32] cf BVerfGE 46, 325, 333 (concerning Art 14 GG); 53, 30 (concerning Art 2(2) GG); 69, 315, 355(concerning Art 8 GG); 52, 391, 407; 56, 216, 236; 60, 253, 294 (concerning Art 16a GG), 52, 380, 389; 84, 34, 45 (concerning Art 12 GG); 69, 1, 25 (concerning Art 4(3); Art 12a(2) GG); 65, 1, 4 (concerning 'informational self-determination'); 61, 82, 110 (concerning Art 19(4) GG); 116, 135, 153 (concerning Art 3 GG).

[33] cf BVerfGE 49, 89, 133, as well as the dissenting opinions (*Sondervoten*) of Helmut Simon und Hermann Heußner in BVerfGE 53, 30, 69.

[34] See W Schmitt Glaeser, 'Partizipation an Verwaltungsentscheidungen' (1973) 31 *Veröffentlichungen der Vereinigung der Deutschen Staatsrechtslehrer* 179, 241.

[35] cf in a comparative perspective Pünder, 'Democratic Legitimation of Delegated Legislation' (n 10).

Although not every breach of statutory procedural rules can be seen as an infraction of constitutional fundamental rights,[36] it is a constitutional obligation of procedural law to guarantee a minimum standard of protection of fundamental rights. This idea is manifested in the various statutory rights given to the citizens concerned. Being that the administrative agency, in contrast to the courts, is not an impartial entity, but a party in the conflict at hand, it is vital to ensure 'equality of arms' (*Waffengleichheit*).[37] Some scholars even feel that involving citizens into administrative proceedings is a realization of the constitutional guarantee of human dignity (*Menschenwürde*) found in Article 1(1) GG.[38] The right to pre-judicial legal relief comprises the right to obtain information. The agency must inform parties of all facts relevant for the pursuance of constitutional rights (§ 25 VwVfG). In addition, they must grant access to all records pertaining to the case (§ 29 VwVfG). This obligation is, however, limited to such information, the disclosure of which does not infringe upon the confidentiality rights of third parties or the state (§ 30 VwVfG). Administrative acts which are disadvantageous for the party receiving them must be accompanied by a statement of grounds (§ 39 VwVfG) to give the party the opportunity to assess the chances before the courts. Furthermore, the constitutional fundamental rights grant citizens the right to state their case before an agency decision is made (§ 28 VwVfG). The Constitution demands that the procedure be fair.[39] The agency is obligated to ascertain all relevant facts itself (§ 24 VwVfG) and to do so in an impartial manner (§§ 21, 22 VwVfG).[40] Moreover, the agency must fulfil its obligation to advise and assist its citizens (§ 25 VwVfG). Each citizen is to be protected against the failure to realize his constitutional rights due to lack of knowledge, inexperience or ineptness. Finally, the citizen must be granted the right to have legal representation during the administrative proceedings (§ 14 VwVfG). If need be, a representative is to be appointed ex officio (§ 16 VwVfG).

C. Legitimation by Procedure

Administrative procedure furthermore contributes to the democratic legitimation of the agency decision. According to the traditional constitutional theory, administrative decisions are legitimized by the continuous 'chain of democratic legitimacy' (*Legitimationskette*) from the Parliament down to the decision-making officer in the administration, and by the courts, which check the content of agency decisions for their compliance with the law passed by Parliament (Article 20(3)

[36] BVerfGE 53, 31, 65. See also the dissenting opinions (*Sondervoten*) of the Justices Helmut Simon und Hermann Heußner in BVerfGE 53, 30, 77.

[37] cf M Fehling, *Verwaltung zwischen Unparteilichkeit und Gestaltungsaufgabe* (Tübingen, Mohr Siebeck, 2001) 297.

[38] See especially Kopp 'Verfassungsrecht und Verwaltungsverfahrensrecht' (n 6) 16.

[39] cf eg BVerfGE 46, 325, 334; 52, 380, 389.

[40] cf BVerwGE 70, 143.

GG).[41] In this way, it is assured that all state power is derived from the people (Article 20(2) (2) GG). This conventional form of democratic legitimation does not, however, always suffice to promote acceptance of an agency decision. In a democracy, it is not enough that government acts lawfully but rather the party involved should be convinced of the decision made. To promote this acceptance is a sign not only of administrative prudence, but also the fulfilment of the constitutional democratic principle.[42] The right to an opportunity to be heard (§ 28 VwVfG) and the right to disclosure of information (§ 29 VwVfG), on the one hand, and the obligation of the agency to inform the party involved (§ 25 VwVfG) and to substantiate decisions made (§ 39 VwVfG), on the other hand, serve to legitimize administrative acts. The legislature is given a broad spectrum of discretion, though, as far as the structure of administrative procedure is concerned. This is especially the case for such procedures which are substantially governed by statutory law and thereby monitored by the courts. The more Parliament fails to implement specific regulations, the more recourse must be taken to general constitutional principles. However, rights of participation cannot entirely replace parliamentary specification.[43] In a conflict situation, the legislative rule must assert itself.

D. Efficiency by Procedure

The constitutional imperatives of efficacy, legal protection and democratic legitimacy would seem to suggest an elaborate administrative procedure. However, such a procedure is costly as it demands a great deal of time, personnel, materials and money. It is often criticized that rights of participation are a hindrance to the efficient fulfilment of administrative duties. It is feared that procedural rights will lead to a prolonged procedure and a delayed decision by way of unnecessary obstacles which, in the end, lead only to a more error-prone procedure.[44] These criticisms are not mere political pandering as the efficiency of administrative action is guaranteed by the Constitution.[45] The effort required by all parties must

[41] cf BVerfGE 83, 60, 73, as well as eg E-W Böckenförde, 'Demokratie als Verfassungsprinzip' in J Isensee and P Kirchhof (eds), *Handbuch des Staatsrechts der Bundesrepublik Deutschland*, vol II, 3rd edn (Heidelberg, CF Müller 2004) § 24, paras 16, 2; H Pünder, 'Wahlrecht und Parlamentsrecht als Gelingensbedingungen repräsentativer Demokratie' (2013) 72 *Veröffentlichungen der Vereinigung der Deutschen Staatsrechtslehrer* 191, 197

[42] Kopp 'Verfassungsrecht und Verwaltungsverfahrensrecht' (n 6) 180. Contrary: Schmitt Glaeser, 'Die Position der Bürger als Beteiligte im Entscheidungsverfahren gestaltender Verwaltung' (n 17) 37, 49.

[43] See for a comparative analysis Pünder, 'Democratic Legitimation of Delegated Legislation' (n 10).

[44] Pietzcker, 'Verwaltungsverfahren zwischen Verwaltungseffizienz und Rechtsschutzauftrag' (n 1) 193, 194.

[45] cf W Hoffmann-Riem, 'Effizienz als Herausforderung an das Verwaltungsrecht' in W Hoffmann-Riem, and E Schmidt-Aßmann (eds), *Effizienz als Herausforderung an das Verwaltungsrecht* (Baden-Baden, Nomos, 1998) 11, 23, 49; Pünder, *Haushaltsrecht im Umbruch* (n 26), 63; R Pitschas, 'Maßstäbe des Verwaltungshandelns' in W Hoffmann-Riem, E Schmidt-Aßmann and A Voßkuhle (eds), *Grundlagen des Verwaltungsrechts*, vol II (Munich, CH Beck, 2008) § 42, para 111; A Voßkuhle, 'Schlüsselbegriffe der Verwaltungsrechtsreform' (2001) 92 *Verwaltungsarchiv* 184, 197.

be as limited as possible. If the realization of a constitutional fundamental right is dependent upon an administrative decision, the citizen can demand that the decision be reached without unnecessary delay.[46]

It is the legislature's responsibility to create a balance between the constitutional guarantees of efficacy, legal remedy and democratic legitimacy on the one hand, and efficiency on the other.[47] The benefit of the administrative procedure must be assessed in relation to the procedural 'transaction costs'.[48] It is important to note, though, that the involvement of those concerned can also be a means to reduce costs for the acting agency, as it is an effective mode of acquiring information. Misunderstandings or unanswered questions can be cleared up quickly through verbal exchanges between the parties. Bothersome costs during the decision-making phase can often become quite cost-effective, if they prevent the agency from reaching a decision, whose errors would, in the long run, induce far greater costs. Most importantly, the involvement of the citizen concerned can help to relieve the workload of the judicial branch, as legal relief acquired through the agency itself can prevent long, drawn-out court litigation. Finally, decisions which come about by means of discussion and the cooperative examination of various viewpoints lead to a greater scope of acceptance, which in itself reduces the costs of enforcement of these decisions.

In the codes concerning administrative procedure, the German legislator has achieved a balance between the various procedural guarantees offered by the Constitution. As a general rule, administrative procedures are to be carried out in an 'easy, practicable and expeditious' way ('*einfach, zweckmäßig und zügig*', pursuant to § 10 VwVfG). The inquisitorial system (§ 24 VwVfG) is a means to this end. The cost of investigating the facts of a particular case are reduced through the incidental obligation (*Mitwirkungsobliegenheit*) of the parties to participate in the procedure (§ 26(2)VwVfG). The duty to give administrative aid between agencies (*Amtshilfe*) prevents an uneconomical administrative procedure due to the diverging responsibilities of various agencies (§ 4 VwVfG). The right to be heard and the right of disclosure are limited where they may inhibit the fulfilment of administrative duties (§§ 28(2), 29(2) VwVfG). Primarily, though, the rules concerning the correction (*Heilung*) or irrelevance (*Unbeachtlichkeit*) of certain procedural errors (§§ 45, 46 VwVfG) help to uphold an efficient administration (section IV). Additional facilitation of administrative procedure is achieved by means of so-called *Massenverfahren* (§§ 17 and following, 69(2), 74(5) VwVfG), whereby petitions of numerous citizens can be decided within one procedure.

[46] cf eg BVerfG (1999) *Neue Zeitschrift für Verwaltungsrecht* 1102, 1103.
[47] K Hesse, *Grundzüge des Verfassungsrechts*, 20th edn (Heidelberg, CF Müller, 1995) para 72.
[48] cf Pünder, 'German Administrative Procedure in a Comparative Perspective' (n 1).

IV. CONSEQUENCES OF PROCEDURAL ERRORS

If an administrative decision is made in breach of procedural provisions, the decision is formally unlawful (*formell rechtswidrig*). The decision may, however, in substance be in full coherence with the material law (*materiell rechtmäßig*). Prior to the codification of administrative procedure in the 1970s, there was controversy among courts and academics as to the consequences of such 'merely' formally unlawful decisions. In accordance with § 45 VwVfG, certain formal errors – insofar as they do not result in absolute nullity (*Nichtigkeit*) of the administrative act (§ 44 VwVfG) – can be corrected (*Heilung*) by repeating the portion of the procedure, which was administered incorrectly (subsection A). Even if a correction is no longer possible, the party does not have a right to a reversal of the decision (*Aufhebungsanspruch*), 'if it is evident that the infringement of regulations governing procedure had not influenced the decision on the matter' (subsection B). This structure finds its roots in the traditional idea that the correct decision according to material law is to be sought, whereas the path leading to it and the form in which it finds its expression are secondary. While this political assessment is not free of doubt, various other legal systems have opted for the same interpretation, as will be shown later (subsection C).[49]

A. Correction of Procedural Errors

The possibility of correcting procedural errors pursuant to § 45 VwVfG facilitates the efficiency of administrative actions, especially the mandate to expedite the administrative decision-making process. Being that these principles are founded in the Constitution itself, and considering the fact that Parliament is given a certain degree of law-making discretion, such corrections are, in general, constitutionally acceptable.[50] The constitutional commitment to lawful decisions (Article 20(2) GG, *Gesetzesbindung*) is ultimately upheld as procedural errors are eliminated. It is, however, of great importance to remember the importance of the procedural edicts for the realization of the constitutional fundamental rights when interpreting the statutes which deal with the correction of administrative errors. The citizens affected may not incur any detriment due to the correction. They must acquire the same legal protection as though the error had not been made in the first place. Thus, a true healing of the error must take place.

[49] cf also E Schmidt-Aßmann, *Das allgemeine Verwaltungsrecht als Ordnungsidee*, 2nd edn (Berlin, Springer, 2004) 305; R Wahl, 'Das Verhältnis von Verwaltungsverfahren und Verwaltungsprozessrecht in europäischer Sicht' in H Hill and R Pitschas (eds), *Europäisches Verwaltungsverfahrensrecht* (Berlin, Duncker & Humblot, 2004) 357, 371; Pünder, 'German Administrative Procedure in a Comparative Perspective' (n 1).

[50] Different opinion VG Arnsberg (1981) *Deutsches Verwaltungsblatt*, 648, 649; M Niedobitek, 'Rechtsbindung der Verwaltung und Effizienz des Verwaltungsverfahrens' (2000) *Die öffentliche Verwaltung* 761.

i. Preconditions and Consequences of Correction of Procedural Errors

Pursuant to § 45(1) VwVfG, a correction of procedural errors can be made above all if the required statement of grounds (*erforderliche Begründung*) is subsequently given or the necessary right to be heard (*erforderliche Anhörung*) is granted. Similar regulations can be found in tax and social security law (with the exception that a breach of a citizen's right to be heard in social security proceedings cannot be corrected).[51] As long as citizens are not limited in their ability to seek remedy, the general rules concerning the corrections of procedural errors can be applied by analogy to other areas of administrative action.[52]

Once the procedural error has been corrected, the breach becomes null and void. From this point on, the administrative measure is viewed as lawful; courts have no right to overturn the decision of the administration pursuant to § 113(1), sentence 1 VwGO. The party can, however, pursue a so-called *Fortsetzungsfeststellungsklage* (§ 113(1), sentence 4 VwGO), a law suit designed to establish that an administrative decision was unlawful until the time of its correction, in addition to the possibility to sue for damages for losses (*Amtshaftungsanspruch*) incurred due to the procedural error (Article 34 GG in conjunction with § 839 *Bürgerliches Gesetzbuch*, Civil Law Code). The widespread opinion that the correction leads to the lawfulness of the act ab initio[53] must be dismissed, as this notion would lead to the original unlawfulness having no consequences whatsoever. If a party fails to file an administrative objection (*Widerspruch* according to § 68 VwGO) or to seek a judicial action against the administrative act (*Anfechtungsklage* according to § 42 VwGO) within the allotted time period of one month (§§ 70, 74 VwVfG) because the administrative decision did not contain the necessary statement of grounds (§ 39 VwVfG) or because the party's right to be heard was not granted (§ 28 VwVfG), the failure to uphold the deadline cannot be construed against the party (§ 45(3), sentence 1 VwVfG). Thus, the party is not limited in its ability to seek administrative or judicial remedy through the correction of the procedural error. The party is granted a *restitutio in integrum* (*Wiedereinsetzung in den vorherigen Stand*) as long as the procedural error causally determined the failure to uphold the deadline. The prerequisites for causality must not be construed too narrowly. The error is causal already if it is not certain that the party would have met the deadline, had the procedural error not occurred.[54] The new time limit begins as soon as the correction is made (§ 45(3), sentence 2 VwVfG).

[51] § 126 Tax Code (*Abgabenordnung*) and § 41 Social Code, volume X (*Sozialgesetzbuch X*).

[52] See eg BayVGH (1999) *Neue Zeitschrift für Verwaltungsrecht–Rechtsprechungsreport* 119, 120; W Durner, 'Die behördliche Befugnis zur Nachbesserung fehlerhafter Verwaltungsakte' (2006) 97 *Verwaltungsarchiv* 345, 356.

[53] cf H Maurer, *Allgemeines Verwaltungsrecht*, 17th edn (Munich, CH Beck, 2009) § 10, para 39.

[54] More strictly BGHZ 144, 210, 218ff, but reversed by BVerfG (2001) *Neue Zeitschrift für Verwaltungsrecht* 1392.

ii. Correction Within the Administrative Procedure and Within Court Proceedings

According to § 45(2) VwVfG, the correction of administrative errors can be made throughout all proceedings up to the superior regional administrative trial courts (*Oberverwaltungsgerichte*). If the agency corrects the error within the administrative procedure itself due to a pre-judicial objection (*Widerspruch*) filed by the party (§ 68 VwGO), the party incurs no costs for these preliminary administrative proceedings (*Widerspruchsverfahren*), as the agency is required to fully bear the expenses (§ 80 VwVfG). The requisite statement of grounds can be submitted by the acting agency itself (*Ausgangsbehörde*) or by the supervising agency (*Widerspruchsbehörde*) ruling on the objection according to § 73 VwGO.[55] As far as the right to be heard is concerned, different rules must apply, however. § 28 VwVfG sets certain standards in regard to the time frames within which a hearing is to take place. Therefore, only the original agency can subsequently grant a hearing and decide to overturn its own decision (*Abhilfe*, according to § 72 VwGO), rather than passing the action on to the supervising agency (§ 73 VwGO). This rule applies even when the supervising agency is granted full competency to change any portion of the administrative decision (*Selbsteintrittsrecht*), as it cannot be ruled out that the original agency may have granted a more advantageous decision.[56] An exception to this rule can be made only in cases in which the agency has no discretion, but can only make one decision (*gebundene Entscheidung*). In this case, even the original agency would not have been able to reach a different decision. Thus, the party is not detrimentally affected. If the hearing is to be granted only by the supervising agency, then the party must be informed of this. The fact that the party filed a pre-judicial objection (*Widerspruch*) – by which it has the possibility to state its point of view – is not sufficient.[57] If this was the case, the agency would have no incentive to uphold the party's right to be heard, as no consequences would result from the omission of such a hearing; the error would automatically be corrected by filing an objection. Should no objection be filed, the decision becomes final despite the procedural mistake.

Pursuant to § 45(2) VwVfG, formal errors can be corrected not only during the administrative process, but even during court proceedings (including summary proceedings for injunctive relief – *einstweiliger Rechtsschutz* – in accordance with § 80(5) and § 123 VwGO respectively). Similar regulations are stipulated within the tax and social security codes.[58] These rules are part of the legislature's efforts to expedite administrative procedure even more. Up until 1996, the

[55] Different opinion: U Kischel, *Folgen von Begründungsfehlern* (Tübingen, Mohr Siebeck, 2004) 177.

[56] BVerwGE 66, 184, 187 (3rd Panel); different opinion: BVerwGE 66, 111, 114 (2nd Panel); BVerwG (1984) *Neue Zeitschrift für Verwaltungsrecht*, 578, 579; C Bumke, 'Verwaltungsakte' in Hoffmann-Riem, Schmidt-Aßmann, and Voßkuhle, *Grundlagen des Verwaltungsrechts* (n 45) § 35, para 181; Durner, 'Die behördliche Befugnis zur Nachbesserung fehlerhafter Verwaltungsakte' (n 52) 352.

[57] BVerwGE 66, 111, 114; 66, 184, 189.

[58] § 126, para 2 Tax Code (*Abgabenordnung*), § 41, para 2 Social Code, volume X (*Sozialgesetzbuch* X).

correction of procedural errors was limited to the time up until an action was filed with the administrative courts (Verwaltungsgerichte). Originally, it had been planned to extend the possibility of error correction until the end of the final appellate court procedure at the Federal Administrative Court (Bundesverwaltungsgericht), the highest German court in administrative matters dealing only with legal questions (*Revisionsverfahren*). This idea was abandoned as the result of strong criticism so that corrections were allowed only through the trial court proceedings (*Tatsacheninstanz*) in lower instances up to the Higher Administrative Courts (Oberverwaltungsgerichte). The possibility to correct procedural errors during court proceedings is precarious, as it is nearly impossible to establish a position for the citizen within court proceedings which would have been reached, had the error not been made in the first place. As far as social security proceedings are concerned, the social courts (Sozialgerichte) have, for this very reason, denied the possibility of correction during a trial.[59] Even the debates preceding the 1973 legislation emphasized the fact that the right to be heard must be granted prior to the filing of any legal action. It would be unjust for the party to be forced to enter court litigation without having had an opportunity to state its views or without having received a statement of grounds for the agency action.[60] Owing to legislative discretion granted in realizing procedural constitutional rights, an error correction during a court trial – which was already recognized by the Prussian Highest Administrative Court (Preußisches Oberverwaltungsgericht)[61] – is not unconstitutional.[62] The party is protected from substantial material damage by § 92(2) and § 161(2) VwGO respectively, which state that the agency must bear all the costs of court proceedings, should the action be withdrawn or discharged owing to the correction of procedural errors. Nevertheless it is essential that the interpretation of the statutes which regulate these corrections is performed in such a way that the correction must be made as soon as possible – in most cases during the administrative procedure itself – so that the purpose of a hearing can still be met. Furthermore, the correction can only make the error obsolete if the party's arguments are subsequently included in the new agency decision.[63] If the agency merely references the arguments in a formal way, without truly dealing with them, merely in order

[59] See for examples Martin, *Heilung von Verfahrensfehlern* (n 18) 62, 289.

[60] BT-Drucks 7/910, 66.

[61] See for details Durner, 'Die behördliche Befugnis zur Nachbesserung fehlerhafter Verwaltungsakte' (n 52) 351.

[62] Different opinions: B Bredemeier, *Kommunikative Verfahrenshandlungen im deutschen und europäischen Verwaltungsrecht* (Tübingen, Mohr Siebeck, 2007) 359; W Erbguth, 'Zum Gehalt und zur verfassungs- wie europarechtlichen Vereinbarkeit der verwaltungsprozessual ausgerichteten Beschleunigungsgesetzgebung' (2000) 20 *Umwelt und Planungsrecht* 81, 85; Martin, 'Heilung von Verfahrensfehlern' (n 18) 286; Niedobitek, 'Rechtsbindung der Verwaltung und Effizienz des Verwaltungsverfahrens' (n 50); H Sodan, 'Unbeachtlichkeit und Heilung von Verfahrens- und Formfehlern' (1999) *Deutsches Verwaltungsblatt* 729, 738; A Hatje, 'Die Heilung formell rechtswidriger Verwaltungsakte im Prozess als Mittel der Verfahrensbeschleunigung' (1997) *Die öffentliche Verwaltung* 477, 483.

[63] cf BVerwGE 66, 111, 114.

to uphold their decision before the courts, the error may not be viewed as corrected.

B. No Entitlement to Judicial Reversal in Spite of Procedural Errors

If procedural errors are not corrected or if a correction is not possible, the party will generally be entitled to have a court reverse the decision of the agency (*Aufhebungsanspruch*, according to § 113(1), sentence 1 VwGO). Pursuant to § 46 VwVfG, this is not the case, however, when it is clear that the breach of formal requirements had no influence on the outcome of the decision made. Similar rules apply to the supervisory phase of the administrative procedure itself (§ 79(2), sentence 2 VwGO), and to tax and social security procedures.[64] This preclusion of the right to a reversal is precarious as it provides a further limitation of procedural rules beyond the scope of § 45 VwVfG and, as such, a cavalier approach to procedural obligations must be feared. The notion may arise that breaching procedural rules are forgivable sins. Naturally, the regulations, which make such errors irrelevant, expedite administrative procedure, which is a constitutional goal. As a result of the legislative discretion granted in realizing these constitutional rights, § 46 VwVfG is not unconstitutional.[65] However, the Constitution must be considered, when interpreting these regulations: the possibility to correct errors must be given priority over the declaration of errors as irrelevant, as the healing strengthens the legitimacy of the decision by observing the legal requirements made (Article 20(3) GG). Therefore, § 46 VwVfG cannot be applied to errors which could still be corrected.

i. Prerequisites for the Denial of a Reversal Decision

In order to preserve the constitutional value of procedural requirements, § 46 VwVfG stipulates that the right to a reversal of the agency decision may only be excluded if it is 'evident' (*offensichtlich*) that the breach of procedure had no effect on the substantive outcome of the administrative act. In other words, the citizen maintains his or her right to a reversal if there is a real possibility that the agency would have reached a different decision, if the procedural requirements had been observed. In cases of uncertainty, the decision in regard to the obviousness is to be made in favour of the citizen and his or her procedural rights. The lack of causality of the procedural mistake for the agency decision must really be 'evident', meaning that it must be distinct and easily discernible. However, in cases in which the agency had no discretion for its decision (*gebundene Entscheidung*), there can be no right to a reversal, because the agency would have had to issue the very same

[64] cf § 127 Tax Code (*Abgabenordnung*) and § 42 Social Code, volume X (*Sozialgesetzbuch* X).
[65] Different opinion: Niedobitek 'Rechtsbindung der Verwaltung und Effizienz des Verwaltungsverfahrens' (n 50).

decision had it observed all the procedural standards.[66] A different scenario would be met where the adherence to procedural standards may have led to a diverging administrative decision. In such cases, the courts may reverse the agency decision without reaching a conclusion about the correct decision (§ 113(3) VwGO).[67] When the agency is granted discretion in its decision-making with regard to the legal consequences (*Ermessen*) or in respect to the ascertainment of the facts (*Beurteilungsspielraum*), § 46 VwVfG may not be applied.[68] In these cases, the procedural standards fulfil the purpose of influencing the decision. Owing to the limited checks by the courts in this area, the breach cannot be corrected by a court decision.

Finally, it is important to note that the rule of § 46 VwVfG whereby procedural breaches are irrelevant cannot be applied to the so-called 'absolute' procedural errors (*absolute Verfahrensfehler*). Those breaches lead to a right of reversal irrespective of their causality for the decision made even if the decision is the only possible lawful result of the proceedings. In part, there are explicit rules which specify this general principle. For example, in social law, § 42 *Sozialgesetzbuch X* (Code of Social Law, volume X) mandates that an agency measure is reversed if the required hearing did not take place. § 46 VwVfG also reveals *e contrario* that breaches of jurisdiction pertaining to the subject matter (*sachliche Zuständigkeit*) or the level of authority (*instanzielle Zuständigkeit*) pose absolute errors in procedure. By means of interpretation, it must be ascertained whether a particular procedural requirement merely orders and facilitates the proceedings or whether it achieves an intended purpose in its own right, so that the citizen is given an independently enforceable procedural position.[69]

ii. Legal Consequences

In the event of one of the cases covered by § 46 VwVfG, a court action filed by a citizen must be dismissed. However, § 46 VwVfG merely precludes the right to have the administrative act reversed by the courts. It changes nothing as far as the unlawfulness of the agency decision is concerned. Thus, the citizen can still file an action to seek to establish that the decision was formally illegal (*Fortsetzungsfeststellungsklage* according to § 113(1), sentence 4 VwGO). In addition, he or she may seek damages (*Amtshaftungsanspruch*). The opinion – often stated by courts and academics alike – that in the case of § 46 VwVfG there can be no violation of individual rights,[70] must be repudiated. § 46 VwVfG merely limits the right to seek reversal, but does not exclude all rights associated with the error.

[66] cf BVerwGE 62, 108, 116; (1988) *Neue Zeitschrift für Verwaltungsrecht* 525, 526.
[67] cf OVG Münster (1989) *Baurecht* 315, 319. Different opinion BVerwGE 65, 287.
[68] cf BVerwGE 61, 45, 50.
[69] cf BVerwGE 41, 58, 64; 44, 235, 239.
[70] cf BVerwGE 65, 287, 289.

C. Consideration of Comparative Law

i. Administrative Procedure in England and France

In a comparative perspective, English and French law are well worth examining.[71] Both countries lack an exhaustive codification of administrative procedural law, in spite of the tendencies toward codification found throughout the European Union.[72] In England, the judiciary – especially the Administrative Court established in 2000 as part of the High Court of Justice – monitors administrative procedure relatively closely. 'Procedural impropriety' represents a cause for legal action.[73] A breach of the 'natural justice' rules – to which *audi alteram partem* belongs – generally leads to nullity of the agency decision. Occasionally though, British judges will deny a 'quashing order', if the procedural error had no consequence for the decision.[74] This jurisprudence corresponds with the German rule set forth in § 46 VwVfG. In addition, British law allows a correction of administrative errors in regard to procedure, similar to § 45 VwVfG under German law.[75]

In France, the situation is comparable. The legal action to seek *annulation* of an agency decision (*recours pour excès de pouvoir*) deals – like in German and English law – not only with material legality, but also with the question of formal legality (*légalité interne* and *externe*). Breaches of form and procedural requirements (*vice de forme ou de procédure*) generally lead to the reversal of the decision at hand.[76] Procedural errors are, however, irrelevant – similar to § 46 VwVfG of German law – when they concern decisions in which the agency had no discretion (*compétence liée*). In regard to discretionary decisions (*pouvoir discrétionnaire*), a breach will only be seen as irrelevant if it represents a mere irregularity (*irrégularité*) and is a breach of unsubstantial formalities (*formalités accessoires* or *non-substantielles*). The distinction between whether or not the error affected the decision or whether the purpose of the procedural regulation was fulfilled in another way is crucial. The correction of fundamental errors is barred, unlike under German law (§ 45 VwVfG).

[71] cf Pünder, 'Verwaltungsverfahren' (n 22) § 13, paras 22–28, and – for more details and including a comparative view on the US-American law – Pünder, 'German Administrative Procedure in a Comparative Perspective' (n 1).

[72] cf Pünder, 'Verwaltungsverfahren' (n 22) § 13, para 25.

[73] cf *Council of Civil Service Unions v Minister for the Civil Service* (1985) AC 374, 410.

[74] cf *Malloch v Aberdeen Corp* (1971) 1 WLR 1578; *Glynn v Keele University* (1971) 1 WLR 487; differing from *Annamunthodo v Oilfields Workers' Trade Union* (1961) AC 945; more restrictive *John v Rees* (1970) Ch 345, 402.

[75] cf *Calvin v Carr* (1980) AC 574.

[76] In a comparative perspective: T von Danwitz, *Europäisches Verwaltungsrecht* (Berlin, Springer, 2008) 59, 65; C Ladenburger, *Verfahrensfehlerfolgen im französischen und im deutschen Verwaltungsrecht* (Berlin, Springer, 1999) 156.

ii. Administrative Procedure in European Union Law

In general, procedural and formal errors can be corrected even in regard to European Union law as – generally speaking – the Member States' procedural law will be applied. However, some European specifics must be adhered to. When European agencies directly execute European law (*direkter Vollzug*), the correction of procedural errors is allowed during the administrative procedure,[77] but not during court proceedings[78] (although the European Court of Justice has seen this differently in the past[79]). The European Court of Justice is particularly strict when it comes to breaches of the right to a statement of grounds or the right to be heard.[80] In order to preserve the uniformity of EU law, these restrictions must also be observed when European law is indirectly executed by the Member States (*indirekter Vollzug*), so that in these cases, § 45 VwVfG may only be applied until the end of the administrative, procedure but not during court proceedings.[81] In addition, according to European law, the subsequent fulfilment of procedural specifications has no retroactive effects, if the practical effect of the procedural rule would otherwise be undermined.[82]

Furthermore, European law does not require procedural errors to always lead to a reversal of agency decisions, irrespective of the consequences of the error for the decision itself. For example, as far as direct execution of EU law goes, only the breach of fundamental procedural provisions qualifies for a nullification action (Article 263(II) TFEU). This so-called 'harmless error principle' can also be applied to indirect execution of EU law by Member States. A procedural stipulation is considered to be fundamental only if its breach can influence the content of an action.[83] Errors have therefore been deemed irrelevant not only where no legal alternative to the decision met existed,[84] but also where there simply was no

[77] cf Case C-107/82 *AEG-Telefunken v Commission* (1983) ECR 3151, para 29; Case C-295/85 *Hochbaum and Rawes v Commission* (1987) ECR 3259, para 10.

[78] cf Case C-329/93 *Germany v Commission* (1996) ECR I-5151, paras 22, 48; Case T-30/91 *Solvay v Commission* (1995) ECR II-1775, paras 98, 103; Case T-32/91 *Solvay v Commission* (1995) ECR II-1825, para 53; Case T-36/91 *ICI v Commission* (1995) ECR II-1847, paras 108, 113; Case T-346/94 *France-aviation v Commission* (1995) ECR II-2841, para 39.

[79] cf Case C-85/76 *Hoffman la Roche v Commission* (1979) ECR 461, para 15.

[80] cf Case C-18/57 *Nold v High Authority* (1958-59) ECR 89, 115–16; Joined Cases C-8 to C–11/66 *Cimenteries v Commission* (1967) 99, 125; Case C-16/76 *France v Commission* (1979) ECR 321, paras 6ff; Case C-138/79 *Roquette Frères v Council* (1980) ECR 3333, para 37; Case C-158/80 *Rewe v Hauptzollamt Kiel* (1981) ECR 1805, paras 26–27; Case C-248/84 *Germany v Commission* (1987) ECR 4013, para 22; Case C-63/95 *Germany v Commission* (1996) ECR I-5151, para 48; Case C-315/99 *Ismeri Europa v Court of Auditors* (2001) ECR I-5281, paras 21–22.

[81] See for details von Danwitz, *Europäisches Verwaltungsrecht* (n 76) 541; W Kahl, 'Grundrechtsschutz durch Verfahren in Deutschland und in der EU' (2004) 95 *Verwaltungsarchiv* 1, 20.

[82] cf Case C-354/90 *FNCE v France* (1991) ECR I-5505, paras 16–17; Case C-39/94 *SFEI v La Poste* (1996) ECR I-3547, para 67.

[83] cf Case C-30/78 *Distillers Company v Commission* (1980) ECR 2229, para 26; Case C-117/81 *Geist v Commission* (1983) ECR 2191, para 7; Case C-301/87 *France v Commission* (1990) ECR I-307, para 31.

[84] cf *Geist v Commission* (n 83) para 7.

factual alternative to the decision, in spite of discretion on the part of the agency.[85] However, as far as breaches of the right to a statement of grounds and of the right to be heard go, the European Court of Justice generally finds these mistakes to be fundamental.[86] Thus, § 46 VwVfG must be interpreted in accordance with European law.[87] The criterion of evidence (*Offensichtlichkeit*) must not be dealt with too generously. A procedural error may only be considered irrelevant if the agency would not have reached a different decision, had the breach not occurred.

V. CONCLUDING REMARKS

In Germany – as well as throughout Europe, which is finding its way to a *ius commune europaeum*[88] – the debate about the importance of administrative procedure is not yet finally concluded. A tendency to underestimate the administrative decision-making can still not be denied. For that reason, it is essential to reiterate that administrative procedure is an independently important instrument through which common welfare can be achieved in cooperation with the citizens affected. The procedural provisions gain relevance especially in areas in which the substantial specifications by statutes are limited and thus the possibility of the court to check the administration are restricted as well. It is in fact rare that a decision is merely the result of a formal, logical process which can lead only to one 'right' result.[89] More often than not, agencies have a plethora of possible decisions which can be reached. This process is steered by means of procedural law as it structures the decision-making process, coordinates the cooperative work of various agencies and guides the participation of the citizens. Thus administrative procedure is not merely an onerous formality. Quite the contrary: administrative procedure is relevant for the efficient and effective fulfilment of administrative duties as well as it is essential for the legal protection of those affected and for the democratic acceptance of administrative decisions among the population.

[85] cf Case C-9/76 *Morello v Commission* (1976) ECR 1415, paras 10-11; Case C-234/84 *Belgium v Commission* (1986) ECR 2263, para 30; Case C-259/85 *France v Commission* (1987) ECR 4393, para 13; Case C-301/87 *France v Commission* (1990) ECR I-307, para 31; Case C-142/87 *Belgium v Commission* (1990) ECR I-959, para 48.

[86] cf Case C-264/82 *Timex Corpn v Council and Commission* (1985) ECR 849, para 31; Case C-304/89 *Oliveira v Commission* (1991) ECR I-2283, para 21; Case C-291/89 *Interhotel v Commission* (1991) ECR I-2257, para 17; Case C-157/90 *Infortec v Commission* (1992) ECR I-3525, para 20; Case C-199/91 *Foyer Culturel du Sart-Tilman v Commission* (1993) ECR I-2667, para 34; Joined Cases C-62 and 63/95 *Germany v Commission* (1996) ECR I-5151, paras 38, 48, 58; Case C-367/95 *Commission v Sytraval and Brink's France* (1998) ECR I-1719, paras 74, 78; Case T-346/94 *France-aviation v Commission* (1995) ECR II-2841, para 65; Case T-16/91 *RV Rendo v Commission* (1996) ECR II-1827; paras 30ff, 55–56.

[87] See for details B Wegener, *Rechte des Einzelnen* (Baden-Baden, Nomos 1998) 296.

[88] cf von Danwitz, '*Europäisches Verwaltungsrecht*' (n 76) 128ff; C Engel, 'Integration durch Koordination und Benchmarking?' in Hill and Pitschas, *Europäisches Verwaltungsverfahrensrecht* (n 49) 409; Pünder, 'German Administrative Procedure in a Comparative Perspective' (n 1).

[89] cf eg F Müller and R Christensen, *Juristische Methodik*, vol I, 9th edn (Berlin, Duncker & Humblot, 2004) 23.

CASES

BVerfGE 46, 325 – *Zwangsversteigerung* (1977)
BVerfGE 52, 380 – *Mündliche Prüfung* (1979)
BVerfGE 52, 391 – *Auslieferung* (1979)
BVerfGE 53, 30 – *Mülheim-Kärlich* (1979)
BVerfGE 60, 253 – *Anwaltsverschulden* (1982)
BVerfGE 69, 1 – *Kriegsdienstverweigerung* (1985)
BVerfGE 69, 315 – *Brokdorf* (1985)
BVerfGE 84, 34 – *Prüfungsentscheidungen* (1991)
BVerwGE 44, 235 – *Wasserrechtliche Unterhaltungspflicht* (1973)
BVerwGE 65, 287 – *Fehlerfolgen im Kriegsdienstverweigerungsverfahren* (1982)
BVerwGE 66, 184 – *Nachholung unterbliebener Anhörung* (1982)
BVerwGE 105, 348 – *Beteiligungsrecht von Naturschutzverbänden* (1997)
BVerwGE 137, 199 – *Genehmigung eines Linienverkehrs* (2010)

SELECTED LITERATURE

Bredemeier B, Kommunikative Verfahrenshandlungen im deutschen und europäischen Verwaltungsrecht (Tübingen, Mohr Siebeck, 2007)

Durner W, 'Die behördliche Befugnis zur Nachbesserung fehlerhafter Verwaltungsakte' (2006) 97 *Verwaltungsarchiv* 345–80

Erbguth W, 'Abbau des Verwaltungsrechtsschutzes' (2009) *Die öffentliche Verwaltung* 921–32

Fehling M, 'Der Eigenwert des Verfahrens im Verwaltungsrecht' (2011) 70 *Veröffentlichungen der Vereinigung der Deutschen Staatsrechtslehrer* 278–337

Hufen F and Siegel T, *Fehler im Verwaltungsverfahren*, 5th edn (Baden-Baden, Nomos, 2013)

Kopp FO, *Verfassungsrecht und Verwaltungsverfahrensrecht* (Munich, CH Beck, 1971)

Ladenburger C, *Verfahrensfehlerfolgen im französischen und im deutschen Verwaltungsrecht* (Berlin, Springer, 1999)

Langrod G, *La doctrine allemande et la procédure administrative non contentieuse* (Bruxelles, Institut International des Sciences Administratives 1961)

Lerche P, Schmitt Glaeser W and Schmidt-Aßmann E (eds), *Verfahren als staats- und verwaltungsrechtliche Kategorie* (Heidelberg, CF Müller, 1984)

Möllers C, 'Materielles Recht – Verfahrensrecht – Organisationsrecht: Zu Theorie und Dogmatik dreier Dimensionen des Verwaltungsrechts' in H-H Trute and others (eds), *Allgemeines Verwaltungsrecht – zur Tragfähigkeit eines Konzepts* (Tübingen, Mohr Siebeck, 2008) 525–50

Pietzcker J, 'Verwaltungsverfahren zwischen Verwaltungseffizienz und Rechtsschutzauftrag' (1983) 41 *Veröffentlichungen der Vereinigung der Deutschen Staatsrechtslehrer* 193–231

Pünder H, 'Verwaltungsverfahren' in H-U Erichsen and D Ehlers (eds), *Allgemeines Verwaltungsrecht*, 14th edn (Berlin, de Gruyter, 2010) 415–583

——'Democratic Legitimation of Delegated Legislation – A Comparative View on the American, British and German Law' (2009) 58 *International and Comparative Law Quarterly* 353–78

Pünder H, 'German Administrative Procedure in a Comparative Perspective – Observations on the Path to a Transnational "Ius Commune Proceduralis" in Administrative Law', *International Journal of Constitutional Law* (no 4, forthcoming)

Schmidt-Aßmann E, 'Verwaltungsverfahren' in J Isensee and P Kirchhof (eds), *Handbuch des Staatsrechts der Bundesrepublik Deutschland*, vol V, 3rd edn (Heidelberg, CF Müller, 2007) § 109

Schmitt Glaeser W, 'Partizipation an Verwaltungsentscheidungen' (1973) 31 *Veröffentlichungen der Vereinigung der Deutschen Staatsrechtslehrer* 179–258

Schoch F, 'Der Verfahrensgedanke im allgemeinen Verwaltungsrecht' (1992) 25 *Die Verwaltung* 21–53

Wahl R, 'Verwaltungsverfahren zwischen Verwaltungseffizienz und Rechtsschutzauftrag' (1983) 41 *Veröffentlichungen der Vereinigung der Deutschen Staatsrechtslehrer* 151–86

Part III

European Integration

14

The Legitimation of the European Union – Democracy versus Integration

MARCEL KAUFMANN

I. POSITIONING OF THE DEBATE

THE DEBATE ON the democratic legitimation of the European Union ('EU') does not deal with one coherent subject for discussion, but rather with a bundle of issues of a legal as well as an extra-legal nature. First, this contribution will describe the dimensions and historic stages of the discussion. Then, I will outline the issues usually addressed in relation to the key concept of the European Union's 'democratic deficit' (section II). For about two decades, there has been a constitutional debate in Germany about the problem of whether and, if so, in what way, democratic statehood is jeopardized by the European Union (section III). This debate has been dramatically intensified by certain decisions of the German Constitutional Court in the course of the Euro crisis. Finally, I will attempt to draw an albeit provisional conclusion (section IV).

The debate on the democratic legitimation of the European Union has been conducted in different technical and legal contexts. It has also been historically marked by characteristic shifts of emphasis.

A. Dimensions of the Debate

In its classical form, the debate on the democratic legitimation of the European Union has been a debate about institutions. It has dealt with the analysis of bodies, competences and procedures in the European Union.

The discussion typically centred around the issue of the competences of the European Parliament. These competences have been compared with the competences of a national parliament. In this context, reference has often been made to typical, ideal conceptions of the powers of the Parliament in a representative democracy. Partially backed by legal policy, there have also been frequent calls for more powers to be conferred upon the European Parliament, in particular with regard to legislation and budget law.

However, the debate could no longer be confined to a mere debate on institutions. Rather, the discussion was extended early on by examining the structural differences of the constitutions of a political body organized as a state and a political body organized as a federation, the respective characteristic principles of legitimation and the consequences for the Constitution of the European Union. One example of the growing intensification of this discussion is the question concerning the voting weight of EU citizens in European Parliament elections. Whilst some critics object to the comparatively weaker voting weight of the citizens of the more populated Member States of the European Union ('Member States') in proportion to the voting weight of the citizens of smaller Member States, based on democratic equality, others consider this very element to reflect the federal nature of the European Union's Constitution.[1]

The debate becomes even more comprehensive when addressing the question of the extra-legal requirements of democracy and democratic legitimation, beyond issues relating to the institutions and the Constitution of the European Union. Some representatives of German political science assume that democracy (as a reference point for democratic equality) requires a similarity or homogeneity (of some nature) amongst a state's citizens.[2] In terms of legitimation, these approaches are considered inappropriate today as they do not sufficiently reflect the process of a democratically obtained consensus and democratic representation. If the focus is on these aspects, the necessity of a common language as a requirement for social discourse, of a common cultural background or of a shared national tradition is all the more important.[3]

The *Maastricht* judgment of the German Federal Constitutional Court (Bundesverfassungsgericht) of 1993[4] marks the third dimension of the debate on the European principle of democracy, in that it voiced concerns regarding the preservation of a democratic political body in the process of European integration. The basic assumption of this discussion is that the Member States' peoples are primarily to be taken into consideration as the subjects of democratic legitimation. In contrast, the path of legitimation from the European Union citizens to the European Parliament has a merely complementary function. Consequently, any transfer of functions from a Member State to the association of sovereign states (*Staatenverbund*), necessarily results in deficits in the legitimation process, which (it is presumed) cannot be compensated by institutions and decision-making processes at the European level.[5] Critics of this 1993 court ruling argue that it perpetuates a 'democratic dilemma' of the European Union. It would not help to remedy the democratic deficits at the European Union level as this would necessarily conflict with the Member States' democratic constitutions.

[1] As to the discussion: CD Classen, 'Europäische Integration und demokratische Legitimation' (1994) 119 *Archiv des öffentlichen Rechts* 238; BVerfG *Neue Juristische Wochenschrift* 1995, 2216; S Hölscheidt in E Grabitz and M Hilf (eds), *Das Recht der Europäischen Union*, 46th edn (Munich, CH Beck, 2011) Art 14 EUV, paras 43–45; BVerG [2009] *Neue Juristische Wochenschrift* 2267.

[2] S Benhabib, 'Demokratie und Differenz' in M Brunlik and H Brunkhorst (eds), *Gemeinschaft und Gerechtigkeit* (Frankfurt, S Fischer, 1993) 105; C Schmitt, *Verfassungslehre*, 8th edn (Berlin, Duncker & Humblot, 1993) 226, 235ff; E-W Böckenförde, 'Demokratie als Verfassungsprinzip' in E-W Böckenförde, *Staat, Verfassung, Demokratie*, 2nd edn (Frankfurt am Main, Suhrkamp, 1992) 332.

[3] J Habermas, 'Staatsbürgerschaft und nationale Identität', in Habermas, *Faktizität und Geltung*, 2nd edn (Frankfurt am Main, Suhrkamp, 1992) 632, 542.

[4] BVerfGE 89, 155.

[5] BVerfG [2009] *Neue Juristische Wochenschrift* 2267; P Kirchhof, 'Der deutsche Staat im Prozeß der europäischen Integration' in J Isensee and P Kirchhof, *Handbuch des Staatsrechts der Bundesrepublik Deutschland*, vol VII (Heidelberg, CF Müller, 1992) § 183, para 38; U Di Fabio, 'Der neue Art. 23 des Grundgesetzes: Positivierung vollzogenen Verfassungswandels oder Verfassungsneuschöpfung?' (1993) 32 *Der Staat* 191, 203ff.

B. Historic Stages of the Debate

During the foundation stage of European integration, the most influential interpretative concept was the so-called functionalist paradigm, which considered the original European communities as constituting models for a 'rule of expertise' limited to defined sectors of specific communitized policies. The counter-model to these ideas was the federalist paradigm, according to which the European Union was considered as a future federal state. In a counter-movement evolving from the idea of the national constitutional state, a stronger emphasis was placed on the federal, non-state element of the EU. This perspective was reflected in the German concept of the *Staatenverbund* (association of sovereign states), coined by the German Federal Constitutional Court in 1993. In the early 1990s, various critics criticized the 'rigid nature' of such paradigmatic ideas, thereby opening the way for alternative views.[6]

i. Functionalism

Historically, the aim of European integration was initially seen as dominating and did not allow for the question of democratic legitimation at a supra-national level. The so-called functionalist paradigm was consistent with the sectoral communitization of individual, previously national functions, to be performed by supranational authorities in their own right, as initiated with the foundation of the European Coal and Steel Community ('ECSC'). This paradigm could be based upon the (retrospectively utopian) ideas of the 1950s and 1960s, according to which specific economic-administrative issues could be handled by transnational agencies in a 'non-political' way. This approach was associated with the idea of transnational administration having an increasing effect on the entirety of the traditional functions of a welfare state (the so-called 'spillover effect').[7]

This mechanism was originally intended to take place on a global scale. The so-called neo-functionalistic theory also referred to the mechanism for setting-up territorially delimited 'political communities'.[8] In Germany, the functionalistic paradigm (with Hans-Peter Ipsen's influential designation of the European Community as *Zweckverbände* (special purpose associations)) probably became the prevailing integration theory of the 1970s. The designation was meant to reveal the 'limited relevance of the functions for economic and social policies, their special purpose being confined to partial functions'.[9]

In the functionalist paradigm, the concept of the democratic legitimation of public power is replaced by the idea of a specific technocratic determination of

[6] M Kaufmann, *Europäische Integration und Demokratieprinzip* (Baden-Baden, Nomos, 1997) 105ff; JHH Weiler, U Haltern and F Mayer, 'European Democracy and its Critique' (1995) 18 *West European Politics* 4, 24ff.

[7] eg D Mitrany, *A Working Peace System* (Chicago, Quadrangle Books, 1966).

[8] EB Haas, *The Uniting of Europe* (Palo Alto, CA, Stanford University Press, 1958)

[9] HP Ipsen, *Europäisches Gemeinschaftsrecht* (Tübingen, Mohr, 1972) 196.

common welfare by functional administration agencies. This idea was consistent with the prominent role of the European Commission in the institutional system of the European Community. At the same time, the integration process was substantially promoted during the early stage of integration (until the 1970s) by the new legal quality of European Community law and its interpretation by the European Court of Justice ('ECJ'). The ECJ distinguished the Community's legal system from traditional international law, using elements of constitutionalism, notably the idea of the priority of application of EU law over national law, in order to protect the Community's competences and enforce the communitized political areas.

In this respect, the ECJ could rely on the cooperation of the Member States' executive and legislative bodies, because the implementation of the common policies was thereby facilitated and 'de-politicized'.[10] From the Member States' perspective, the practical and legal constraints of integration served as some form of 'protective shield' for the enforcement of unpopular measures in the domestic context. The 'practical constraints' of the integration are particularly important, given the background that the political integration process stagnated from the mid-1960s to the mid-1980s. The Member States' participation in the European Community's legislation was hampered by the Luxemburg compromise and the national veto option. In this context, Ulrich Haltern correctly speaks of two trends in opposing directions, namely the erosion of 'decisional supra-nationalism', on the one hand, and the intensification of 'normative supra-nationalism', on the other hand.[11]

This process could not be satisfactorily considered from a perspective oriented towards classical patterns of the theories of democracy. For example, court rulings are not considered as a driving force for communitization and an extension of competences. According to the constitutional understanding of the democratic constitutional state, characterized by the division of powers, courts are confined to the role of the 'neutral third party', deciding on disputes between citizens or between a citizen and the state in accordance with (democratically legitimized) parliamentary law. The Member States, of course, emphasize their role as the 'Masters of the Treaties', even though this role (save for the veto option) is a reserve competence rather than a role with any influence on political shaping. At a European level, this mix of functionalistic ideas of rule, integration based on practical constraints and court rulings, as well as the withdrawal of the political integration process, has resulted in the democratic legitimation continuing to be considered an issue of secondary importance.

ii. Federalism

During the period from the 1960s to the 1980s, the federalist paradigm was the only paradigm available as a conceptual alternative to the functionalist paradigm.

[10] cf U Haltern, *Europarecht*, 2nd edn (Tübingen, Mohr Siebeck, 2007) 16.
[11] Haltern, *Europarecht* (n 10) 17.

In the federalist paradigm, the idea of the European Union as a future federal state dominates and contrasts with the traditional union of states. In this comparison, the traditional idea of the union of states, which was determined by where sovereignty rested – at the level of the Member States – was increasingly deemed inappropriate compared to the federal state, where sovereignty rests at the federal level.[12] This could not satisfactorily explain the process of integration, the scope of the communitized political areas and the influence of the European Commission and the European Court of Justice.

A typical notion of the federalist paradigm was the 'United States of Europe', referred to as the aim of integration – a notion chosen by the founder of the Pan-European Union, Richard Graf Coudenhove-Kalergi. From this perspective, European integration already seemed to be on its way to a federal state in 1953. Historic federations, and in particular the United States of America, were referred to as 'archetypes' of European integration. The dominating ideas for the integration process were that a constituent assembly might serve as an institutional framework for Europe's transition to a state. These ideas necessarily considered the body of the European Community's Parliament (as a representative of a future European 'people') to be at the heart of the integration model.[13] This is also the origin of the theory of the Community's deficit of democracy, which (according to a federalist interpretation) is primarily a deficit of Parliament (see further details in section II below).

iii. The Staatenverbund

The more recent constitutional discussion in Germany has been characterized by the debate on the concept of the *Staatenverbund* (association of sovereign states), as set out in more detail by the German Federal Constitutional Court in its *Maastricht* decision and further developed in its decision on the Lisbon Treaty. After the functionalist theory had increasingly lost credibility as a model of legitimation for European integration since the end of the 1970s, the two essential models remaining since the beginning of the 1990s were the traditional federalist model and the new concept of the *Staatenverbund*. According to this concept, the peoples (in the sense of the national citizens) of the Member States form the subjects of the democratic legitimation. A legitimation by the European institutions (in particular the European Parliament) may be considered, if at all, as a complementary legitimation. In the opinion of the German Federal Constitutional Court, this legitimation is ultimately an aliud to the genuinely democratic legitimation in the sense of structural decisions, in accordance with the German Basic Law

[12] P Laband, *Das Staatsrecht des Deutschen Reiches*, vol I, 5th edn (Tübingen, Mohr, 1911) 55ff; cf G Waitz, 'Das Wesen des Bundesstaats' [1853] *Allgemeine Monatsschrift für Wissenschaft und Literatur* 494; G Jellinek, *Allgemeine Staatslehre*, 3rd edn (Heidelberg, Springer, 1928) 768.

[13] cf RN von Coudenhove-Kalergi, *Die europäische Nation* (München, Deutsche Verlags-Anstalt, 1953); A Spinelli, 'Ein "europäisches Europa"' in G Ziebura (ed), *Nationale Souveränität oder übernationale Integration* (Berlin, Colloqium Verlag, 1966) 42; in this context H Schneider, *Rückblick für die Zukunft* (Bonn, Europa Union Verlag, 1986) 50ff.

(Article 20(2) *Grundgesetz*, 'GG'). As shown in detail below, the concept of the *Staatenverbund* has its origins in both constitutional and non-legal presumptions. The most important of these non-legal premises is that democracy requires a 'national reservation' in favour of such type of (genuinely political) decisions that particularly depend on previous understandings as regards culture, history and language and which unfold in discourses amongst a political public that is organized by party politics and Parliament.[14]

For some German constitutional law scholars, this approach marked the end of the discussion. Others continue to refer to the insufficiencies of the *Staatenverbund* model. They point to the increasing shift of democratic legitimation from the European Union citizens to the European institutions and the increasing establishment of a democratic public and democratic institutions in Europe. At the same time, issues such as identity, shared myths or normative legitimation generate new scientific interest.[15] This discussion is directly related to the existing common cultural or intangible values that are considered to form the breeding ground of democratic communication and decision-making processes.

II. 'DEMOCRATIC DEFICIT' OF THE EUROPEAN UNION

A. Parliamentary Deficit

As already pointed out above, the European democratic deficit was originally an element of 'federalist' thinking and essentially designated a parliamentary deficit of the European Union. The theory of the parliamentary deficit was more closely specified by way of a comparison of the competences of the European Parliament with those of a parliament in the democratic constitutional state – for example, with regard to the controlling function, the legislative function or the issue of representation. In particular, the comparatively weak competences of the European Parliament in the area of law-making, for example, the lack of any right of initiative and the limited powers to make 'final decisions', were key arguments for the theory of the European democratic deficit.[16]

The European Parliament seemed to have deficits not only in respect of its competences, but also with regard to its functions within the European constitutional structure. There was considered to be an inherent deficit, for example, in the feedback function of the European Parliament as a 'body for the public and a body of the public', which was already considered in classical theories of parliaments to be a 'function of teaching and opinion forming' (ie parliament as a political forum of the nation). Furthermore, the European Parliament's function of representation was compared with that of national parliaments. An essential deficit here was the fact that the European Parliament was, in principle, not allowed to define its role as

[14] BVerfG [2009] *Neue Juristische Wochenschrift* 2267.

[15] Haltern (n10) 20.

[16] Kaufmann, *Europäische Integration und Demokratieprinzip* (n 6) 241.

a body representing a European citizenship. This problem was enhanced by the fact that both the European executive in the form of the European Commission and the national governments acting through the Council of the European Union had a comparatively strong influence on EU legislation.

B. Representation of a Multiplicity

The typical argument was that the European Parliament does not embody one entity, but several entities, a multiplicity. In the discussion so far, the European Parliament has not been deemed to be a representation of one European people, but essentially a body representing the Member States.[17] The core of the problem with the representation issue was considered to be the fact that a democratic people's representation requires all individuals to have equal political rights of participation. Democratic homogeneity in the sense of a substantial identity of the nationals (emanating from the concept of a people's sovereignty being based upon a social contract) was considered on this basis to be the requirement of democratic representation in parliament.

From this perspective, the allocation of national quotas to the European Parliament, which would result in a different weighting of the votes of the citizens of smaller Member States compared with those of the larger Member States, was already inconsistent with the European Parliament's function of representation in the traditional sense of democratic theories. The next step was not far away, to consider the European Parliament as a mere 'assembly of states', which was essentially composed according to the principle of a federalist equal representation of the Member States, rather than according to the principle of the democratic equality of the citizens of Europe.[18] It seemed problematic to describe the functions of the European Parliament according to the model of the parliamentary democracy of the constitutional state. References to the German Bundesrat or comparable representative bodies of the federal states were open to attack for applying the federal union-related legitimation principle of a political entity rather than the democratic legitimation principle requiring the democratic equality of all nationals.

C. Identity Deficit

The fact that the European Union also lacked the 'pre-legal conditions' of the Constitution as a parliamentary democracy was even more significant than the aforementioned conceptual dilemma.

[17] J Isensee, 'Integrationsziel Europastaat?' in O Due (ed), *Festschrift für Ulrich Everling* (Baden-Baden, Nomos, 1995) 567, 579; J Isensee, *Europa als politische Idee und rechtliche Form*, 2nd edn (Berlin, Duncker & Humblot, 1994) 254.

[18] ibid 133; Kaufmann (n 6) 260.

i. Political Unity

In this context, reference could first be made to political unity or homogeneity patterns as conceived by various German constitutional law scholars. On the one hand, the requirement of social homogeneity was emphasized as a prerequisite for the formation of a political entity.[19] Other authors pointed to the idea that political unity relies upon the formulation of an identity that creates a specific difference by which it can be distinguished from other identities.[20] These descriptions may be applicable to the political unity organized in a national state. However, they need not necessarily serve as a standard or even as a defined target for the European Union. Numerous efforts were made towards modifying or even abolishing the traditional semantics of political unity. This applied, for example, to the proposal made by Jürgen Habermas that a European constitutional patriotism at the European level should form a social substrate of democratic processes, similar to the national consciousness which served as a political-cultural anchor for the universalistic principles of the modern democratic constitutional state.[21] More recently, reference has been made to ideas such as the 'principle of constitutional tolerance' or Christian tradition as the basis of a European identity.[22]

The counter-argument remains that such universal moral concepts or fundamental ideas are highly generalized ideologies, which cannot substitute the specific orientations that have so far been the characteristic features of the legitimation of political power in national states. Empirically the integrative contribution of universal moral or legal rules is, in any case, a controversial issue. Furthermore, such ideas based upon the 'general equality of human beings' are hardly suitable to form a political unity as opposed to other political entities. In particular, they are hardly appropriate to distinguish 'Europe from other entities creating a political unity on this basis.

ii. Plurality of Political Loyalties

Against this background, it seems more consistent to generally criticize the basic idea of identity-oriented or homogeneity-oriented democracy. This criticism starts with the question of whether the alliance between democracy and the national state is a historically accidental or conceptually compulsory alliance. It was argued against the latter theory (and the reflection by the German Federal Constitutional Court in the *Maastricht* judgment) that it involves a quasi-theological exaggeration of people and state *über alles* (above all). This exaggeration is said not only to cause nationalistic wrongdoings in politics, but also to obstruct the plurality of political loyalties required in the European context.[23]

[19] H Heller, *Politische Demokratie und soziale Homogenität* (Berlin, 1928) 13.
[20] Schmitt, *Verfassungslehre*, (n 2) 227.
[21] Habermas, *Faktizität und Geltung* (n 3) 642.
[22] JHH Weiler, *Ein christliches Europa* (Salzburg-München, Pustet, 2004).
[23] JH Weiler, 'The State "über alles"' in Due, *Festschrift für Ulrich Everling* (n 17) 1651.

Irrespective of this fundamental criticism, there is the widespread theory that, in the European context, there would need to be a second European citizenship in addition to a citizen's national identity or loyalty. This second identity (in addition to the national level) could be a further yardstick of democratic identification[24]. The problem of 'double loyalties' does not exist, according to Joseph H Weiler, because the European citizenship has quite a different significance than the national citizenship and thus they could not compete with each other at the same level.[25]

D. Communication Deficit

Finally, another deficit identified at the European level was the absence of a political public – the absence of a common language, of a European media and of European parties and associations. Accordingly, there was considered to be a transparency deficit for political decisions at the European level. In particular, the European Parliament, largely acting (as stated at the time) in a 'political vacuum', was said to be unable to perform its feedback function that might act as a means of legitimation.[26]

E. Democratization as a Substitute for the Constituent Power

Taking this criticism of the EU's 'democratic deficit', based upon federalism, to its logical conclusion, must necessarily result in a conflict of constitutional principles. This was particularly the case with interpreting the progressing integration from a federal perspective, because the federal optimization was necessarily effected to the detriment of the European Union's structure as a union of Member States. Among constitutional law scholars, this conflict was known as a potential antinomy between the democratic and the federal principle of a supra-national community.[27]

From the classical federalist perspective, a full democratization of the EU is ultimately only possible as an act of 'revolutionary power' outside EU primary law. After all, such a form of democratization would have to be the creation of a constitution by a European legislator, and thus a replacement of the *pouvoir constituant*. The creation of such a constitution would mean (in the classical categories of constitutional theory) a destruction of the existing constitution by exchanging the constituent power.[28] Finally, the federalist paradigm is likely to

[24] cf E Grabitz, 'Der Verfassungsstaat in der Gemeinschaft' [1977] *Deutsches Verwaltungsblatt* 786, 793.

[25] Weiler, 'The State "über alles"' (n 23) 1651, 1686ff.

[26] JA Frowein, 'Verfassungsperspektiven der Europäischen Gemeinschaft' [1992] *Europarecht Beiheft* 1, 71.

[27] Schmitt (n 2) 388.

[28] Di Fabio, 'Der neue Art. 23 des Grundgesetzes' (n 5) 205.

have been marked by this hope – for a revolutionary leap into the European democratic statehood. This hope was not very realistic in its theoretical heyday, nor has it become a realistic hope over the following decades of integration, in spite of its extension and intensification. Furthermore, over the years resistance has become stronger, pointing to the danger that may result from progressing the integration of the democratic statehood of the Member States.

III. DANGERS TO DEMOCRATIC STATEHOOD

The *Maastricht* decision of the German Federal Constitutional Court marks a significant counter-movement. While functionalism had side-stepped the issue of legitimation and while federalism was dependent upon the assumption of a European national people, the German Federal Constitutional Court emphasized the role of the Member States' peoples as subjects of the democratic legitimation. Conceptually, the process of European integration was thereby considerably curtailed, resulting (according to the critics of the court ruling) in a democracy dilemma of the European Union.

A. Concept of the *Staatenverbund* (Association of Sovereign States)

The starting point for the concept of the *Staatenverbund* was the German Federal Constitutional Court's *Maastricht* judgment, which described the basis of the democratic legitimation of the *Staatenverbund* as follows:

> The European Union is, according to its understanding of itself as a union of the peoples of Europe (. . .), a federation of democratic states whose objectives include a dynamic development (. . .). If the Union carries out sovereign tasks and exercises sovereign powers for those purposes, it is first and foremost the national peoples of the Member States who, through their national parliaments, have to provide the democratic legitimation for its so doing.[29]

The German Federal Constitutional Court thereby referred to a view previously expressly by Josef H Kaiser at a meeting of constitutional law scholars in 1964: the holders of the European Community's *pouvoir constituant* are, according to democratic theory, the peoples of the Member States of such Community. They act not through the European Parliament, but through their own national parliaments if and to the extent the development of the Community's Constitution is effected by way of an amendment or supplement to the treaties subject to ratification. In other cases, they act through the representatives of their states in the Council.[30]

[29] BVerfG 89, 155, 184; Kirchhof, 'Der deutsche Staat im Prozeß der europäischen Integration (n 5) 877.

[30] JH Kaiser, 'Bewahrung und Veränderung demokratischer und rechtsstaatlicher Verfassungsstruktur in den internationalen Gemeinschaften' (1966) 23 *Veröffentlichungen der Vereinigung der Deutschen Staatsrechtslehrer* 19.

The constitutional basis of the doctrine of the *Staatenverbund* is a reference to the state in an extension of the provision set out in Article 79(3) GG. The provision actually merely protects specific substantive core issues of the German Constitution from being amended, namely the principles laid down in Article 1 GG (human dignity) as well as the structural decisions under Article 20(1) GG. In the German Federal Constitutional Court's rulings, the provision is given an additional meaning.

The German Federal Constitutional Court argues that Article 79(3) GG relies, in respect of its guarantees, upon the premise that the association it seeks to qualify substantively is and remains a sovereign state. As the German Basic Law is, as stated by Paul Kirchhof, based upon this assumption of sovereign statehood, statehood itself is said to be part of the guarantees of the constitutional structural elements of Article 20(1) GG.[31]

Furthermore, the *Staatenverbund* doctrine considers the principle of democracy to be associated in a specific, normatively qualified manner with the guarantee of sovereign statehood. Article 20(2) GG combines (according to this idea) statehood, democracy and sovereignty to form a constitutionally intended entity, in which sovereignty, in its function of implementation, stands for the normative premise of the political self-determination of the community.[32] This entity is protected by Article 23(1), sentence 3 GG in conjunction with Article 23(3), Article 20(1) and (2) GG against the power of integration and European law.

B. Sovereign Power to Determine One's Competences as a Yardstick of the Principle of Democracy

As a necessary consequence of the doctrine, the sovereignty of the Federal Republic of Germany must be protected from integration. This does not refer to any specific spheres of activity of the state, but designates the Member States as 'Masters of the Treaties', having the sovereign power to determine their own competences. This key element of the doctrine of the *Staatenverbund* is also reflected in the most recent decision of the German Federal Constitutional Court on the Treaty of Lisbon. The German Federal Constitutional Court emphasizes that the fundamental order of the European Union may be determined by the Member States alone.

However, the German Federal Constitutional Court allowed, in this respect, a certain erosion by permitting certain amendments to the law laid down in the Lisbon Treaty without a ratification procedure, as long as a special responsibility is incumbent on the legislative bodies, apart from the German federal government.[33] Although the German Federal Constitutional Court thus allows certain modifications to the principle of the sovereign power to determine one's compe-

[31] Kirchhof (n 5) 883.
[32] Di Fabio (n 5) 200ff.
[33] BVerfG [2009] *Neue Juristische Wochenschrift* 2267.

tences, it makes such modifications subject to special requirements as to the national democratic legitimation of such decisions.

C. Areas Protected from Integration

Furthermore, the German Federal Constitutional Court already held in its *Maastricht* judgment that the extension of the EU's functions and powers is subject to limits by virtue of the democratic principle. The Member States need sufficiently important spheres of activity of their own in which the people of each state can develop and articulate themselves in a process of political will-formation, which they legitimate and control in order to give legal expression to what binds the people together (to a greater or lesser degree of homogeneity) spiritually, socially and politically.[34]

In its most recent judgment on the Lisbon Treaty, the German Federal Constitutional Court again stated that the Member States must retain sufficient

> room for the political formation of the economic, cultural and social circumstances of life. This applies in particular to areas which shape the citizens' circumstances of life, in particular the private space of their own responsibility and of personal and social security, which is protected by the fundamental rights, and to political decisions that particularly depend on previous understandings as regards culture, history and language and which unfold in discourses in the space of a political public that is organised by party politics and Parliament.[35]

A problem with the *Maastricht* judgment had been that the principle of democracy (conceptually) basically implies neither a specific sphere of activity nor a specific level of activity that would be protected against the integration legislator. According to the long-prevailing constitutional understanding, the guarantees involved in the principle of democracy are void of contents as they merely refer to the 'how' (ie the way of a state's formation of will), rather than the 'what' (ie the contents and scope of a state's activities). Democracy as an organizational principle of the state's form responds

> to the question of the holder and owner rather than the contents of the power to rule in a state; it refers to the formation, legitimation and control of the bodies exercising a state's organised power to rule and performing a state's functions.[36]

i. Procedural or Substantive Interpretation of Democracy

However, there will be conceptual difficulties in deriving the requirement of specific public functions from the organizational formal principle of democracy. Any communitization of material political areas must then be deemed to involve

[34] BVerfG 89, 155, 186.
[35] BVerfG [2009] *Neue Juristische Wochenschrift* 2267.
[36] Böckenförde, 'Demokratie als Verfassungsprinzip' (n 2) 365.

democratic deficits compared with the initial condition of a state's all-embracing competence. It seems to be more plausible to interpret the principle of democracy subject to the conditions of globalization and integration under procedural rather than substantive aspects. This is a consequence of the development according to which political self-determination, under the influence of functional globalization, worldwide interdependence and interconnection, increasingly depends upon participation in a cooperative exercise of authority. The former sovereign power of the state in performing its functions, once deemed to be comprehensive, is now only abstractly available with the increasing progress of integration. It now requires cooperation within the *Staatenverbund*. The principle of democracy laid down in the German Basic Law as a formal principle of organization may put up only a little resistance to the globalization and interdependence of a state's core functions. Rather, the focus of the principle of democracy (the core idea of the principle of 'integrated statehood') is on the question of how state participation in the cooperative exercise of sovereign power within the *Staatenverbund* can be democratically embedded in the will of the state's people.[37]

ii. Areas Protected From Integration

It remains to be seen whether the criteria mentioned in the *Lisbon* judgment for 'political areas protected from integration' will become more plausible. According to the German Federal Constitutional Court, these criteria in particular comprise citizenship, the civil and military monopoly on the use of force, revenue and expenditure, including external financing and all elements of encroachment that are decisive for the realization of fundamental rights, and in particular intensive encroachments on fundamental rights such as the deprivation of liberty in the administration of criminal law or placement in an institution. According to the German Federal Constitutional Court, these important areas also include cultural issues such as language, the shaping of circumstances concerning the family and education, freedom of opinion, of the press and of association and profession of faith or ideology.[38]

This approach is at least partially consistent with the idea of protecting such areas that are functionally assigned to the principle of democracy. Accordingly, the principle of democracy covers, for example, the principles of the democratic formation of will, the law on parties, provisions on language and the education system. The connection appears to be less stringent for the other matters mentioned by the German Federal Constitutional Court. It may be doubted, for example, whether the communitization of the shaping of the social welfare system is in fact a breach of the constitutional principle of democracy.[39] The same applies

[37] M Kaufmann, 'Integrierte Staatlichkeit als Staatsstrukturprinzip' [1999] *Juristenzeitung* 814ff.

[38] BVerfG [2009] *Neue Juristische Wochenschrift* 2274.

[39] CD Classen in *von Mangoldt/Klein/Starck: Kommentar zum Grundgesetz*, vol II, 6th edn (Munich, CH Beck, 2010) Art 23, para 29; M Ruffert, 'An den Grenzen des Integrationsverfassungsrechts: Das Urteil des Bundesverfassungsgerichts zum Vertrag von Lissabon' [2009] *Deutsches Verwaltungsblatt* 1097.

to the deprivation of liberty in the administration of criminal law. Both the punishment of criminal offences and the conflicting positions of fundamental rights are actually part of the core essence of the universal convictions which were intended to be developed in the European Union, regardless of previous understandings regarding culture, history and language.

From the perspective of the theories of democracy, it must further be doubted whether there are in fact any political decisions that are based upon a previous understanding of culture, history or language; or rather whether they are preconditions of a democratic formation of will, providing a special line of delimitation on whether matters can or cannot be communitized. On the whole, the impression remains that the positioning of the principle of democracy as a *katechon*, an obstacle to the European integration process, (though comprehensible in light of integration policy) is difficult to justify on the basis of constitutional theory.

iii. Euro Stabilization – Democracy and Fundamental Budgetary Decisions

Most recently, however, the discussion about the role of the Parliament in the participation of Germany in the euro stabilization measures on the European level has added further aspects. In a couple of decisions, the German Federal Constitutional Court ruled that the principles of German parliamentarianism (Article 38 GG) in conjunction with the principle of democracy demand that – as a fundamental part of the ability of a constitutional state to democratically shape itself – the decisions on public revenue and public expenditure must remain in the hand of the German Parliament. As elected representatives of the people, the members of the Parliament must retain control of fundamental budgetary decisions. This applies to systems of intergovernmental governing (such as the euro stabilization facilities European Financial Stability Facility and European Stability Mechanism). Therefore, the Parliament is prohibited from establishing permanent mechanisms that are tantamount to accepting liability for decisions taken by the free will of other states, above all if they entail consequences that are difficult to calculate. An individual approval of the Parliament is required for every large-scale federal aid measure on the international or the European Union level.[40]

In these decisions, the court found new 'protected areas' by bringing together the democratic principle with the budget competence (*Budgethoheit*) that has always been seen as a core parliamentary competence. This approach has to be considered as a new dimension in the question, how the European integration affects the balance between the institutions of the Member States. Above all, it will further strengthen the role of the Parliament as controller of the government on the supra-national level.

[40] BVerfG BvR 1390/12, decision of 9 September 2012.

D. Criticism

The state-centred understanding of the German Federal Constitutional Court has met with significant resistance.

It is argued, for example, that the traditional understanding of the coherence between a national people and democracy is, in principle, hardly suitable to capture European integration.[41] On this basis, the growing significance of the 'second chain of legitimation' (from the citizens of the European Union to the European Parliament) is stressed. It is argued that the deviations from the principle of democratic equality are justified in order to represent the citizens from the various Member States. Moreover, the European Parliament is said to have been given more and more competences and thus is thought to have increased in importance as the second track of legitimation, based on the European Union citizens.

Ultimately, a structured political discourse is increasingly noticeable. The differences amongst the European public (language, media and institutions) are said to be increasingly overcome by way of cross-border discourses. The Lisbon Treaty is said to have addressed the problem of strengthening 'democratic life' in the European Union, including for example, the possibility of a Europe-wide plebiscite (Article 11(4) of the EU Treaty).[42]

Apart from this criticism concerning the requirements of the democratization of Europe, there is further criticism pointing to the negative consequences of the German Federal Constitutional Court's rulings on the further course of integration. The German Federal Constitutional Court (according to the criticism) has brought the European Union to a hopeless impasse by complaining about the democratic deficit on the one hand and by excluding measures required to overcome such democratic deficit, on the other hand.[43] The *Lisbon* decision of the German Federal Constitutional Court is said to prohibit conferring specific competences upon the EU, to prohibit establishing a European federal state and forming a European people.[44] This means cementing the current two-pillar model of the democratic legitimation of the EU, according to which the European Parliament is assigned merely a supplementary legitimation function. This would make the responsibilities at the European Union level even more unclear and sets limits on a further parliamentarianization of the EU. Finally, the approach of the

[41] I Pernice, 'Carl Schmitt, Rudolf Smend und die europäische Integration' (1995) 120 *Archiv des öffentlichen Rechts* 100, 103; A von Bogdandy, 'Das Leitbild der dualistischen Legitimation für die europäische Verfassungsentwicklung' [2000] *Kritische Vierteljahresschrift für Gesetzgebung und Rechtswissenschaft* 284, 295.

[42] M Nettesheim in E Grabitz and M Hilf (eds), *Das Recht der Europäischen Union*, 46th edn (Munich, CH Beck, 2011) Art 10 EUV, para 54; Classen in *von Mangoldt/Klein/Starck: Kommentar zum Grundgesetz* (n 39); emphasizing the citizen as holder of European democracy: C Calliess in C Calliess and M Ruffert (eds), *Das Verfassungsrecht der Europäischen Union*, 3rd edn (Munich, CH Beck, 2007) Art 1 EUV, para 19.

[43] Calliess (n 42).

[44] A Hatje, 'Demokratische Kosten souveräner Staatlichkeit im europäischen Verfassungsverbund' [2010] *Europarecht Beiheft*, 123, 126ff.

German Federal Constitutional Court is said to have placed excessive demands on national parliaments structurally and procedurally.

It is claimed that this leads to a 'democratic dilemma'. On the one hand, the European Union has to comply with the democratic requirements set out in the German Basic Law; on the other hand, the German Constitution is interpreted as making the implementation of these principles at a European level almost impossible. This criticism is surely correct – but it is based upon the assumption that democracy on a European as well as national scale has to be realized in a similar manner. Thus, the structure of the debate on the European democratic deficit has not changed since the *Maastricht* judgment.

IV. CONCLUSION

In retrospect, the concept of the democratic deficit has proven to be versatile. In the functionalist paradigm, the term had no conceptual role, but rather designated the idea of statehood, which was meant to be overcome with the technocratic idea of a special purpose association during the 1950s and 1960s. Based on the federalist paradigm, however, the concept of the democratic deficit grew stronger and became the basis of a fundamental criticism of the European Union's institutional structure, which was compared with the federal state and consequently considered to have deficits, in particular regarding the Parliament's competences. From the perspective of the *Staatenverbund* doctrine, the notion of the democratic deficit finally became the decisive lever for exempting specific elements of democratic statehood (such as sovereign power regarding the transfer of competences, national people, specific political areas) from integration. The further democratization of Europe thus requires the statehood of Europe, and thus a replacement of the national constitution. The respective national people act as the sole subject of democratic legitimation of the public power in the European Union, while the community of the European Union citizens can merely provide a supplementary legitimation. Although this doctrine has proven influential (in particular in view of the German Federal Constitutional Court's rulings), it has at the same time been criticized as regards both the institutional requirements and the dogmatic outline, as well as the state-theoretical requirements of the principle of democracy at a national and European level.

What can still be attributed to the term 'democratic deficit of the European Union' is questionable. Looking back, the discrepancy between the theoretical concerns about a democratic deficit (especially from a constitutional perspective with regard to the 'inviolability' of the principle of democracy, Article 79(3) GG)) and its practical relevance is particularly striking. Practically, the term 'democratic deficit' does not involve any deficits of legitimation of the process of European integration that would in any way amount to the conceptual drama of a failure to comply with democratic standards. Even the risks invoked for decades in legal literature (such as alienation between European Union citizens and the

European Union regime) have not been able to stop the process of integration and the effectiveness of decisions and law-making in the European Union. The same also applies – mutatis mutandis – to the national level.

Therefore, the primary function of the democratic deficit seems to be that of a term of conflict (or a scheme for looking for reasons in the arguments) between the European institutions seeking larger influence in the EU's institutional system, on the one hand, and the defence of national residual areas in the process of European integration, on the other. In this context, it should be noted that, given the variety of potential democratic problems of the European Union and, furthermore, the variety of possibilities of interpretation, it is inappropriate to infer simple theories such as those previously put forward in respect of the steady extension of the European Parliament's competences. It also seems to be too early to hope for a reawakening of European democracy by transferring the meanings associated with the national communities' associations to Europe and by developing a rudimentary European identity.[45]

On the one hand, it may be expedient to understand the increasing democratization of Europe as a challenge to the respective national political arenas. This challenge consists of the task of mirroring the process of European integration from the outside to the inside of the political discourse, thereby contributing to the creation of a common European consciousness of the (to date) nationally fragmented political discourses. On the other hand, it will be a task of legal science to reconcile the dogma of a principle of democracy pursuant to Article 20(2) GG, to date related to the constitutional state, with the forms of democratic legitimation outside the state on the supra-national level.

CASES

BVerfGE 37, 271 – *Solange I* (1974)
BVerfGE 73, 339 – *Solange II* (1986)
BVerfGE 89, 155 – *Maastricht* (1993)
BVerfGE 102, 147 – *Bananenmarkt* (2000)
BVerfGE 113, 273 – *Europäischer Haftbefehl* (2005)
BVerfGE 123, 267 – *Lissabon* (2009)
BVerfGE 126, 286 – *Honeywell* (2010)
BVerfG 2 BvR 1390/12 of 12 September 2012 – *ESM*

SELECTED LITERATURE

von Bogdandy A, 'Das Leitbild der dualistischen Legitimation für die europäische Verfassungsentwicklung' [2000] *Kritische Vierteljahresschrift für Gesetzgebung und Rechtswissenschaft* 284

[45] Haltern (n 10) 140.

Böckenförde EW, 'Demokratie als Verfassungsprinzip' in EW Böckenförde, *Staat, Verfassung, Demokratie*, 2nd edn (Frankfurt am Main, Suhrkamp, 1992)
Classen CD, 'Europäische Integration und demokratische Legitimation' (1994) 119 *Archiv des öffentlichen Rechts* 238
Di Fabio U, 'Der neue Art. 23 des Grundgesetzes: Positivierung vollzogenen Verfassungswandels oder Verfassungsneuschöpfung?' (1993) 32 *Der Staat* 191
Haltern U, *Europarecht und das Politische* (Tübingen, Mohr Siebeck 2005)
Jellinek G, *Allgemeine Staatslehre*, 3rd edn (Heidelberg, Springer, 1928)
Kaufmann M, *Europäische Integration und Demokratieprinzip* (Baden-Baden, Nomos 1997)
—— 'Integrierte Staatlichkeit als Staatsstrukturprinzip' [1999] *JuristenZeitung* 814
Kirchhof P, 'Der deutsche Staat im Prozeß der europäischen Integration' in J Isensee and P Kirchhof, *Handbuch des Staatsrechts der Bundesrepublik Deutschland*, vol VII (Heidelberg, CF Müller, 1992) § 183
Ruffert M, 'An den Grenzen des Integrationsverfassungsrechts: Das Urteil des Bundesverfassungsgerichts zum Vertrag von Lissabon' [2009] *Deutsches Verwaltungsblatt* 1097
Schmitt C, *Verfassungslehre* (Berlin, Duncker & Humblot, 1928)
Waitz G, 'Das Wesen des Bundesstaats' [1853] *Allgemeine Monatsschrift für Wissenschaft und Literatur* 494

Appendix
The Basic Law (Grundgesetz)*

PREAMBLE

CONSCIOUS OF THEIR responsibility before God and men, moved by the purpose to serve world peace as an equal part in a unified Europe, the German People have adopted, by virtue of their constituent power, this Constitution. [2]The Germans in the States [Länder] of Baden-Wurttemberg, Bavaria, Berlin, Brandenburg, Bremen, Hamburg, Hesse, Lower Saxony, Mecklenburg-Western Pomerania, North Rhine-Westphalia, Rhineland-Palatinate, Saarland, Saxony, Saxony-Anhalt, Schleswig-Holstein and Thuringia have achieved the unity and freedom of Germany in free self-determination. [3]This Constitution is thus valid for the entire German People.

Chapter I

Basic Rights

Article 1 [Human Dignity]

(1) Human dignity is inviolable. [2]To respect and protect it is the duty of all state authority.
(2) The German People therefore acknowledge inviolable and inalienable human rights as the basis of every human community, of peace, and of justice in the world.
(3) The following basic rights are binding on legislature, executive, and judiciary as directly valid law.

Article 2 [Liberty]

(1) Everyone has the right to free development of his personality insofar as he does not violate the rights of others or offend against the constitutional order or morality.
(2) Everyone has the right to life and to physical integrity. [2]The freedom of the person is inviolable. [3]Intrusion on these rights may only be made pursuant to a statute.

* Translation by Axel Tschentscher, *The Basic Law (Grundgesetz) – The Constitution of the Federal Republic of Germany (May 23rd, 1949)*, 3rd edn (Würzburg, Jurisprudentia Verlag, 2013).

Article 3 [Equality]

(1) All humans are equal before the law.
(2) Men and women are equal. [2]The state supports the effective realization of equality of women and men and works towards abolishing present disadvantages.
(3) No one may be disadvantaged or favored because of his sex, parentage, race, language, homeland and origin, his faith, or his religious or political opinions. [2]No one may be disadvantaged because of his handicap.

Article 4 [Faith, Religion, Conscience, Creed]

(1) Freedom of creed, of conscience, and freedom to profess a religious or non-religious faith are inviolable.
(2) The undisturbed practice of religion is guaranteed.
(3) No one may be compelled against his conscience to render war service involving the use of arms. [2]Details are regulated by a federal statute.

Article 5 [Expression]

(1) Everyone has the right to freely express and disseminate his opinion in speech, writing, and pictures and to freely inform himself from generally accessible sources. [2]Freedom of the press and freedom of reporting by means of broadcasts and films are guaranteed. [3]There may be no censorship.
(2) These rights are subject to limitations in the provisions of general statutes, in statutory provisions for the protection of the youth, and in the right to personal honor.
(3) Art and science, research and teaching are free. [2]The freedom of teaching does not release from allegiance to the constitution.

Article 6 [Marriage, Family, Children Out of Wedlock]

(1) Marriage and family are under the special protection of the state.
(2) Care and upbringing of children are the natural right of the parents and primarily their duty. [2]The state supervises the exercise of the same.
(3) Against the will of the persons entitled to their upbringing, children may only be separated from the family, pursuant to a statute, where those so entitled failed or where, for other reasons, the children are endangered to become seriously neglected.
(4) Every mother is entitled to protection by and care of the community.
(5) Children out of wedlock, by legislation, have to be provided with the same conditions for their physical and mental development and for their place in society as are legitimate children.

Article 7 [Education]

(1) The entire schooling system stands under the supervision of the state.
(2) Persons entitled to the upbringing of a child have the right to decide whether the child has to attend religion classes.

(3) Religion classes form part of the ordinary curriculum in state schools, except for secular schools. [2]Without prejudice to the state's right of supervision, religious instruction is given in accordance with the tenets of the religious communities. [3]No teacher may be obliged against his will to give religious instruction.
(4) The right to establish private schools is guaranteed. [2]Private schools, as a substitute for state schools, require the approval of the state and are subject to the statutes of the States [Länder]. [3]Such approval has to be given where private schools are not inferior to the state schools in their educational aims, their facilities, and the professional training of their teaching staff, and where segregation of pupils according to the means of their parents is not encouraged. [4]Approval has to be withheld where the economic and legal position of the teaching staff is not sufficiently assured.
(5) A private elementary school has to be permitted only where the education authority finds that it serves a special pedagogic interest, or where, on the application of persons entitled to upbringing of children, it is to be established as an interdenominational school or as a school based on a particular religious or non-religious faith and only if a state elementary school of this type does not exist in the commune.
(6) Preliminary schools remain abolished.

Article 8 [Assembly]

(1) All Germans have the right, without prior notification or permission, to assemble peaceably and unarmed.
(2) With regard to open-air assemblies, this right may be restricted by or pursuant to a statute.

Article 9 [Association]

(1) All Germans have the right to form clubs and societies.
(2) Associations, the purposes or activities of which conflict with criminal statutes or which are directed against the constitutional order or the concept of international understanding, are prohibited.
(3) The right to form associations to safeguard and improve working and economic conditions is guaranteed to everyone and for all professions. [2] Agreements which restrict or seek to impair this right are null and void, measures directed to this end are illegal. [3]Measures taken pursuant to Articles 12a, 35 (2) & (3), 87a (4), or 91 may not be directed against industrial conflicts engaged in by associations to safeguard and improve working and economic conditions in the sense of the first sentence of this paragraph.

Article 10 [Letters, Mail, Telecommunication]

(1) The privacy of letters as well as the secrecy of post and telecommunication are inviolable.

(2) Restrictions may only be ordered pursuant to a statute. [2]Where a restriction serves the protection of the free democratic basic order or the existence or security of the Federation or a State [Land], the statute may stipulate that the person affected shall not be informed and that recourse to the courts shall be replaced by a review of the case by bodies and auxiliary bodies appointed by Parliament.

Article 11 [Movement]

(1) All Germans enjoy freedom of movement throughout the federal territory.
(2) This right may be restricted only by or pursuant to a statute and only in cases in which an adequate basis for personal existence is lacking and special burdens would result therefrom for the community, or in which such restriction is necessary to avert an imminent danger to the existence or the free democratic basic order of the Federation or a State [Land], to combat the danger of epidemics, to deal with natural disasters or particularly grave accidents, to protect young people from neglect, or to prevent crime.

Article 12 [Work, Forced Labor]

(1) All Germans have the right to freely choose their occupation, their place of work, and their place of study or training. [2]The practice of an occupation can be regulated by or pursuant to a statute.
(2) No person may be forced to perform work of a particular kind except within the framework of a traditional compulsory community service that applies generally and equally to all.
(3) Forced labour may be imposed only on persons deprived of their liberty by court sentence.

Article 12a [Military and Other Service]

(1) Males who have attained the age of eighteen years can be required to serve in the Armed Forces, in the Federal Border Guard, or in a civil defence organisation.
(2) A person who refuses, on grounds of conscience, to render war service involving the use of arms can be required to render a substitute service. [2]The duration of such substitute service may not exceed the duration of military service. [3]Details are regulated by a statute which may not interfere with the freedom to take a decision based on conscience and which must also provide for the possibility of a substitute service not connected with units of the Armed Forces or of the Federal Border Guard.
(3) Persons liable to military service who are not required to render service pursuant to Paragraph I or II can, during a state of defense, be assigned by or pursuant to a statute to an employment involving civilian services for defense purposes, including the protection of the civilian population; assignments to employments subject to public law are only admissible for the purpose of discharging police functions or such other functions of public administra-

tion as can only be discharged by persons employed under public law. [2]Employments according to the first sentence of this paragraph can also be established with the Armed Forces, in the area of their supply services, or with public administrative authorities; assignments to employment connected with supply services for the civilian population are only admissible to provide for their vital provisions or to guarantee their safety.

(4) Where, during a state of defense, civilian service requirements in the civilian health system or in the stationary military hospital organization cannot be met on a voluntary basis, women between eighteen and fifty-five years of age can be assigned to such services by or pursuant to a statute. [2]They may in no case be obliged to render service involving the use of arms.

(5) Prior to the existence of a state of defense, assignments under Paragraph III may only be made where the requirements of Article 80a I are satisfied. [2]To prepare services mentioned in Paragraph III for which special knowledge or skills are required, persons can be obliged by or pursuant to a statute to attend training courses. [3]Insofar, the first sentence of this paragraph does not apply.

(6) Where, during a state of defense, staffing requirements for the purposes referred to in Paragraph III 1 cannot be met on a voluntary basis, the freedom of Germans to quit the pursuit of his occupation or quit his place of work may be restricted by or pursuant to a statute in order to meet these requirements. [2]Paragraph V 1 equally applies prior to the existence of a state of defense.

Article 13 [Home]

(1) The home is inviolable.

(2) Searches may be ordered only by a judge or, in the event of danger resulting from any delay, by other organs legally specified, and they may be carried out only in the form prescribed by law.

(3) If specific facts lead to the assumption that someone has committed a very grave crime, technical means of eavesdropping in homes where that person probably stays may be ordered by court if the investigation by other means would be disproportionately obstructed or without chance of success. [2]The measure has to be limited. [3]The order is issued by a court of three justices. [4]In the event of danger resulting from any delay, the order can be issued by a single judge.

(4) To avoid urgent danger to public safety, particularly general or mortal danger, technical means of eavesdropping in homes may only be used on the order of a judge. [2]In the event of danger resulting form any delay, those actions may be ordered by other authorities empowered by law; the subsequent decision of a judge has to be arranged for without delay.

(5) In the case of technical means being exclusively ordered for the protection of investigators during their activity in homes, the measure can be ordered by those authorities empowered by law. [2]Evidence from such investigation

may be used for other purposes only to conduct criminal prosecution or avoid danger and only if the legality of the measure has been stated by court order; in the event of danger resulting form any delay, a subsequent court order has to be arranged for without delay.

(6) The Government provides yearly reports to the House of Representatives [Bundestag] about those measures conducted according to Paragraph III as well as according to Paragraph IV and, as far as court orders are necessary, Paragraph V in the domain of federal authority. [2]A committee elected by the House of Representatives [Bundestag] conducts parliamentary control on the basis of this report. [3]The States [Länder] provide for equivalent control.

(7) Intrusions and restrictions may otherwise only be made to avert a general danger or a mortal danger to individuals, or, pursuant to a statute, to prevent present danger to public safety and order, particularly to relieve a housing shortage, to combat the danger of epidemics, or to protect endangered juveniles.

Article 14 [Property, Inheritance, Expropriation]

(1) Property and the right of inheritance are guaranteed. [2]Their content and limits are determined by statute.

(2) Property imposes duties. [2]Its use should also serve the public weal.

(3) Expropriation is only permissible for the public good. [2]It may be imposed only by or pursuant to a statute regulating the nature and extent of compensation. [3]Such compensation has to be determined by establishing an equitable balance between the public interest and the interests of those affected. [4]Regarding disputes about the amount of compensation, recourse to the courts of ordinary jurisdiction is available.

Article 15 [Socialization]

Land, natural resources, and means of production can, for the purpose of socialization, be transferred to public ownership or other forms of collective enterprise by a statute regulating the nature and extent of compensation. [2]Regarding such compensation, Article 14 III 3 & 4 also applies.

Article 16 [Citizenship, Extradition]

(1) German citizenship may not be taken away. [2]The loss of citizenship may only be imposed pursuant to a statute and against the will of the person affected only where such person does not become stateless as a result thereof.

(2) No German may be extradited to a foreign country. [2]The law can provide otherwise for extraditions to a member state of the European Union or to an international court of justice as long as the rule of law is upheld.

Article 16a [Asylum]

(1) Persons persecuted on political grounds enjoy the right of asylum.

(2) The right of Paragraph I cannot claim who enters from a European Communities country or from another country where the application of the Convention on the Legal Status of Refugees and the Convention to Protect

Human Rights and Civil Liberties is ensured. [2]Countries outside of the European Communities for which the prerequisites of the first sentence hold true are determined by a statute requiring the consent of the Senate [Bundesrat]. [3]In the cases of the first sentence, measures to end a stay can be effectuated independent of recourse to the course sought against these measures.

(3) By statute requiring the consent of the Senate [Bundesrat], countries can be determined in which on the basis of law, law application, or general political conditions it seems to be guaranteed that neither persecution on political grounds nor inhuman or derogatory punishment and treatment takes place. [2]A foreigner from such a state is presumed to not being persecuted unless he asserts facts supporting that, contrary to this presumption, he is politically persecuted.

(4) The effectuation of measures to end a stay will, in the cases of Paragraph III and in other cases where the claim to stay is obviously unfounded or is regarded as obviously unfounded, only be suspended by court order if serious doubts arise concerning the legality of the measure; the scope of scrutiny can be limited and delayed assertions ignored. [2]Details are regulated by a statute.

(5) Paragraphs I to IV are not contrary to public law contracts of European Communities member states among each other and with other countries which, honouring the obligations arising from the Convention on the Legal Status of Refugees and the Convention to Protect Human Rights and Civil Liberties the application of which has to be ensured in the contracting countries, regulate responsibilities to examine claims of asylum including mutual acknowledgement of asylum decisions.

Article 17 [Petition]

Everyone has the right, individually or jointly with others, to address written requests or complaints to the competent agencies and to parliaments.

Article 17a [Defense and Substitute Service]

(1) Statutes concerning military service and substitute service can, by provisions applying to members of the Armed Forces and of the substitute services during their period of military or substitute service, restrict the basic right to freely express and disseminate opinions in speech, writing, and pictures (first half sentence of Article 5 I), the basic right of assembly (Article 8), and the right of petition (Article 17) insofar as this right permits the submission of requests or complaints jointly with others.

(2) Statutes serving defense purposes including the protection of the civilian population can provide for the restriction of the basic rights of freedom of movement (Article 11) and inviolability of the home (Article 13).

Article 18 [Forfeiture of Basic Rights]

Whoever abuses freedom of expression of opinion, in particular freedom of the press (Article 5 I), freedom of teaching (Article 5 III), freedom of assembly (Article 8), freedom of association (Article 9), privacy of letters and secrecy of post and telecommunication (Article 10), property (Article 14), or the right to asylum (Article 16a) in order to combat the free democratic basic order forfeits these basic rights. [2]Such forfeiture and the extent thereof is determined by the Federal Constitutional Court.

Article 19 [Restriction of Basic Rights]

(1) Insofar as a basic right may, under this Constitution, be restricted by or pursuant to a statute, such statute must apply generally and not solely to an individual case. [2]Furthermore, such statute must name the basic right, indicating the relevant Article.
(2) In no case may the essence of a basic right be infringed.
(3) Basic rights also apply to domestic corporations to the extent that the nature of such rights permits.
(4) Should any person's rights be violated by public authority, recourse to the court is open to him. [2]Insofar as no other jurisdiction has been established, recourse is available to the courts of ordinary jurisdiction. [3]Article 10 II 2 is not affected by the provisions of this paragraph.

Chapter II

Federation and States

Article 20 [Basic Principles of State, Resistance]

(1) The Federal Republic of Germany is a democratic and social federal state.
(2) All state authority emanates from the people. [2]It is being exercised by the people through elections and voting and by specific organs of the legislature, the executive power, and the judiciary.
(3) Legislation is subject to the constitutional order; the executive and the judiciary are bound by law and justice.
(4) All Germans have the right to resist any person seeking to abolish this constitutional order, should no other remedy be possible.

Article 20a [Protection of Natural Resources]

The state, also in its responsibility for future generations, protects the natural foundations of life and the animals in the framework of the constitutional order, by legislation and, according to law and justice, by executive and judiciary.

Article 21 [Political Parties]

(1) The political parties participate in the forming of the political will of the people. [2]They may be freely established. [3]Their internal organization must conform to democratic principles. [4]They have to publicly account for the sources and use of their funds and for their assets.

(2) Parties which, by reason of their aims or the behaviour of their adherents, seek to impair or abolish the free democratic basic order or to endanger the existence of the Federal Republic of Germany are unconstitutional. [2]The Federal Constitutional Court decides on the question of unconstitutionality.
(3) Details are regulated by federal statutes.

Article 22 [Capital, Federal Flag]

(1) The capital of the Federal Republic of Germany is Berlin. [2]The representation of the whole state in the capital is a task of the federation. [3]Details are regulated by federal statute.
(2) The federal flag is black, red, and gold.

Article 23 [European Union]

(1) To realize a unified Europe, Germany participates in the development of the European Union which is bound to democratic, rule of law, social, and federal principles as well as the principle of subsidiarity and provides a protection of fundamental rights essentially equivalent to that of this Constitution. [2]The federation can, for this purpose and with the consent of the Senate [Bundesrat], delegate sovereign powers. [3]Article 79 II & III is applicable for the foundation of the European Union as well as for changes in its contractual bases and comparable regulations by which the content of this Constitution is changed or amended or by which such changes or amendments are authorized.
(1a) The House of Representatives [Bundestag] and the Senate [Bundesrat] have the right to challenge violations of the principle of subsidiarity by legislative acts of the European Union before the Court of the European Union. [2]The House of Representatives [Bundestag] is duty bound to do so upon the motion of one quarter of its members. [3]By statute requiring the consent of the Senate [Bundesrat], regarding the exercise of rights of the House of Representatives [Bundestag] and the Senate [Bundesrat] under the contractual bases of the European Union, exceptions may be authorized to Article 42 II 1 and Article 52 III 1.
(2) The House of Representatives [Bundestag] and the States [Länder], by their representation in the Senate [Bundesrat], participate in matters of the European Union. [2]The Government has to thoroughly inform House of Representatives [Bundestag] and Senate [Bundesrat] at the earliest possible time.
(3) The Government allows for statements of the House of Representatives [Bundestag] before it takes part in drafting European Union laws. [2]The Government considers statements of the House of Representatives [Bundestag] during deliberations. [3]Details are regulated by federal statute.
(4) The Senate [Bundesrat] has to be included in the deliberations of the House of Representatives [Bundestag] insofar as it would have to participate in a domestic measure or insofar as the States [Länder] would be accountable domestically.

(5) Insofar as, in the area of exclusive legislative competence of the Federation, the interests of the States [Länder] are affected or insofar as, in all other cases, the Federation has legislative competence, the Government considers the statement of the Senate [Bundesrat]. [2]If legislative competencies of the States [Länder], the installation of their agencies, or their procedures are centrally affected, the opinion of the Senate [Bundesrat] has to be considered as decisive for the Federation's deliberation; the responsibility of the Federation for the whole state has to be maintained in the process. [3]The consent of the Government is necessary in matters possibly resulting in higher expenses or lower revenues for the Federation.

(6) Where exclusive legislative competencies of the States [Länder] are centrally affected in the areas of school education, culture, or broadcasting, the exercise of the Federal Republic of Germany's rights as member state of the European Union is delegated to a representative of the States [Länder] assigned by the Senate [Bundesrat]. [2]These rights are exercised with participation of and in coordination with the Government; the responsibility of the Federation for the whole state has to be maintained in the process.

(7) Details of Paragraphs IV to VI are regulated by a statute requiring the consent of the Senate [Bundesrat].

Article 24 [Collective Security System]

(1) The Federation may by legislation transfer sovereign powers to intergovernmental institutions.

(1a) Insofar as the States [Länder] are responsible for the exercise of state rights and the discharge of state duties, they can, with consent of the Government, delegate sovereign powers to institutions for neighbourhood at state borders.

(2) For the maintenance of peace, the Federation may join a system of mutual collective security; in doing so it will consent to such limitations upon its rights of sovereignty as will bring about and secure a peaceful and lasting order in Europe and among the nations of the world.

(3) For the settlement of disputes between States [Länder], the Federation will accede to agreements concerning international arbitration of a general, comprehensive, and obligatory nature.

Article 25 [Public International Law]

The general rules of public international law constitute an integral part of federal law. [2]They take precedence over statutes and directly create rights and duties for the inhabitants of the federal territory.

Article 26 [Ban on War]

(1) Acts with the potential to and undertaken with intent to disturb the peaceful relations between nations, especially to prepare war or aggression, are unconstitutional. [2]They have to be made a criminal offence.

(2) Weapons designed for warfare may not be manufactured, transported, or marketed except with the permission of the Government. [2]Details are regulated by a federal statute.

Article 27 [Merchant Fleet]

All German merchant vessels form one merchant fleet.

Article 28 [Self-Government]

(1) The constitutional order in the States [Länder] must conform to the principles of the republican, democratic, and social state under the rule of law, within the meaning of this Constitution. [2]In each of the States [Länder], counties, and communes, the people has to be represented by a body chosen in general, direct, free, equal, and secret elections. [3]During elections in counties and communes, persons who possess the citizenship of a European Community country are eligible to vote and being elected according to the laws of the European Community. [4]In communes, the communal assembly can take the place of an elected body.
(2) The communes must be guaranteed the right to regulate, on their own responsibility, all the affairs of the local community within the limits set by statute. [2]Within the framework of their statutory functions, the associations of communes have such right to self-government as may be provided by statute. [3]The right to self-government also encompasses the foundations of financial accountability; part of this foundation is the communes' right to raise their tax shares according to local economic performance.
(3) The Federation ensures that the constitutional order of the States [Länder] conforms to the basic rights and to the provisions of Paragraphs I & II.

Article 29 [States Boundaries]

(1) A new delimitation of federal territory may be made to ensure that the States [Länder] by their size and capacity are able effectively to fulfil their functions. [2]Due regard has to be given to regional, historical, and cultural ties, economic expediency, and the requirements of regional policy and planning.
(2) Measures for a new delimitation of federal territory are effected by federal statutes requiring confirmation by referendum. [2]The States [Länder] thus affected have to be consulted.
(3) A referendum is held in the States [Länder] from whose territories or partial territories a new State [Land] or a State with redefined boundaries is to be formed (affected States). [2]The referendum is held on the question whether the affected States [Länder] are to remain within their existing boundaries or whether the new State [Land] or State with redefined boundaries should be formed. [3]The referendum is deemed to be in favor of the formation of a new State [Land] or of a State [Land] with redefined boundaries where approval is given to the change by a majority in the future territory of such State [Land] and by a majority in all the territories or partial territories of an

affected State [Land] whose assignment to a State [Land] is to be changed in the same sense. [4]The referendum is deemed not to be in favor where in the territory of one of the affected States [Länder] a majority reject the change; such rejection is, however, of no consequence where in one part of the territory whose assignment to the affected State [Land] is to be changed a majority of two-thirds approve of the change, unless in the entire territory of the affected State [Land] a majority of two-thirds reject the change.

(4) Where in a clearly definable area of interconnected population and economic settlement, the parts of which lie in several States [Länder] and which has a population of at least one million, one tenth of those of its population entitled to vote in House of Representatives [Bundestag] elections petition by popular initiative for the assignment of that area to one State [Land], provision is made within two years in a federal statute determining whether the delimitation of the affected States [Länder] is changed pursuant to Paragraph II or determining that a plebiscite is held in the affected States [Länder].

(5) The plebiscite establishes whether approval is given to a change of States [Länder] delimitation to be proposed in the statute. [2]The statute may put forward different proposals, not exceeding two in number, for the plebiscite. [3]Where approval is given by a majority to a proposed change of States [Länder] delimitation, provision is made within two years in a federal statute determining whether the delimitation of the States [Länder] concerned is changed pursuant to Paragraph II. [4]Where approval is given, in accordance with Paragraph III 3 & 4, to a proposal put forward for the plebiscite, a federal statute providing for the formation of the proposed State [Land] is enacted within two years of the plebiscite and no longer requires confirmation by referendum.

(6) A majority in a referendum or in a plebiscite consists of a majority of the votes cast, provided that they amount to at least one quarter of the population entitled to vote in House of Representatives [Bundestag] elections. [2]Other detailed provisions concerning referendums, popular petitions, and plebiscites is made in a federal statute; such statute may also provide that popular petitions may not be repeated within a period of five years.

(7) Other changes concerning the territory of the States [Länder] may be effected by state agreements between the States [Länder] concerned or by a federal statute with the approval of the Senate [Bundesrat] where the territory which is to be the subject of a new delimitation does not have more than 50,000 inhabitants. [2]Detailed provision are made in a federal statute requiring the approval of the Senate [Bundesrat] and the majority of the members of the House of Representatives [Bundestag]. [3]It makes provision for the affected communes and districts to be consulted.

(8) The States [Länder] can change the delimitation of their territory or parts thereof deviating from the provisions in Paragraphs II to VII by state contract. [2]Affected communes and counties have to be consulted. [3]The state contract needs to be confirmed by public referendum in each participating

State [Land]. [4]If a state contract affects only parts of the territory of a State [Land], the public referendum can be limited to these parts; Sentence 5 Half-Sentence 2 is not applicable. [5]The public referendum requires a majority of votes cast if such majority contains at least one fourth of the votes of all persons eligible for elections of the House of Representatives [Bundestag]; details are regulated by a federal statute. [6]The state contract requires the consent of the House of Representatives [Bundestag].

Article 30 [Governmental Powers]

Except as otherwise provided or permitted by this Constitution, the exercise of governmental powers and the discharge of governmental functions is incumbent on the States [Länder].

Article 31 [Precedence of Federal Law]

Federal law takes precedence over State [Land] law.

Article 32 [Foreign Relations]

(1) Relations with foreign countries are a responsibility of the Federation.
(2) Before the conclusion of a treaty affecting the special circumstances of a State [Land], that State [Land] has to be consulted in time.
(3) Insofar as the States [Länder] have power to legislate, they may, with the consent of the Government conclude treaties with foreign countries.

Article 33 [Equality of Status and Office]

(1) Every German has in every State [Land] the same political rights and duties.
(2) Every German is equally eligible for any public office according to his aptitude, qualifications, and professional achievements.
(3) Enjoyment of civil and political rights, eligibility for public office, and rights acquired in the public service are independent of religious denomination. [2]No one may suffer any disadvantage by reason of his adherence or non-adherence to a denomination or to a philosophical persuasion.
(4) The exercise of state authority as a permanent function is, as a rule, entrusted to members of the public service whose status, service and loyalty are governed by public law.
(5) The law of the public service is regulated and developed with due regard to the traditional principles of the professional civil service.

Article 34 [Liability of Officers and State]

Where any person, in the exercise of a public office entrusted to him, violates his official obligations to a third party, liability rests in principle on the state or the public body which employs him. [2]In the event of wilful intent or gross negligence, the right of recourse against the holder of a public office is reserved. [3]In respect of the claim for compensation or the right of recourse, the jurisdiction of the ordinary courts may not be excluded.

Article 35 [Legal, Administrative, Emergency Assistance]

(1) All federal and State [Land] authorities render each other legal and administrative assistance.

(2) In order to maintain or to restore public security or order, a State [Land] may, in cases of particular importance, call upon forces and facilities of the Federal Border Guard to assist its police where without this assistance the police could not, or only with considerable difficulty, fulfill a task. [2]In order to deal with a natural disaster or an especially grave accident, a State [Land] may request the assistance of the police forces of other States [Länder] or of forces and facilities of other administrative authorities or of the Federal Border Guard or the Armed Forces.

(3) Where the natural disaster or the accident endangers a region larger than a State [Land], the Government may, insofar as this is necessary to effectively deal with such danger, instruct the State [Land] governments to place their police forces at the disposal of other States [Länder], and may use units of the Federal Border Guard or the Armed Forces to support the police forces. [2]Measures taken by the Government pursuant to the first sentence of this paragraph have to be revoked at any time at the demand of the Senate [Bundesrat], and otherwise immediately upon removal of the danger.

Article 36 [Federal Civil Servants]

(1) Civil servants employed in the highest federal authorities are drawn from all States [Länder] in appropriate proportion. [2]Persons employed in other federal authorities should, as a rule, be drawn from the State [Land] in which they serve.

(2) Military laws also have to take into account the division of the Federation into States [Länder] and the regional ties of their populations.

Article 37 [Federal Coercion]

(1) Where a State [Land] fails to comply with its obligations of a federal character imposed by this Constitution or another federal statute, the Government may, with the consent of the Senate [Bundesrat], take the necessary measures to enforce such compliance by the State [Land] by way of federal coercion.

(2) For the purpose of exercising federal coercion, the Government or its commissioner has the right to give binding instructions to all States [Länder] and their authorities.

Chapter III

House of Representatives

Article 38 [Elections]

(1) The deputies to the German House of Representatives [Bundestag] are elected in general, direct, free, equal, and secret elections. [2]They are repre-

sentatives of the whole people, not bound by orders and instructions, and subject only to their conscience.

(2) Anyone who has attained the age of eighteen years is entitled to vote; anyone who has attained majority is eligible for election.

(3) Details are regulated by a federal statute.

Article 39 [Sessions, Legislative Term]

(1) The House of Representatives [Bundestag] is elected, except for the following provisions, for a four year term. [2]Its legislative term ends with the assembly of a new House of Representatives [Bundestag]. [3]New elections are held forty-six months at the earliest, and forty-eight months at the latest after the beginning of the legislative term. [4]In the case of dissolution of the House of Representatives [Bundestag], the new election is held within sixty days.

(2) The House of Representatives [Bundestag] assembles, at the latest, on the thirtieth day after the election.

(3) The House of Representatives [Bundestag] determines the termination and resumption of its meetings. [2]The President of the House of Representatives [Bundestag] may convene it at an earlier date. [3]He does so where one third of its members or the President or the Chancellor so demand.

Article 40 [President, Rules of Procedure]

(1) The House of Representatives [Bundestag] elects its President, vice presidents, and secretaries. [2]It draws up its rules of procedure.

(2) The President exercises proprietary and police powers in the House of Representatives [Bundestag] building. [2]No search or seizure may take place on the premises of the House of Representatives [Bundestag] without his permission.

Article 41 [Scrutiny of Elections]

(1) The scrutiny of elections is the responsibility of the House of Representatives [Bundestag]. [2]It also decides whether a deputy has lost his seat in the House of Representatives [Bundestag].

(2) Complaints against such decisions of the House of Representatives [Bundestag] may be lodged with the Federal Constitutional Court.

(3) Details are regulated by a federal statute.

Article 42 [Proceedings, Voting]

(1) The debates of the House of Representatives [Bundestag] are public. [2]Upon a motion of one tenth of its members, or upon a motion of the Government, the public may be excluded by a two-thirds majority. [3]The decision on the motion is taken at a meeting not open to the public.

(2) Decisions of the House of Representatives [Bundestag] require a majority of the votes cast unless this Constitution provides otherwise. [2]The rules of procedure may provide for exceptions in respect of elections to be conducted by the House of Representatives [Bundestag].

(3) True and accurate reports on the public meetings of the House of Representatives [Bundestag] and of its committees does not give rise to any liability.

Article 43 [Presence of Government and Senate]

(1) The House of Representatives [Bundestag] and its committees may demand the presence of any member of the Government.
(2) The members of the Senate [Bundesrat] and of the Government as well as persons commissioned by them have access to all meetings of the House of Representatives [Bundestag] and its committees. [2]They are heard at any time.

Article 44 [Committees of Investigation]

(1) The House of Representatives [Bundestag] has the right, and upon the motion of one quarter of its members the duty, to set up a committee of investigation, which takes the requisite evidence at public hearings. [2]The public may be excluded.
(2) The rules of criminal procedure equally apply to the taking of evidence. [2]The privacy of letters and the secrecy of post and telecommunication remain unaffected.
(3) Courts and administrative authorities are bound to render legal and administrative assistance.
(4) The decisions of committees of investigation is not subject to judicial consideration. [2]The courts are free to evaluate and judge the facts on which the investigation is based.

Article 45 [Committee on the European Union]

The House of Representatives [Bundestag] establishes a committee for European Union matters. [2]It can empower the committee to exercise the rights of the House of Representatives [Bundestag] under Article 23 in its contact with the Government. [3]It can also empower the committee to exercise the rights of the House of Representatives [Bundestag] under the contractual bases of the European Union.

Article 45a [Committees on Foreign Affairs and Defense]

(1) The House of Representatives [Bundestag] appoints a Committee on Foreign Affairs and Committee on Defense.
(2) The Committee on Defense also has the rights of a committee of investigation. [2]Upon the motion of one quarter of its members it has the duty to make a specific matter the subject of investigation.
(3) Article 44 I does not apply to defense matters.

Article 45b [Defense Commissioner]

A Defense Commissioner of the House of Representatives [Bundestag] is appointed to safeguard the basic rights and to assist the House of Representatives

[Bundestag] in exercising parliamentary control. [2]Details are regulated by a federal statute.

Article 45c [Petitions Committee]

(1) The House of Representatives [Bundestag] appoints a Petitions Committee to deal with requests and complaints addressed to the House of Representatives [Bundestag] pursuant to Article 17.
(2) The powers of the Committee to consider complaints is regulated by a federal statute.

Article 45d Parliamentary Control Body

(1) The House of Representatives [Bundestag] appoints a Body to control the intelligence services of the Federation.
(2) Details are regulated by a federal statute.

Article 46 [Indemnity and Immunity]

(1) A deputy may not at any time be subjected to court proceedings or disciplinary action or otherwise called to account outside the House of Representatives [Bundestag] for a vote cast or a statement made by him in the House of Representatives [Bundestag] or in any of its committees. [2]This does not apply to defamatory insults.
(2) A deputy may not be called to account or arrested for a punishable offense except by permission of the House of Representatives [Bundestag], unless he is apprehended during commission of the offense or in the course of the following day.
(3) The permission of the House of Representatives [Bundestag] also is necessary for any other restriction of the personal liberty of a deputy or for the initiation of proceedings against a deputy under Article 18.
(4) Any criminal proceedings or any proceedings under Article 18 against a deputy, any detention or any other restriction of his personal liberty is suspended at the demand of the House of Representatives [Bundestag].

Article 47 [Right to Refuse Evidence]

Deputies may refuse to give evidence concerning persons who have confided facts to them in their capacity as deputies, or to whom they have confided facts in such capacity, as well as evidence concerning these facts themselves. [2]To the extent that this right of refusal to give evidence exists, no seizure of documents is permissible.

Article 48 [Entitlements]

(1) Any candidate for election to the House of Representatives [Bundestag] is entitled to the leave necessary for his election campaign.
(2) No one may be prevented from accepting and exercising the office of deputy. [2]He may not be given notice of dismissal nor dismissed from employment on this ground.

(3) Deputies are entitled to adequate remuneration ensuring their independence. [2]They are entitled to the free use of all state-owned means of transport. [3]Details are regulated by a federal statute.

Article 49 [repealed]

Chapter IV

Senate

Article 50 [Functions]

The States [Länder] participate through the Senate [Bundesrat] in the legislation and administration of the Federation and in European Union matters.

Article 51 [Composition]

(1) The Senate [Bundesrat] consists of members of the State [Land] governments which appoint and recall them. [2]Other members of such governments may act as substitutes.

(2) Each State [Land] has at least three votes; States [Länder] with more than two million inhabitants have four, States [Länder] with more than six million inhabitants five, and States [Länder] with more than seven million inhabitants six votes.

(3) Each State [Land] may delegate as many members as it has votes. [2]The votes of each State [Land] may be cast only as a block vote and only by members present or their substitutes.

Article 52 [President, Rules of Procedure]

(1) The Senate [Bundesrat] elects its President for one year.

(2) The President convenes the Senate [Bundesrat]. [2]He convenes the Senate [Bundesrat] where delegates from at least two States [Länder] or the Government so demand.

(3) The Senate [Bundesrat] takes its decisions with at least the majority of its votes. [2]It draws up its rules of procedure. [3]Its meetings are public. [4]The public may be excluded.

(3a) For European Union matters, the Senate [Bundesrat] can establish a European Chamber whose decisions are considered decisions of the Senate [Bundesrat]; the number of State [Land] votes cast in unison are determined according to Article 51 II.

(4) Other members of or persons commissioned by State [Land] governments may serve on the committees of the Senate [Bundesrat].

Article 53 [Presence of Government]

The members of the Government have the right, and on demand the duty, to attend the meetings of the Senate [Bundesrat] and of its committees. [2]They have the right to be heard at any time. [3]The Senate [Bundesrat] is being kept informed by the Government as regards the conduct of affairs.

Chapter IVa

Joint Committee

Article 53a [Composition, Rules of Procedure]

(1) Two thirds of the members of the Joint Committee are deputies of the House of Representatives [Bundestag] and one third are members of the Senate [Bundesrat]. [2]The House of Representatives [Bundestag] delegates its deputies in proportion to the relative strength of its parliamentary groups; deputies may not be members of the Government. [3]Each State [Land] is represented by a Senate [Bundesrat] member of its choice; these members are not bound by instructions. [4]The establishment of the Joint Committee and its procedures are regulated by rules of procedure to be adopted by the House of Representatives [Bundestag] and requiring the consent of the Senate [Bundesrat].

(2) The Government informs the Joint Committee about its plans in respect of a state of defense. [2]The rights of the House of Representatives [Bundestag] and its committees under Article 43 I remain unaffected by the provision of this paragraph.

Chapter V

Federal President

Article 54 [Election]

(1) The President is elected, without debate, by the Federal Convention. [2]Every German who is entitled to vote in House of Representatives [Bundestag] elections and has attained the age of forty years is eligible for election.

(2) The term of office of the President is five years. [2]Reelection for a consecutive term is permitted only once.

(3) The Federal Convention consists of the members of the House of Representatives [Bundestag] and an equal number of members elected by the parliaments of the States [Länder] according to the principles of proportional representation.

(4) The Federal Convention meets no later than thirty days before the expiration of the term of office of the President or, in the case of premature termination, not later than thirty days after that date. [2]It is convened by the President of the House of Representatives [Bundestag].

(5) After the expiration of a legislative term, the period specified in Paragraph IV 1 begins with the first meeting of the House of Representatives [Bundestag].

(6) The person receiving the votes of the majority of the members of the Federal Convention is elected. [2]Where such majority is not obtained by any candidate in two ballots, the candidate who receives the largest number of votes in the next ballot is elected.

(7) Details are regulated by a federal statute.

Article 55 [Incompatibilities]

(1) The President may not be a member of the government nor of a legislative body of the Federation or of a State [Land].
(2) The President may not hold any other salaried office, nor engage in an occupation, nor belong to the management or the board of directors of an enterprise carried on for profit.

Article 56 [Oath of Office]

On assuming his office, the President takes the following oath before the assembled members of the House of Representatives [Bundestag] and the Senate [Bundesrat]:

> "I swear that I will dedicate my efforts to the wellbeing of the German people, enhance their benefits, avert harm from them, uphold and defend the Constitution and the statutes of the Federation, fulfill my duties conscientiously, and do justice to all. So help me God."

[2] The oath may also be taken without religious affirmation.

Article 57 [Representation]

Where the President is prevented from acting, or where his office falls prematurely vacant, his powers are exercised by the President of the Senate [Bundesrat].

Article 58 [Countersignature]

Orders and directions of the President require, for their validity, the countersignature of the Chancellor or the appropriate Minister. [2]This does not apply to the appointment and dismissal of the Chancellor, the dissolution of the House of Representatives [Bundestag] under Article 63 and a request made under Article 69 III.

Article 59 [Representation in International Relations]

(1) The President represents the Federation in its international relations. [2]He concludes treaties with foreign countries on behalf of the Federation. [3]He accredits and receive envoys.
(2) Treaties which regulate the political relations of the Federation or relate to matters of federal legislation requires the consent or participation, in the form of a federal statute, of the bodies competent in any specific case for such federal legislation. [2]As regards administrative agreements, the provisions concerning the federal administration are applicable.

Article 59a [repealed]

Article 60 [Appointments, Pardon]

(1) The President appoints and dismisses the federal judges, the federal civil servants, the officers and noncommissioned officers, except as may otherwise be provided for by statute.

(2) He exercises the right of pardon in individual cases on behalf of the Federation.
(3) He may delegate these powers to other authorities.
(4) Article 46 II to IV also apply to the President.

Article 61 [Impeachment]

(1) The House of Representatives [Bundestag] or the Senate [Bundesrat] may impeach the President before the Federal Constitutional Court for willful violation of this Constitution or any other federal statute. [2]The motion of impeachment is filed by at least one quarter of the members of the House of Representatives [Bundestag] or one quarter of the votes of the Senate [Bundesrat]. [3]A decision to impeach requires a majority of two thirds of the members of the House of Representatives [Bundestag] or of two thirds of the votes of the Senate [Bundesrat]. [4]The impeachment is pleaded by a person commissioned by the impeaching body.
(2) Where the Federal Constitutional Court finds the President guilty of a willful violation of this Constitution or of another federal statute, it may declare him to have forfeited his office. [2]After impeachment, it may issue an interim order preventing the President from exercising his functions.

Chapter VI

Federal Government

Article 62 [Composition]

The Government consists of the Chancellor and the Ministers.

Article 63 [Election of Chancellor]

(1) The Chancellor is elected, without debate, by the House of Representatives [Bundestag] upon the proposal of the President.
(2) The person obtaining the votes of the majority of the members of the House of Representatives [Bundestag] is elected. [2]The person elected is appointed by the President.
(3) Where the person proposed is not elected, the House of Representatives [Bundestag] may elect within fourteen days of the ballot a Chancellor by more than one half of its members.
(4) Where no candidate has been elected within this period, a new ballot takes place without delay in which the person obtaining the largest number of votes is elected. [2]Where the person elected has obtained the votes of the majority of the members of the House of Representatives [Bundestag], the President appoints him within seven days of the election. [3]Where the person elected did not obtain such a majority, the President, within seven days, either appoints him or dissolves the House of Representatives [Bundestag].

Article 64 [Appointment of Ministers]

(1) The Ministers are appointed and dismissed by the President upon the proposal of the Chancellor.
(2) The Chancellor and the Ministers, on assuming office, take before the House of Representatives [Bundestag] the oath provided for in Article 56.

Article 65 [Governmental Powers]

The Chancellor determines and is responsible for the general policy guidelines. [2]Within the limits set by these guidelines, each Minister conducts the affairs of his department independently and on his own responsibility. [3]The Government decides on differences of opinion between Ministers. [4]The Chancellor conducts the affairs of the Government in accordance with rules of procedure adopted by it and approved by the President.

Article 65a [Command Over Armed Forces]

Power of command in respect of the Armed Forces is be vested in the Minister of Defense.

Article 66 [Incompatibilities]

The Chancellor and the Ministers may not hold any other salaried office, nor engage in an occupation, nor belong to the management or, without the consent of the House of Representatives [Bundestag], to the board of directors of an enterprise carried on for profit.

Article 67 [Lack of Confidence]

(1) The House of Representatives [Bundestag] can express its lack of confidence in the Chancellor only by electing a successor with the majority of its members and by requesting the President to dismiss the Chancellor. [2]The President complies with the request and appoints the person elected.
(2) Forty-eight hours must elapse between the motion and the election.

Article 68 [Dissolution of Parliament]

(1) Where a motion of the Chancellor for a vote of confidence is not carried by the majority of the members of the House of Representatives [Bundestag], the President may, upon the proposal of the Chancellor, dissolve the House of Representatives [Bundestag] within twenty-one days. [2]The right of dissolution lapses as soon as the House of Representatives [Bundestag] elects another Chancellor with the majority of its members.
(2) Forty-eight hours must elapse between the motion and the vote thereon.

Article 69 [Members of Government]

(1) The Chancellor appoints a Minister as his deputy.
(2) The tenure of office of the Chancellor or a Minister end in any event on the assembly of a new House of Representatives [Bundestag]; the tenure of office

of a Minister also end on any other termination of the Chancellor's tenure of office.

(3) At the request of the President, the Chancellor – or at the request of the Chancellor or of the President, a Minister – is bound to continue managing the affairs of his office until the appointment of a successor.

Chapter VII

Federal Legislative Powers

Article 70 [General Principle]

(1) The States [Länder] have the right to legislate insofar as this Constitution does not confer legislative power on the Federation.

(2) The division of competence between the Federation and the States [Länder] are determined by the provisions of this Constitution concerning exclusive and concurrent legislative powers.

Article 71 [Exclusive Legislative Power]

In matters within the exclusive legislative power of the Federation, the States [Länder] have power to legislate only where and to the extent that they are given such explicit authorization by a federal statute.

Article 72 [Concurrent Legislative Power]

(1) In the field of concurrent legislative power, the States [Länder] have power to legislate as long as and to the extent that the Federation does not exercise its right to legislate by statute.

(2) In the areas of Article 74 I No. 4, 7, 11, 13, 15, 19a, 20, 22, 25 and 26, the Federation has legislation if and insofar as the establishment of equal living conditions in the federal territory or the preservation of legal and economic unity necessitates, in the interest of the state at large, a federal regulation.

(3) If the Federation has used its legislative competence, the States [Länder] may adopt differing rules by statute regarding:

1. hunting (without the right to hunting licences);
2. natural protection and land cultivation (without the general principles of natural protection, the law of species protection or of protecting the nature of the sea);
3. distribution of land;
4. zoning arrangements;
5. protection of water (without regulation about substances or installations);
6. university admission and university degrees.

[2]Federal statutes regarding these matters come into force, at the earliest, six months after their promulgation as long as the Senate [Bundesrat] does not

decide otherwise. [3]Regarding the matters of sentence 1, the latest statute takes precedence within the concurrence of federal and state law.

(4) A federal statute can stipulate that a federal regulation for which the conditions of Paragraph II no longer hold true is replaced by law of the States [Länder].

Article 73 [Exclusive Legislation]

(1) The Federation has exclusive power to legislate in the following matters:

1. foreign affairs and defense, including the protection of the civilian population;
2. citizenship in the Federation;
3. freedom of movement, passport, registration and individual document matters, immigration, emigration and extradition;
4. currency, money and coinage, weights and measures, as well as the determination of standards of time;
5. the unity of the customs and trading area, treaties on commerce and on navigation, the freedom of movement of goods, and the exchange of goods and payments with foreign countries, including customs and other frontier protection;

5a. the protection of German cultural items against being moved abroad;

6. air transport;

6a. the traffic of railroads owned completely or mainly by the Federation (railroads of the Federation), the construction, maintenance, and operation of railway tracks and railroads of the Federation as well as the charging for the use of these railways;

7. postal affairs and telecommunication;
8. the legal status of persons employed by the Federation and by federal corporate bodies under public law;
9. industrial property rights, copyrights and publishing law;

9a. fight against dangers of international terrorism by the Federal Criminal Police [Bundeskriminalpolizei] in cases where the danger is transcending State [Länder] boundaries, where the competence of a State Police Agency is not established, or where the supreme State Agency asks for a discharge;

10. cooperation between the Federation and the States [Länder] concerning

    a) criminal police,
    b) protection of the free democratic basic order, of the existence and the security of the Federation or of a State [Land] (protection of the constitution) and
    c) protection against activities in the federal territory which, through the use of force or actions in preparation for the use of force, endanger the foreign interests of the Federal Republic of Germany,

as well as the establishment of a Federal Criminal Police Office and the international control of crime;

11. statistics for federal purposes;
12. laws on weapons and explosives;
13. care for people handicapped by war, widowed or orphaned by war, and help for former prisoners of war;
14. production and use of nuclear power for peaceful means, construction and operation of plants furthering these goals, protection against dangers resulting from exposition of nuclear energy or ionizing rays, and disposition of radioactive substances.

(2) The consent of the Senate [Bundesrat] is necessary for statutes according to Paragraph I No. 9a.

Article 74 [Concurrent Legislation]

(1) Concurrent legislative powers cover the following matters:

1. civil law, criminal law, the organization and procedure of courts (excluding the law governing pre-trial confinement), the legal profession, notaries and legal advice;
2. registration of births, deaths and marriages;
3. the law of association;
4. the law relating to residence and settlement of aliens;

4a. [repealed]

5. [repealed]
6. refugee and expellee matters;
7. public welfare (excluding the law on asylums);
8. [repealed]
9. war damage and reparations;
10. war graves of soldiers, graves of other victims of war and of victims of despotism;
11. the law relating to economic matters (mining, industry, supply of power, crafts, trades, commerce, banking, stock exchanges and private insurance) excluding the law on shop opening hours, restaurants, gaming parlours, presentations by people, exhibitions, expositions, and markets;

11a. [repealed]

12. Labor law, including the legal organization of enterprises, protection of workers, employment exchanges and agencies, as well as social insurance, including unemployment insurance;
13. the regulation of educational and training grants and the promotion of scientific research;
14. the law regarding expropriation, to the extent that matters enumerated in Articles 73 and 74 are concerned;

15. transfer of land, natural resources and means of production to public ownership or other forms of collective enterprise for the public benefit;
16. prevention of the abuse of economic power;
17. promotion of agricultural production and forestry (excluding the law on land consolidation), securing the supply of food, the importation and exportation of agricultural and forestry products, deep sea and coastal fishing, and preservation of the coasts;
18. property sales according to town planning, land law (excluding the law of charges for development) and aid for rent, relief regarding old debts, aid for construction of apartments, miners' apartment construction law and miners' settlement law;
19. measures against human or animal diseases that are communicable or otherwise endanger public health, admission to the medical profession and to other medical occupations or practices as well as the law on pharmacy, drugs, medical products, health products, narcotics and poisons;

19a. the economic viability of hospitals and the regulation of hospitalization fees;

20. the law on food including animals for slaughter, the law on products of indulgence, articles of daily use, fodder as well as the protection of the sale of agricultural and forest seeds and seedlings, and the protection of plants against diseases and pests as well as the protection of animals;
21. ocean and coastal shipping, as well as sea marks, inland navigation, meteorological services, sea routes, and inland waterways used for general traffic;
22. road traffic, motor transport, construction and maintenance of long distance highways, as well as the collection of charges or fees for the use of public highways by vehicles and the allocation of revenue therefrom;
23. railroads which are not railroads of the Federation, except mountain railroads;
24. garbage collection, protection against air pollution and noise (excluding protection against voluntary noise);
25. state liability;
26. medically enhanced production of human life, research on manipulations of genes, and regulations for transplantation of organs, tissues and cells;
27. rights and duties regarding the status of civil servants in the States [Länder], communes and other public law bodies as well as judges in the States [Länder] excluding their career, remuneration and pensions;
28. hunting;
29. conservation of nature and landscape;
30. distribution of real estate;
31. land use planning;
32. water supply;
33. academic admission and academic degrees.

(2) The consent of the Senate [Bundesrat] is necessary for statutes according to Paragraph I No. 25 and 27.

Article 74a [repealed]

Article 75 [repealed]

Article 76 [Bills]

(1) Bills are introduced in the House of Representatives [Bundestag] by the Government or by members of the House of Representatives [Bundestag] or by the Senate [Bundesrat].

(2) Bills of the Government first have to be submitted to the Senate [Bundesrat]. [2]The Senate [Bundesrat] is entitled to state its position on such bills within six weeks. [3]If, for important reasons and particularly with regard to the volume of the bill, the Senate [Bundesrat] asks for deferral, the period is nine weeks. [4]A bill which, on submission to the Senate [Bundesrat], is exceptionally specified by the Government to be particularly urgent may be submitted by the latter to the House of Representatives [Bundestag] three weeks later, or, if the Senate [Bundesrat] asked for deferral according to Sentence 3, six weeks later, even though the Government may not yet have received the statement of the Senate's [Bundesrat] position; upon receipt, such statement has to be transmitted to the House of Representatives [Bundestag] by the Government without delay. [5]The time limit for statements to bills changing this Constitution or delegating sovereign powers according to Article 23 or 24 is nine weeks; Sentence 4 is not applied.

(3) Bills of the Senate [Bundesrat] have to be submitted to the House of Representatives [Bundestag] by the Government within six weeks. [2]In doing so, the Government should state its own view. [3]If, for important reasons and particularly with regard to the volume of the bill, the Government asks for deferral, the period is nine weeks. [4]The time limit for a bill which is exceptionally specified by the Senate [Bundesrat] to be particularly urgent is three weeks or, if the Government asked for deferral according to Sentence 3, six weeks. [5]The time limit for statements to bills changing this Constitution or delegating sovereign powers according to Article 23 or 24 is nine weeks; Sentence 4 is not applied. [6]The House of Representatives [Bundestag] has to debate about bills within adequate time and reach a decision.

Article 77 [Legislative Procedure]

(1) Federal statutes are enacted by the House of Representatives [Bundestag]. [2]Upon their adoption they have to be transmitted, without delay, to the Senate [Bundesrat] by the President of the House of Representatives [Bundestag].

(2) The Senate [Bundesrat] may, within three weeks of the receipt of the adopted bill, demand that a committee for joint consideration of bills, composed of members of the House of Representatives [Bundestag] and members of the

Senate [Bundesrat], be convened. [2]The composition and the procedure of this committee is regulated by rules of procedure to be adopted by the House of Representatives [Bundestag] and requiring the consent of the Senate [Bundesrat]. [3]The members of the Senate [Bundesrat] on this committee are not bound by instructions. [4]Where the consent of the Senate [Bundesrat] is required for a bill to become a statute, the House of Representatives [Bundestag] and the Government may also demand that the committee be convened. [5]Should the committee propose any amendment to the adopted bill, the House of Representatives [Bundestag] again votes on the bill.

(2a) Insofar as a statute requires the consent of the Senate [Bundesrat], the Senate [Bundesrat], if no demand according to Paragraph II 1 was issued or if the committee for joint consideration has concluded its procedures without suggesting changes, has to debate about its consent within adequate time and reach a decision.

(3) Insofar as the consent of the Senate [Bundesrat] is not required for a bill to become a statute, the Senate [Bundesrat] may, when the proceedings under Paragraph II are completed, enter an objection within two weeks against a bill adopted by the House of Representatives [Bundestag]. [2]The period for entering an objection begins, in the case of the last sentence of Paragraph II, on the receipt of the bill as readopted by the House of Representatives [Bundestag], and in all other cases on the receipt of a communication from the chairman of the committee provided for in Paragraph II to the effect that the committee's proceedings have been concluded.

(4) Where the objection was adopted with the majority of the votes of the Senate [Bundesrat], it can be rejected by a decision of the majority of the members of the House of Representatives [Bundestag]. [2]Where the Senate [Bundesrat] adopted the objection with a majority of at least two thirds of its votes, its rejection by the House of Representatives [Bundestag] requires a majority of two thirds, including at least the majority of the members of the House of Representatives [Bundestag].

Article 78z [Adopting Bills]

A bill adopted by the House of Representatives [Bundestag] becomes a statute where the Senate [Bundesrat] consents to it, or fails to make a demand pursuant to Article 77 II, or fails to enter an objection within the period stipulated in Article 77 III, or withdraws such objection, or where the objection is overridden by the House of Representatives [Bundestag].

Article 79 [Amendment of the Constitution]

(1) This Constitution can be amended only by statutes which expressly amend or supplement the text thereof. [2]In respect of international treaties, the subject of which is a peace settlement, the preparation of a peace settlement or the phasing out of an occupation regime, or which are intended to serve the

defense of the Federal Republic, it is sufficient, for the purpose of clarifying that the provisions of this Constitution do not preclude the conclusion and entry into force of such treaties, to effect a supplementation of the text of this Constitution confined to such clarification.

(2) Any such statute requires the consent of two thirds of the members of the House of Representatives [Bundestag] and two thirds of the votes of the Senate [Bundesrat].

(3) Amendments of this Constitution affecting the division of the Federation into States [Länder], the participation on principle of the States [Länder] in legislation, or the basic principles laid down in Articles 1 and 20 are inadmissible.

Article 80 [Government Ordinances]

(1) The Government, a Minister or the State [Land] governments may be authorized by statute to issue ordinances. [2]The content, purpose, and scope of the authorization so conferred must be laid down in the statute concerned. [3]This legal basis has to be stated in the ordinance. [4]Where a statute provides that such authorization may be delegated, such delegation requires another ordinance.

(2) The consent of the Senate [Bundesrat] is required, unless otherwise provided by federal legislation, for ordinances of the Government or a Minister concerning basic rules or charges for the use of facilities of postal affairs and telecommunication, concerning the basic rules for charges and use of facilities of railroads of the Federation, or concerning the construction and operation of railroads, as well as for ordinances issued pursuant to federal statutes that require the consent of the Senate [Bundesrat] or that are executed by the States [Länder] as agents of the Federation or as matters of their own concern.

(3) The Senate [Bundesrat] can submit such bills for ordinances to the Government that require its consent.

(4) Insofar as, by or on the basis of federal statutes, Governments of the States [Länder] are empowered to adopt ordinances, the States [Länder] are also allowed to regulate the matter by statute.

Article 80a [State of Defense]

(1) Where this Constitution or a federal statute on defense, including the protection of the civilian population, stipulates that legal provisions may only be applied in accordance with this Article, their application is, except in a state of defense, admissible only after the House of Representatives [Bundestag] has determined that a state of tension exists or where it has specifically approved such application. [2]In respect of the cases mentioned in Article 12a V 1 & VI 2, such determination of a state of tension and such specific approval requires a two-thirds majority of the votes cast.

(2) Any measures taken by virtue of legal provisions enacted under Paragraph I have to be revoked whenever the House of Representatives [Bundestag] so demands.

(3) In derogation of Paragraph I, the application of such legal provisions is also admissible by virtue of and in accordance with a decision taken with the consent of the Government by an international body within the framework of a treaty of alliance. [2]Any measures taken pursuant to this paragraph have to be revoked whenever the House of Representatives [Bundestag] so demands with the majority of its members.

Article 81 [State of Emergency]

(1) Should, in the circumstances of Article 68, the House of Representatives [Bundestag] not be dissolved, the President may, at the request of the Government and with the consent of the Senate [Bundesrat], declare a state of legislative emergency with respect to a bill, where the House of Representatives [Bundestag] rejects the bill although the Government has declared it to be urgent. [2]The same applies where a bill has been rejected although the Chancellor had combined with it the motion under Article 68.
(2) Where, after a state of legislative emergency has been declared, the House of Representatives [Bundestag] again rejects the bill or adopts it in a version stated to be unacceptable to the Government, the bill is deemed to have become a statute to the extent that the Senate [Bundesrat] consents to it. [2]The same applies where the bill is not passed by the House of Representatives [Bundestag] within four weeks of its reintroduction
(3) During the term of office of a Chancellor, any other bill rejected by the House of Representatives [Bundestag] may become a statute in accordance with Paragraphs I and II within a period of six months after the first declaration of a state of legislative emergency. [2]After the expiration of this period, a further declaration of a state of legislative emergency is inadmissible during the term of office of the same Chancellor.
(4) This Constitution may not be amended nor repealed nor suspended in whole or in part by a statute enacted pursuant to Paragraph II.

Article 82 [Promulgation, Validity]

(1) Statutes enacted in accordance with the provisions of this Constitution are, after countersignature, signed by the President and promulgated in the Federal Law Gazette. [2]Ordinances are signed by the agency which issues them and, unless otherwise provided by statute, are promulgated in the Federal Law Gazette.
(2) Every statute or every ordinance should specify its effective date. [2]In the absence of such a provision, it takes effect on the fourteenth day after the end of the day on which the Federal Law Gazette containing it was published.

Chapter VIII

Execution of Statutes and Federal Administration

Article 83 [General Principle]

The States [Länder] execute federal statutes as matters of their own concern insofar as this Constitution does not otherwise provide or permit.

Article 84 [State Execution With Federal Supervision]

(1) Where the States [Länder] execute federal statutes as matters of their own concern, they provide for the establishment of authorities and the regulation of administrative procedures. [2]If federal statutes provide something else, the States [Länder] may adopt divergent regulation. [3]If a State [Land] has adopted divergent regulation according to Sentence 2, federal regulation adopted later regarding the establishment of authorities and the regulation of administrative procedures will enter into force no earlier then six months after promulgation, provided nothing else is prescribed with approval by the Senate [Bundesrat]. [4]Article 72 III 3 is applicable. [5]In exceptional cases, the Federation may, because of particular need for federal uniformity, adopt regulation without the States' [Länder] power to deviate. [6]These statutes require approval by the Senate [Bundesrat]. [7]Federal statutes may not delegate powers to communes or associations of communes.

(2) The Government may, with the consent of the Senate [Bundesrat], issue general administrative rules.

(3) The Government exercises supervision to ensure that the States [Länder] execute the federal statutes in accordance with applicable law. [2]For this purpose the Government may send commissioners to the highest State [Land] authorities and, with their consent or, where such consent is refused, with the consent of the Senate [Bundesrat], also to subordinate authorities.

(4) Should any shortcomings which the Government has found to exist in the execution of federal statutes in the States [Länder] not be corrected, the Senate [Bundesrat] decides, at the request of the Government or the State [Land] concerned, whether such State [Land] has violated the law. [2]The decision of the Senate [Bundesrat] may be challenged in the Federal Constitutional Court.

(5) With a view to the execution of federal statutes, the Government may be authorized by a federal statute requiring the consent of the Senate [Bundesrat] to issue individual instructions for particular cases. [2]They are addressed to the highest State [Land] authorities unless the Government considers the matter urgent.

Article 85 [State Execution as Federal Agency]

(1) Where the States [Länder] execute federal statutes as agents of the Federation, the establishment of the requisite authorities remains the concern of the States [Länder], except insofar as federal statutes consented to by the Senate

[Bundesrat] otherwise provide. [2]Federal statutes may not delegate powers to communes or associations of communes.

(2) The Government may, with the consent of the Senate [Bundesrat], issue general administrative rules. [2]It may regulate the uniform training of civil servants and other salaried public employees. [3]The heads of authorities at the intermediate level are appointed with its agreement.

(3) The State [Land] authorities are subject to the instructions of the competent highest federal authorities. [2]Such instructions are addressed to the highest State [Land] authorities unless the Government considers the matter urgent. [3]Execution of the instructions is ensured by the highest State [Land] authorities.

(4) Federal supervision covers the lawfulness and appropriateness of execution. [2]The Government may, for this purpose, require the submission of reports and documents and send commissioners to all authorities.

Article 86 [Direct Federal Administration]

Where the Federation executes statutes by means of direct federal administration or by federal corporate bodies or institutions under public law, the Government issues, insofar as the statute concerned contains no special provision, pertinent general administrative rules. [2]The Government provides for the establishment of the requisite authorities insofar as the statute concerned does not otherwise provide.

Article 87 [Matters for Direct Federal Administration]

(1) The foreign service, the federal finance administration and, in accordance with the provisions of Article 89, the administration of federal waterways and of shipping is conducted as matters of direct federal administration with their own administrative substructures. [2]Federal legislation may be enacted to establish Federal Border Guard authorities and central offices for police information and communications, for the criminal police and for the compilation of data for the purposes of protection of the constitution and of protection against activities on federal territory which, through the use of force or acts preparatory to the use of force, endanger the foreign interests of the Federal Republic of Germany.

(2) Social insurance institutions whose sphere of competence extends beyond the territory of one State [Land] are administered as direct federal corporate bodies under public law. [2]Social insurance institutions whose sphere of competence extends beyond the territory of one State [Land], but not beyond that of more than three States [Länder], are administered, differing from the first sentence, as direct State [Land] corporate bodies under public law if the supervising State [Land] is determined by the States [Länder] involved.

(3) In addition, independent federal higher authorities as well as new federal corporate bodies and institutions under public law may be established by federal legislation for matters on which the Federation has the power to

legislate. [2]Where new functions arise for the Federation in matters on which it has the power to legislate, federal authorities at the intermediate and lower levels may be established, in case of urgent need, with the consent of the Senate [Bundesrat] and of the majority of the members of the House of Representatives [Bundestag].

Article 87a [Establishment of Armed Forces]

(1) The Federation establishes Armed Forces for defense purposes. [2]Their numerical strength and general organizational structure must be shown in the budget.
(2) Apart from defense, the Armed Forces may only be used insofar as explicitly permitted by this Constitution.
(3) While a state of defense or a state of tension exists, the Armed Forces have the power to protect civilian property and discharge functions of traffic control insofar as this is necessary for the performance of their defense mission. [2]Moreover, the Armed Forces may, when a state of defense or a state of tension exists, be entrusted with the protection of civilian property also in support of police measures; in this event the Armed Forces cooperate with the competent authorities.
(4) In order to avert any imminent danger to the existence or to the free democratic basic order of the Federation or a State [Land], the Government may, should conditions as envisaged in Article 91 II obtain and the police forces and the Federal Border Guard be inadequate, use the Armed Forces to support the police and the Federal Border Guard in the protection of civilian property and in combatting organized and militarily armed insurgents. [2]Any such use of the Armed Forces has to stop whenever the House of Representatives [Bundestag] or the Senate [Bundesrat] so demands.

Article 87b [Administration of Armed Forces]

(1) The Federal Armed Forces Administration is conducted as a direct federal administration with its own administrative substructure. [2]Its function are to administer personnel matters and directly to meet the material requirements of the Armed Forces. [3]Tasks connected with benefits to disabled persons or with construction work are not assigned to the Federal Armed Forces Administration except by federal legislation requiring the consent of the Senate [Bundesrat]. [4]Such consent is also required for any statutes to the extent that they empower the Federal Armed Forces Administration to interfere with rights of third parties; this does not apply, however, in the case of statutes concerning personnel matters.
(2) Moreover, federal statutes concerning defense, including recruitment for military service and protection of the civilian population, may, with the consent of the Senate [Bundesrat], provide that they are executed, wholly or in part, either by means of direct federal administration having its own administrative substructure or by the States [Länder] acting as agents of the Federation.

[2]Where such statutes are executed by the States [Länder] acting as agents of the Federation, they may, with the consent of the Senate [Bundesrat], provide that the powers vested in the Government or appropriate highest federal authorities by virtue of Article 85 are transferred wholly or in part to higher federal authorities; in such an event it may be enacted that these authorities do not require the consent of the Senate [Bundesrat] in issuing general administrative rules as referred to in Article 85 II 1.

Article 87c [Nuclear Energy]

Statutes enacted under Article 73 I No. 14 may, with the consent of the Senate [Bundesrat], provide that they are executed by the States [Länder] acting as agents of the Federation.

Article 87d [Aviation]

(1) Aviation administration is conducted as federal administration. [2]Tasks of air-traffic control can also be conducted by foreign air-traffic control organizations accredited under the law of the European Community. [3]Details are regulated by a federal statute.
(2) Through federal legislation requiring the consent of the Senate [Bundesrat], functions of aviation administration may be transferred to the States [Länder] acting as agents of the Federation.

Article 87e [Railroads]

(1) The administration for traffic of railroads of the Federation is conducted as a direct federal administration. [2]By federal statute, tasks of the administration for traffic of railroads can be delegated to the States [Länder] as their own tasks.
(2) The Federation undertakes the tasks to administer traffic of railroads of the Federation as are assigned to it by federal statute.
(3) Railroads of the Federation are managed in the form of private law businesses. [2]They are owned by the Federation as far as the activities of the business encompass construction, maintenance, or operation of railways. [3]The sale of shares of the Federation in the businesses mentioned in the second sentence is regulated on the basis of a statute; the Federation retains a majority of shares in those businesses. [4]Details are regulated by federal statute.
(4) The Federation guarantees that the public weal, particularly the interest in traffic, in the development and preservation of the railway network of railways of the Federation as far as it is used for local railway transport of persons is considered. [2]Details are regulated by federal statute.
(5) Statutes based on Paragraphs I to IV need the consent of the Senate [Bundesrat]. [2]Furthermore, the consent of the Senate [Bundesrat] is necessary for statutes that dissolve, merge, or split railroads of the Federation, convey railways of railroads of the Federation to third parties as well as

discontinue railways of railroads of the Federation, or affect the local railway transport of persons.

Article 87f [Mail, Telecommunication]

(1) Regulated by a federal statute requiring the consent of the Senate [Bundesrat], the Federation guarantees a comprehensive and adequate coverage with mail services and telecommunication.

(2) Services in the sense of Paragraph I are organized as private law activities by those businesses originating in the special property Deutsche Bundespost. [2]Sovereign tasks in the area of mail and telecommunication are organized as direct federal administration.

(3) Notwithstanding Paragraph II 2, the Federation, in the public law form of a direct federal agency, discharges certain duties regarding businesses originating in the special property Deutsche Bundespost, as are assigned to it by federal statutes.

Article 88 [Federal Bank]

The Federation establishes a note-issuing and currency bank as the Federal Bank [Bundesbank]. [2]Its tasks and powers can, in the context of the European Union, be transferred to the European Central Bank which is independent and primarily bound by the purpose of securing stability of prices.

Article 89 [Federal Waterways]

(1) The Federation is the owner of the former Reich waterways.

(2) The Federation administers the federal waterways through its own authorities. [2]It exercises those governmental functions relating to inland shipping which extend beyond the territory of one State [Land], and those governmental functions relating to maritime shipping which are conferred on it by statute. [3]Upon request, the Federation may transfer the administration of federal waterways, insofar as they lie within the territory of one State [Land], to that State [Land] as its agent. [4]Where a waterway touches the territories of several States [Länder], the Federation may delegate one State [Land] to be its agent where so requested by the States [Länder] concerned.

(3) In the administration, development, and new construction of waterways, the needs of land improvement and of water economy are safeguarded in agreement with the States [Länder].

Article 90 [Federal Highways]

(1) The Federation is the owner of the former Reich streets and Reich highways.

(2) The States [Länder], or such self-governing corporate bodies as are competent under State law, administer as agents of the Federation the federal streets and other federal highways used for long-distance traffic.

(3) At the request of a State [Land], the Federation may place federal streets and other federal highways used for long distance traffic under direct federal administration insofar as they lie within the territory of that State [Land].

Article 91 [Internal Emergency]

(1) In order to avert any imminent danger to the existence or to the tree democratic basic order of the Federation or a State [Land], a State may request the services of the police forces of other States [Länder], or of the forces and facilities of other administrative authorities and of the Federal Border Guard.
(2) If the State [Land] where such danger is imminent is not itself willing or able to combat the danger, the Government may place the police in that State [Land] and the police forces of other States [Länder] under its own instructions and use units of the Federal Border Guard. [2]The order for this has to be revoked after the removal of the danger or else at any time at the demand of the Senate [Bundesrat]. [3]Where the danger extends to a region larger than a State [Land], the Government may, insofar as is necessary for effectively combatting such danger, issue instructions to the State [Land] governments; the first and second sentences of this paragraph are not affected by this provision.

Chapter VIIIa

Joint Tasks

Article 91a [Participation of the Federation]

(1) The Federation participates, in the following sectors, in the discharge of responsibilities of the States [Länder], provided that such responsibilities are important to society as a whole and that federal participation is necessary for the improvement of living conditions (joint tasks):

1. improvement of regional economic structures,
2. improvement of the agrarian structure and of coast preservation.

(2) Joint tasks as well as details of coordination are defined in detail by a federal statute requiring the consent of the Senate [Bundesrat].
(3) In cases to which Paragraph I No. 1 applies, the Federation pays for one half of the expenditure in each State [Land]. [2]In cases to which Paragraph I No. 2 applies, the Federation pays for at least one half of the expenditure, and such proportion is the same for all the States [Länder]. [3]Details are regulated by statute. [4]Provision of funds are subject to appropriation in the budgets of the Federation and the States [Länder].

Article 91b [Funding of Research, Performance of the Educational System]

(1) The Federation and the States [Länder] may, pursuant to agreements, cooperate in cases of supra-regional importance to promote:

1. institutions and projects of scientific research outside of universities;
2. projects of science and research at universities;
3. research facilities at universities including large scale equipment.

Agreements according to Sentence 1 No. 2 require the approval by all States [Länder].

(2) The Federation and the States [Länder] may, pursuant to agreements, cooperate in order to internationally compare the performance of the educational system and to participate in reports and recommendations in that respect.

(3) The allocation of costs is determined by the agreement.

Article 91c [Systems of Information Technology]

(1) Federation and States [Länder] may cooperate in the planning, installation, and operation of systems of information technology needed for their tasks.

(2) Federation and States [Länder] may by agreement establish standards and security requirements necessary for the communication between their systems of information technology. [2]Agreements about the basis of cooperation according to sentence 1 may for tasks of specific substance and extent provide that detailed regulation is adopted on the consent of a qualified majority of Federation and States [Länder] as specified in the convention. [3]They require the consent of the House of Representatives [Bundestag] and of the Houses of Representatives of participating States [Länder]; the right to cancellation of these agreements cannot be excluded. [4]The agreement also determines the allocation of costs.

(3) Furthermore, the States [Länder] may agree on the joint operation of systems of information technology as well as the establishment of specific installations.

(4) For the connection of information technology networks of the Federation and the States [Länder], the Federation establishes a connection network. [2]Details regarding the installation and operation of the connection network are regulated by a federal statute requiring the consent of the Senate [Bundesrat].

Article 91d [Comparative Surveys]

Federation and States [Länder] may, to establish and improve the performance of their administrations, conduct comparative surveys and publish the results.

Article 91e [Job Centres]

(1) In the execution of federal law regarding the basic benefits for the unemployed, Federation and States [Länder] or those communes or associations of communes competent according to state law are, in principle, cooperating by shared institutions.

(2) The Federation can allow for a limited number of communes or association of communes, on their request and with the consent of the supreme State Agency, to exclusively fulfill the tasks according to Paragraph (1). Necessary expenses including administrative costs are borne by the Federation insofar as the tasks in executing federal law according to Paragraph (1) are the duty of the Federation.

(3) Details are regulated by a federal statute requiring the consent of the Senate [Bundesrat].

Chapter IX

Judiciary

Article 92 [Court Organization]

Judicial power is vested in the judges; it is exercised by the Federal Constitutional Court, by the federal courts provided for in this Constitution, and by the courts of the States [Länder].

Article 93 [Federal Constitutional Court]

(1) The Federal Constitutional Court decides:

1. on the interpretation of this Constitution in the event of disputes concerning the extent of the rights and duties of a highest federal body or of other parties concerned who have been vested with rights of their own by this Constitution or by rules of procedure of a highest federal body;
2. in case of differences of opinion or doubts on the formal and material compatibility of federal law or State [Land] law with this Constitution, or on the compatibility of State [Land] law with other federal law, at the request of the Government, of a State [Land] government, or of one fourth of the House of Representatives [Bundestag] members;

2a. in case of differences of opinion on the compatibility of federal law with Article 72 II, at the request of the Senate [Bundesrat], of a State [Land] government, or of a State [Land] parliament;

3. in case of differences of opinion on the rights and duties of the Federation and the States [Länder], particularly in the execution of federal law by the States [Länder] and in the exercise of federal supervision;
4. on other disputes involving public law, between the Federation and the States [Länder], between different States [Länder] or within a State [Land], unless recourse to another court exists;

4a. on complaints of unconstitutionality, being filed by any person claiming that one of his basic rights or one of his rights under Article 20 IV or under Article 33, 38, 101, 103 or 104 has been violated by public authority;

4b. on complaints of unconstitutionality filed by communes or associations of communes on the ground that their right to self-government under Article 28 has been violated by a statute other than a State [Land] statute open to complaint to the respective State [Land] constitutional court;

4c. on complaints by associations against their nonadmission as a political party to the election for the House of Representatives [Bundestag]

5. in the other cases provided for in this Constitution.

(2) The Federal Constitutional Court also decides, at the request of the Senate [Bundesrat], a State [Land] Government or State [Land] Parliament, whether in the case of Article 72 IV the necessity of federal regulation according to Article 72 II no longer prevails or federal law could no longer be adopted in the cases of Article 125a II 1. [2]The declaration that the necessity no longer prevails or that federal law no longer could be adopted replaces a federal statute based on Article 72 IV or Article 125a II 2. [3]The request according to Sentence 1 is only admissible once a bill based on Article 72 IV or 125 a II 2 has been denied in the German House of Representatives [Bundestag] or not been deliberated and decided within one year or if such a bill has been denied in the Senate [Bundesrat].

(3) The Federal Constitutional Court also acts in such other cases as are assigned to it by federal legislation.

Article 94 [Composition of Constitutional Court]

(1) The Federal Constitutional Court consists of federal judges and other members. [2]Half of the members of the Federal Constitutional Court are elected by the House of Representatives [Bundestag] and half by the Senate [Bundesrat]. [3]They may not be members of the House of Representatives [Bundestag], the Senate [Bundesrat], the Government, nor of any of the corresponding bodies of a State [Land].

(2) The constitution and procedure of the Federal Constitutional Court are regulated by a federal statute which specifies in what cases its decisions have the force of law. [2]Such statute may require that all other legal remedies must have been exhausted before a complaint of unconstitutionality can be entered, and may make provision for a special procedure as to admissibility.

Article 95 [Highest Courts of Justice, Joint Panel]

(1) For the purposes of ordinary, administrative, fiscal, labor, and social jurisdiction, the Federation establishes as highest courts of justice the Federal Court of Justice, the Federal Administrative Court, the Federal Finance Court, the Federal Labor Court, and the Federal Social Court.

(2) The judges of each of these courts are selected jointly by the competent Minister and a committee for the selection of judges consisting of the competent State [Land] ministers and an equal number of members elected by the House of Representatives [Bundestag].

(3) In order to preserve uniformity of decisions, a Joint Panel of the courts specified in Paragraph I is set up. [2]Details are regulated by a federal statute.

Article 96 [Other Federal Courts]

(1) The Federation may establish a federal court for matters concerning industrial property rights.

(2) The Federation may establish military criminal courts for the Armed Forces as federal courts. [2]They may only exercise criminal jurisdiction while a state

of defense exists, and otherwise only over members of the Armed Forces serving abroad or on board warships. [3]Details are regulated by a federal statute. [4]These courts are within the competence of the Minister of Justice. [5]Their full time judges are persons qualified to hold judicial office.

(3) The highest court of justice for appeals from the courts mentioned in Paragraphs I and II is the Federal Court of Justice.

(4) The Federation may establish federal courts for disciplinary proceedings against, and for proceedings in pursuance of complaints by, persons in the federal public service.

(5) With respect to criminal proceedings for the following crimes, a federal statute requiring the consent of the Senate [Bundesrat] may provide that State [Land] courts exercise federal jurisdiction over:

1. genocide;
2. crimes against humanity under international public law;
3. war crimes;
4. other acts with the potential to and undertaken with intent to disturb the peaceful relations between nations (Article 26 I);
5. protection of the state.

Article 96a [repealed]

Article 97 [Independence of Judges]

(1) The judges are independent and subject only to the law.

(2) Judges appointed permanently on a full time basis in established positions cannot, against their will, be dismissed or permanently or temporarily suspended from office or given a different posting or retired before the expiration of their term of office except by virtue of a judicial decision and only on the grounds and in the form provided for by statute. [2]Legislation may set age limits for the retirement of judges appointed for life. [3]In the event of changes in the structure of courts or in their districts, judges may be transferred to another court or removed from office, provided they retain their full salary.

Article 98 [Legal Status of Judges]

(1) The legal status of the federal judges is regulated by a special federal statute.

(2) Where a federal judge, in his official capacity or unofficially, infringes the principles of this Constitution or the constitutional order of a State [Land], the Federal Constitutional Court may decide by a two-thirds majority, upon the request of the House of Representatives [Bundestag], that the judge be given a different office or retired. [2]In a case of intentional infringement, his dismissal may be ordered.

(3) The legal status of the judges in the States [Länder] is regulated by special State [Land] statutes, insofar as Article 74 I No. 27 does not provide otherwise.

(4) The States [Länder] may provide that the State [Land] minister of Justice

together with a committee for the selection of judges decides on the appointment of judges in the States [Länder].

(5) The States [Länder] may, in respect of State [Land] judges, enact provisions corresponding to those of Paragraph II. [2]Existing State [Land] constitutional law remains unaffected. [3]The decision in a case of impeachment of a judge rests with the Federal Constitutional Court.

Article 99 [Disputes Concerning State Law]

The decision on constitutional disputes within a State [Land] may be assigned by State [Land] legislation to the Federal Constitutional Court, and the decision at last instance in matters involving the application of State [Land] law to the highest courts of justice referred to in Article 95 I.

Article 100 [Constitutionality of Laws]

(1) Where a court considers that a statute on whose validity the court's decision depends is unconstitutional, the proceedings have to be stayed, and a decision has to be obtained from the State [Land] court with jurisdiction over constitutional disputes where the constitution of a State [Land] is held to be violated, or from the Federal Constitutional Court where this Constitution is held to be violated. [2]This also applies where this Constitution is held to be violated by State [Land] law or where a State [Land] statute is held to be incompatible with a federal statute.

(2) Where, in the course of litigation, doubt exists whether a rule of public international law is an integral part of federal law and whether such rule directly creates rights and duties for the individual (Article 25), the court obtains a decision from the Federal Constitutional Court.

(3) Where the constitutional court of a State [Land], in interpreting this Constitution, intends to deviate from a decision of the Federal Constitutional Court or of the constitutional court of another State [Land], it obtains a decision from the Federal Constitutional Court.

Article 101 [Ban on Extraordinary Courts]

(1) Extraordinary courts are inadmissible. [2]No one may be removed from the jurisdiction of his lawful judge.

(2) Courts for special fields of law may be established only by Legislation.

Article 102 [Abolishment of Capital Punishment]

Capital punishment is abolished.

Article 103 [Due Process]

(1) In the courts, everyone is entitled to a hearing in accordance with the law.

(2) An act can be punished only where it constituted a criminal offense under the law before the act was committed.

(3) No one may be punished for the same act more than once under general criminal legislation.

Article 104 [Legal Guarantees to Protect Liberty]

(1) The liberty of the individual may be restricted only by virtue of a formal statute and only in compliance with the forms prescribed therein. [2]Detained persons may not be subjected to mental or to physical ill treatment.
(2) Only judges may decide on the admissibility or continuation of any deprivation of liberty. [2]Where such deprivation is not based on the order of a judge, a judicial decision has to be obtained without delay. [3]The police may hold no one on their own authority in their own custody longer than the end of the day after the day of apprehension. [4]Details are regulated by legislation.
(3) Any person provisionally detained on suspicion of having committed an offense has to be brought, not later than the day following the day of apprehension, before a judge who has to inform him of the reasons for the detention, examine him, and give him an opportunity to raise objections. [2]The judge, without delay, has to either issue a warrant of arrest setting forth the reasons therefor or order his release from detention.
(4) A relative or a person enjoying the confidence of the person detained has to be notified without delay of any judicial decision imposing or ordering the continuation of his deprivation of liberty.

Chapter X

Finance

Article 104a [Apportionment of Expenditure]

(1) The Federation and the States [Länder] separately meet the expenditure resulting from the discharge of their respective tasks insofar as this Constitution does not provide otherwise.
(2) Where the States [Länder] act as agents of the Federation, the Federation meets the resulting expenditure.
(3) Federal statutes to be executed by the States [Länder] and granting money payments may make provision for such payments to be met wholly or in part by the Federation. [2]Where any such statute provides that the Federation meets one half of the expenditure or more, it is implemented by the States [Länder] as agents of the Federation.
(4) Federal statutes establishing duties of the States [Länder] to contribute money, benefits in kind, or similar services towards third parties and executed as matters of their own concern or according to Paragraph III 2 as agents of the Federation require the consent of the Senate [Bundesrat] if resulting expenses are to be met by the States [Länder].
(5) The Federation and the States [Länder] meet the administrative expenditure incurred by their respective authorities and are responsible to each other for ensuring proper administration. [2]Details are regulated by a federal statute requiring the consent of the Senate [Bundesrat].

(6) Federation and States [Länder] carry the burden resulting from supranational and international responsibilities of Germany according to the national division of competencies and responsibilities. [2]In cases of financial adjustments by the European Union affecting more than one State [Land], Federation and States [Länder] carry the burden at the ratio of 15 to 85. [3]The States at large provide 35% of the total burden in solidarity according to an allocation key; the States [Länder] which have caused the obligation carry 50% of the total burden according to their share in the funds received. [4]Details are regulated by a federal statute requiring the consent of the Senate [Bundesrat].

Article 104b [Financial Support for Investments]

(1) The Federation may, as far as this Constitution grants federal legislative power, provide the States [Länder] with financial support for particularly important investments by the States [Länder] or Communes (associations of communes), if such support is necessary

1. for the defense against a disturbance of the overall economic equilibrium, or
2. to equalize differences of economic performance throughout the federal territory, or
3. for the advancement of economic growth.

[2] In deviation from sentence 1, the Federation may, in the case of natural catastrophes or exceptional emergencies outside of state control and with serious negative impact on public finances, grant financial support even without legislative power.

(2) Details, in particular the kinds of investments to be supported, are regulated by a federal statute requiring the consent of the Senate [Bundesrat] or by administrative agreement on the basis of the federal statute about the budget. [2]The funds are provided with a time limit and are subject to periodic examination regarding their utilization. [3]Financial support has to be designed with decreasing yearly payments during its duration.

(3) On their request, House of Representatives [Bundestag], Government, and Senate [Bundesrat] have to receive a report about the implementation of the measures and about the improvements achieved.

Article 105 [Legislative Powers]

(1) The Federation has exclusive power to legislate on customs duties and fiscal monopolies.

(2) The Federation has concurrent power to legislate on all other taxes the revenue from which accrues to it wholly or in part or where the conditions provided for in Article 72 II apply.

(2a) The States [Länder] have power to legislate on local excise taxes as long and insofar as they are not identical with taxes imposed by federal legislation. [2]They have the power to set the rate for the tax on real estate sales.

(3) Federal laws relating to taxes the receipts from which accrue wholly or in part to the States [Länder] or communes or associations of communes require the consent of the Senate [Bundesrat].

Article 106 [Apportionment of Revenue]

(1) The yield of fiscal monopolies and the revenue from the following taxes belongs to the Federation:

1. customs duties;
2. excise taxes insofar as they do not accrue to the States [Länder] pursuant to Paragraph II, or jointly to the Federation and the States [Länder] in accordance with Paragraph III, or to the communes in accordance with Paragraph VI;
3. road freight tax, motor vehicle tax and other traffic taxes related to motorized vehicles;
4. capital transaction taxes, the insurance tax, and the bill of exchange tax;
5. nonrecurrent levies on property, and contributions imposed for the purpose of implementing the equalization of burdens legislation;
6. income and corporation surtaxes;
7. charges imposed within the framework of the European Communities.

(2) Revenue from the following taxes belong to the States [Länder]:

1. wealth tax;
2. inheritance tax;
3. such taxes on transactions as do not accrue to the Federation pursuant to Paragraph I or jointly to the Federation and the States [Länder] pursuant to Paragraph III;
4. beer tax;
5. gaming casinos levy.

(3) Revenues from income taxes, corporation taxes, and turnover taxes belong jointly to the Federation and the States [Länder] (joint taxes) to the extent that the revenue from the income tax and turnover tax is not allocated to the communes pursuant to Paragraphs V and Va respectively. [2]The Federation and the States [Länder] equally share the revenues from income taxes and corporation taxes. [3]The respective shares of the Federation and the States [Länder] in the revenue from the turnover tax are determined by a federal statute requiring the consent of the Senate [Bundesrat]. [4]Such determination is based on the following principles:

1. The Federation and the States [Länder] have an equal claim to coverage from current revenues of their respective necessary expenditures. [2]The extent of such expenditures is determined giving due consideration to financial planning for several years ahead.
2. The coverage requirements of the Federation and of the States [Länder] are coordinated in such a way that a fair balance is struck, any overbur-

dening of taxpayers precluded, and uniformity of living conditions in the federal territory ensured.

[5] In addition, for the apportionment of the value added tax to Federation and States [Länder] it will be taken into account that after 1 Jan. 1996 the States' [Länder] income tax revenues will be reduced due to child benefits. [6] Details are regulated by the federal statute according to Sentence 3.

(4) The respective shares of the Federation and the States [Länder] to the revenue from the turnover tax are newly apportioned whenever the relation of revenues to expenditures in the Federation develops substantially differently from that of the States [Länder]; this does not apply to reduced tax revenues which are included into the calculation of the apportionment of value added tax according to Paragraph III 5. [2]Where federal legislation imposes additional expenditures on or withdraws revenue from the States [Länder], the additional burden may be compensated for by allocation of federal grants under a federal statute requiring the consent of the Senate [Bundesrat], provided such additional burden is limited to a short period of time. [3]Such statute lays down the principles for calculating such grants and distributing them among the States [Länder].

(5) A share of the revenue from the income tax belongs to the communes, to be passed on by the States [Länder] to their communes on the basis of income taxes paid by the inhabitants of the latter. [2]Details are regulated by a federal statute requiring the consent of the Senate [Bundesrat]. [3]Such statute may provide that communes assess the rate which is applicable to this communal share.

(5a) From 1 Jan 1998, a share of the revenue from the turnover tax belongs to the communes. [2]This share is to be passed on by the States [Länder] to their communes on the basis of an index about locality and economic power. [3]Details are regulated by a federal statute requiring the consent of the Senate [Bundesrat].

(6) Revenue from taxes on real estate and on local industry and trade belongs to the communes; revenue from local excise taxes belongs to the communes or, as may be provided for by State [Land] legislation, to associations of communes. [2]Communes are authorized to assess, within the framework of the relevant statutes, the rates at which the taxes on real estate and on local industry and trade are levied locally. [3]Where there are no communes in a State [Land], revenue from taxes on real estate and on local industry and trade as well as from local excise taxes belongs to the State [Land]. [4]The Federation and the States [Länder] may participate, by virtue of an apportionment, in the revenue from the tax on local industry and trade. [5]Details regarding such apportionment are regulated by a federal statute requiring the consent of the Senate [Bundesrat]. [6]In accordance with State [Land] legislation, taxes on real estate and on local industry and trade as well as the communes' share of revenue from the income tax may be taken as a basis for calculating the amount of apportionment.

(7) An overall percentage, to be determined by State [Land] legislation, of the State [Land] share of total revenue from joint taxes belongs to the communes or associations of communes. [2]In all other respects State [Land] legislation determines whether and to what extent revenue from State [Land] taxes belong to communes or associations of communes.
(8) Where in individual States [Länder] or communes or associations of communes the Federation causes special facilities to be provided which directly result in an increase of expenditure or a loss of revenue (special burden) to these States [Länder] or communes or associations of communes, the Federation grants the necessary compensation where and insofar as such States [Länder] or communes or associations of communes cannot reasonably be expected to bear such special burden. [2]In granting such compensation, due account is being taken of third party indemnities and financial benefits accruing to the States [Länder] or communes or associations of communes concerned as a result of provision for such facilities.
(9) For the purpose of this Article, revenues and expenditures of communes or associations of communes are deemed to be State [Land] revenues and expenditures.

Article 106a [State Share for Public Local Transport]

Starting 1 Jan. 1996, the States [Länder] can claim a sum out of federal tax revenues for the public local transport of persons. [2]Details are regulated by a federal statute requiring the consent of the Senate [Bundesrat]. [3]The sum mentioned in the first sentence is not included in the calculation of financial strength according to Article 107 II.

Article 106b [Compensation for Transfer of Motor Vehicle Tax]

Starting 1 July 2009, the States [Länder] can claim a sum out of federal tax revenues for the transfer of the motor vehicle tax to the Federation. [2]Details are regulated by a federal statute requiring the consent of the Senate [Bundesrat].

Article 107 [Financial Equalization]

(1) Revenue from State [Land] taxes and the State [Land] share of revenue from income and corporation taxes belongs to the individual States [Länder] to the extent that such taxes are collected by revenue authorities within their respective territories (local revenue). [2]A federal statute requiring the consent of the Senate [Bundesrat] may provide in detail for the delimitation as well as the manner and scope of allotment of local revenue from corporation and wage taxes. [3]Such statute may also provide for the delimitation and allotment of local revenue from other taxes. [4]The State [Land] share of revenue from the turnover tax belongs to the individual States [Länder] on a per capita basis; a federal statute requiring the consent of the Senate [Bundesrat] may provide for supplementary shares not exceeding one quarter of a State [Land] share to be granted to States [Länder] whose per capita revenue from

State [Land] taxes, from the income and corporation taxes and according to Article 106b is below the average of all the States [Länder] combined; in the case of real estate transfer tax, the difference in revenue has to be taken into account.

(2) It has to be ensured by statute, that a reasonable equalization between financially strong and financially weak States [Länder] is achieved; due consideration being given to financial capacity and financial requirements of communes or associations of communes. [2]Such statute has to specify the conditions governing equalization claims of States [Länder] entitled to equalization payments and equalization liabilities of States [Länder] owing equalization payments as well as the criteria for determining the amounts of equalization payments. [3]Such statute may also provide for grants to be made by the Federation from federal funds to financially weak States [Länder] in order to complement the coverage of their general financial requirements (supplementary grants).

Article 108 [Revenue Administration]

(1) Customs duties, fiscal monopolies, excise taxes subject to federal legislation, including the import turnover tax, motor vehicle tax and other traffic taxes related to motorized vehicles as well as charges imposed within the framework of the European Communities are administered by federal revenue authorities. [2]The organization of these authorities is regulated by federal statute. [3]Where authorities at the intermediate level are established, their heads are appointed in consultation with the respective State [Land] governments.

(2) All other taxes are administered by State [Land] revenue authorities. [2]The organization of these authorities and the uniform training of their civil servants may be regulated by a federal statute requiring the consent of the Senate [Bundesrat]. [3]Where authorities at the intermediate level are established, their heads are appointed in agreement with the Government.

(3) To the extent that taxes accruing wholly or in part to the Federation are administered by State [Land] revenue authorities, those authorities act as agents of the Federation. [2]Article 85 III & IV applies with the Minister of Finance being substituted for the Government.

(4) Regarding the administration of taxes, a federal statute requiring the consent of the Senate [Bundesrat] may provide for collaboration between federal and state revenue authorities as well as, for taxes according to Paragraph I, for their administration by state revenue authorities, and, in the case of other taxes, for their administration by federal revenue authorities, if and insofar as the implementation of revenue statutes is substantially improved or facilitated. [2]Regarding taxes the revenue from which belongs exclusively to communes (associations of communes), the administration may completely or in part be transferred by the States [Länder] from the appropriate state revenue authorities to communes (associations of communes).

(5) The procedure to be applied by federal revenue authorities is laid down by federal legislation. [2]The procedure to be applied by State revenue authorities or, as envisaged in Paragraph IV 2, by communes or associations of communes may be laid down by a federal statute requiring the consent of the Senate [Bundesrat].
(6) The jurisdiction of revenue courts is uniformly regulated by federal legislation.
(7) The Government may issue appropriate general administrative rules which, to the extent that administration is entrusted to State revenue authorities or communes or associations of communes, require the consent of the Senate [Bundesrat].

Article 109 [Budget Management]

(1) The Federation and the States [Länder] are autonomous and independent of each other in their budget management.
(2) The Federation and the States [Länder] give due regard in their budget management to the requirements of overall economic equilibrium.
(3) The budgets of Federation and States [Länder] principally have to be balanced without revenue from credits. [2]Federation and States [Länder] may adopt rules to symmetrically balance in boom and bust periods the effects of economic cycles deviating from normality as well as exceptions for natural catastrophes or exceptional emergencies outside of state control and with serious negative impact on public finances. [3]Equivalent amortization rules have to be adopted for exceptions. [4]Details are regulated for the budget of the Federation according to Article 115, provided that sentence 1 is complied with if revenues from credits do not exceed 0.35 percent in relation to the nominal gross domestic product. [5]Details are regulated for the budget of the States [Länder] within their constitutional competencies, provided that sentence 1 is only complied with if no revenues from credits are admitted.
(4) Through federal legislation requiring the consent of the Senate [Bundesrat] principles applicable to both the Federation and the States [Länder] may be established governing budgetary law, responsiveness of budget management to economic trends, and financial planning to cover several years ahead.
(5) Sanctions by the European Community with regard to provisions in Article 104 of the Treaty establishing the European Community about the observance of fiscal discipline are borne by the Federation and the States [Länder] in the ratio 65 to 35.

Article 109a [Stability Council]

To prevent budget emergencies, a federal statute requiring the consent of the Senate [Bundesrat] provides for

1. continuous control of the budget management of Federation and States [Länder] by a common body (stability council),
2. preconditions and procedure for the declaration of an imminent budget emergency,

3. principles for the establishment and implementation of restructuring programs to prevent budget emergencies.

[2]The decisions of the stability council and the documentation of its deliberation have to be published.

Article 110 [Budget Law]

(1) All revenues and expenditures of the Federation are included in the budget; in respect of federal enterprises and special assets, only allocations thereto or remittances therefrom need be included. [2]The budget has to be balanced as regards revenue and expenditure.
(2) The budget is laid down in a statute covering one year or several fiscal years separately before the beginning of the first of those fiscal years. [2]Provision may be made for parts of the budget to apply to periods of different duration, but divided into fiscal years.
(3) Bills within the meaning of Paragraph II 1 as well as bills to amend the budget statute and the budget are submitted simultaneously to the Senate [Bundesrat] and to the House of Representatives [Bundestag]; the Senate [Bundesrat] is entitled to state its position on such bills within six weeks or, in the case of amending bills, within three weeks.
(4) The budget statute may contain only such provisions as apply to revenues and expenditures of the Federation and to the period for which the budget statute is being enacted. [2]The budget statute may stipulate that these provisions cease to apply only upon the promulgation of the next budget statute or, in the event of an authorization pursuant to Article 115, at a later date.

Article 111 [Interim Budget]

(1) Where, by the end of a fiscal year, the budget for the following year has not been laid down by statute, the Government may, until such statute comes into force, make all payments which are necessary:

    (a) to maintain statutory institutions and to carry out measures authorized by statute;
    (b) to meet the Federation's legal obligations;
    (c) to continue building projects, procurements, and other services, or to continue to grant subsidies for these purposes, provided that amounts have already been appropriated in the budget of a previous year.

(2) To the extent that revenues provided by specific legislation and derived from taxes or duties or any other sources, or the working capital reserves, do not cover the expenditures referred to in Paragraph I, the Government may borrow the funds necessary for the conduct of current operations up to a maximum of one quarter of the total amount of the previous budget.

Article 112 [Excessive Expenditures]

Expenditures in excess of budgetary appropriations and extra budgetary expenditures require the consent or the Minister or Finance. [2]Such consent may be given only in the case of an unforeseen and compelling necessity. [3]Details may be regulated by federal legislation.

Article 113 [Changing of Expenditures/Revenues]

(1) Statutes increasing the budget expenditures proposed by the Government or involving or likely in future to cause new expenditures requires the consent of the Government. [2]This also applies to statutes involving or likely in future to cause decreases in revenue. [3]The Government may demand that the House of Representatives [Bundestag] postpone its vote on such bills. [4]In this case the Government states its position to the House of Representatives [Bundestag] within six weeks.
(2) Within four weeks after the House of Representatives [Bundestag] has adopted such a bill, the Government may demand that it votes on that bill again.
(3) Where the bill has become a statute pursuant to Article 78, the Government may withhold its consent only within six weeks and only after having initiated the procedure provided for Paragraph I 3 & 4 or in Paragraph II. [2] Upon the expiry of this period such consent is deemed to have been given.

Article 114 [Audit]

(1) The Minister of Finance on behalf of the Government has to submit annually to the House of Representatives [Bundestag] and to the Senate [Bundesrat] for their approval an account, covering the preceding fiscal year, of all revenues and expenditures as well as of property and debt.
(2) The Federal Audit Office, the members of which enjoy judicial independence, audits the account and examines the management of the budget and the conduct of business as to economy and correctness. [2]The Federal Audit Office submits an annual report directly to the Government as well as to the House of Representatives [Bundestag] and to the Senate [Bundesrat]. [3]In all other respects the powers of the Federal Audit Office are regulated by federal legislation.

Article 115 [State Credit]

(1) The borrowing of funds and the assumption of pledges, guarantees or other commitments, as a result of which expenditure may be incurred in future fiscal years, requires federal legislative authorization indicating, or permitting computation of, the maximum amounts involved.
(2) Revenue and expenditure are principally to be balanced without revenues from credits. [2]This principle is satisfied if revenues from credits do not exceed 0.35 percent in relation to the nominal gross domestic product.

[3]Furthermore, in the case of economic cycles deviating from normality, effects on the budget have to be factored in by symmetrically balancing boom and bust periods. [4]Deviations of actual borrowing from the credit limit outlined by sentences 1 to 3 are to be registered on a control account; debits exceeding the threshold of 1.5 percent in relation to the nominal gross domestic product have to be reduced with the economic cycle. [5]Details, particularly the balancing of revenue and expenditure by financial transactions and the procedure for the calculation of the yearly limit of net borrowing in consideration of the economic cycle on the basis of an economic cycle equalization procedure as well as the control and readjustment of effective borrowing against the credit limit, are regulated by a federal statute. [6]In the case of natural catastrophes or exceptional emergencies outside of state control and with serious negative impact on public finances, these credit limits may be exceeded by a decision of the majority of the members of the House of Representatives [Bundestag]. [7]The decision has to be combined with an amortization plan. [8]The readjustment of borrowing according to sentence 6 has to be carried out within an adequate space of time.

Chapter Xa

State of Defense

Article 115a [State of Defense]

(1) The determination that federal territory is being attacked by armed force or that such an attack is directly imminent (state of defense) are made by the House of Representatives [Bundestag] with the consent of the Senate [Bundesrat]. [2]Such determination are made at the request of the Government and require a two-thirds majority of the votes cast, which include at least the majority of the members of the House of Representatives [Bundestag].

(2) Where the situation imperatively calls for immediate action and where insurmountable obstacles prevent the timely assembly of the House of Representatives [Bundestag], or where there is no quorum in the House of Representatives [Bundestag], the Joint Committee makes this determination with a two-thirds majority of the votes cast, which includes at least the majority of its members.

(3) The determination is promulgated in the Federal Law Gazette by the President pursuant to Article 82. [2]Where this cannot be done in time, the promulgation is effected in another manner; subsequently, it has to be printed in the Federal Law Gazette as soon as circumstances permit.

(4) Where the federal territory is being attacked by armed force and where the competent bodies of the Federation are not in a position at once to make the determination provided for in Paragraph I 1, such determination is deemed to have been made and promulgated at the time the attack began. [2]The President announces such time as soon as circumstances permit.

(5) Where the determination of the existence of a state of defense has been promulgated and where the federal territory is being attacked by armed force, the President may, with the consent of the House of Representatives [Bundestag], issue declarations under international law regarding the existence of such state of defense. [2]Where the conditions mentioned in Paragraph II apply, the Joint Committee acts in substitution for the House of Representatives [Bundestag].

Article 115b [Command of the Chancellor]

Upon the promulgation of a state of defense, the power of command over the Armed Forces passes to the Chancellor.

Article 115c [Extension of Legislative Powers]

(1) The Federation has the right to legislate concurrently in respect of a state of defense even on matters within the legislative powers of the States [Länder]. [2]Such statutes require the consent of the Senate [Bundesrat].
(2) Federal legislation to be applicable upon the occurrence of a state of defense to the extent required by conditions obtaining while such state of defense exists may make:

   1. preliminary provision for compensation to be made in the event of property being taken, in derogation of Article 14 III 2;
   2. provision for a time limit other than that referred to in Article 104 II 3 & III 1 in respect of deprivations of liberty, but not exceeding four days at the most, in a case where no judge has been able to act within the time limit applying in normal times.

(3) Federal legislation to be applicable upon the occurrence of a state of defense to the extent required for averting an existing or directly imminent attack may, subject to the consent of the Senate [Bundesrat], regulate the administration and the financial system of the Federation and the States [Länder] in derogation of Sections VIII, VIIIa and X, provided that the viability of the States [Länder], communes and associations of communes is safeguarded, particularly in financial matters.
(4) Federal statutes enacted pursuant to Paragraph I or Subparagraph 1 of Paragraph II may, for the purpose of preparing for their enforcement, be applied even prior to the occurrence of a state of defense.

Article 115d [Legislative Process for Urgent Bills]

(1) While a state of defense exists, the provisions of Paragraphs II and III apply in respect of federal legislation, in derogation of the provisions of Articles 76 II, 77 I 2 & II to IV, 78, and 82 I.
(2) Bills submitted as urgent by the Government are forwarded to the Senate [Bundesrat] at the same time as they are submitted to the House of Representatives [Bundestag]. [2]The House of Representatives [Bundestag] and

the Senate [Bundesrat] debate such bills together without delay. [3]Insofar as the consent of the Senate [Bundesrat] is necessary, the majority of its votes is required for any such bill to become a statute. [4]Details are regulated by rules of procedure adopted by the House of Representatives [Bundestag] and requiring the consent of the Senate [Bundesrat].

(3) Article 115a III 2 also applies in respect of the promulgation of such statutes.

Article 115e [Powers of Joint Committee]

(1) Where, in a state of defense, the Joint Committee determines with a two-thirds majority of the votes cast, which includes at least the majority of its members, that insurmountable obstacles prevent the timely assembly of the House of Representatives [Bundestag] or that there is no quorum in the House of Representatives [Bundestag], the Joint Committee has the status of both the House of Representatives [Bundestag] and the Senate [Bundesrat] and exercises their rights as one body.

(2) The Joint Committee may not enact any statute to amend this Constitution or to deprive it of effect or application either in whole or in part. [2]The Joint Committee is not authorized to enact statutes pursuant to Articles 23 I 2, 24 I, or 29.

Article 115f [Powers of Government]

(1) In a state of defense, the Government may, to the extent necessitated by circumstances:

1. use the Federal Border Guard throughout the federal territory;
2. issue instructions not only to federal administrative authorities but also to State [Land] governments and, where it deems the matter urgent, to State [Land] authorities, and may delegate this power to members of State [Land] governments to be designated by it.

(2) The House of Representatives [Bundestag], the Senate [Bundesrat] and the Joint Committee is informed without delay of the measures taken in accordance with Paragraph I.

Article 115g [Functions of Federal Constitutional Court]

The constitutional status and the performance of the constitutional functions of the Federal Constitutional Court and its judges may not be impaired. [2]The Federal Constitutional Court Act may not be amended by a statute enacted by the Joint Committee except insofar as such amendment is required, also in the opinion of the Federal Constitutional Court, to maintain the capability of the Court to function. [3]Pending the enactment of such a statute, the Federal Constitutional Court may take such measures as are necessary to maintain the capability of the Court to carry out its work. [4]Any decisions by the Federal Constitutional Court in pursuance of the second and third sentence of this Article requires a two-thirds majority of the judges present.

Article 115h [Constitutional Institutions]

(1) Any legislative terms of the House of Representatives [Bundestag] or of State [Land] parliaments due to end while a state of defense exists end six months after the termination of such state of defense. [2]A term of office of the President due to expire while a state of defense exists, and the exercise of his functions by the President of the Senate [Bundesrat] in case of the premature vacancy of the President's office, ends nine months after the termination of such state of defense. [3]The term of office of a member of the Federal Constitutional Court due to expire while a state of defense exists ends six months after the termination of such state of defense.
(2) Should the necessity arise for the Joint Committee to elect a new Chancellor, the Committee does so with the majority of its members; the President proposes a candidate to the Joint Committee. [2]The Joint Committee can express its lack of confidence in the Chancellor only by electing a successor with a two-thirds majority of its members.
(3) The dissolution of the House of Representatives [Bundestag] is impossible during a state of defense.

Article 115i [State Governments]

(1) Where the competent federal bodies are incapable of taking the measures necessary to avert the danger, and where the situation imperatively calls for immediate independent action in individual parts of the federal territory, the State [Land] governments or the authorities or commissioners designated by them are authorized to take, within their respective spheres of competence, the measures provided for in Article 115f I.
(2) Any measures taken in accordance with Paragraph I of the present Article may be revoked at any time by the Government, or, in relation to State [Land] authorities and subordinate federal authorities, by State [Land] minister presidents.

Article 115k [Extraordinary Legal Provisions]

(1) Statutes enacted in accordance with Articles 115c, 115e, and 115g, as well as ordinances issued by virtue of such statutes, for the duration of their applicability suspend law which is inconsistent with such statutes or ordinances. [2]This provision does not apply to earlier legislation enacted by virtue of Articles 115c, 115e or 115g.
(2) Statutes adopted by the Joint Committee, as well as ordinances issued by virtue of such statutes, cease to have effect not later than six months after the termination of a state of defense.
(3) Statutes containing provisions that diverge from Articles 91a, 91b, 104a, 106 and 107 applies no longer than the end of the second fiscal year following upon the termination of a state of defense. [2]After such termination they may, with the consent of the Senate [Bundesrat], be amended by federal legislation so as to return to the provisions made in Sections VIIIa and X.

Article 115l [Repeal of Extraordinary Measures]

(1) The House of Representatives [Bundestag], with the consent of the Senate [Bundesrat], may at any time repeal statutes enacted by the Joint Committee. [2]The Senate [Bundesrat] may demand that the House of Representatives [Bundestag] make a decision on such matter. [3]Any measures taken by the Joint Committee or the Government to avert a danger has to be revoked where the House of Representatives [Bundestag] and the Senate [Bundesrat] so decide.
(2) The House of Representatives [Bundestag], with the consent of the Senate [Bundesrat], may at any time declare a state of defense terminated by a decision to be promulgated by the President. [2]The Senate [Bundesrat] may demand that the House of Representatives [Bundestag] make a decision on such matter. [3]The state of defense has to be declared terminated without delay where the prerequisites for its declaration no longer exist.
(3) The conclusion of peace is subject to federal statute.

Chapter XI

Transitional and Concluding Provisions

Article 116 [Definition of "a German"]

(1) Unless otherwise provided by statute, a German within the meaning of this Constitution is a person who possesses German citizenship or who has been admitted to the territory of the German Reich within the frontiers of 31 December 1937 as a refugee or expellee of German ethnic origin or as the spouse or descendant of such a person.
(2) Former German citizens who, between 30 January 1933 and 8 May 1945, were deprived of their citizenship on political, racial or religious grounds, and their descendants, are re-granted German citizenship on application. [2]They are considered as not having been deprived of their German citizenship where they have established their residence in Germany after 8 May 1945 and have not expressed a contrary intention.

Article 117 [Articles 3 II, 11]

(1) Law which is inconsistent with Article 3 II remain in force until adapted to that provision of this Constitution, but not beyond 31 March, 1953.
(2) Statutes which restrict the right of freedom of movement in view of the present housing shortage remain in force until repealed by federal legislation.

Article 118 [Baden, Wurttemberg]

A new demarcation of the territory comprising the States [Länder] of Baden, Wurttemberg-Baden and Wurttemberg-Hohenzollern may be effected, in derogation of the provisions of Article 29, by agreement between the States [Länder] concerned. [2]Where no agreement is reached, the reorganization is effected by federal legislation which provides for a plebiscite.

Article 118a [Berlin, Brandenburg]

The new delimitation of boundaries between Berlin and Brandenburg can, differing from the provisions of Article 29, be constituted by agreement between both States [Länder] under participation of their electorate.

Article 119 [Refugees, Expellees]

In matters relating to refugees and expellees, in particular as regards their distribution among the States [Länder], the Government may, with the consent of the Senate [Bundesrat], issue ordinances having statutory effect, pending the settlement of the matter by federal legislation. [2]The Government may in this matter be authorized to issue individual instructions for particular cases. [3]Except where there is danger resulting in any delay in taking action, such instructions are addressed to the highest State [Land] authorities.

Article 120 [Occupation Expenditure]

(1) The Federation meets the expenditure for occupation costs and the other internal and external burdens caused by the war, as regulated in detail by federal legislation. [2]To the extent that these costs and other burdens have been regulated by federal legislation on or before 1 Oct. 1969, the Federation and the States [Länder] meet such expenditure between them in accordance with such federal legislation. [3]Insofar as expenditures for such of these costs and burdens as neither have been nor will be regulated by federal legislation have been met on or before I October 1965 by States [Länder], communes, associations of communes or other entities performing functions of the States [Länder] or the communes, the Federation is not obliged to meet expenditure of that nature even where it arises after that date. [4]The Federation pays the subsidies towards the burdens of social insurance institutions, including unemployment insurance and public assistance to the unemployed. [5]The distribution between the Federation and the States [Länder] of costs and other burdens caused by the war, as regulated in this paragraph, does not affect any statutory regulation of claims for indemnification in respect of the consequences of the war.
(2) Revenues pass to the Federation at the same time as the latter assumes responsibility for the expenditure referred to in this Article.

Article 120a [Equalization of Burdens]

(1) Statutes serving to implement the equalization of burdens may, with the consent of the Senate [Bundesrat], stipulate that they are executed, as regards equalization benefits, partly by the Federation and partly by the States [Länder] acting as agents of the Federation, and that the relevant powers vested in the Government and the competent highest federal authorities by virtue of Article 85 are wholly or partly delegated to the Federal Equalization Office. [2]In exercising these powers, the Federal Equalization Office does not require the consent of the Senate [Bundesrat]; with the exception of urgent

cases, its instructions has to be given to the highest State [Land] authorities (State Equalization Offices).

(2) The provisions of Article 87 III 2 are not affected hereby.

Article 121 [Definition of "Majority"]

Within the meaning of this Constitution, a majority of the members of the House of Representatives [Bundestag] and a majority of the members of the Federal Convention are the majority of the respective statutory number of their members.

Article 122 [Transfer of Legislative Powers]

(1) From the date of the assembly of the House of Representatives [Bundestag], statutes are enacted exclusively by the legislative bodies recognized in this Constitution.

(2) Legislative bodies as well as those bodies participating in legislation in an advisory capacity, whose competence ends by virtue of Paragraph I, are dissolved with effect from that date.

Article 123 [Validity of Old Law and Treaties]

(1) Law in force before the first assembly of the House of Representatives [Bundestag] remains in force insofar as it does not conflict with this Constitution.

(2) Subject to all rights and objections of the interested parties, the treaties concluded by the German Reich concerning matters which, under this Constitution, are within the legislative competence of the States [Länder], remain in force, provided they are and continue to be valid in accordance with general principles of law, until new treaties are concluded by the agencies competent under this Constitution, or until they are in any other way terminated pursuant to their provisions.

Article 124 [Sphere of Exclusive Legislative Power]

Law affecting matters subject to the exclusive legislative power of the Federation becomes federal law in the area in which it applies.

Article 125 ["Inherited" Federal Law]

Law affecting matters subject to the concurrent legislative power of the Federation becomes federal law in the area in which it applies:

1. insofar as it applies uniformly within one or more zones of occupation;
2. insofar as it is law by which former Reich law has been amended after 8 May 1945.

Article 125a [Old Federal Law as State Law]

(1) Law adopted as federal law which, because of changes in Article 74 I, insertion of Articles 84 I 7, 85 I 2 or 105 IIa 2 or because of the repeal of Articles 74a, 75 or 98 III 2, could no longer be adopted as federal law continues to be federal law. [2]It can be replaced by State [Land] law.

(2) Law adopted on the basis of Article 72 II in the version valid until 15 Nov. 1994, but no longer admissible as federal statute because of the change in Article 72 II, continues to be federal law. [2]Federal statutes can stipulate its replaceability by State [Land] law.
(3) Law adopted as State [Land] law, but no longer adoptable as State [Land] law due to Article 73, continues to be valid as State [Land] law. [2]It may be replaced by federal law.

Article 125b [Framework Legislation, Deviation]

(1) Law adopted on the basis of Article 75 in the form valid until 1st September 2006 and still adoptable as federal law thereafter continues to be valid as federal law. [2]In this respect, the States' [Länder] powers and responsibilities to legislate continue to exist. [3]Regarding the subjects mentioned in Article 72 III 1, the States [Länder] may adopt divergent rules, however, regarding the subjects of Article 72 III 1 Numbers 2, 5, and 6 only if and insofar as the Federation, after 1st September 2006, has used its legislative power, in the case of Numbers 2 and 5 on 1st January 2010 at the latest, in the case of Number 6 on 1st August 2008 at the latest.
(2) The States [Länder] may adopt rules diverging from federal statutes adopted on the basis of Article 84 I in the form valid until 1st September 2006, however, regarding administrative procedures only until 31st December 2008 and only if the administrative procedures in the respective federal statute have been changed after 1st September 2006.

Article 125c [Law Regarding Joint Tasks]

(1) Law adopted on the basis of Article 91a II in conjunction with Paragraph I Number 1 in the form valid until 1st September 2006 continue to be valid until 31st December 2006.
(2) Rules regarding financial assistance to communes and for rent-controlled apartments adopted on the basis of Article 104a IV in the form valid until 1st September 2006 continue to be valid until 31st December 2006. [2]Special programs regarding financial assistance for traffic in communes based on § 6 I of the Statute About Communal Traffic Financing as well as other rules adopted on the basis of Article 104a IV in the form valid until 1st September 2006 continue to be valid until 31st December 2019, provided no earlier expiration date has been or will be set.

Article 126 [Applicability of Law as Federal Law]

Differences of opinion regarding the applicability of law as federal law are settled by the Federal Constitutional Court.

Article 127 [Bi-zonal Economic Administration]

Within one year of the promulgation of this Constitution the Government may, with the consent of the governments of the States [Länder] concerned, extend to the States [Länder] of Baden, Greater Berlin, Rhineland-Palatinate and Wurttemberg-

Hohenzollern any legislation of the Bi-zonal Economic Administration, insofar as it continues to be in force as federal law under Article 124 or 125.

Article 128 [Continuance of Powers to Give Instructions]

Insofar as law continuing in force provides for powers to give instructions within the meaning of Article 84 V, these powers remain in existence until otherwise provided by statute.

Article 129 [Applicability of Authorizations]

(1) Insofar as legal provisions which continue in force as federal law contain authorizations to issue ordinances or to issue general administrative rules or to perform administrative acts, such authorizations pass to the agencies henceforth competent in the matter. [2]In cases of doubt, the Government decides in agreement with the Senate [Bundesrat]; such decisions are published.
(2) Insofar as legal provisions which continue in force as State [Land] law contain such authorizations, they are exercised by the agencies competent under State [Land] law.
(3) Insofar as legal provisions within the meaning of Paragraphs I and II authorize their amendment or supplementation or the issue of legal instead of statutory provisions, such authorizations are deemed to have expired.
(4) The provisions of Paragraphs I and II also apply where legal provisions refer to regulations no longer valid or to institutions no longer in existence.

Article 130 [Control Over Existing Institutions]

(1) Administrative agencies and other institutions which serve the public administration or the administration of justice and are not based on State [Land] law or treaties between States [Länder], as well as the Administrative Union of South West German Railroads and the Administrative Council for the Postal Services and Telecommunications of the French Zone of Occupation, are placed under the control of the Government. [2]The Government provides, with the consent of the Senate [Bundesrat], for their transfer, dissolution, or liquidation.
(2) The highest disciplinary superior of the personnel of these administrative bodies and institutions is the appropriate Minister.
(3) Corporate bodies and institutions under public law not directly subordinate to a State [Land] nor based on treaties between States [Länder] are under the supervision of the competent highest federal authority.

Article 131 [Former Public Service Personnel]

Federal legislation is passed to regulate the legal position of persons, including refugees and expellees, who, on 8 May, 1945, were employed in the public service, have left the service for reasons other than those arising from civil service regulations or collective agreement rules, and have not until now been reinstated or are employed in a position not corresponding to their former one. [2]The same rule is applicable to persons, including refugees and expellees, who, on 8 May, 1945, were entitled to a pension and who no longer receive any such pension or any commensurate pension for reasons other than those arising from civil service regulations or collective agreement rules. [3]Until the pertinent federal statute comes into force, no legal claims can be made, unless otherwise provided by State [Land] legislation.

Article 132 Public Service Rights]

(1) Civil servants and judges who, when this Constitution comes into force are appointed for life, may, within six months after the first assembly of the House of Representatives [Bundestag], be retired or temporarily retired or be given a different office with lower remuneration where they lack the personal or professional aptitude for their present office. [2]This provision also applies to salaried public employees, other than civil servants or judges, whose service cannot be terminated by notice. [3]Where, however, such service can be terminated by notice, periods of notice in excess of the periods fixed by collective agreement rules may be cancelled within the six months referred to above.
(2) The preceding provision does not apply to members of the public service who are not affected by the provisions regarding the "Liberation from National Socialism and Militarism" or who are recognized victims of National Socialism, except on important grounds relating to themselves as individuals.
(3) Those affected may have recourse to the courts in accordance with Article 19 IV.
(4) Details are specified by an ordinance of the Government requiring the consent of the Senate [Bundesrat].

Article 133 [Bi-zonal Economic Administration]

The Federation succeeds to the rights and obligations of the Bi-zonal Economic Administration.

Article 134 [Reich Property]

(1) Reich property on principle becomes federal property.
(2) Insofar as such property was originally intended to be used predominantly for administrative tasks which, under this Constitution, are not administrative tasks of the Federation, it is transferred without compensation to the agencies now charged with such tasks, and to the States [Länder] insofar as it is being used at present, and not merely temporarily, for administrative tasks which under this Constitution are now within the administrative competence of the States [Länder]. [2]The Federation may also transfer other property to the States [Länder].
(3) Property which was placed at the disposal of the Reich by States [Länder] or communes or associations of communes without compensation again becomes the property of such States [Länder] or communes or associations

of communes, insofar as it is not required by the Federation for its own administrative tasks.

(4) Details are regulated by a federal statute requiring the consent of the Senate [Bundesrat].

Article 135 [Property of Old States]

(1) Where after 8 May 1945 and before the coming into force of this Constitution an area has passed from one State [Land] to another, the State [Land] to which the area now belongs is entitled to the property located therein of the State [Land] to which it belonged.

(2) Property of States [Länder] or corporate bodies or institutions under public law which no longer exist passes, insofar as it was originally intended to be used predominantly for administrative tasks or is being used at present, and not merely temporarily, predominantly for administrative tasks, to the State [Land] or the corporate body or institution under public law which now discharges these tasks.

(3) Real estate of States [Länder] which no longer exist, including accessories, passes to the State [Land] within which it is located, insofar as it is not included among property within the meaning of Paragraph I.

(4) Where an overriding interest of the Federation or the particular interest of an area so requires, a settlement other than in Paragraphs I to III may be effected by federal legislation.

(5) In all other respects, the succession in title and the settlement of the property, insofar as it has not been effected before 1 January 1952 by agreement between the States [Länder] or corporate bodies or institutions under public law concerned, is regulated by federal legislation requiring the consent of the Senate [Bundesrat].

(6) Interests of the former State of Prussia in enterprises under private law passes to the Federation. [2]A federal statute, which may also diverge from this provision, regulates the details.

(7) Insofar as property which on the coming into force of this Constitution would devolve upon a State [Land] or a corporate body or institution under public law pursuant to Paragraphs I to III has been disposed of through or by virtue of a State [Land] law or in any other manner by the party thus entitled, the transfer of the property is deemed to have taken place before such disposition.

Article 135a [Old Liabilities]

(1) The legislation reserved to the Federation in Article 134 IV and in Article 135 V may also stipulate that the following liabilities are not discharged, or not to their full extent:

1. Liabilities of the Reich or liabilities of the former State of Prussia or liabilities of such corporate bodies and institutions under public law as no longer exist;

2. such liabilities of the Federation or corporate bodies and institutions under public law as are connected with the transfer of properties pursuant to Articles 89, 90, 134 or 135, and such liabilities of these entities as arise from measures taken by the entities mentioned under No. 1;
3. such liabilities of States [Länder] or communes or associations of communes as have arisen from measures taken by these legal entities before 1 August 1945 within the framework of administrative functions incumbent upon or delegated by the Reich to comply with regulations of occupying powers or to put an end to a state of emergency due to the war.

(2) Paragraph I above also applies to liabilities of the German Democratic Republic or its legal entities as well as to liabilities of the Federation or other corporate bodies and institutions under public law which are connected with the transfer of properties of the German Democratic Republic to the Federation, States [Länder] and communes, and to liabilities arising from measures taken by the German Democratic Republic or its legal entities.

Article 136 [First Assembly of Senate]

(1) The Senate [Bundesrat] assembles for the first time on the day of the first assembly of the House of Representatives [Bundestag].
(2) Until the election of the first President, his powers are exercised by the President of the Senate [Bundesrat]. [2]He does not have the right to dissolve the House of Representatives [Bundestag].

Article 137 [Eligibility of Civil Servants]

(1) The right of civil servants, of other salaried public employees, of professional soldiers, of temporary volunteer soldiers or of judges to stand for election in the Federation, in the States [Länder] or in the communes may be restricted by legislation.
(2) The electoral statute to be adopted by the Parliamentary Council applies to the election of the first House of Representatives [Bundestag], of the first Federal Convention and of the first President of the Federal Republic.
(3) The function of the Federal Constitutional Court pursuant to Article 41 II, pending its establishment, is exercised by the German High Court for the Combined Economic Area, which decides in accordance with its rules of procedure.

Article 138 [Southern German Notaries]

Changes in notarial institutions as presently existing in the States [Länder] of Baden, Bavaria, Wurttemberg-Baden and Wurttemberg-Hohenzollern require the consent of the governments of these States [Länder].

Article 139 [Denazification Laws]

The legislation enacted for the "Liberation of the German People from National Socialism and Militarism" is not affected by the provisions of this Constitution.

Article 140 [Law of Religious Bodies]

The provisions of Articles 136, 137, 138, 139 and 141 of the German Constitution of 11 August 1919 are integral parts of this Constitution.

Article 136 WRV [Civil and Political Rights]

(1) Civil and political rights and duties are neither dependent on nor restricted by the exercise of the freedom of religion.
(2) Enjoyment of civil and political rights and eligibility for public office are independent of religious denomination.
(3) No one is bound to disclose his religious convictions. [2]The authorities have no right to inquire into a person's membership of a religious body except to the extent that rights or duties depend thereon or that a statistical survey ordered by law makes it necessary.
(4) No one may be compelled to perform any religious act or ceremony or to participate in religious exercises or to use a religious form of oath.

Article 137 WRV [State Church]

(1) There is no state church.
(2) Freedom of association to form religious bodies is guaranteed. [2]The union of religious bodies within the territory of the Reich is not subject to any restrictions.
(3) Every religious body regulates and administers its affairs autonomously within the limits of the law valid for all. [2]It confers its offices without the Participation of the state or the civil community.
(4) Religious bodies acquire legal capacity according to the general provisions of civil law.
(5) Religious bodies remain corporate bodies under public law insofar as they have been such heretofore. [2]The other religious bodies are granted like rights upon application, where their constitution and the number of their members offers an assurance of their permanency. [3]Where several such religious bodies under public law unite in one organization, such organization is a corporate body under public law.
(6) Religious bodies that are corporate bodies under public law are entitled to levy taxes in accordance with State [Land] law on the basis of the civil taxation lists.
(7) Associations whose purpose is the common cultivation of a philosophical persuasion have the same status as religious bodies.
(8) Such further regulation as may be required for the implementation of these provisions is a matter for State [Land] legislation.

Article 138 WRV [Church Property]

(1) State [Land] contributions to religious bodies, based on law or contract or special legal title, are redeemed by means of State [Land] legislation. [2]The principles for such redemption are established by the Reich.

(2) The right to own property and other rights of religious bodies or associations in respect of their institutions, foundations, and other assets destined for purposes of worship, education or charity are guaranteed.

Article 139 WRV [Sunday and Holidays]

Sunday and the public holidays recognized by the state remain legally protected as days of rest from work and of spiritual edification.

Article 141 WRV [Religious Services]

To the extent that there exists a need for religious services and spiritual care in the army, in hospitals, prisons, or other public institutions, the religious bodies is permitted to perform religious acts; in this context there is no compulsion of any kind.

Article 141 ["Bremen Clause"]

Article 7 III 1 does not be applied in any State [Land] in which different provisions of State [Land] law were in force on 1 Jan. 1949.

Article 142 [Basic Rights in State Constitutions]

Notwithstanding the provision of Article 31, such provisions of State [Land] constitutions also remain in force as guarantee basic rights in conformity with Articles 1 to 18 of this Constitution.

Article 142a [repealed]

Article 143 [Limitation of Deviations]

(1) Law in the territory specified in Article 3 of the Unification Treaty may deviate from provisions of this Constitution for a period not extending beyond 31 December 1992 in so far as and as long as no complete adjustment to the order of the Constitution can be achieved as a consequence of the different conditions. [2]Deviations must not violate Article 19 II and must be compatible with the principles set out in Article 79 III.
(2) Deviations from sections II, VIII, VIIIa, IX, X and XI are permissible for a period not extending beyond 31 December 1995.
(3) Notwithstanding Paragraphs I & II above, Article 41 of the Unification Treaty and the rules for its implementation remain valid in so far as they provide for the irreversibility of intrusion on property in the territory specified in Article 3 of the said Treaty.

Article 143a [Railway Administration]

(1) The Federation has exclusive legislation in all matters arising from the transformation of railroads of the Federation from direct federal administration to businesses. [2]Article 87e V is applicable. [3]Officials of railroads of the Federation can, by statute preserving their legal position and the responsibility of their former employer, be assigned to work at railroads of the Federation organized under private law.

(2) Statutes according to Paragraph II are administered by the Federation.
(3) The discharge of all duties in the area of local railway transport of persons by former railroads of the Federation is a responsibility of the Federation until 31 Dec. 1995. [2]This provision also applies to tasks of railway traffic administration. [3]Details are regulated by federal legislation requiring the consent of the Senate [Bundesrat].

Article 143b [Deutsche Bundespost]

(1) The special property Deutsche Bundespost will be transformed into private law businesses according to a federal statute. [2]The Federation has exclusive legislation over all related matters.
(2) Exclusive rights of the Federation prior to the transformation can be delegated preliminarily to businesses originating in the Deutsche Bundespost Postdienst and Deutsche Bundespost Telekom. [2]The Federation may sell the majority of shares in the business originating in the Deutsche Bundespost Postdienst no earlier than five years after enacting the statute. [3]For this measure, a federal statute with consent of the Senate [Bundesrat] is required.
(3) Federal officers of the Deutsche Bundespost are being employed by the businesses preserving their legal position and the responsibility of their former employer. [2]These businesses exercise the rights of the former employer. [3]Details are regulated by a federal statute.

Article 143c [Compensation for the Abolishment of Joint Tasks and Financial Support]

(1) Between 1st January 2007 and 31st December 2019, the States [Länder] may claim yearly contributions from the federal budget for the abolishment of joint tasks regarding extension and construction of universities including university hospitals and educational planning as well as for the abolishment of financial support to improve traffic conditions within communes and rent-controlled apartments. [2] Until 31st December 2013, these contributions will be calculated on the basis of average federal support during the reference period of 2000 to 2008.
(2) Until 31st December 2013, the contributions according to Paragraph I are distributed among the States [Länder]:

1. as yearly fixed amounts according to the average share of each State [Land] during the period 2000 to 2003;
2. according to the purpose of the task in the case of former mixed financing.

(3) Federation and States, until the end of 2013, reappraise the sufficiency and necessity of the funds assigned to the States [Länder] according to Paragraph I for fulfilling the responsibilities of the States [Länder]. [2]Starting 1st January 2014, the limitation to the purpose as established by Paragraph II Number 2 for the funds provided according to Paragraph I is abolished; the share of investment within the total of funds remains fixed. [3]Agreements in the Solidarity Pact II remain unaffected.

(4) Details are regulated by a federal statute requiring the consent of the Senate [Bundesrat].

Article 143d [Consolidation Support]

(1) Articles 109 and 115 in the version valid until 31 July 2009 are applicable for the last time on the 2010 budget. [2]Articles 109 and 115 in the version in force on 1 Aug. 2009 are applicable for the first time on the 2011 budget; provided that credit authorizations existing on 31 Dec. 2010 for separate assets remain untouched. [3]The States [Länder] may, for the period 1 Jan. 2011 to 31 Dec. 2019, following applicable rules of State [Land] regulation, deviate from the provisions of Article 109 III. [4]The budgets of the States [Länder] have to be planned in a way that the budget 2020 satisfies the requirements of Article 109 III 5. [5]The Federation may, for the period 1 Jan. 2011 to 31 Dec. 2015 deviate from the provision of Article 115 II 2. [6]The reduction of existing deficits should commence with the budget 2011. [7]The yearly budgets have to be planned in a way that the budget 2016 satisfies the requirement of Article 115 II 2; details are regulated by a federal statute.

(2) To help observing the provisions of Article 109 III after 1 Jan. 2020, the States [Länder] of Berlin, Bremen, Saarland, Saxony-Anhalt, and Schleswig-Holstein for the period 2011 to 2019 may receive consolidation support out of the federal budget to the total extent of 800 million Euro per year. [2]The shares are 300 million Euro for Bremen, 260 million Euro for Saarland, and 80 million Euro each for Berlin, Saxony-Anhalt, and Schleswig-Holstein. [3]The support is extended on the basis of an administrative agreement according to a federal statute requiring the consent of the Senate [Bundesrat]. [4]Receipt of the support requires a complete reduction of financial deficits until the end of 2010. [5]The details, particularly regarding the yearly steps of reduction in financial deficits, the supervision of the reduction of financial deficits by the stability council as well as the sanctions in case of non-compliance with the steps of reduction, are regulated by federal statute requiring the consent of the Senate [Bundesrat] and by administrative agreement. [6]The simultaneous receipt of consolidation support and reorganization support in case of extreme budget emergency is excluded.

(3) The financial burden resulting from consolidation support is carried by Federation and States [Länder] to one half each, the latter financing it from their share of the value added tax. [2]Details are regulated by federal statute requiring the consent of the Senate [Bundesrat].

Article 144 [Ratification of the Constitution]

(1) This Constitution requires ratification by the parliaments of two thirds of the German States [Länder] in which it is for the time being to apply.

(2) Insofar as the applications of this Constitution is subject to restrictions in any State [Land] listed in Article 23 or in any part thereof, such State [Land]

or part thereof has the right to send representatives to the House of Representatives [Bundestag] in accordance with Article 38 and to the Senate [Bundesrat] in accordance with Article 50.

Article 145 [Promulgation of the Constitution]

(1) The Parliamentary Council confirms in public session, with the participation of the deputies of Greater Berlin, the fact of ratification of this Constitution and signs and promulgates it.
(2) This Constitution comes into force at the end of the day of promulgation.
(3) It is published in the Federal Law Gazette.

Article 146 [Validity of the Constitution]

This Constitution, which is valid for the entire German people following the achievement of the unity and freedom of Germany, ceases to be in force on the day on which a constitution adopted by a free decision of the German people comes into force.

Index

www.ingramcontent.com/pod-product-compliance
Lightning Source LLC
Chambersburg PA
CBHW071305180926
51613CB00001B/129
9781849464727